Criminal Psychology and the Criminal Justice System in India and Beyond

Sanjeev P. Sahni · Poulomi Bhadra
Editors

Criminal Psychology and the Criminal Justice System in India and Beyond

Springer

Editors
Sanjeev P. Sahni
Jindal Institute of Behavioural Sciences
O.P. Jindal Global University
Sonipat, Haryana, India

Poulomi Bhadra
Jindal Institute of Behavioural Sciences
O.P. Jindal Global University
Sonipat, Haryana, India

ISBN 978-981-16-4569-3 ISBN 978-981-16-4570-9 (eBook)
https://doi.org/10.1007/978-981-16-4570-9

This Springer imprint is published by the registered company Springer Nature Singapore Pte Ltd.
The registered company address is: 152 Beach Road, #21-01/04 Gateway East, Singapore 189721, Singapore

Preface

The role of psychology in the criminal justice system has been increasingly realized in the last few decades, with criminal psychology and behavioural profiling gaining prominence in public interest and media attention. Since the 1800s, criminal psychology and profiling has evolved as an investigative tool, whether in fiction, from Doyle's *Sherlock* to Poe's *Dupin*, or in academic practice, from Freud to Bowlby. Since then, many distinguished scholars have published many books in this field, their works documenting and furthering the interdisciplinarity between law, psychology, and crime studies. *Criminal Psychology and the Criminal Justice System in India and Beyond* attempts to advance this area of study by introducing a comprehensive resource for understanding the theoretical foundations of criminal psychology, and expanding the purview of discussion from the Global West to the Global South, specifically India, to illustrate how they apply to different investigative regimes.

This book is especially designed to convey the knowledge simply and succinctly, so that it may cater to the interests of all kinds of readers, whether it be the student interested in enrolling for criminal psychology or forensic psychology programmes or the professional intending to begin a career in law enforcement or looking to expand their knowledge in alternative investigative approaches. The need and use for criminal psychology in legal processes, criminal jurisprudence, and corrective rehabilitation is expanding in many countries and becoming increasingly interdisciplinary. At the same time, there is an increasing need for trained scholars and practitioners who are adept at translating various alternative approaches from theory to practice. The purpose of this book is to provide valuable contribution in training and education by proving to be an indispensable resource on important topics such as detecting deceit, eyewitness testimony, juvenile delinquency, jury and judiciary decision-making, cognitive biases in forensic examinations, and psychology as applied to law and policy. To this end, we have curated this volume with contributions authored and co-authored by accomplished scholars and practitioners in their respective areas. These authors have endeavoured to address the enduring issues at the interface of psychology and the criminal justice system, and frame these issues in the light of contemporary research and prevailing conceptual formations.

The content of this volume has been divided into three parts, preceded by an abridged introduction to the evolution of psychological theories, to set the background for an independent study. The sequence of the chapters has been framed in order of their relevance to the three aspects of the criminal justice process—investigation, prosecution, and rehabilitation. Statutory case laws and case studies have been abundantly incorporated to elucidate theories and emerging trends in forensic procedures. We hope that all readers of this book will appreciate the collaborative efforts of the authors and the editors to present an array of topics dealing with the theoretical, systematic, and scientific processes involved in fusing psychological theories and processes to criminal investigations and consequent restorative endeavours.

Sonipat, India

Sanjeev P. Sahni
Poulomi Bhadra

Acknowledgements

It has been our pleasure and honour to work with many distinguished scholars from various institutions whose valuable contributions have resulted in this engaging publication. We sincerely thank our contributors for their hard work, extensive efforts, and commitment to deliver their chapters, despite the challenges that the pandemic has presented towards our productivity. In this regard, we would also like to thank the team at Springer Publication Singapore, especially Satvinder Kaur, Gowrishankar Ayyasamy and Lokeshwaran M., who have consistently supported us from the conception to the publication of this book.

As editors of the book and faculty members of O.P. Jindal Global University, we would like to take this opportunity to express our sincere gratitude to the founding Chancellor, Mr. Naveen Jindal, and to Dr. C. Rajkumar, founding Vice Chancellor, O.P. Jindal Global University, for their continued support of academic freedom and research opportunities. My appreciation also goes to those students and research assistants who have rendered helpful assistance in completing this book, both to the authors and to the editors. Editing a contributed volume can be an isolating and tedious process, made more so by the challenges of 2020. On a personal note, we would like to extend our appreciation to our families for their support towards our academic efforts and a special thanks to Bhadra's editorial companion, Cleo, for her motivating purrs.

As editors, we have strived our best to incorporate a comprehensive and substantiated outlook on the subject, while also valuing each author's perspective and work. We apologize for any shortcomings and hope that any errors made on our part do not compromise your educational experience of the book. We look forward to hearing any suggestions or feedback you may have for us or the authors.

Sanjeev P. Sahni
Poulomi Bhadra

Contents

Editors and Contributors

About the Editors

Prof. (Dr.) Sanjeev P. Sahni is presently Professor at O.P. Jindal Global University and Principal Director of the Jindal Institute of Behavioural Sciences (JIBS), Director for the Center for Victimology and Psychological Studies and the Centre for Criminology and Forensic Studies, Member of the Governing Body and Advisor to the Vice Chancellor at O.P. Jindal Global University. He holds a Ph.D. in Psychology and possesses an extensive and rich experience of over 32 years in academia, industry and government sector. His work spans in the areas of criminal psychology, victimology, policing and law enforcement. He has trained over 75,000 professionals in over 50 countries and was a visiting professor in criminal psychology to China several times. Dr. Sahni has recently been nominated as Member of the Board of Directors to the International Society of Criminology. He is also a UN Liaison Committee Member of World Society of Victimology (WSV). Among his several academic endeavours, he has been regularly representing India at United Nations Office on Drugs and Crime (UNODC—Austria, Doha, Japan) and Academic Council on the United Nations System. He has published more than 35 research articles in international and national indexed journals and about 20 book chapters. He has also authored/edited 15 books, some of the recent ones being: The Death Penalty (Springer), Internet Infidelity (Springer), Piracy in the Digital Era (Springer).

Poulomi Bhadra is presently an Assistant Professor and Assistant Director at the Jindal Institute of Behavioural Sciences (JIBS) and also Research Fellow at the Centre for India China Studies (CICS). She founded the Centre for Criminology and Forensic Studies (CCFS) at JIBS in 2020 in recognition of a need to integrate scientific and legal education. She holds degrees in Forensic Science from King's College London and Criminology and Criminal Psychology from University of Essex, UK. Prior to joining JGU, she has worked as a researcher with the Natural History Museum, London, and the London Metropolitan Police. She is presently associated with the South Asian Society of Victimology and Criminology, the International Society of

Criminology and the Chartered Society of Forensic Science, UK. She is also affiliated to the research think-tank Centre for Forensic Studies in Criminal Justice. As an early career academic, she has publications in national and international journals and books ranging from a variety of topics such as forensic entomology to criminal law in refugee jurisprudence. Her research interests are built on a multidimensional, interdisciplinary profile that is predominantly focused at the intersection of forensics, law, forensic psychology and criminology as well as cultural studies.

Contributors

Kartik Adlakha Student Researcher, Jindal Global Law School, O.P. Jindal Global University, Sonipat, Haryana, India

Poulomi Bhadra Jindal Institute of Behavioural Sciences, O.P. Jindal Global University, Sonipat, Haryana, India

Bhavya Chhabra Jindal Institute of Behavioural Sciences, O.P. Jindal Global University, Sonipat, Haryana, India

Tanni Choudhury Jindal Institute of Behavioural Sciences, O.P. Jindal Global University, Sonipat, Haryana, India

S. A. Deepak D.D.G.D. Vaishnav College, Chennai, India

Mohita Junnarkar Jyoti Dalal School of Liberal Arts, NMIMS Deemed University, Mumbai, India

Karishma Jindal Institute of Behavioural Sciences, O.P. Jindal Global University, Sonipat, Haryana, India

Kulpreet Kaur Jindal Global Business School & Jindal Institute of Behavioural Sciences, O.P. Jindal Global University, Sonipat, Haryana, India

Pulkit Khanna Jindal Institute of Behavioural Sciences, O.P. Jindal Global University, Sonipat, Haryana, India

Akshaya Krishnakumar Jindal Institute of Behavioural Sciences, O.P. Jindal Global University, Sonipat, Haryana, India

Sweta Lakhani Jindal Global Law School, O.P. Jindal Global University, Sonipat, Haryana, India

Swikar Lama Criminology and Police Studies, Sardar Patel University of Police, Security and Criminal Justice, Jodhpur, India

Lukus Langan Jindal Institute of Behavioural Sciences, O.P. Jindal Global University, Sonipat, Haryana, India

Tanay Maiti Department of Psychiatry, Jagannath Gupta Institute of Medical Science and Hospital, Kolkata, West Bengal, India

Vipin Vijay Nair Jindal Institute of Behavioural Sciences, O.P. Jindal Global University, Sonipat, Haryana, India

Manjushree Palit Jindal School of Psychology and Counselling, O.P. Jindal Global University, Sonipat, Haryana, India

Nisha Phakey Jindal Institute of Behavioural Sciences, O.P. Jindal Global University, Sonipat, Haryana, India

Sanjeev P. Sahni Jindal Institute of Behavioural Sciences, O.P. Jindal Global University, Sonipat, Haryana, India

Shankey Verma Jindal Institute of Behavioural Sciences, O.P. Jindal Global University, Sonipat, Haryana, India

Chapter 1
Psychology: The Science of Mental Processes

Kulpreet Kaur

Abstract The complexity of human behaviour has intrigued mankind because of its conscious and subconscious motivations. Psychologists try to find the causes for these complexities and reasons of individual differences. The best evolved definition of psychology is that it is a scientific study of behaviour and mental processes. To elaborate, psychology as a science uses systematic and objective scientific methods to study overt (observable) behaviour like facial expressions, gestures, endocrine reactions and such, and covert (hidden/unobservable) behaviour or cognitive or mental processes like thinking, remembering, feelings and so on. This chapter summarizes the fundamental theories of psychology to assist in understanding the chapters that follow.

1.1 Early Influencers and Followers

Psychology, as a discipline, was influenced by ancient Greek philosophers such as Plato (428-348 B.C.E) and Aristotle (384-322 B.C.E) who tried to explain the connection of human mind to the physical body. While Plato spoke about psychological problems which emphasized on innate characteristics rather than experiences, Aristotle, also Plato's favourite student, considered mind as a function of bodily processes and experience. Descartes (1596-1650), a French philosopher, propagated dualism by suggesting that mind and body are two distinctly different entities and interact through a gland located within the brain.

Wilhelm Wundt (1832–1920), a physiologist known as the 'founder of experimental psychology', established the first formal psychology laboratory in Leipzig, Germany, in 1879. This historic event gave psychology a modern experimental beginning. He introduced the process of objective introspection with which one's own thought and mental activities could be objectively examined. Edward Titchener (1867–1927) agreed with Wundt's views that every individual experience can be

K. Kaur (✉)
Jindal Global Business School & Jindal Institute of Behavioural Sciences, O.P. Jindal Global University, Sonipat, Haryana, India
e-mail: kkaur@jgu.edu.in

S. Sahni et al. (eds.), *Criminal Psychology and the Criminal Justice System in India and Beyond*, https://doi.org/10.1007/978-981-16-4570-9_1

broken down into its emotions and experience. He added that introspection can be used on thoughts and sensations alike. He named his school as Structuralism. But introspection as a procedure soon lost its influence due to lack of scientific verification from outside observers.

Meanwhile, William James (1842–1910), who was influenced by Charles Darwin's theory of 'natural selection', came up with a different school of thought, Functionalism, which focused on explaining how the mental state is a function of sensory stimulation. Functionalism gradually faded away leaving behind only a few traces on evolutionary psychology—one of the contemporary perspectives.

Max Wertheimer (1880–1943), Kurt Koffka (1886–1941) and Wolfgang Kohler (1887–1967) devoted their efforts to study sensation and perception to propagate Gestalt principles that focused on the tendency of organizing perceptual experiences into whole rather than sum of its parts. Gestalt's ideas are an important part of a contemporary field of psychology called cognitive psychology. Cognitive psychology focuses on how people perceive, store, think, and use information, and became a widely accepted idea in 1960s. Extension of this view is the relatively new field of cognitive neuroscience which includes the study of the working brain and nervous system during various cognitive processes. Constructivism, a view in modern cognitive psychology, propounded that human beings are constantly building up their minds through continuous interaction and exploration into physical and social world. Jean Piaget (1896–1980) and Lev Vygotsky (1896–1934) further used this view to construct their theories of development.

While Structuralists, Functionalists, and Gestaltists were trying to promote their perspective on the study of human mind and behaviour to different corners of the world, Sigmund Freud (1856–1939), a neurologist, believed that unconscious leftovers of earlier experiences accounted for neurotic behaviour. Later, neo-Freudians like Alfred Adler (1870–1937), Carl Jung (1875–1961), Karen Horney (1885–1952), and Anna Freud (1895–1982) modified the psychoanalytic viewpoints. Freudian psychoanalysis has been the basis of modern psychotherapy. Contemporary psychodynamic perspective focuses on the influence of the unconscious mind on the development of self, social, intra-personal, and interpersonal relationships.

By the early 1900s, psychologist John B. Watson (1878–1958) challenged all the prevailing schools of psychology with his own school of Behaviourism which explained behaviour as an outcome of stimulus–response relationship. His 'Little Albert' experiment on the process of conditioning along with Ivan Pavlov's experiment on dogs called classical conditioning and B.F Skinner's Operant conditioning experiments became landmarks in the history of experimental psychology. Behaviourism is still a major perspective in psychology and has influenced the field of cognitive psychology and various techniques of psychotherapy.

A relatively new perspective focused on people's freedom to choose their own follow-up path and strive for self-actualization to unfold their inner potential. This Humanistic perspective was founded by Abraham Maslow (1908–1970) and Carl Rogers (1902–1987). Contemporary psychotherapy aimed at positive outlook of human nature is inspired by the Humanistic views.

Table 1.1 Evolution and growth of psychology in India (Source: Baron & Misra, 2018)

Year	Events
1916	First psychology laboratory established in Calcutta university with Dr. N. N. Sengupta as founder in-charge
1922	Psychology was included in Indian Science Congress Association
1922	Indian psychoanalytic society was formed by Girindra Shekhar Bose
1924	Indian psychological association was founded by N. N. Sengupta
1940	Lumbini Park, The first Mental Hospital was founded at Calcutta
1954	Bureau of Psychology was established at Allahabad
1955	National Institute of Mental Health was founded in Bangalore
1968	Indian association of clinical psychologists is formed
1972	First survey of research in India is published by the Indian Council of social research
1989	National Academy of Psychology (NAOP) established
1997	National Brain Research Centre (NBRC) was established in Gurgaon, Haryana
2009	NAOP's Journal of Psychological Studies becomes international (springer)

Another modern perspective which combines social psychology and cultural psychology is the socio-cultural perspective. This perspective emphasizes on the effect of the social (groups, surroundings, social roles, and relationships) and the cultural (class differences, cultural ethnicity, cultural norms, values, and expectations) on the behaviour of an individual. It also studies the contrast and compares an issue between two or more cultures.

The evolutionary perspective, a combination of the sociocultural and the bio-psychological perspective (behaviour seen as a result of physiological changes in the body), focuses on the biological bases for explaining general mental strategies and traits. Some of these disciplinary changes happened simultaneously globally, and some ideas were slow in arriving to different parts of the world. Below is a summary of the landmarks in the evolution and growth of psychology in India (Table 1.1).

1.1.1 Various Fields of Psychology

Intense exploration of psychology has led to advent of several sub-fields of study, diversifying its scope. The American Psychological Association (APA), established in 1892 by G. Stanley Hall, is the strongest professional body of psychologists, and has more than fifty divisions of psychology. The major fields and their area of concerns are listed below (Table 1.2).

The interdisciplinary focus on research and application of psychological theories have found its way into varied areas like aviation psychology, military psychology, engineering psychology, and psychology of women.

Table 1.2 Overview of fields of psychology (Source: Baron & Misra, 2018)

Sub-fields	Area of concern
Clinical psychology	Studies diagnosis, causes and intervention of mental disorders
Cognitive psychology	Investigates all aspects of cognition-perception, sensation, learning, memory, language acquisition, thinking, decision-making, problem solving, and so on
Counselling psychology	Help people to deal with personal problems, mal adjustment, and career choices
Criminal psychology	The study of the views, thoughts, intentions, actions, and reactions of criminals and all others who are associated in the criminal behaviour
Cross-cultural psychology	Studies variability in behaviour among cultural groups around the world and investigates the mutual correlation. It also explains that meanings and practice of concepts not only vary across cultures but are rooted in cultures
Developmental psychology	Studies bodily, cognitive, social, and emotional changes throughout the life process
Educational psychology	Studies all aspects of teaching–learning process such as increasing attention and memory, training techniques for better understanding, improving the performance of all the stakes holders of an institute and so on
Experimental psychology	Studies all aspects of perception, attention, learning, perception based on experimental research
Industrial/organizational psychology	Studies all aspects of behaviour in work settings such as group dynamics, team work, improving the efficiency and so on
Positive psychology	Studies optimal human functioning with a focus on human virtues, well-being, and meaningful life. The role of positive emotions, happiness, etc., enhancing the quality of life is also its focus
Psychobiology and evolutionary psychology	Investigates biological bases of behaviour and role of evolution in human behaviour
Social/applied social psychology	Studies social interaction as a function of social thought and experiences and its application in various fields like education, work, health, and so on
Sports psychology	It applies psychological principles to improve sports performance by altering the perception and in turn the motivation of the players

1.2 Evolution of Psychology via Research

Psychology is a diverse field with professionals working in various subfields which require specialized trainings, focus, and entails different goals from the familiar professional umbrella of a psychologist. A psychologist does not possess any medical training but has advanced degrees (doctoral degree) in a specific area and undergoes intense learning about different areas of psychology before choosing their specialization. A psychiatrist, on the other hand, has a medical degree and specializes in diagnosis and treatment (prescription, medication, and therapy) of psychological disorders. Although many psychologists help people through therapy, there are many others who are involved in teaching and researching.

The goals of psychological enquiry are description, prediction, explanation, control of behaviour, and application of knowledge. Various research methodologies are used to generate these goals in an objective manner. All research methods used in psychology can be categorized as either quantitative or qualitative.

The aim of the quantitative research is usually to present trends and laws in form of numerical data that characterize behaviour of large groups of individuals. Qualitative research uses non-numeric data like texts and pictorial stimulations. Since internal characteristics are not overtly observable, like violence, love, anxiety, they are called 'constructs' because constructs are constructed or defined based on the theories which delineates it from similar constructs. For the purpose of research, these constructs need to be operationalised. Operationalization of the construct means expressing it in terms of observable behaviour. For example, to operationalize construct of aggression, one might look at the 'number of insulting comments per hour' or to operationalize anxiety, one might look at the scored on an anxiety questionnaire.

The three main types of quantitative research are Experimental research, Causal-Comparative/Quasi-Experimental and Correlational research.

Experimentation is the scientific method that establishes cause and effect relationship through manipulation of a variables to identify any changes in behaviour. The variable that is manipulated in the experiment is an independent variable (IV). The change in the behaviour of the participants as an effect of change in independent variable is known as dependent variable (DV). Besides independent variable, confounding variable are those variables that may interfere with the cause-and-effect relationship between IV and DV, and hence, they need to be controlled. The control of confounding variables, also called controlled variable (CV), can be done either by eliminating them or keeping them constant for all participants. Confounding variables can also be controlled by using two groups of participants, the experimental group and the control group. The experimental group is exposed to independent variable and controlled group gets no treatment or gets different treatment than the experimental group.

Experimental design refers to allocation of participants to the different groups or treatments (or IV levels) in an experiment. These are of three types:

1. Independent measures/between groups: Random distribution of different subjects in each condition of the independent variable.

2. Repeated measures/within groups: The same subjects take part in each condition of the independent variable. This design is vulnerable to order effects (results may differ depending on which condition comes first). To overcome this effect, researchers use the techniques of counter-balancing.
3. Matched pairs: Each condition uses different subjects, but they are not randomly distributed, instead they are grouped under various characteristics, e.g., gender, age, intelligence, and other variable relevant to the experiment.

In causal–comparative/quasi-experimental, naturally formed, or pre-existing groups are used to establish cause–effect relationships among the variables. An independent variable is identified. The effects of the independent variable on the dependent variable are measured without any manipulation of the independent variable.

When two or more variables are measured and the relationship between them is mathematically quantified, it is a correlational research. A positive correlation indicates the tendency for one variable to increase with increase in another variable. A negative correlation signifies the inverse tendency: when one variable increases the other decreases. When plotted on a graph, a perfect correlation of 1 or -1 is a straight line with the slope of 45°. This happens when one variable increases or decreases by exactly same unit as the other variable. A correlation close to zero is a flat line which shows no relationship between two variables.

The most common qualitative methods are participant observation, in-depth interviews, case studies, and surveys. Each method is particularly suited for getting a specific type of data.

Observation technique enables a researcher to gain first-hand knowledge by observing into the studied phenomenon in depth, and at times, even becoming part of it. Observation can be laboratory versus naturalistic, structured versus unstructured, or participant versus non-participant, each of which will have broad implication on credibility, reflexivity, generalization, and ethics. Participant observation is appropriate for collecting data on natural behaviours in their natural settings.

In-depth interview is one of the most popular qualitative research methods that enables direct contact between the interviewer and the interviewee. The sequence of the question determines if the interview is structured, semi-structured, unstructured, open-ended, or closed-ended. In-depth interviews are optimal for collecting data on individuals' personal histories, episodes, perspectives, and behaviours, particularly when delicate topics are being explored.

A case study is an in-depth investigation of an individual and/or a group. Case studies can involve a variety of other methods (observation, testing, interviews and so on), which deepens the understanding of an individual.

Research in human development faces a constant challenge of age. Since the scientific study of human development involves studying the changes that occur in people throughout their lifetime, three special designs are used to study the age-related changes. In longitudinal design, same group of subjects is repeatedly studied, observed, and assessed to notice the changes over time as the group ages, whereas the cross-sectional design can be used to study different age groups at one given time.

Features of both longitudinal and cross—sectional design are used in the cross-sequential design.

1.3 Fundamentals of Psychological Theories

From the moment of foetal conception, we are each headed down individual pathways of physical, cognitive, and social changes. These changes are an interplay of nature and nurture. The contribution of each has given rise to long-lasting debate in psychology that attempts to establish whether human behaviour is determined primarily by biological factors such as genetics and brain structure (nature) or environmental factors such as education, parenting styles, friends (nurture), and how it contributes towards the individual differences among each one of us. Genes provide a distinguishable combination for the development of individual differences. Not only genetics, but development occurs in relation to an individual's environment as well. This is what makes each one of us unique in the way we organize information, interpret our world, and react to stimulus and sensations.

1.3.1 Reaction to Stimulus

Sensation occurs due to activation of receptors in the sense organs. The stimulus from sense organs is converted into the neural signals in the brain through the process of transduction. Based on one's interests and motivations, as well as the nature of the stimuli which impinge on us, we pay attention to a few things out of the innumerable stimuli with which we are bombarded. Sensory modality, clarity of the stimulus, temporal uncertainty, and spatial uncertainty can facilitate or inhibit an individual's sustained attention to what one hears, sees, smells, tastes, and otherwise experiences. Furthermore, it is influenced not only by stimulating circumstances, but also by our past experience and present psychological state. The process by which we identify, organize, recognize, interpret, understand the information provided by the sense organs is called perception. No matter how individually determined perception might be, there are some similarities in how people perceive the world around them. These similarities are called perceptual constancies of shape, size, and brightness.

Prominent Gestalt psychologists like Köhler et al. (1925) indicate that human analytic processes are generally focused towards making the complex figures appear simple through the perception of good figure or *pragnanz*. They explained basic principles of human perceptual tendency to group objects into meaningful forms and perceive the object as whole instead of sum of its parts. Humans' impressive capability to see the world in three dimensions is called depth perception. Different monocular and binocular cues are used in forming the judgement of depth and distance.

Several psychologists have studied the processes of perception in different sociocultural settings. Sinha and Mishra (1996) have carried out several studies on pictorial presentation using a variety of pictures with people with diverse cultural settings, such as hunters and gatherers living in forests, agriculturists living in villages, and people employed and living in cities. Their studies indicate that interpretation of pictures is strongly related to cultural experiences and learning of people.

1.3.2 Behavioural Conditioning

Learning is a key process in human behaviour. It refers to the gamut of changes that take place in behaviour because of one's own experience. These changes are relatively permanent. One type of learning is conditioning, which is a relatively simple modification of behaviour. Classical conditioning is a basic form of learning in which two stimuli when administered in a pattern gives rise to a new conditioned (learned) response. Basic vocabulary in the area of classical conditioning originated with Ivan Pavlov's work in 1927 on the process of digestion on dogs. Salivation in response to food placed is a natural response, an unlearned or unconditioned response (UCR). Because it elicited the unconditional response, the food is called unconditional stimulus (UCS). When Pavlov sequenced ringing of the bell followed by presentation of food repeatedly, the dog learned to salivate in response to the sound of the bell alone and this salivation was called conditioned response (CR), which indicated that arousal of the response was dependent upon a stimulus (bell) other than the natural one (food). Since salivation on ringing the bell was a conditioned response, hence the bell was labelled as conditioned stimulus (CS). Although, psychologist initially believed that conditioning was determined primarily by the number of conditioned–unconditioned stimulus pairing, several other studies revealed that delay conditioning, trace conditioning, simultaneous conditioning, backward conditioning, and familiarity can affect conditioning to a large extent.

Classical conditioning was concerned about involuntary responses elicited by specific identifiable stimuli, but in everyday life, much of our behaviour are voluntary or 'operant' or under one's control. Conditioning of operant behaviour is called operant conditioning. Edward L. Thorndike (1874–1949) was one of the first researchers to explore the laws of learning on voluntary responses but the procedure in operant conditioning is best illustrated by a typical training session used by B. F Skinner (1904–1990). He used the research device known as 'Skinner box' by placing the rat in this box and training it to press the lever inside the box to get the food. In Skinner's view, reinforcement or punishment is the reason that the rat learned to press the lever after several trial and errors. Reinforcement is any event or stimulus that increases the likelihood of reoccurrence of a response, whereas punishment is a procedure by which the application or removal of a stimulus decreases the strength of the behaviour.

Many behavioural psychologists further developed cognitive learning theories to study the influence of thinkings, feelings, and expectations on the observable behaviour. Tolman (1932) in his experiments on rats concluded that the group who was given reinforcement soon after expected behaviour learned to navigate the maze quickly. However, although the unrewarded rats had also learned the way out of the maze during exploration, this unrewarded group never displayed their hidden leaning to find the way out faster until reinforcement was provided. This hidden learning was labelled as latent learning by Tolman. During the process of exploration, the rats developed mental representation of the locations, paths, and directions needed to reach the goal. These mental representations are called cognitive maps.

Another exploration of cognitive elements of learning that involved problem solving was given by Wolfgang Kohler (1887–1967) when he experimented with chimpanzees. In these experiments, when chimpanzee used boxes, tolls, and sticks to reach the food placed beyond the reach of the animal, learning not only occurred as a result of trial and error or reinforcement, but came out as sudden flashes of insight which Köhler (1925) labelled as insight learning. Insight learning is the sudden perception of relationship also called AHA experience among various parts of the problem, allowing the solution of the problem to come as a flash suddenly. Such rapid solutions depend upon the type of task involved, the subject's level of mental development, their prior experience, and their use of trial and error procedures.

Seligman (1975) discovered another form of avoidable situation caused due to repeated failures in the past known as learned helplessness. Another kind of learning through observing the actions of others is called observational learning. Albert Bandura's social learning theory refers to acquiring behaviour through social interaction. His bobo doll experiments showed that children displayed violent behaviour towards their toy after witnessing, and hence imitating, a violent role model. Bandura (1986) concluded from his studies that attention, memory, imitation, and motivation were the four important elements of observational learning.

1.3.3 Memory Retention

Once the information is paid attention to, perceived, processed, and learnt, it is important to retain and retrieve the information as well. Retention is one of the three processes of memory. Memory is an active system that receives information from the senses, organizes, and stores it away to retrieve when needed. Atkinson and Shiffrin (1968) noted that human memory must accomplish three basic tasks of encoding, storage, and retrieval. This approach focuses on the way information is handled and processed through three different systems of memory—sensory memory, short-term memory, and long-term memory. Sensory memory stores the information in form of iconic (visual) memory and echoic (auditory) memory. Long-term memory stores information of skills, procedures, habits, and conditioned responses and are called non-declarative (implicit) memory. Declarative (explicit) memory stores facts and knowledge which is conscious and known. Semantic memory and episodic memory are types of declarative memory. Each of these systems must deal with three tasks of encoding, storing, and retrieving the information (Fig. 1.1).

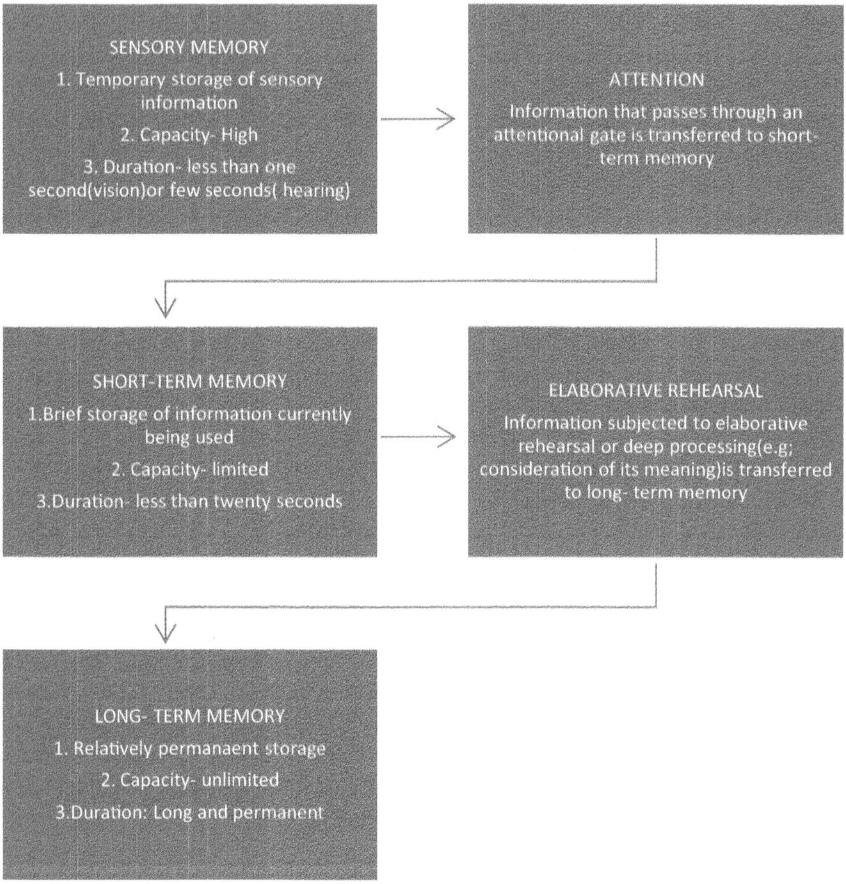

Fig. 1.1 Overview of information—processing model of memory (2016) (Source: Based on model by Atkinson & Shiffrin, 1968 mentioned in Baron & Misra, 2018)

The levels of processing view of memory were given by Craik and Lockhart (1972). This view suggested that level of retention of the information depends upon the depth to which an information is processed (deeper the processing, better the retention). This theory projects that the information can be encoded at the structural, the phonetic, and the semantic levels. Semantic encoding is considered as the deepest level of processing which leads to better retention (Fig. 1.2).

Parallel distribution processing model assumes that all memory processes take place at the same time over a large matrix of interwoven neural connections. This model, proposed by McClelland (1988), consists of simultaneous processing of the information that enables people to retrieve many and different information from memory all at once enabling faster reactions and decisions. Chunking method, deep-level processing, minimizing interference, and forming enough retrieval cues are

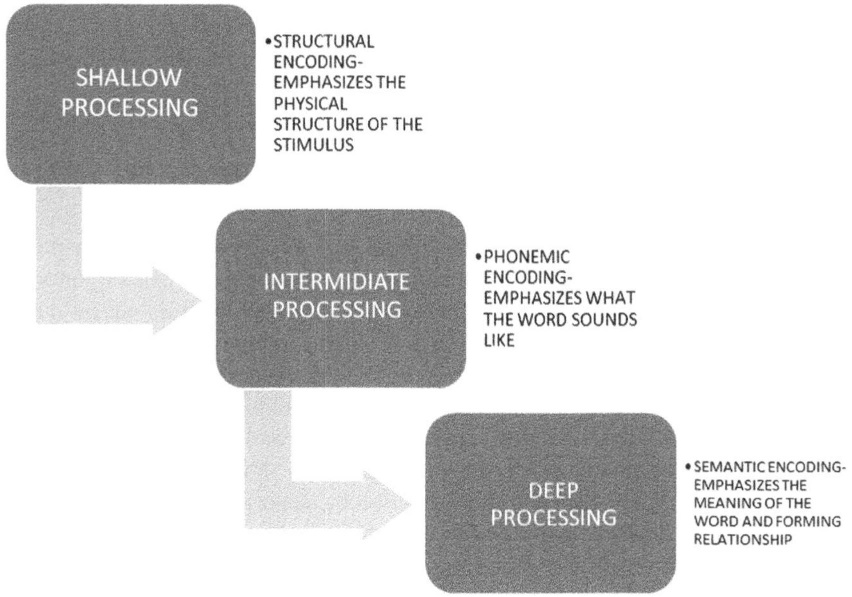

Fig. 1.2 Overview of level of processing model of memory (Source: Based on view by Craik & Lockhart, 1972 & suggested in Baron & Misra, 2018)

techniques of mnemonics using organization. These models formed the fundamental research in eyewitness testimony, as you will read later in the book.

One of the most important and ultimate tasks of memory is to retrieve the stored information. There are two types of retrieval of memory, recall and recognition. During recall, the information is retrieved from storage with fewer external cues, whereas recognition is an ability to match a piece of information with the stored fact.

Failure to retrieve an information is called forgetting. The first systematic attempt to understand the nature of forgetting was made by Ebbinghaus (1885). He presented forgetting in a graphical manner called forgetting curve, indicating a distinct pattern in which forgetting happens predominantly within the first hour after learning, and then the phenomenon tapers off gradually. One of the simplest views of forgetting is that some things fail to get encoded which is known as encoding failure, i.e., failure to process information into memory. The earliest view of forgetting was fading or decaying of information in long-term memory within due course of time if not put in use for a long time. Memory trace decay theory was not found verifiable on several occasions when less used information could be recalled successfully. A possible explanation of long-term forgetting is that though information in long-term memory is relatively permanent, it may not always be accessible due to interference cause by other information. Interference can come in form of retroactive inhibition or proactive inhibition. Besides the cognitive causes, forgetting can occur due to biological causes like amnesia and Alzheimer's disease. Short-term memory is encoded in the form of sound and visual images, forming a mental image. These mental images or mental representations of an object form an important tool for thinking process.

1.3.4 Cognition, Decision-Making, and Problem-Solving

The base of all cognitive processes is thinking that clearly differentiates human from other species. Thinking is a higher mental process where already existing information is manipulated and analysed. Such manipulation and analysis occurs during formation of concepts and processes such as reasoning, imagining, problem-solving, judging, and decision-making. Convergent thinking is a type of thinking in which all paths of thinking lead to a single answer. Divergent thinking is a type of thinking in which diverse possibilities and ideas are run through mentally for solving a problem.

Besides mental images, another important aspect of thought process is concept. Concepts are the ideas that represent a class or categories of objects or events. Concepts help in thinking and act as an important instrument for problem-solving. Problem-solving is the process that occurs when a goal must be reached by thinking and behaving appropriately to the situation. The process of cognition that involves identifying, evaluating, and choosing among several alternatives is called decision-making. The simplest form of problem-solving is trial and error. A rule that guarantees a solution to a specific type of problem is called algorithm. Heuristics, unlike algorithms, are less time consuming. Heuristics are rules of thumb, guided by previous experiences. Finally, analogy is an approach of applying similar techniques of problem-solving that were previously successful to similar problems.

Creativity is the process of solving a problem by combining ideas in new ways. Study of creative thinking suggests four general aspects which are preparation—the gathering of relevant information, incubation—a period of relative inactivity, illumination—sudden insight and verification—the evaluation of idea. Sometimes despite our best efforts, certain problems cannot be solved. Our strong tendency to think of using objects only as they have been used in the past is one of the reasons for this. This is called functional fixedness. Another factor that interferes in problem-solving is mentality which involves sticking to tried-and-tested means even if better alternatives are available.

Solving problems involves using one's experience, knowledge, and resources effectively. How effectively one solves the problem indicates one's intelligence. Intelligence is the ability to understand, think rationally, and use resources effectively to adapt to new challenges. Several theories offer an explanation to a number of intelligence-related abilities. Spearman (1904) proposed general intelligence or g-factor as an ability to reason and solve problems where as specific intelligence or s-factor was related to task-specific abilities. Gardner (1999), on the other hand, proposed nine different types of intelligence. Sternberg (1988) proposed analytical, creative, and practical as three types of intelligence. PASS theory of intelligence by Das et al. (1994) proposes planning, attention, simultaneous, and successive as four kinds of competence for intelligence. The more recent Cattell–Horn–Carroll (CHC) theory of intelligence includes general intelligence, sixteen major abilities, and many minor abilities within each broad area. Intelligence Quotient is a measure of intelligence which is calculated by dividing the mental age with the chronological age and multiplying by hundred. Individual tests of intelligence, such as the Standford–Binet or Wechsler Scales, help identification of children at the extremes of the normal probability curve. Extremes of normal distribution curves can be estimated through classification of intelligence quotient. Extremes of normal distribution curves can be estimated through classification of intelligence quotient which considers 90–110 as an average IQ. Increase in IQ depicted on the right-hand side of the normal probability curve ranges between high average to very superior. Below average IQ is depicted on the left side of the curve.

1.4 Motivation as a Causal Factor

Perceiving, memorizing, learning, thinking, and problem-solving using one's intelligence are all guided by the process of motivation. Motivation is the force that initiates the activities, gives them a direction, and pushes to be continued for the fulfilment of physical or psychological needs. When the motivation comes from outside of oneself like awards, salary, or appreciation, it is called extrinsic motivation. Intrinsic motivation is the type of motivation in which a person performs an action because the act itself is rewarding or satisfying to one's own self. Below are discussed several approaches to understanding the key elements of motivation. These form the foundational background on which theories of crime explained criminal tendencies.

Early attempts to understand motivation focused primarily on innate patterns of behaviour that were biologically determined called instincts. The next approach to understanding motivation focused on drive—reduction of inner physical needs. McClelland's (1961) theory of affiliation, power, and achievement need focused on importance of psychological needs. Another explanation for human motivation involves the recognition of the need for stimulation. Incentive approaches to motivation involves behaviour as a response to rewards. The most acceptable approach to motivation is the humanistic model based on Maslow's theory, and places the needs in a hierarchy of needs where primary needs are met before the higher order needs (Table 1.3).

Motives are often accompanied by emotions, and emotions have tendency to influence motivational. Motivation and emotions are closely related concepts because motives and the arousal of emotion activate behaviour. Emotions is the 'feeling' aspect of consciousness and includes affective, behavioural, and cognitive elements. Physical arousal is associated with activation of the sympathetic nervous system, and the amygdala plays a key role in emotional processing. Early theory of emotion was called common-sense theory as it believed that a feeling stimulates arousal, which is followed by a response. Ever since, several theories have been proposed by various psychologists. James–Lange theory proposed by James (1894) and Lange

Table 1.3 Overview of approaches to motivation (Source: Based on information given by Ciccarelli & White, 2018)

Approaches	Proposed by	Key elements
Instincts and the evolutionary approaches	McDougall (1908)	Human beings are governed by instincts which are biologically determined and are innate patterns of behaviour
Drive-reduction theory	Clark Hull (1943)	Approach assumes behaviour arises from internal drives that push the organism to satisfy the need to reduce the tension arising out of need
McClelland's theory	McClelland (1961, 1988)	Highlights the importance of need for affiliation (nAff), need for power (nPow), and need for achievement (nAch) in motivation
Dweck's self-theory	Carol Dweck (1999)	Suggests that the need for achievement is linked to a person's locus of control and view of self
Arousal approaches	Robert Yerkes and John Dodson (1908)	Suggests level of tension ranges from low to high depending on individual differences. Optimal level of stress leads to optimum performance. Yerkes–Dodson law states that when tasks are less complex and similar, a higher level of motivation leads to better performance; and when tasks are difficult and new, lower level of arousal lead to better performance
Incentive approaches	Tolman(1932) and Kurt Lewin (1936s)	Early works by Tolman and Lewin focused on expectancy values or how much importance one attaches to beliefs and thoughts affect our actions
Humanistic approaches (Maslow's hierarchy of needs)	Abraham Maslow (1943, 1987)	Based primarily on Maslow's hierarchy of needs; i.e., primary, basic needs must be met before higher levels can be fulfilled. Physiological needs are the most basic needs followed by safety, belongingness and love, esteem. This is followed by cognitive needs, aesthetic needs, and at the top of the pyramid, self-actualization needs

(continued)

Table 1.3 (continued)

Approaches	Proposed by	Key elements
Renovating the pyramid of needs	Kenrick et al. (2010)	This revision preserves several Maslow's ideas of need such as physiological, safety, and esteem and integrates life-history development with it. It studies human motives at three different levels of analysis (a) their ultimate evolutionary function, (b) their developmental sequencing, and (c) their cognitive priority as triggered by proximate inputs The model also outlines the subsequent developing goal systems as overlapping with earlier developing systems
Humanistic approaches (ERG motivation theory)	Alderfer (1969)	Condenses Maslow's needs into only three levels: existence, relatedness, and growth
Humanistic approaches (self-determination theory)	Richard Ryan and Edward Deci (2000)	Similar to Maslow's hierarchy. States that the three universal needs are autonomy, competence, and relatedness

(1885) suggests that environmental stimuli give rise in physiological arousal, which helps in labelling of the emotion. Later, Cannon (1927) and Philip Bard (1934) propounded the Cannon–Bard theory that suggests that emotion and physiological arousal occur simultaneously leading to a specific response. According to the cognitive arousal two-factor theory, physiological arousal and its interpretation are based on environmental clues known as labelling. Physiological arousal must occur before experiencing emotion. The facial feedback hypothesis (Laird et al., 1974) suggests that facial expressions (and other behaviours) provide estimation to the brain that can cause or escalate experience of a specific emotion. Lastly, the cognitive mediational theory by Lazarus (1991) suggests that the cognitive appraisal and interpretation of the stimulus cause the emotional reaction. These theories are useful in laying the background for lie-detection techniques in the future.

Motivation and one's interaction with the psychological environment determine the personality of the person. Personality is the unique and relatively stable ways in which people think, feel, and behave. Personality, unlike other constructs, is difficult to be measured precisely and scientifically, and hence, different perspectives on personality has arisen.

The psychodynamic perspective had its beginnings in the work of Sigmund Freud (1856–1939) and still exists today. It focuses on the influence of the unconscious mind in the development of personality. The structure of mind, divisions of personality, and

Table 1.4 Divisions of personality according to Sigmund Freud (Source: Based on structure of personality suggested by Freud, 1933)

Divisions	Level of consciousness	Principle
Id	Part of the personality from birth to early years and is completely unconscious	Pleasure principle-principle by which the id functions and aims for immediate gratification of needs without considering its consequences
Ego	Part of the personality that develops deals with reality in conscious, rational, and logical manner	Reality principle–principle by which the ego functions and enables gratification of the demands of the id only when it will not result in negative consequences
Superego	Part of the personality that acts as the moral police	Conscience part of the superego that produces guilt during unacceptable behaviour

the psycho-sexual stages given by Freud show the causes of differences in personality during the process of development. Defence mechanisms are sub-conscious, psychologically manipulative behaviour or thoughts that reduce the anxiety arising out of guilt and shame. These behaviours can be in form of denial or distorted reality to defend against unacceptable impulses.

According to the psychodynamic theory, the structure of the mind can be divided in threefold. The preconscious mind contains memories, information, and events of which one can easily become aware of through focusing. Conscious mind consists of one's present awareness, whereas the unconscious mind contains thoughts, feelings, memories, and information that are not easily brought into the consciousness. Id, ego, superego are in constant state of conflict in Freud's view of how personality works. When anxiety created by their conflict gets unbalanced, abnormal behaviour arises. In order to deal with stress, psychological defence mechanisms unconsciously distort one's perception of reality (Table 1.4).

Freud (1933) believed that personality is a product of tension and pleasure build around libido (sexual energy) and over or under satisfaction of the energy leads to fixation to a particular stage. While this may not be held true at the moment, the sexual tension Freud researched forms the basis of interrogating motivations and offender behaviour in sexual crimes.

1.5 Conclusion

The behaviourist and social cognitive perspectives are based on the theories of learning. This approach focuses on the effect of the environment on behaviour. For behaviourists, personality is a set of learned responses and habits, gained through classical and operant conditioning, including reinforcement and punishments, individual social learnings and imitation (social processes) and cognitive processes (such as anticipation and memory) are important. The humanistic perspective focuses on the role of individual and subjective life experiences and personal preferences in personality development, absolutely contradicting the psychoanalytic and behaviourist perspective. The psychoanalytic, behaviourist, and humanistic perspectives seek to explain the causes that lead to uniqueness of the characteristics, whereas trait theorists concern themselves with the characteristics. Personality traits are specific dimensions along which individuals differ in consistent and stable ways. Some trait postulates that traits are biologically determined while others attribute them to the environment. You will read more about the development of these theories in Chap. 3.

Personality can be assessed through various methods based on validation of the perspective. Interview techniques are largely self-reports through unstructured or semi-structured interviews which may incur the problem of halo effect. Behavioural assessment is a method of direct observation used to quantify behaviour through rating scales. Observer's bias and lack of environmental control prevent it from yielding correct results. Projective tests are ambiguous visual stimuli used for clients to describe what they see, with an expectation that unconscious concerns or fears will be 'projected' onto stimulus (e.g., Rorschach Inkblot Test and TAT). Another measure used are personality inventories which includes standard list of objective, reliable, and valid questions with a broad range of structured answers.

These scientific techniques to measure the psychological constructs effectively link psychology to all fields of study, and thereby increases its relevance to interdisciplinary studies. Since psychology concerns itself with studying perception, attitude formation, motivation, emotions, and cognitive processes like memory, learning, thinking, and intelligence and their domino effect on behaviour, the influence of all these psychological processes on our behavioural outcome can be seen in our everyday functioning, including criminal tendencies and offending behaviour. Recognition and changing the behaviour can be easily felicitated through understanding psychology of the criminal and the victim, as well as the societal systems within which it exists.

Strong relevance of stress coping mechanisms to disentangle major physical and mental health problems such as obesity, anxiety, drug, insomnia, alcohol, tobacco abuse, media addiction, and inclination for violent behaviour and crime cannot be belittled. The one end of the spectrum has its focus on genetics, interpersonal, group, and societal behaviour and on the other end, importance of self and personality as key factors that underlie the complex mental health problems besetting our society.

Inspiring those susceptible or born into crime by adding excitement or interest through productive tasks, orienting individuals towards goal attainment and implicating a drive towards an action requires motivational techniques ranging from external motivators, such as monetary and emotional benefits, to intrinsic motivators, such as instilling enthusiasm through inspiring talks and team involvements. Positive attitude provides positive results not only to the workplace but interpersonal and intrapersonal relationships too. Familial happiness has direct linage to the self-esteem and self-identity. Positive attitude towards self and things around improves the value of existence. We will expound more on this in terms of offenders and their behaviour towards the end of this book.

Attitude depends on our perceptual biases, prejudice, and stereotypes acquired through the entire learning process. The real situation may be different from the perceived one, as the possibility that perceived attitude may be formed due to inaccurate information. Hence, developing perceptual abilities in order to establish positive thinking may prove advantageous in the attainment of goals. Attitude towards religious group or community, specific gender and race impacts our behaviour in a positive or a negative manner. Negative behaviour attracts the same from the other group and strains the relationship. Techniques to understand the perceptual bias and its influence on attitude formation, and in turn, its effects on one's behaviour and future goal orientation can easily be guided through structural analysis of the factors that govern it. For example, before addressing how to change attitudes and behaviours around AIDS or homosexuality, one needs to know how attitudes develop and change. Before addressing memory decline in the elderly or susceptibility of children to suggestions, one must know the basics of learning and memory and how that changes with age. Before changing the violent and imbalance emotional adolescent, one must understand the factors that led to its acquisition. Similarly, before convicting any person, one not only needs to know in-depth similar case studies and offender profiling, but also ways of rehabilitation to reduce re-offending. The field of criminal psychology is also concerned with analysing and improving the criminal justice system; enhancing police interviewing, detecting deception, or examining courtroom psychology and jury decision-making. Moving forward in the book, we will examine these topics closely in each chapter.

References

Alderfer, C. P. (1969). An empirical test of new theory of human need. *Organizational Behavior and Human Performance, 4*(1), 142–175.

Atkinson, R. C., & Shiffrin, R. M. (1968). Human memory: A proposed system and its control processes. In K. W. Spence & J. T. Spence (Eds.), *The psychology of learning and motivation* (Vol. 2, pp. 89–105). Academic Press.

Bandura, A. (1986). *Social foundations of thought and action: A social cognitive theory*. Prentice Hall.

Bard, P. (1934). On emotional expression after decortication with some remark on certain theoretical views. *Psychological Review, 41*, 309–329, 424–449.

Baron, R. B., & Misra, G. (2018). *Psychology-Indian subcontinent edition* (5th ed.). Pearson.

Cannon, W. B. (1927). The James-Lange theory of emotion: A critical examination and an alternative theory. *American Journal of Psychology, 39*, 10–124.

Ciccarelli, S. K., & White, J. N. (2018). (Adapted by Misra, G) *Psychology* (5th ed.). Pearson.

Craik, F. I. M., & Lockhart, R. S. (1972). Levels of processing. A framework for memory research. *Journal of Verbal Learning and Verbal Behaviour, 11*, 671–684.

Das, J. P. (1994). Eastern views of intelligence. In R. J. Sternberg (Ed.), *Encyclopedia of human intelligence* (pp. 387–391). Macmillan Publishing Company.

Dweck, C. S. (1999). *Self-theories: Their role in motivation, personality and development*. Psychology Press.

Ebbinghaus, H. (1885). *Memory: A contribution to experimental psychology*. Dover Publications.

Freud, S. (1900). *The interpretation of dreams*. S.E., 4–5. (cf. J. Crick, Trans., 1999).

Freud, S. (1933). *New introductory lectures on psycho-analysis*. Hogarth.
Gardner, H. (1999). *Intelligence reframed: Multiple intelligences for the 21st century*. Basic Books.
Hull, C. L. (1943). *Principles of behavior*. Appleton-Century.
James, W. (1894). The physical basis of emotion. *Psychological Review, 1*, 516–529.
Kenrick, D. T., Griskevicius, V., Neuberg, S. L., & Schaller, M. (2010). Renovating the pyramid of needs: Contemporary extensions built upon ancient foundations. *Perspectives on Psychological Science, 5*(3), 292–314.
Köhler, W. (1925, 1992). Gestalt psychology: An introduction to new concepts in modern psychology (reissue). Liveright.
Laird, J. D. (1974). Self-attribution of emotion: The effects of expressive behavior on the quality of emotional experience. *Journal of Personality and Social Psychology, 29*(4), 475–486.
Lange, C. (1885). The emotions. Reprinted in C. G. Lange & W. James (Eds.), *The emotions*. Harner.
Lazarus, R. S. (1991). *Emotion and adaptation*. Oxford University Press.
Lewin, K. (1936). *Principles of topological psychology*. McGraw Hill.
Maslow, A. (1943). A theory of human motivation. *Psychological Review, 50*, 370–396.
Maslow, A. (1987). *Motivation and personality* (3rd Ed.). Harper & Ro.
McClelland, D. C. (1961). *The achieving society*. Van Nostrand.
McClelland, D. C. (1988). *Human motivation*. Cambridge University Press.
McDougall, W. (1908). *An introduction to social psychology*. Methuen & Co.
Mishra, R. C., Sinha, D.,& Berry, J. W. (1996). *Ecology, acculturation and psychological adaptation: A study of adivasis in Bihar*. Sage.
Ryan, R. M., & Deci, E. L. (2000). Self-determination theory and the facilitation of intrinsic motivation, social development, and well-being. *American Psychologist, 55*, 68–78.
Seligman, M. (1975). *Helplessness: Depression, development and death*. W. H. Freeman.
Spearman, C. (1904). "General intelligence" objectively determined and measured. *American Journal of Psychology, 15*, 201–293.
Sternberg, R. J. (1988). *The triarchic mind: A new theory of human intelligence*. Viking-Penguin.
Tolman, E. C. (1932). *Purposive behavior in animals and man*. Century.
Yerkes, R. M., & Dodson, J. D. (1908). The relation of strength of stimulus to rapidity of habit formation. *Journal of Comparative Neurology and Psychology, 18*, 459–482.

Chapter 2
Criminal Psychology: Understanding Criminal Behaviour

Sanjeev P. Sahni and Nisha Phakey

Abstract Criminal psychology is a field involving an amalgamation of psychology, criminology, and the law. This discipline was conceived in the mid-twentieth century, when psychologists began offering expert perspectives on criminal behaviour and speculate about the possible causes that push one to commit such acts. This chapter will expound upon the purview of criminal psychology, how it emerged as a specialized field of study, and how it is different from related disciplines such as forensic psychology. Further, this chapter will cover the role and responsibilities of a criminal psychologist in criminal justice proceedings as a clinician, experimentalist, actuarial, and advisor in criminal proceedings. It will also briefly encapsulate the role played by a criminal psychologist in investigation, trial, conviction, and rehabilitation of convicts. Then, next section will deal with scope of this field realized by different institutions and individuals globally, and what are the applications of this discipline in different countries of the world and India.

Keywords Criminal psychology · Forensic psychology · Psychology and law · Criminal behaviour · Criminal psychologist

2.1 Introduction

Many might derive their understanding of what being a criminal psychologist involves from popular TV series and crime thrillers, such as the Netflix series *Mindhunter*, which is based on a true-crime book with the same title, written by John E. Douglas and Mark Olshaker. It follows two FBI Agents, Holden Ford and Bill Tench, as they interview a plethora of serial killers who were serving life sentences to gain insights into what caused them to commit such heinous crimes. While these depictions in media do portray some aspects of the work done by a criminal psychologist correctly, nevertheless, it also fails to represent the diverse variety of other roles that a criminal psychologist can perform. A criminal psychologist's work profile is not

S. P. Sahni (✉) · N. Phakey
Jindal Institute of Behavioural Sciences, O. P. Jindal Global University, Sonipat, Haryana, India
e-mail: drspsahni@jgu.edu.in

S. Sahni et al. (eds.), *Criminal Psychology and the Criminal Justice System in India and Beyond*, https://doi.org/10.1007/978-981-16-4570-9_2

merely limited to interviewing witnesses or suspects of crimes, it also involves planning and working towards rehabilitation of the offenders, serving as expert witnesses in the courtroom, and conducting research on emerging topics in criminal psychology. In this chapter, we will introduce the discipline of criminal psychology and how criminal psychologists function.

2.1.1 What Classifies as a Crime?

To understand the scope of criminal psychology, it is necessary to first define the concept of crime. In legal terms, crime can be defined as an act or omission punishable by law (Mclaughlin & Munice, 2001). But the definition of crime is dynamic—what qualifies as a crime depends on the place and time of committing the act, and the prevalent societal norms of that particular place (Newburn, 2013). For example, the usage of various drugs such as marijuana, homosexuality, prostitution, and marital rape is legal in some countries, but a criminal act in others.

This variance in classifying crime gives rise to the dilemma of providing psychological explanations for criminal behaviour. As Wortley contemplates, if someone can be called a criminal today for an act, but not tomorrow, then nothing meaningful can be said about the criminal nature. Robert Agnew tried to address this ambiguity in his definition of crime. He proposes that crime should be defined as 'acts that cause blameworthy harm, is condemned by the public, and/or are not sanctioned by the state'. This definition shifted the load away from the deeds that are currently prohibited by the law to a wider array of destructive human actions (Durrant, 2018).

Our ideas about the criminal world are formed through multiple sources—media, social media, the government, and personal experiences of the general population. Although all these sources seem to influence each other, media—with its widespread reach—particularly dominates in influencing people's perception of crime. Media coverage majorly focuses on the sensationalization of events rather than a realistic coverage of crime phenomena, such as property crime or theft that are often underrepresented in the newspapers. On the other hand, violent crimes such as homicide and rape are overtly reported in the news (Howitt, 2006).

The National Crime Records Bureau of India, in its recent report of 2018, shows an increase of 1.3% in the registration of crimes, although the crime rate per lakh population has come down marginally from 388.6 in 2017 to 383.5 in 2018. Higher numbers of crimes against women, suicides, economic offenses, and cybercrime offenses have been reported in 2018 in comparison with similar crime statistics of 2017 (NCRB, 2018).

It is important for practicing criminal psychologists to be familiar with the recent trends in crime, both globally as well as within their own regions (Howitt, 2006). This can be estimated via different methods such as general population and offender surveys, surveys involving victims of crime, police records or reports of crime, prison statistics of members imprisoned, and court statistics of convicted crimes. Interpretation of the information correctly requires expertise and experience as each source of information has to be considered mindful of particular characteristics and influencing factors.

2.1.2 What is Criminal Psychology?

Criminology involves the study of crime, criminal behaviour, and responses to crime (Newburn, 2013), whereas criminal psychology involves an influx of both criminology and psychology to explain the causes of criminal behaviour. The term 'criminal psychology' has been defined in many ways. One definition from Gudjonsson and Haward (1998) reads as 'that branch of applied psychology which is concerned with the collection, examination, and presentation of evidence for judicial purposes'. This explanation reflects that criminal psychology is concerned with investigative and judicial processes. However, for years, the involvement of criminal psychologists has also been in the assessment and rehabilitation of criminal offenders following their sentencing. A more comprehensive definition was proffered by an American psychologist, Wrightsman (2001), who described criminal psychology as any application of psychological knowledge or methods to a task faced by the legal system. Criminal psychologists can deal in all areas of the criminal justice system, even post-sentence, and thus, an elaborate definition is needed to encompass all the roles which a criminal psychologist can perform. There is, as yet, a lack of consensus on the meaning of criminal psychology.

Some other terms are frequently used interchangeably with criminal psychology—such as forensic psychology or legal psychology. However, these disciplines are totally different from the field of criminal psychology. Forensic psychology deals with the psychological aspects of legal processes, including applying theory to criminal investigations, understanding psychological problems associated with criminal behaviour, and the treatment of criminals (Bull et al., 2009). Forensic Psychology usually involves professional practice by any psychologist working within any subdiscipline of psychology such ad clinical psychology, developmental psychology, social or cognitive psychology. The psychologist involved applies his/her subject knowledge to the law while addressing legal and administrative matters (Vaya, 2015).

Both forensic and criminal psychology are quite similar in scope, but criminal psychology focuses more on the offender. However, criminality is not solely a characteristic of an individual; it is contingent on the social context of crime and the criminal justice system which also includes the wider aspects of the criminal's experience, i.e. in courts or while imprisoned. In this way it can be said that the role of both criminal and forensic psychologists are quite overlapping. The major difference between the two is that forensic psychology finds its application in both criminal and civil law.

2.1.3 History and Evolution of Criminal Psychology

The origin of criminal psychology as a discipline is rooted in the allied fields, especially psychology, sociology, and criminology. The history of criminal psychology can be traced back to the era of Charles Darwin where writings about lie detection based on hidden emotional cues can be found. He offered that an angry person can regulate or manipulate their body movements, but not the facial muscles which are not under voluntary control. These ideas were reflected in the approach followed by Paul Eckman to detect lies through facial micro-expressions.

In the UK, the origin of forensic and criminal psychology could be found when Sir Francis Galton devised a word association test that would assist in the lie detection procedure. In this, the assessor would say a word linked to the crime and will subsequently study the suspect's response to it closely (Matte, 2007). The establishment of the psychological laboratory by Wilhelm Wundt in 1875 also serves as an important keystone in the development of forensic and criminal psychology, as many students and coworkers of Wundt were instrumental in developing the field of criminal psychology. In 1985, James McKeen Cattell, former student of Wundt, used structured and controlled laboratory experiments into human memory to investigate the quality of eyewitness testimony. He investigated the individual differences in situational influence on eyewitness accuracy. Alfred Binet in France and William Stern in Germany also researched on similar lines. Around 1905, in Germany, Carl Gustav Jung also experimented on a criminal suspect using word association test.

Then came Hugo Münsterberg, an applied psychologist, who worked as a pioneer in applying psychological principles to the legal field. In his book, *On the Witness Stand* (1908), he debated the role of psychological research in legal proceedings and how psychologists can provide objective data to support evidence and testimony. He did this at a time when psychology was a relatively new science and was not perceived to have a legitimate role in the judicial proceedings in the court.

In the United Kingdom, Lionel Haward from University of Surrey began to advocate for the psychologist to play a role in legal proceedings, especially in defence. He conducted a study testing the accuracy of a police officer's claim that he recorded the license plate of a speeding motorcycle correctly. About a hundred trained observers participated this experiment, but none of them, surprisingly, was able to correctly identify the license numbers.

Studies in criminal psychology were on a steady rise at the end of World War II. In 1960, Hans Eysenck proposed a general theory of crime. Through the 1970s and 1980s, forensic and criminal psychology not only developed extensively as a discipline but also developed in its institutional basis. Royo, in 1996, suggested that the discipline can be further consolidated by the formation of associations, the creation of specialized books and journals, the official institutionalization of the discipline as part of the criminal justice process, and the creation of university courses devoted to the subject. Some of these institutional happenings include.

Formation of Associations: Meetings and associations of like-minded researchers are important for the development of a field because it helps to form research relationships between universities and other organizations, both nationally and internationally. With this purpose, The American Psychology-Law Association was established in 1969 and was instrumental in the creation of the Psychology and Law division (division 41) of the American Psychological Association (APA), with which it finally merged in 1981. The association began publishing the highly influential journal *Behavioral Sciences and the Law* in 1977.

The Division of Criminological and Legal Psychology was established by the British Psychological Society in 1977 but renamed the Division of Forensic Psychology in 1999. The division publishes the journal *Legal.* The Australia and New Zealand Association of Psychiatry, Psychology and Law was founded in 1972 and in 1993, respectively, publishes its first issue of the journal *Psychiatry, Psychology and Law.*

The European Association of Psychology and Law initially began with small meetings until their first European conference on psychology and law was held in Maastricht, Netherlands, in 1988. This led to a second larger congregation in Nuremberg, Germany, which led to the founding of the European Association of Psychology and Law. The Nordic Network for Research on Psychology and Law began in Sweden in 2004 (VandenBos, 2007).

Professional Education: Postgraduate psychology and law programs are to be found in many countries. There are over thirty courses in the USA, around twenty in the UK, nine in Australia, four in Germany, four in Spain, three in Russia, three in Canada, and one in Sweden. Around seven colleges in India offer postgraduate diplomas or degrees in criminal psychology in India. Structured and accessible education contributes greatly to the future of any discipline.

Publications: There are many journals that publish articles in the field of psychology and the law, including important mainstream journals such as *Psychological Bulletin.* There are also some specialized journals catering solely to research in forensic/criminal/legal psychology. It was observed that the top 68 most frequently cited journals that accounted for only 47% of the total number of citations, contained 15 journals specific to legal psychology (Howitt, 2006).

2.1.4 History and Evolution of Criminal Psychology in India

Criminal psychology is a relatively new and evolving field that rose in the early nineteenth century. In India, the foundations of criminal psychology were laid in 1916, with the establishment of the first Department of Experimental Psychology at Calcutta University followed by the establishment of Lok Nayak Jayprakash Narayan National Institute of Criminology and Forensic Sciences in Delhi in 1972. Since 1985, forensic psychological assessment was introduced for examining crime suspects (actual case studies), as and when needed, using various projective tests such as Henry Murray's Thematic Apperception Test, Draw a Person, Bender Gestalt

Tests, Carl Jung's Word Association Test, Sentence Completion Test, and Rorschach Inkblot Test. Between 1985 and 1988, this had facilitated in assimilating psychological insights that aided suspect interrogations. The clinical approach was amalgamated with investigative skills to examine the suspects which resulted in the advent of forensic interview techniques.

With the emergence of criminal psychology, clinical psychologists were empowered with administrative authority and extended their services to civil and criminal cases to assess competency to stand trial, reconciliation in family courts, and victim rehabilitation. Investigation methods such as psychological assessment, hypnosis, statement analysis, modified polygraph technique, and narcoanalysis have progressed from heuristic techniques developed to meet the requirement of the investigation to more empirical methodologies. In India, criminal psychology is still in its infancy but is continuously evolving as an independent discipline (Vaya S. L).

2.2 Roles of a Criminal Psychologist

The roles that psychologists perform when they become professionally involved in criminal proceedings were first listed by Professor Lionel Haward, one of the founding fathers of criminal psychology in the UK. These are as follows:

Clinical: Here, the psychologist usually assesses the individual to provide a clinical judgement, using interviews, various psychometric tests, and other assessment tools, to inform the police, jurors, and probation services about the psychological functioning of the individual. A psychologist may be asked to assess individuals to determine whether the suspect is fit to stand the trial or not, whether the person under the trial will be able to understand the court proceedings or not, or to rule whether the persons under trial are suffering from any mental illness. These assessments will aid and influence the functioning of the criminal justice system and how the trials will proceed.

Experimental: In this role, the expert is involved in research to provide objective evidence for the case in hand. This involves carrying out assessments using psychological tools to opine on a question or to provide further information to assist the courts' decision-making process (e.g. how likely it is that someone can correctly identify an individual driving on the highway, from a distance, in the dark). Alternatively, it can also involve psychologists providing the summary to the court of current research findings that are relevant to the case in question.

Actuarial: This role involves the use of statistics to provide information to the court relating to the probability of an event occurring, such as, how likely is it for an offender to reoffend. In such a case, a psychologist could be called upon to weigh in on the pre- or post-sentence report to the court.

Advisory: In this role, the psychologist may help the police in issues guiding an investigation. An offender's profile delivered by a criminal psychologist could help inform the investigation, or a criminal psychologist's advice could assist in interviewing a particular suspect or cross-examining witnesses in court. In this role, a psychologist advises the police, courts, prison, and probation services.

The above-stated roles of psychologists describe the array of different circumstances within the criminal justice system where inputs from psychologists are needed. Among all the roles performed by a criminal psychologist, the most important is the assistance they provide towards a criminal investigation. Professor Laurence Alison of the University of Liverpool advocated the ways the expertise provided by a psychologist can support the police in the work they do. From assistance in profiling offenders to suggesting measures to improve techniques of interviewing victims, offenders, and witnesses, criminal psychologists can also help in increasing the accuracy of methods of collecting, collating, and analysing the obtained data. They can also aid in the development of empirically based suspect prioritization systems. Thus, from this description, it is apparent that the role of a criminal psychologist in assisting police is essential and widespread (Durrant, 2018).

2.2.1 *Crime Analysis*

Intelligence analysis draws heavily upon methods used in psychology. Criminal psychologists are usually employed by the policing agencies to investigate and examine crime data to aid police in their work. As a crime analyst, the most common task is linking crimes based on similarities found in the behaviour of the offender, as recounted by the victim or inferred from the crime scene. For example, let us examine the murder of a woman who was walking home alone in the night, on her way back from work. Crime analysts could pick up some useful information in this case—the fact that she had just left from office, that the perpetrator took some of her belongings away from the scene with him, and the way she was murdered, the choice of weapon—to check against pre-existing records of similar crimes to flag any similarities to past crimes. If matches are found—either the same kind of weapon was used, similar items were taken by a murderer from the victims, or it was in a close geographical location to another murder—then all this information can be used by the police to consider the possibility that the same individual offender or a specific group has committed both crimes. This allows more focused investigation and avoids wasting time and labour.

2.2.2 *Offender Profiling*

Usually, criminal profiling involves using information from the crime sites and then combining it with testimony from eyewitnesses and victims, so that meaningful conclusions can be drawn about the person who committed the crime. Such a profile answers various related questions, such as the gender and age of the offender, whether the crime was impulsive or planned, and others. This information assists investigation agencies in arriving at a set of possible suspects. Offender profiling by criminal psychologists has grabbed a lot of media attention in recent years, both in fiction and in real-life high-profile cases. While this may have popularized the disciplinary profile, yet the sensationalized portrayal has, to some extent, compromised the science behind it for the general population.

2.2.3 Interviewing Victims and Suspects

The most crucial part of an investigation involves collecting reliable evidence to understand what happened at the crime scene. Reliable information from witnesses and victims requires good interviewing skills through which the investigators can get accurate information without biasing or coercing the testimony. The skills required to interview suspects are very different than that needed for eyewitnesses. There is empirical evidence that the recall of events by eyewitnesses is vulnerable to manipulation by the interviewer, intentionally or otherwise. Hence, the mode of the interview and the way it is conducted for different people involved in the case is extremely important. Psychologists are instrumental in guiding and training police personnel in techniques to interview suspects or witnesses. The investigative agencies can also utilize the expertise of psychologists to gain advice on interviewing particularly difficult witnesses or suspects, for example, children or the elderly.

2.2.4 Expert Witness

Sometimes, court cases might involve complex issues of mental ability and cognition that might require the expertise of a criminal psychologist. Under such circumstances, expert witnesses are called upon to give their opinion on the issue in question, although this procedure may vary from one jurisdiction to another. For example, in European countries, the court itself calls the expert witness to give an opinion or provide information, when required. In the USA & UK, the experts are instructed by either the defence or prosecution to testify in support of their claims. In the past, the admissibility of a psychologist's opinion often uses to be limited to issues related to psychological functioning or intellectual impairment of an individual. Over the recent years, the opinion by psychologists has been increasingly sought in a wide number of issues, such as the influence of interviewing techniques, reliability of eyewitness testimony, psychometric or clinical assessment of a suspect or witness, or regarding profiling techniques used during the investigation.

2.2.5 Assessment and Rehabilitation of Offenders

In countries like Australia, Canada, and UK, criminal psychologists are comprehensively involved in activities concerning the assessment, rehabilitation, and management of criminals, during the detention period and afterwards. This work might range from working with offenders to reduce their tendency to reoffend to looking after the psychological needs of offenders, such as counselling prisoners suffering from depression due to the secluded environment in prisons or other stress such as bullying and trauma.

Pre- and post-sentence assessment of the offenders comprises assessing their risk of reoffending, of harming themselves and/or others, and also assessing their mental health needs. These assessments can be further used in planning the release and rehabilitation of the offenders. If an offender has been identified as posing a high risk to the public, then psychologists provide input at an operational level to monitor his/her activity and also managerial and advisory support in delivering interventions to reduce the risk. Apart from this, criminal psychologists are involved in training of prison or probation staff, preparing reports elaborating the risk level for courts, and emphasizing the needs of individual offenders for their welfare.

2.2.6 Academia and Research

With the growing interest in criminal psychology over the years, there has been a rise in such courses, also an increase in the number of psychologists specializing in various aspects of this discipline. Undergraduate and postgraduate studies should not only involve theory but also its practical application in understanding criminal behaviour, in the courtroom, in the investigation, rehabilitation, and assessment of offenders. Also, criminal psychologists in academia should be actively engaged in researching emerging phenomena and lacunas in this discipline (Newburn, 2013).

2.3 Conclusion

In this chapter, we have tried to define the area of criminal psychology and how it evolved as a discipline over the years. This chapter also elaborates the multiple roles they perform in criminal justice proceedings. From aiding the police in investigations, in selection of police officers, carrying out psychological assessment of offenders, victims, or suspects, providing intervention and planning management and rehabilitation of offenders, conducting research in this area and also to provide training to future investigators and criminalists, the work of a criminal psychologist is widespread. Over the years, the field of criminal psychology has witnessed tremendous growth, and with time, the role of criminal psychologists has now attained recognition by courts and other investigative agencies. Although in India, the field is still evolving, its popularity predicts that psychologists will only increasingly be involved in criminal justice proceedings in the future.

References

Bull, R., Bilby, C., Cooke, C., & Grant, T. (2009). *Criminal psychology: A beginner's guide*. Oneworld Publications.
Durrant, R. (2018). *An introduction to criminal psychology*. Routledge.
Gudjonsson, G. H., & Haward, L. R. C. (1998). *Forensic psychology: A guide to practice*. Routledge.
Howitt, D. (2006). *Introduction to forensic and criminal psychology*. Pearson Education.
Matte, J. A. (2007). Psychological structure and theoretical concept of the Backster Zone Comparison Technique and the Quadri-Track Zone Comparison Technique. *Polygraph, 36*(2), 84–90.
McLaughlin, E., & Muncie, J. (Eds.). (2001). *Controlling crime* (vol. 2). Sage.
National Crime Records Bureau. (2018). *Crime in India*. Ministry of Home Affairs, Government of India.
Newburn, T. (2013). *Criminology* (2nd ed.). Routledge.
VandenBos, G. R. (2007). *APA dictionary of psychology*. American Psychological Association.
Vaya, S. L. (2015). Forensic Psychology in India. *International Research Journal on Police Science, 1*(1), 29.
Wrightsman, L. S. (2001). *Forensic psychology*. Thomson Learning.

Chapter 3
Theoretical Approaches to Understanding Criminal Behaviour

Sanjeev P. Sahni and Akshaya Krishnakumar

Abstract Why do some people commit crimes? Since the early period, scholars have tried to answer this question by attributing criminal behaviour to various factors such as physical characteristics, heredity, socialization, and even supernatural elements. This chapter will look at theories that have evolved over time that seeks to understand criminal behaviour from various perspectives. Broadly, this chapter will approach to understand criminal behaviour from three popular perspectives—biological, psychological, and sociological. The focus will be to understand whether criminality is inherited; a result of individual experiences or influenced by societal factors, or whether it is a combination of all the three.

Keywords Theories of crime · Physical anomalies · Genetics and crime · Learning criminality · Criminal thinking · Anomie · Culture conflict · Self-fulfilling prophecy

3.1 Introduction

More often, when we think of people who commit crimes and what motivates them, we are compelled to think of them as outliers in the society. From an early period, scholars have tried to explain criminal behaviour by attributing them to various factors, most of which reflected the thinking and beliefs of the people at the time when these were propounded. In the early days, when people were dominated by spiritualistic notions, the explanation to criminal behaviour was mostly attributed to religious and supernatural elements. It was perceived that people were driven to commit crimes by forces beyond their self-control. This naturally meant that little or no attention was given to motive, psyche, or any other aspects that could have contributed to the concerned criminal behaviour. As there were no specific legislation or rules on how to treat criminals, closed trials were held and the punishments that were administered were often very inhuman, arbitrary, and torturous (Burke, 2009).

S. P. Sahni (✉) · A. Krishnakumar
Jindal Institute of Behavioural Sciences, O.P. Jindal Global University, Sonipat, Haryana, India
e-mail: drspsahni@jgu.edu.in

S. Sahni et al. (eds.), *Criminal Psychology and the Criminal Justice System in India and Beyond*, https://doi.org/10.1007/978-981-16-4570-9_3

This kind of spiritualistic notion of crime prevailed in ancient India as well. Ordeals by fire and oaths were used to determine the guilt of the offender until the advent of British Rule (Paranjape, 2017).

As the society progressed, the theories explaining criminal behaviour also took new shapes. The classical theory of crime, which emerged in the eighteenth century, moved away from the spiritualistic notions of crime, and free will was seen as the central concept to explain criminal behaviour. Cesare Beccaria and Jeremy Bentham are considered to be the two major contributors to classical theory of crime. Beccaria considered people to be rational beings and believed that they have the free will to choose and control their behaviour. In his work from 1819, *An Essay on Crimes and Punishments,* he states that pleasure and pain are the only springs of action in humans, a concept known as hedonism, which was integral to the classical theory. He was also concerned about the kinds of existing punishment for crimes during his period which were cruel and torturous, and advocated for the punishment administered to be proportional to the crime committed.

Jeremy Bentham had similar ideas as that of Beccaria, he also believed that as rational beings, people will seek to gain pleasure by trying to avoid pain (Burke, 2009). He postulated that the punishment for a crime must outweigh any pleasure derived from it. Bentham also formulated a number of rules by which the administration of punishment was to be regulated (Hollin, 2013).

In the late nineteenth century, the popularity of the Classical School began to dwindle but the ideas propounded by this school of thought continued to influence the criminal justice systems in Europe, America, and many other countries.

3.2 Physical Features and Criminal Behaviour

With the emergence of new and innovative ways to explain criminal behaviour, the validity of the Classical School of Thought was challenged. The Positivist School eliminated the free will notion of the Classical School and replaced it with a science of society, which explained and enabled eradication of crime (Taylor, Walton, & Young, 2013). The Positivist School of Thought stressed on the application of scientific methods in understanding criminal behaviour. The early criminological positivists were mostly biological theorists who attributed criminal behaviour to certain physical characteristics, such as the shape of the skull, ears, and forehead; type of hair and biological factors such as genetics, biochemical irregularities, chromosomal abnormalities, and so on (Siegel, 2011).

One of the earliest theories in this field was given by Cesare Lombroso in his work, *Criminal Man,* published in 1875. He studied both criminals and non-criminals and found some correlation between the individual characteristics of the criminals, mostly physical (Heidt & Wheeldon, 2014). He then argued that anthropologically, criminals were less evolved than non-criminals, and some of their criminal tendencies might be contingent on their primitive natures.

His theory of Atavism argued that some criminals were not fully evolved and had observable *stigmata* or markers such as thinness of body hair, thick skull, jug ears, sloping foreheads, overdeveloped jaws and cheekbones, oblique eyes, dark skin, thick and curly hair, low degrees of strength, below-average weight, absence of remorse, insensitivity to pain, lack of moral sense, lack of foresight, underdeveloped concepts of divinity and morality (Lombroso, 2006).

Based on his study, he also developed a classification of criminals which evolved with each edition of his book *Criminal Man*. He classified criminals into four categories, namely- born criminals, insane criminals, occasional criminals, and criminals of passion (Lombroso, 2006). The 'born criminals' were those who had distinguishable physical atavistic characteristics. Imbeciles, alcoholics, 'idiots', and epileptics constituted the insane criminals under his theory. Physical deformities such as abnormal eyes, arrested physical development, scanty beard were observable in these types of criminals along with other characteristics such as insensitivity to pain and emotional imbalance. The occasional criminals were those criminals whose crimes are explained primarily by opportunity. Although they too were presumed to have innate traits that predisposed them to criminality, it was comparatively less than the born and insane criminals. He further subdivides occasional criminals into three categories—pseudo-criminal, criminaloids, and habitual criminals. And finally, there were criminals of passion who committed crimes because of anger, love, or honour (Lombroso, 2006).

The concept of born criminals inadvertently led to the persecution of certain communities, or, as was seen in colonial India, tribes as well. The term, criminal tribes (now known as denotified tribes) referred to people who were born in a particular group or caste that was known to have 'criminal tendencies'; i.e. they were assumed to be destined or addicted to the commission of criminal activities because of their ancestors' crimes or criminal associations (Kapadia, 1952).

> These tribes were known as criminal tribes because the men and women born within it take to crime just as a duck takes to water... (Kapadia, 1952)

Just like Lombroso, the authorities who designated the title of 'born criminal' to the people belonging to this tribe, also blatantly ignored the social and environmental factors that could have contributed to their 'criminal tendencies' or the consequent persecution that prevented the tribe from alleviating their social status. Till date, the members of these tribes face a lot of discrimination because of their historic label.

Lombroso's theory was heavily criticized for the primitive methodology relying on limited data, and for the underlying racial discrimination. Even though Lombroso's theory fell into disrepute, many researchers were still interested in the relationship between physical features, body type, and criminality.

William Sheldon posited his Constitutional theory of crime in the 1940s, wherein he identified three types of physique related to temperament styles that were responsible for criminal behaviour. The three types of physique—somatotypes—were: endomorphs, people who are large and heavy; ectomorphs, who are thin and bony; and mesomorphs, who are broad and muscular (Heidt & Wheeldon, 2014).

He suggested that each body type is characterized by a specific type of temperament. The endomorphs have a viscerotonic temperament, which includes characteristics such as sociable, easy-going, and extroverted. The ectomorphs have a cerebrotonic temperament, characterized by high intelligence, introversions and are often seen to have various ailments and allergies. Those with the mesomorphic body type have a somotonic temperament, which is characterized by aggressiveness, assertiveness, and activeness (Heidt & Wheeldon, 2014). Each individual, according to their somatotype, would display a mixture of these traits.

Sheldon studied 400 men in a rehabilitation centre, classifying their somatotypes, and found that most of the delinquents were mesomorphs, and a few were endomorphs. According to his records, there was a clear absence of ectomorphs among the delinquents that he studied (Hollin, 2013). Hence, he concluded that the mesomorphs were most likely to produce criminal behaviour.

Enrico Ferri, Rafael Garafalo, Ernst Kretschmer, and many others also looked at associating body types and other physical characteristics to criminal behaviour. In fact, theorists of biological positivism extended their research to even look at how genes, chromosomes, and certain hormones contribute to criminal behaviour.

3.3 Genetical Influence on Criminal Behaviour

Whether crime is caused by nature or nurture is a popular debate that continues till date in criminology. Many researchers continue to look at family and genealogical studies in order to explain criminal behaviour. This branch of biological positivism includes studies focused on family, twins and adoption, which attempts to understand the effect of familial relationships and the role of genetics on criminal behaviour.

When it comes to family research, the focus has been mostly on two questions—firstly, is there any difference in the functioning of families of criminals and those of non-offenders; and secondly, is there any similarity in the behaviour of the criminal and his biological relatives (Hollin, 2013). Much work has been particularly centred around the second question. The argument governing these studies is that criminal families will invariably produce criminal children since biological relatives share certain genes. Richard L. Dugdale's and Henry Herbert Goddard's study on criminal families are the two famous studies where criminality was traced back to a person's ancestry.

In Dugdale's study of the Juke family in 1877, he tracked 709 members of the family and found that a large number of them exhibited criminality over successive generation. He believed that criminality was passed down in family, but he also strongly believed that the external environment also plays a major role. A criminal is built both by the genes and the bad environment he inherits from his family (Heidt & Wheeldon, 2014).

In 1912, Henry Herbert Goddard examined two families, the Kallikak family, fathered by the same man. The mother of one family was a 'feeble-minded' woman that the father, Martin Kallikak Sr., met at a tavern, while the other family was from his legal wife, who was a 'quaker woman' from a 'good family' (Goddard, 2009). According to his observations, the majority of descendants of the 'feeble-minded' woman were also 'feeble-minded', either prostitutes, alcoholics or criminals. On the other hand, the descendants of the 'quaker woman from a good family' were found to be law-abiding citizens who married into respectable families. He attributed criminality to feeble-mindedness and said that criminals were not born but were formed by feeble-mindedness (Goddard, 2009). He believed that environment had little or no effect upon criminality and it was only the inherited feeble mind that played a major role.

The critique for these, and other similar, studies is that it is impossible to disentangle the contributions of both genetics and environment towards criminality. Also, certain social and psychological factors within the family can be found to equally contribute to criminal behaviour.

The study of twins, according to many researchers, gave a clearer picture of the influence of genetics on criminality. Identical twins (monozygotic twins) have the same DNA, thereby the same genes; unlike fraternal twins (dizygotic twins) or family members, who only share some genes in common. Most of the twin studies measured the concordance rate, that is, the likelihood of a twin developing the same trait as that of the other twin, expressed as a percentage.

One of the earliest studies of twins was conducted by Johannes Lange in 1930. He examined 30 pairs of men, comprising of 13 identical twins, and 17 fraternal twins. He found that the concordance rate for identical twins was 77%, whereas for fraternal twins, only 12% (Hollin, 2013). Similar study was done by Christiansen on a larger scale. He examined the official records to identify how many of the 3586 pairs of twins born in the eastern half of Denmark between the years 1881 and 1910 had criminal records against them. The concordance rate for male identical twins was found to be 35% whereas for male fraternal twins, it was only 13%. Similarly, the concordance rate for female identical twins was found to be 21%, whereas for female fraternal twins it was only 8% (Christiansen, 1977).

A recent research that looked at twin studies to establish a link between genetics and offending behaviour has established that the monozygotic twins in one cohort were more similar in their criminal offending than the dizygotic twins. This according to the authors indicated the influence of genetics (Wertz et al., 2018).

The adoption studies, on the other hand, addressed the nature versus nurture debate, which forms the basis of the most popular criticisms of the family and twin studies. The adoptee receives his/her genes from one set of parents while another set of parents raise them, and hence, this allows the researchers to study whether genes or the social environment has more influence on behaviour.

Mednick's Danish Adoption studies are one of the most popularly cited studies where his team researched 13,194 adoptees, among which 6129 were male and 7065 were female. For the purposes of this study, criminal behaviour was limited to those with a record of court conviction (Joseph, 2001) and the researchers also checked for conviction records of the adoptive and biological parents. The research discovered that when both adoptive and biological parents had a criminal record, the adoptee was 24.5% more likely to have committed a crime. In this study, it was also found that when an adoptive parent does not have a criminal record, but the biological parent does, then 20% of the sons were found to be having a criminal record (Joseph, 2001). Similar results were found in the female sample as well.

There are many other studies on adoption which also found similar results, where the possibility of an adoptee having a criminal record was high when both the adoptive and biological parents had a criminal record. These studies suggest the possibility of a partial genetic aetiology (Burke, 2009).

Recently researchers have also attempted to associate particular genes to criminal and aggressive behaviour. One of the most popular ones that has created controversy in recent times for being associated with criminal behaviour is the monoamine oxidase A (MAOA) gene. According to many contemporary researchers, low activity MAOA gene (MAOA–L) predisposes people to criminal behaviour as it makes the individual more prone to express aggression when they are provoked or socially excluded (Baum, 2011). An Italian appeals court recently made news when it reduced the defendant's sentence after the defence team presented evidence of the individual having a genetic predisposition to violence (Feresin, 2009). A similar incident followed in 2011, as an Italian court again in a separate case, reduced the sentence of a convicted murderer from life term to 20 years on the grounds that the defendant had a low activity version of the MAOA gene (which is also commonly known as the 'warrior gene') (Feresin, 2011). While many lawyers continue attempts to use this as a defence advocating for lighter sentences, many researchers have raised concern over the scientific validity of such claim.

The studies on family, twins, and adoption do indicate that genetic factors do play a role in criminality, but it is also important to understand that these factors do not solely predetermine if a person is going to have criminal tendencies. The genetic potential might be realized due to any environmental event(s), and hence, the environmental factors cannot be totally ignored. As Rutter and Giller state, '*The question of just what is inherited remains unanswered. It is unlikely to be criminality as such*' (Canter, 2017).

By introducing the scientific method, the biological positivists innovated the way criminal behaviour was being studied. Indeed, this school of thought introduced us to the possible association between criminality and biological factors, but the major shortcoming is that they failed to acknowledge the various social and individual factors that also play a major role in the making of a criminal, along with the biological factors. For example, in the 1960s, the city of Mumbai (then Bombay) was terrorized by a serial killer for three years, who had murdered 41 people. Raman Raghav, the infamous serial killer of Mumbai, targeted poor people who either slept on the pavements or stayed in small huts in the northern suburbs of the city. He attacked his targets at night, by smashing their heads, while they were sleeping, with a hard and blunt instrument. When he was finally apprehended in 1968, in his confession to the magistrate he said that he committed the murders voluntarily and it was 'God' who had asked him to do so. He also believed that he had to kill people in order to prevent himself from being forced into homosexuality (BBC News, 2015). A panel of three psychiatrists, after examining Raghav, diagnosed him with schizophrenia and also observed that he suffered from delusions (BBC News, 2015). Cases such as that of

Raman Raghav reinforce the concept that in order to understand criminal behaviour, one has to move beyond factors such as gender, race, and physical characteristics. Individual thought and social factors can better explain these cases, which then brings us to the next section of the chapter.

3.4 Psychoanalysis and Criminal Behaviour

The psychology–crime link is not a new field of study; it had intrigued the interest of various psychologists and criminologists since the late nineteenth century. The development of psychological theory in relation to crime began with the idea of uncovering hidden unconscious forces within the individual's mind. When it comes to the conscious and unconscious part of the human mind, the psychoanalysis theory, origins of which can be traced back to the works of Viennese psychiatrist Sigmund Freud, still remains a prominent theory in psychology.

Sigmund Freud argued that much of our personality is determined by the unconscious, which is a part of an individual's personality that comprises of memory, beliefs, knowledge, urges, feelings, instincts, and drives, that one is not aware of, and which lie dormant in our inner conscious (Feldman, 2011).

In the essay *Criminals from a Sense of Guilt,* Freud suggested that for some, criminal behaviour was preceded by guilt (Goldberg, 2003). He claimed that a child progresses through three distinct, yet overlapping, stages of sexual development which culminates in an oedipal conflict between the child and his parents. In his studies, he found that some criminals were not able to overcome their oedipal conflict, which is an unconscious feeling of desire for their parent of the opposite sex and jealousy, envy, and a feeling to eliminate the parent of the same sex (Fitzpatrick, 1976). Because they were not able to overcome their oedipal conflict in their childhood, '*they suffer from an acute, albeit unconscious, sense of guilt that seeks alleviation through punishment*'. Freud further believed that some people in their adulthood steal or murder mostly because of this sense of unconscious guilt (Fitzpatrick, 1976).

> In many criminals, especially youthful ones, it is possible to detect a very powerful sense of guilt which existed before the crime, and is therefore not its result but its motive. It is as if it was a relief to be able to fasten this unconscious sense of guilt on to something real and immediate. (Freud, 1923)

Freud did not work much on building a connection between psychoanalysis and crime or delinquency, but other psychoanalysts such as August Aichhorn, Franz Alexander, and Hugo Staub did explore this aspect. Originally a teacher, Aichhorn, worked with disturbed and delinquent children to understand and treat them. Following in the footsteps of Freud, Aichhorn also focused on how delinquency resulted from neurosis, when the psychological conflict was poorly resolved, rather than wickedness (Galatzer-Levy & Galatzer-Levy, 2007). He further stated that environmental factors cannot solely be a cause for criminal behaviour, but there is some underlying predisposition that also contributes towards criminality. The term that he used to describe this was *latent delinquency,* which he believed predisposes a child to criminal behaviour. Aichhorn believes that latent delinquency is partially innate and is partially attributed to a child's early emotional relationships (Hollin, 1989). He suggested that every child is asocial when they deal with the world for the first time; that is, a child is only concerned about their own wellbeing, which is an idea that is based on Freud's pleasure principle. He further suggests that as the child develops, their behaviour becomes more socialized due to the emergence of ego and development of reality principle (Hollin, 1989). In some children, this process of psychological development goes astray and the child ends up not being able to '*postpone pleasure in the moment in response to social or societal constraints*', (Galatzer-Levy & Galatzer-Levy, 2007) which in turn allows the latent delinquency to be dominant. Hence, according to Aichhorn, failure of the psychological development leads to criminal or delinquent behaviour.

Alexander and Staub, in their book *The Criminal, the Judge and the Public,* also presented similar views as that of Aichhorn; that is, they also suggested that the criminal was someone who failed to resolve his internal psychological conflict (Hollin, 1989). David Abrahamsen, on the other hand, suggested that criminal tendencies are caused when the ego is damaged, and not just weak; this meant that the criminal was unable to postpone seeking instant gratification through pleasure-seeking activity of the Id. He, in fact, attributed damaged or weak ego and superego to form an attachment and connection with their parents (Einstadter & Henry, 2006).

Psychoanalysis and crime have been studied by many other scholars; the focus of these studies later moved on to explaining criminal behaviour from a psychodynamic framework, one example being John Bowlby's theory of maternal deprivation. From his study of 44 juvenile thieves, Bowlby inferred that early maternal separation was higher in case of delinquents rather than non-delinquents. He stated that separation from the mother had an adverse effect on the psychological development of the child. His theory was based on two main propositions—one, that a close and unbroken relationship between the mother and the child is an important aspect of mental health; and second, that separation from the mother or rejection by the mother leads to serious cases of delinquency (Hollin, 1989). He further argued that children who do not have a secure maternal bonding tend to develop anxiety and also avoid developing a relationship with others. This, in turn, makes them affectionless children due to which they even fail to empathize with others, which eventually makes them prone to displaying antisocial behaviour (Einstadter & Henry, 2006).

The psychoanalytic and psychodynamic theories look at criminal behaviour as a result of internal conflicts and the inner process that works at an unconscious level. Due to this, these theories have been criticized by many for their lack of use of scientific method. It was also stated by many that most of the concepts that are central to these theories are very vague and untestable (Hollin, 1989).

When it comes to personality traits and criminal behaviour, one of the most popular theories is that of Hans Eysenck, who believed that an individual's personality is made of up a cluster of traits. He developed the PEN model of personality where he identified three dimensions of personality—*extroversion, neuroticism, and psychoticism*. Each of these dimensions runs from high to low for different people based on biological and conditioning processes.

An extrovert is considered as cortically under-aroused, because of which they keep seeking stimulation to maintain the cortical arousal at optimum. An introvert, on the other hand, is cortically over-aroused, due to which they try to avoid seeking simulation to keep their arousal levels low (Hollin, 1989). Neuroticism is considered to be related to the functioning of the autonomic nervous system. Individuals with a high level are characterized by a very imbalanced autonomic nervous system that causes strong reactions to painful or unpleasant stimuli (Hollin, 1989). The final dimension is that of psychoticism has been associated with both psychotic episode and aggression. This dimension too has a biological basis in, increased levels of testosterone (Hollin, 1989).

These personality dimensions have different characteristics, such as an individual who scores high on extroversion is someone who is sociable, impulsive, and outgoing, whereas an individual who scores low on extroversion is someone who is quiet, unsociable, and reserved. According to Eysenck, a normal human personality is emotionally stable and is neither highly introverted nor extroverted. Whereas a person who scores high on extroversion, neuroticism, and psychoticism has greater predisposition to crime (Lanier & Henry, 2010). He further elaborated that such people require more stimulation those with normal personality, and they achieve that by indulging in crime, violence, and drug abuse. They were also found to be difficult to condition and had a higher tolerance to pain (Lanier & Henry, 2010). Over the years, many researchers have tried to test Eysenck's theory of criminal personality and have found many drawbacks to it. One of the most commonly listed drawbacks to his theory is that it fails to be an integrative theory of criminality as it completely ignores the socio-economic variables that could contribute in the making of a criminal (Goldsmith, 1981; Reid, 2011).

3.4.1 Learning Criminal Behaviour

Many sociologists and social psychologists assert that just like any other behaviour, criminal behaviour is also learnt by processes such as conditioning, observation, and association. The social learning theory, proposed by the American psychologist, Albert Bandura, posits that behaviour can be learnt by observing other people. He is famously known for his Bobo doll experiment, in which he studied how children acquire social behaviours, such as aggression, by observation and imitation. According to Bandura's theory, criminals and delinquents observe and learn from poor role models and tend to imitate the socially undesirable behaviour of the models, as they might assume it to be acceptable behaviour.

There have been several real-life cases where the criminals have claimed to have learned violent behaviour by observing characters in movies, cartoons, video games, etc. For example, an Indian man in Australia, aged 32, who was a huge fan of

Bollywood films, was accused of stalking a woman. His actions were inspired by the Hindi movies that he was exposed to, where stalking was an acceptable way of pursuing a woman (Pearlman, 2015). Not only does observation and imitation of poor role models causes delinquency and crime, even our associations with our close family and friends who are into unacceptable behaviour, play an important role in deciding whether we take to a life of crime.

Edwin H. Sutherland's Theory of Differential Association is another theory that advocates that criminal behaviour is learnt just like any other behaviour. According to Sutherland's theory, criminal behaviour is learned from interactions with other criminals and this learning occurs within intimate personal groups. He also furthered that not only does one learn a behaviour, but they also learn the techniques, rationalizations, motives, and drives behind these behaviours (Siegel, 2011). These and similar ideas were discussed in the nine postulates that he gave in his theory which conclude that one takes to a life of crime if they learn values and behaviours that are not consistent with the conventionally accepted values and behaviour (Siegel, 2011).

There are numerous case studies that support Sutherland's theory, such as that of the famous sandalwood smuggler from South India, Veerappan, who grew up exposed to a lot of close relations who were smugglers and poachers. Applying Sutherland's theory, Veerappan learned the criminal behaviour from these people as they were his close relations and he was constantly exposed to their law-breaking behaviour from a very young age (Manoharan, 2004). This, of course, does not absolve his choices, but it does help us understand what could surely have been the possible reason why he took to criminal activities.

3.4.2 A Criminal's Thought Process

Scholars from the field of psychology also looked at the possibility of criminals having different thinking processes or patterns that in fact motivate them to indulge in criminal activities. Samuel Yochelson and Stanton Samenow (1976) gave the first prominent conceptualization of criminal thinking, noting that the differential thinking processes of criminals are prevalent throughout every aspect of their lives (Mandracchia, Morgan, Garos, & Garland, 2007). For their study, they relied on in-depth interviews with incarcerated prisoners to understand the different thinking processes of these criminals. They identified 52 thinking patterns in criminals, which they referred to as 'errors', because it was devoid of responsibility and formed the basis of their criminal behaviour. They also claimed that the individuals were usually unaware of their erroneous nature of thinking. These errors were further divided into three broad categories (Mandracchia, Morgan, Garos, & Garland, 2007)

- *criminal thinking patterns*, included errors such as excessive levels of pride, anger, and fear.
- *automatic errors of thinking*, included errors in lack of empathy, self-victimization, etc.

- *thinking errors from idea through execution*, included the ability to see oneself as a good person only by cutting oneself off from their conscience.

It was observed that even though these tendencies exist in the minds of the criminals, these never directly cause criminal behaviour; but it is the cluster of dysfunctional thoughts that have not been acted upon that leads to criminal behaviour (Mandracchia, Morgan, Garos, & Garland, 2007). They even worked on creating a treatment programme for these offenders and found that the first step to that is to alter or amend their maladaptive thinking patterns.

They further identified certain cognitive process that operates in an individual before, during and after the commission of a crime. Before the commission of a crime, an individual experiences a mental process which they called 'corrosion' which acts as a technique to eliminate the deterrents to crime (Mandracchia, Morgan, Garos, & Garland, 2007). While committing a crime, an individual uses 'cut-off mechanism', which they identified as a mechanism that instantly gets rid of fear or guilt and also boosts the self-confidence of the individual which in turn facilitates the commission of the crime. Finally, after the commission of the crime, the cognitive process of 'power thrust' increases the perception of self-importance which functions as a reinforcement for the criminal behaviour (Mandracchia, Morgan, Garos, & Garland, 2007).

Glenn Walters criticized this theory because of difficulties in empirical evaluation and lack of generalized applicability. He also critiqued that they failed to recognize the effect of environment on erroneous thinking. Walters gave his own theory, based on Yochelson's and Samenow's, that proffered that 'crime is a lifestyle' with a beliefs system that provides rationalizations, justifications, etc., for the criminal act (Mandracchia, Morgan, Garos, & Garland, 2007). Walters believed that criminal lifestyle is a result of the choices that one makes, and these choices are further dependent on various individual and environmental conditions. These conditions and choices go on to affect the cognitive or thinking style that they develop. He identified various cognitive patterns that describe the thinking patterns seen in criminals, such as mollification (rationalizing one's own behaviour by blaming external factors), cut-off (instantly getting rid of thoughts that can deter oneself from committing a crime), entitlement (permitting criminal behaviour by associating antecedents and consequences for that behaviour) (Mandracchia, Morgan, Garos, & Garland, 2007).

The claim that criminals have a different thinking process which is the cause of their criminality is still often debated and needs a lot more formative research. Another similar psychological claim that is highly debated even today is the relationship between intelligence and criminal behaviour.

3.4.3 The IQ—Crime Connection

The early studies on criminals were mainly focused on the intelligent quotient (IQ) of the delinquent and criminals which were found to be below average, and it was assumed that it was the low IQ that caused criminality (Siegel, 2011). The criminals and delinquents were believed to have substandard intelligence and were thought to be more prone to committing crimes than the rest of the people. It was also assumed earlier that by identifying individuals with low IQ, the authorities could deter the potential criminals from indulging in harmful behaviour (Siegel, 2011). The mainstream criminologists, however, did not give much importance to this connection between crime and intelligence as it was difficult to prove a link between the two, and this theory fell out of popularity until the late 1900s. In 1977, Travis Hirschi and Michael Hindelang published an article that linked both of these variables, where they advocated an indirect link between IQ and crime. They argued that youths with lower IQs tend to perform poorly in school, which leads to school failure and academic incompetence, which are two variables that are highly associated with delinquency and later, with adult criminality (Siegel, 2011). Similar claims were advocated by various other studies as well. However, the American Psychological Association, after evaluating various researches, has come to a conclusion that the link between IQ and crime is very low (Siegel, 2011).

The debate regarding the validity of this connection is still continuing; particularly since research in this area is plagued by methodological issues, such as biases against certain racial groups and socio-economic disadvantages of some groups. Therefore, unless there is a strong scientific evidence proving the IQ-crime link, it does not, at present, hold much strength as an explanation to criminality.

So far, we can see that in the discussions of factors leading to criminality, sociological factors such as culture, economy, employment, and mobility have taken a back seat. Much of the focus was on biological and psychological factors, and sociological factors were seen as secondary to these. The following section would focus primarily on theories of crime that included various sociological factors that contributed to the making of a criminal.

3.5 Social Disorganization and Crime

The term social disorganization in this context is understood as the failure of the community to achieve shared values and to solve chronic problems (Bursik, 1988). One of the early theories in this area was propounded by Clifford R. Shaw and Henry D. Mckay in the late 1900s. Shaw and Mckay conducted their study in the city of Chicago and came to the conclusion that the ecological conditions of a neighbourhood shaped the crime rates. Their study focused on the urban areas which at that time were experiencing rapid changes in the economic and social structure. Shaw and McKay did not establish a direct relationship between economic status and crime, but instead proposed that the areas where economic deprivation was prevalent also saw high rates of population turnover, residential mobility, and racial heterogeneity (Bursik, 1988). These neighbourhoods were seen as 'socially disorganized' because the social control mechanisms were weak in these areas because of the high population turnover and residential mobility. High racial heterogeneity also impedes establishing common goals and solving shared problems (Bursik, 1988).

Shaw and McKay's theory was tested by Robert J. Sampson and W. Byron Groves in 1989, by using data from British communities. The results of the study by Sampson and Groves supported the claims of Shaw and McKay and established that social disorganization does in fact lead to crime (Sampson & Groves, 1989). More specifically, Sampson and Groves found that in communities where friendship networks were scarce; teenage peer-groups were unsupervised; and organizational participation was low, were characterized by high rates of delinquency and crime (Sampson & Groves, 1989). This British study was further tested in the year 2003, and the result that they established was consistent with that of Sampson & Groves' study (Lowenkamp, Cullen, & Pratt, 2003).

Anomie and Strain Theories of Crime

Emile Durkheim, a sociologist, emphasized that crime is a normal phenomenon and that no society can be totally devoid of it. According to him, crime originates from within the society, and at times, can also be useful in paving the way for social change (Siegel, 2011). In his work, he dealt with the consequences that follow the shift from a traditional rural society, which he called the 'mechanical society', to a modern one—the 'organic society'—that brings along division of labour and more personal isolation (Rock, 2012). He claimed that when societies evolve rapidly from a traditional one to a modern one, there occurs a breakdown of norms and collective consciousness. The structural changes in the society then lead to what he termed as anomie—a state of normlessness or lack of clear social standards—which lead to role confusion, crisis, and disorder, thus contributing to criminal behaviour (Siegel, 2011).

Building on Durkheim's theory of anomie, sociologist Robert K. Merton identified two elements of culture that interact to produce potentially anomic condition—culturally defined goals, and legitimate means of obtaining them. Merton argues that even if the culturally defined goals are uniform throughout the society, the access to legitimate means of achieving them is bound by various factors such as class, status, economic conditions, and so on. The inequality of resources results in societal strain that produces anomie among those individuals who cannot access the legitimate opportunity structure (Siegel, 2011). As a result, they will take to deviant ways to attain their goals. Merton further states that there are individual differences in defining socially accepted goals and the legitimate means of obtaining them, proposing these five modes of social adaptations (Table 3.1).

Among these forms of social adaptations, innovation is most closely associated with criminal behaviour. According to Merton, people who cannot access the legitimate opportunity structure, which mostly constitutes people from the lower strata of the society, tend to resort to illegitimate means to attain goals. One of the commonly accepted goals in the society, for example, is to earn money to have a comfortable lifestyle. In order to achieve this goal, most people choose the legitimate means of finding a job that abides with the law. But some people—thieves, gamblers, gangsters, corrupt officials—prefer taking short-cuts and end up doing illegal activities in order to earn more and rapidly, to achieve their goal.

Table 3.1 Merton's mode of adaptation (Murphy & Robinson, 2008)

Mode of social adaptations	Societal goals	Legitimate means
Conformity	Accept	Accept
Retreatism	Reject	Reject
Ritualism	Reject	Accept
Innovation	Accept	Reject
Rebellion	Rejects and creates new goals	Rejects and creates new means

Robert Agnew took Merton's theory a little further and developed what is known as the General strain theory (GST). Before looking into his theory, it is important to understand what the term 'strain' means in this context. Strain, Agnew notes, are the events and conditions that individuals dislike (Agnew, 1992, 2006). According to the GST, strains increase the likelihood of negative emotions such as anger and frustration in an individual, which then promotes delinquent behaviour in the absence of necessary coping skills (Agnew, 2001). One of the key takeaways from Agnew's theory, which he has evolved over the years is that, not all strains lead to crime. Strains are likely to lead to crime when they (1) *'are seen as unjust'* (2) *'are seen as high in magnitude'* (3) *'are associated with low social control'*, and (4) *'create some pressure or incentive to engage in criminal coping'* (Agnew, 2001). Agnew was also able to establish that failure to achieve success in education and career, which were previously seen as one of those strains that lead to crime, were very weakly or entirely unrelated to crime (Agnew, 2001). The GST, over the years, has found its place in many research studies and is still seen as a relevant theory of crime.

3.5.1 Cultural and Subcultural Theories of Crime

Thorsten Sellin proffered the Cultural Conflict theory, which states that the root cause of criminality can be found in a clash of values, between differently socialized groups, over what is acceptable and proper behaviour. As societies become more heterogenous, shared norms and values begin to lessen and this creates a conflict, which in turn contributes to higher crime rates (Black, 2014). He also talked about primary and secondary culture conflict, wherein primary culture conflicts occur between two different cultures, for example, a colonizer replacing the norms of the colonized groups with their own, or when an external group migrates to a host territory, etc. (Black, 2014); and secondary culture conflict occurs between different subcultures or between the dominant culture and the subcultures, such as during internal migration in most countries, where rural populations move into urban environment (Black, 2014).

The culture conflict theory is easily understood from an Indian perspective, because of its history of migration, both external and internal. India is a diverse country with a lot of mixed cultures, which according to Sellin's theory, would mean that there are lesser shared norms and values between the subpopulation demographics. This would explain the arising of conflict with outsiders from across national borders, as seen in civil disobedience, army mutiny, and other related freedom movements when the British colonizers tried to impose their norms and values on the indigenous population. Secondary conflict can be seen in recent years between different religious and ethnic groups, where the dominant subculture has resorted to violence to compel the minority(ies) to conform to their beliefs and norms, such as the violence and killing of Muslims for violating the ban on consumption and selling beef. While certain groups of Hindu majorities consider the cow to be holy and, by extension, making it criminal to consume its meat, there are other groups, even within the Hindu community in India who consume beef as part of their food culture, and who do not consider it a crime to do so. This dissent of religious beliefs created a conflict of norms within a society, which has led to violent crimes such as mob lynching and manslaughter.

Many theories of crime have evolved over the years, and subcultural theories are an interesting addition to this list. These theories have borrowed ideas from various others like social disorganization, anomie, and strain theories, to come up with a new explanation of criminal behaviour. One such theory is the status frustration theory by Albert Cohen. Cohen believed that one of the main shortcomings of Merton's theory was that it failed to explain the non-utilitarian or non-economic nature of delinquency. In his theory, he argued that boys who perform poorly in school tend to lack social status and out of frustration they are likely to develop their own norms and values which they can accomplish and which are often completely opposite to that of the mainstream society (Lanier & Henry, 2010). In short, when these boys end up being a failure at school, they turn to gangs and subcultures for respect and status.

Richard A. Cloward and Lloyd Ohlin's differential opportunity theory also looks at the delinquent subculture. The main difference between these two theories is that while Cohen's theory looked at the motivation behind delinquent behaviour, Cloward and Ohlin's theory mostly deals with the opportunities to engage in delinquent behaviour. Cloward and Ohlin believed that even to engage in delinquent activities, one needs to have access to illegitimate means (Lanier & Henry, 2010). That is, for example, if a boy who is a failure in school decides to engage in drug trafficking, he should firstly have access to the people who supply drugs and also to the people who buy these drugs. The accessibility to these does not come that easy, which means that when choosing between whether to indulge in legitimate acts or illegitimate acts, one needs to have means to do so.

3.5.2 Criminal Behaviour as a Self-fulfilling Prophecy

Another oft-discussed theory from the sociological school of thought in criminology is the Labelling theory. Essentially, the labelling theorists questioned if it was possible to affect people's behaviour towards certain deviances by associating labels to them? They looked at how and why certain people are defined as being deviant and what were the consequences of associating such labels to people.

Edwin Lemert's early work on primary and secondary deviance is an important precursor to labelling theory. According to him, primary deviance constituted the spontaneous and sporadic minor rule violations that almost all of us engage in—smoking or littering in public places, speeding, etc. Secondary deviance was the response to society's reaction to primary deviance, which often includes the offending individual to be labelled as a criminal and has major consequences on a person's status, relationships, and future behaviour. This label contradicts the self-image of the individual and would, in turn, create a cognitive dissonance within self. The individual, then, will ultimately adopt the label of criminal or deviant given to them and will behave accordingly in future—a concept otherwise known as a self-fulfilling prophecy (Triplett & Upton, 2016).

Howard S. Becker further elaborated on the concept of secondary deviance through his study on the development of deviant careers. He discussed three phases that lead to the development of a criminal or a deviant career. The first phase is similar to that of Lemert's primary deviance, i.e. the initial act of deviance, which may not always be intentional. The second phase begins when the individual who breaks the 'rule' is caught and labelled deviant. The label attached to the rule-breaking individual is important as it will show how the society views and reacts to the individual and how she/he will see themselves. The final phase in the development of a criminal career is when the individual who is labelled as a criminal moves into a deviant group that will further affect his/her self-image, social interaction, and social identity. By moving into a deviant group, the individual is provided with rationalizations and motives that support the deviant behaviour (Triplett & Upton, 2016). It can be deduced from the above discussions that, labelling theorists believed that people become criminals as a result of negative labelling and stereotyping, especially by the control agents of the society (Lanier & Henry, 2010). Criminal behaviour can then be seen as a self-fulfilling prophecy.

3.5.3 Routine Activity and Criminal Behaviour

Does the way one lives their routine lives contribute to one's criminality or victimhood? Lawrence Cohen and Marcus Felson tried to answer this through their routine activity theory which looks at how the characteristics of one's activities and interactions of individuals can dictate the temporal and spatial distribution of offenders and victims (Bruinsma & Weisburd, 2014). As a phenomenon, three ingredients that are an absolute necessity for a crime to happen are—a motivated offender, a suitable victim or target, and absence of a capable guardian.

A motivated offender can be anyone who has criminal intention, and also, the ability to act on these intentions. A suitable victim or target can be any person or object, that is, attractive to the offender for any number of reasons, including easy accessibility and value. And finally, the absence of a capable guardian implies the absence of an effective deterrent to crime, it can be a person or a thing (e.g. CCTV cameras). The routine activity theory states that the absence of even one of these three ingredients will decrease the likelihood of a crime from happening. Most of the cases of kidnapping and rape can actually be understood from the perspective of the routine activity theory. It is the absence of a capable guardian, in this case street traffic or policemen, and a vulnerable victim that provides the perfect opportunity to a person to commit the crime.

3.6 Conclusion

Through these theoretical discussions, we can infer that there is no one particular reason why people commit crimes; different people commit crimes because of different reasons, or a combination thereof. Understanding these individual differences in patterns of offending is important to understand crime trends and criminal behaviour. Human beings are unique and complex themselves and exist within complex structures of society and law. Causes of criminal behaviour cannot be fathomed by one universal theory, but is a combination of various biological, psychological, and sociological factors. Jim Clemente, a retired FBI Behavioural analyst and criminal profiler, while addressing the nature vs. nurture debate, observed something that holds true for most criminal deviance—'*Genetics loads the gun, personality and psychology aim it, and your experiences pull the trigger*'.

References

Agnew, R. (2001). Building on the foundation of general strain theory: Specifying the types of strain most likely to lead to crime and delinquency. *Journal of Research in Crime Delinquency, 38*, 319–361.

Agnew, R. (1992). Foundation for a general strain theory of crime and delinquency. *Criminology, 30*, 47–87.

Agnew, R. (2006). *Pressured into crime: An overview of general strain theory*. Oxford University Press.

Baum, M. L. (2011). The Monoamine Oxidase A (MAOA) genetic predisposition to impulsive violence: Is it relevant to criminal trials? *Neuroethics, 6*(2), 1–20. https://doi.org/10.1007/s12152-011-9108-6

BBC News. (2015, November 5). *Raman Raghav: When India's 'Jack the Ripper' terrorised Mumbai*. Retrieved November 14, 2019, from BBC News: https://www.bbc.com/news/world-asia-india-34719646

Black, P. (2014). Conflict theories of crime. In J. M. Miller (Ed.), *The encyclopaedia of criminology and criminal justice*. Wiley Blackwell.

Bruinsma, G., & Weisburd, D. (2014). *Encyclopedia of criminology and criminal justice*. Springer.

Burke, R. H. (2009). *An introduction to criminological theory*. Willan Publishing.

Canter, D. (2017). *Criminal psychology*. Taylor & Francis.

Christiansen, K. O. (1977). *Preliminary study of criminality among twins*. Gardner Press Inc.

Einstadter, W. J., & Henry, S. (2006). *Criminological theory: An analysis of its underlying assumptions*. Rowman & Littlefield.

Feldman, R. S. (2011). *Understanding psychology*. McGraw Hill Education (India).

Feresin, E. (2009, October 30). *Lighter sentence for murderer with 'bad genes'*. Retrieved May 5, 2021, from Nature: https://www.nature.com/news/2009/091030/full/news.2009.1050.html.

Feresin, E. (2011, September 01). *Italian court reduces murder sentence based on neuroimaging data*. Retrieved May 04, 2021, from Nature: http://blogs.nature.com/news/2011/09/italian_court_reduces_murder_s.html.

Fitzpatrick, J. J. (1976). Psychoanalysis and crime—A critical survey of salient trends in the literature. *Annals of the American Academy of Political and Social Science, 423*, 67–74.

Freud, S. (1923). *The ego and the id*. Simon and Schuster.

Galatzer-Levy, I. R., & Galatzer-Levy, R. M. (2007). August Aichhorn—A different vision of psychoanalysis, children and society. *The Psychoanalytic Study of the Child, 62*(1), 153–179.

Goddard, H. H. (2009). *The Kallikak family: A study of the heredity of feeble-mindedness*. Retrieved from Buck v Bell Documents, 7. https://readingroom.law.gsu.edu/buckvbell/7.

Goldberg, A. (2003). Addendum to Freud's "Criminals from a Sense of Guilt." *The Psychoanalytic Quarterly, 72*(2), 465–468.

Goldsmith, A. J. (1981). Eysenck's theory of criminal personality—A review of recent evidence and the implications for criminological theory and social practice. *Canadian Criminology Forum, 4*(2), 88–102. Retrieved May 04, 2021, from https://www.ojp.gov/ncjrs/virtual-library/abstracts/eysencks-theory-criminal-personality-review-recent-evidence-and#:~:text=Virtual%20Library-,Eysenck's%20Theory%20of%20Criminal%20Personality%20%2D%20A%20Review%20of%20Recent%20Evidence,Criminological%20Th.

Heidt, J., & Wheeldon, J. P. (2014). *Introducing criminological thinking—Maps, theories, and understanding*. Sage Publications.

Hollin, C. R. (2013). *Psychology and crime: An introduction to criminological psychology*. Routledge.

Hollin, C. R. (1989). *An introduction to criminological psychology*. Routledge.

Joseph, J. (2001). Is crime in the genes? A critical review of twin and adoption studies of criminality and antisocial behaviour. *The Journal of Mind and Behaviour, 22*(2), 179–218.

Kapadia, K. M. (1952). The criminal tribes of India. *Sociological Bulletin, 1*(2), 99–125. Retrieved from https://journals.sagepub.com/doi/abs/10.1177/0038022919520203?journalCode=soba.

Lanier, M. M., & Henry, S. (2010). *Essential criminology*. Westview Press.

Lombroso, C. (2006). *Criminal Man*. (M. Gibson, N. H. Rafter, Eds., M. Gibson, M. Seymour, & N. H. Rafter, Trans.). Duke University Press.

Mandracchia, J. T., Morgan, R. D., Garos, S., & Garland, J. T. (2007). Inmate thinking patterns: An empirical investigation. *Criminal Justice and Behavior, 34*(8). Retrieved October 5th, 2019, from https://pdfs.semanticscholar.org/ed49/de45a99b20a0147c1b36e032f1afe61b2e8f.pdf.

Manoharan, N. (2004, October 29). *Profiling a poacher: The rise and fall of Veerappan*. Retrieved April 25, 2020, from Institute of Peace and Conflict Studies : http://www.ipcs.org/comm_select.php?articleNo=1547.

Murphy, D., & Robinson, M. (2008). The maximizer: Clarifying Merton's theories of anomie and strain. *Theoretical Criminology, 12*(4), 501. https://libres.uncg.edu/ir/asu/f/Murphy_Robinson_2008_The_Maximizer.pdf.

Paranjape, N. (2017). *Criminology, penology and victimology*. Central Law Publications.

Pearlman, J. (2015, January 29). Australian man accused of stalking escapes conviction after blaming Bollywood. *The Telegraph*. Retrieved April 01, 2020, from https://www.telegraph.co.uk/news/worldnews/australiaandthepacific/australia/11377511/Australian-man-accused-of-stalking-escapes-conviction-after-blaming-Bollywood.html.

Reid, J. A. (2011). Crime and personality: Personality theory and criminality examined. *Inquiries Journal, 03*(1). Retrieved May 04, 2021, from http://www.inquiriesjournal.com/articles/1690/crime-and-personality-personality-theory-and-criminality-examined.

Rock, P. (2012). Sociological theories of crime. In M. Maguire, R. Morgan, & R. Reiner (Eds.), *The Oxford handbook of criminology* (pp. 51–82). Oxford University Press.
Siegel, L. J. (2011). *Criminology—The core*. Wadsworth, Cengage Learning.
Stochholm, K., Bojesen, A., Jensen, A. S., Juul, S., & Gravholt, C. H. (n.d.). Criminality in Men with Klinefelter's syndrome and XYY syndrome: A Cohort study . *BMJ Open, 2*(1). https://doi.org/10.1136/bmjopen-2011-000650.
Taylor, I., Walton, P., & Young, J. (2013). *The new criminology: For a social theory of deviance*. Routledge.
Triplett, R., & Upton, L. (2016). Labeling theory: Past, present and future. In A. R. Piquero (Ed.), *The handbook of criminological theory* (pp. 271–289). Wiley Blackwell.
Wertz, J., Caspi, A., Belsky, D. W., Beckley, A. L., Arseneault, L., Barnes, J. C., … Moffitt, T. E. (2018). Genetics and crime: Integrating new genomic discoveries into psychological research about antisocial behavior. *Psychological Science, 29*(5). https://doi.org/10.1177/0956797617744542.

Chapter 4
The Science of Criminal Profiling

Sanjeev P. Sahni and Tanni Choudhury

Abstract Criminal profiling has been in existence since the 1960s. It is a global practice followed to lead to accurate cognizance of the crime. The first section of the chapter will examine the concepts and approaches towards criminal profiling. Familiarity with the why and how of the offender will strengthen the accuracy rate of the apprehension of offenders. The second section will provide an overview of the techniques or strategies that are used in front-line profiling across the world. The global best practices, and the differences between them, would also be focused here. The third section of the chapter will focus on the Indian practice of criminal profiling through the policies and implementations that are currently effective in the country. The fourth section of the chapter would conclude with the presentation of case studies that are crucial to the process of unravelling the concept of criminal profiling. It will pay particular attention to the psychological beliefs that have insisted on the link between psychopathy and crime, along with the questioning of such understanding.

Keyword Criminal profiling · Techniques · Approaches · Applications

4.1 Introduction

The abundance of movies and television shows that focus on the invention and use of criminal profiling, presently and in the past, is testament to the prolonged media interest in the science of looking into the criminal mind. The idea of being able to identify the offender through his or her behaviour where the crime has taken place always captivated the minds of not only the general masses, but also the law enforcement and legal agencies. The aim of criminal profiling has always been to find the person who committed the crime. Usually, this could be accomplished through forensic tests or speaking with eye-witnesses at the scene of the crime. But running forensic tests take time, and may not always provide a conclusive result, or when they do, it might only provide support to some of the questions in the case trial.

S. P. Sahni (✉) · T. Choudhury
Jindal Institute of Behavioural Sciences, O.P. Jindal Global University, Sonipat, Haryana, India
e-mail: drspsahni@jgu.edu.in

S. Sahni et al. (eds.), *Criminal Psychology and the Criminal Justice System in India and Beyond*, https://doi.org/10.1007/978-981-16-4570-9_4

Similarly, eyewitness accounts may not always be available or reliable. Psychological profiling presents the most suitable alternative to identifying the perpetrator by gleaning aspects of the perpetrator's mental, sometimes physical and social, profile depending on the behavioural evidence at the crime scene.

4.2 History of Criminal Profiling

The technique of criminal profiling has a brief but interesting history. The primal birthplace of profiling can be drawn from as early as the Middle Ages. Later on, scholars like Cesare Lombroso, Hans Gross, Alphonse Bertillon, Jacob Fries, and others recognized the importance and use of profiling. Informally, criminal profiling began as early as the 1880s when two physicians, George Philips and Thomas Bond, made predictions using crime scene clues about the British serial killer, Jack the Ripper. It was at the same time that profiling started sprouting in policing practices in the USA as well.

The FBI was the first to use the terminology of criminal profiling in the 1970 s as a means to develop an inventory of their criminal investigative analysis work (Canter, 1994). It was developed by the Behavioral Science Unit (BSU) that was established with the intention to assist the law enforcement in cases of serial homicide or serial rape (Homant & Kennedy, 1998). Criminal profiling is the technique to identify the offender from what we gather about the crime itself. Various other terms have been created for these techniques such as offender profiling, criminal investigative analysis, crime scene analysis, behaviour profiling, and psychological profiling.

Modern practitioners of profiling do not, for obvious reasons, seem to agree upon a single methodology or terminology as conclusively defining the field or its purview. Profiling was viewed as reading 'criminal shadows'. Profiling does not yield the exact identification of the offender but one indicates the certain behavioural and personality characteristics of the type of person who is obvious to have committed the crime (Douglas & Burgess, 1986). Author and psychologist, Dr. David Canter, scrutinized and concluded that a criminal *'leaves psychological traces, tell-tale patterns of behaviour that indicate the sort of person he is. Clues gleaned from the crime scene and reports from witnesses indicate these traces are more ambiguous and subtle than those examined scientifically by the biologist or physicist. These cannot be taken into a laboratory and dissected under the microscope. They are more like shadows, which undoubtedly are connected to the criminal who cast them, but they flicker and change, and it may not always be conclusive as to their origin. Yet, if they can be fixed and interpreted, criminal shadows can merely indicate directions as to where investigators should look and what sort of characteristic of a person they should be looking for'* (Douglas & Burgess, 1986).

He also cultivated that *'a criminal leaves, among other things, evidence of his personality through his actions in relation to a crime. Any person's behaviour exhibits characteristics unique to that person, as well as patterns and consistencies which are typical of the upbringing and subgroup to which he or she belongs*' (Douglas & Burgess, 1986).

The theoretical concept of psychological examination soon evolved with appropriate methodologies and techniques. The clinically oriented practice of profiling crimes is now understood as diagnostic evaluation (Des). The oldest examples of such evaluation can be seen in the Jack the Ripper case aka the Whitechapel murders and case of the Mad Bomber of New York. Till date, diagnostic evaluations are the most common and easily available method to obtain a criminal profile. These methodologies have been utilized in assorted locations, ranging from crimes such as rapes and arsons to hostage kidnapping (Reiser, 1982). It was found that through careful and incisive interviews, one can develop a profile about certain behaviour that helps the law enforcement personnel build and classify a profile. This approach compiles information accumulated from the scene of crime, witnesses, victims, forensic notes in order to construct the offender's profile which can be developed as to pinpoint the most likely person to commit the said crime (Kocsis, 2006). Profiling has always been used as a supportive technique in crime scene investigation.

The key assertion of criminal profiling is situated on the ground that the method of operation (modus operandi) at the crime scene or other locations related to the crime may lead to direct clues about the suspect and hence help in the unravelling of a personality characteristic of a particular perpetrator (Egger, 1999a, b). The rationale behind criminal profiling is the method of operation is related to the offender and his behaviour. By developing a behavioural composite, combining sociological and psychological assessments from clues left at the scene, the profiler may eventually determine a certain pattern for the crime or extrapolate a type of offender (Douglas & Burgess, 1986). While profiling, the relevant information that a profiler needs to note are individual traits, physical description from witnesses/victims, any different behaviour and records of anything that the perpetrator did or said during the crime. Along with such information, the profiler can also be helped if information is available about the offender's age, race, gender, occupation, and criminal records (Ebisike, 2008). As stated by Douglas and Olshaker (2000), 'the primary goal is to aid local police in limiting and refining their suspect list so that they can zero in on and direct their resources where they might do the most good'. This also helps in avoiding wastage of time and resources.

According to Holmes and Holmes (1996), there are three main objectives of profiling. They are as follows.

4.3 Assessment of Offender (Social and Psychological)

The analysis of the social and psychological aspects of the offender is the necessary first steps of criminal profiling. The social and psychological core variables of the offender's personality under consideration include the offender's race, age, employment status and type, religion, marital status, and level of education. This psychological information are parameters based on which the police can narrow its range and focus the investigation better, which in turn, will have a direct bearing upon the duration the police spends to produce fruitful results (Holmes, 1996).

4.3.1 Psychological Evaluation of Belongings of the Offenders

This involves a thorough investigation of any items left at the suspect's home or place of work. The items could vary from souvenirs taken from the scene of crime, videos, magazines, books, or any other item that may point and link the suspect to the crime. This would also include any item unintentionally dropped or left hastily at the scene of the crime by the suspect. The investigators need to be sharp and trained at picking up the most insignificant clues from the scene of crime or from suspect's home.

4.3.2 Approaches and Methods to Conduct Interviews for the Suspected Offenders

As suggested by Holmes and Holmes (1996), not every offender, even those guilty of the same type of crime, would react similarly to a particular interviewing strategy during interrogation. There must be some basic uniformity in following strategies, but there obviously is no 'one-size-fits-all' questionnaire. Just as offenders may be motivated by different reasons to commit a crime, their responses to interrogation may also vary. The basic principle to a successful interviewing strategy is to not generalize, for each crime has its own peculiarities.

4.4 Development of Criminal Profiling Techniques

Since the 1970s, investigators at the Behavioral Science Unit of FBI have been interpreting crime scenes and developing extensive data compiled on criminal profiles. The aim of the FBI was initially to study serial rape and homicides, incidents that were on a surge at the time and majorly unsolved. The resulting frustration brewing when physical evidence could not yield any suitable perpetrator is what inspired the heuristic profiling technique as an alternate strategy. Thirty-six convicted serial killers were firstly interviewed by the FBI where they made the assertion that their crimes were mostly sexually driven. The central idea about analysing these interviews was to catalogue specific personal traits and behavioural aspects of these killers.

In the beginning, there were three principal ways to criminal profiling—Diagnostic Evaluation or Clinical, Crime Investigative Analysis or the FBI approach, and the Investigative Psychology for Environmental Psychology Approach. Contemporary approaches have come to include geographical profiling, behavioural evidence analysis, and crime action profiling.

4.4.1 Diagnostic Evaluations

Diagnostic evaluation or clinical approach is regarded as the most common and oldest method in criminal profiling. This avenue to offender profiling is usually adopted by mental health professionals such as psychiatrists and clinical psychologists. The cardinal notion of diagnostic evaluation approach is to make a clinical assessment of the perpetrator from a mental illness perspective (Ainsworth, 2001). Through their expertise in clinical experiences, these practitioners deduce the type of offenders most likely to commit certain crimes by intimate knowledge of mental health processes and psychological disorders.

The DE approach is premised on the proposition that the clinical experience of psychiatrists equip them to offer informed insights into extreme or bizarre behavioural patterns, even if they are not directly related to criminal behaviour. This is especially handy when police encounter baffling patterns that are not usually characteristic of that kind of crime. A clinical psychologist may be able to offer an offender's perspective that may explain behaviour which the police may find 'senseless', or struggle to make sense of at first glance (Ainsworth, 2001). In 1956, DE approach was found to be very useful in the case of 'New York Mad Bomber' and 'Jack the Ripper', conducted by Dr. James Brussel and Dr. Thomas Bond, respectively.

Since the DE approach depends on a practitioner's expertise in psychopathology to construct an accurate profile, such a diagnosis can vary widely depending on the knowledge and experience of different practitioners consulted. This is one of its predominant critiques.

There has been a general consensus among practitioners that certain forms of mental illness may predispose one more or less towards certain types of criminal behaviours. That is the main reason why clinical psychologists and psychiatrists reiterate the requirement of criminal profiling. With the proficiency of their learning, it gives them a leverage to produce profiles based on crimes that lean towards psychopathology, paraphilias, and sadomasochistic personality types. Indeed, Badcock (1997) noted that 'the mental disorders most commonly associated with offenders are the psychoses, sociopathic personality disorder, and drug/alcohol addictions'.

As with any heuristic technique dependent on individual subject knowledge and experience of the experts, DE is bound to be flawed in its scientific ramifications. It is generally agreed upon by researchers that psychiatrists and clinical psychiatrists do not have any law enforcement training and as such lacked concrete legal evaluations (Egger, 1999a, b). Wilson et al. (1997) suggests that the individualistic approach of DE prevents the methodology to gain 'adequate comparative assessments of validity, utility and process'. Ainsworth (2001) declared that DE's single case-study approach may help consider in detail all aspects of the case and glean information that may otherwise not be obvious, however, its specificity to that incident may also prevent one from extrapolating the findings to other similar investigations.

4.4.2 Criminal Investigative Analysis/FBI Approach or Crime Scene Analysis

According to the FBI, criminal investigative analysis involves reviewing crimes from both a behavioural and investigative perspective. This process includes 'reviewing and assessing the facts of a criminal act, interpreting offender behaviour, and interaction with the victim, as exhibited during the commissioning of the crime, or as displayed in the crime scene'. This method was innovated when the Behavioural Analysis Unit (previously Behavioural Sciences Unit) of the FBI saw the need for a multidisciplinary approach to criminal profiling. In the 1970s, the FBI was stumped in several investigations when physical evidence did not yield any information and they were unable to create a profile on the basis of just physical evidence. Keeping this in mind, they recycled data from previous serious crimes such as sexual assaults and murders to establish behavioural traits of such perpetrators. They carried out interviews with 36 convicted serial killers in their pursuit to criminal profiling.

This technique majorly relies on a careful documentation and analysis of information stored in the database against these important parameters of match: (1) aspects of the crime scene, (2) nature of the attacks themselves, (3) the medical examiner's report, (4) the characteristics of the type of victim selected (Ainsworth, 2001). Through this approach, FBI classified the crime scene of the offenders into organized and disorganized categories. They believed the classification assisted in their understanding of the behavioural characteristics of the most likely offender.

4.4.3 Organized Offenders

As per the FBI, these are some of the common features among organized offenders.

- The crime shows some kind of planning.
- The crime scene shows that the offender was in some kind of control.
- The crime scene also highlights the awareness of forensic knowledge.

Ressler et al. (1992) upheld the following features for organised offenders:

- They are often the firstborn in the family and have inconsistent parental discipline.
- Work history of the father is found to be generally stable.
- Have transportability and most likely to choose a stranger as the victim.
- They are intelligent but possibly an underachiever.
- Socially skilled and sexually competent.

- Likely to be living with a partner.
- At the time of the attack they are experiencing a great amount of anger and also found to be depressed.
- They leave the area of the attack by following news report about the attack.

4.4.4 *Disorganized Offenders*

- Contrarily, the following features are mostly shared by the disorganised offenders at the crime scene:
- The crime shows no sign of planning.
- The crime indicates being random.
- The crime scene shows a sense of confusion and frightened state of the offender.
- There are signs of other disorganised behaviour.
- The crime scene displays the use of incidental weapon that may have been available at the scene of crime.
- The crime scene is loaded with evidences which shows the offender's surrender to leaving clues at the scene.
- Disorganized offender shares the following features as well (Ressler, 1992):
- They are likely to live near the location of the crime and preferably alone.
- They display inefficiency in social and sexual aspects.
- They exhibit below average intelligence.
- Suffers from some form of mental health issues.
- Likely to have suffered childhood abuse (physical or sexual).
- Likely to be of low birth status in the family.
- Unstable work of their fathers accompanied with harsh parental discipline.
- Poor work history is displayed by this type of offender.

Within the possibility of organised and disorganised crimes, it can be inferred whether the crime involved a single individual or multiple individuals.

4.4.5 *Organization of Crime Scenes*

The FBI also formulated crime scenes into organized, disorganized crime scene, mixed and atypical. As we have seen, organized crime scene has been known to show elements of planning and intention along with the pursuit to bury physical traces. The disorganized crime scene has high aspects of disorganised behaviour along with no sign of planning and high focus on being random and laden with physical traces. As evident with the nomenclature, mixed crime scene shows traits of both organized and disorganized crime scenes. Davies (1999) noted that this maybe because there were more than one perpetrator, either in execution, or alternatively in planning and execution; or that the crime scene was purposefully staged to mislead.

The atypical crime scene is where it is difficult to ascertain any classification due to lack of concrete evidence for the same, usually seen in crimes that have been uncovered several years later.

4.4.6 Types of Rapists

The FBI further classified rapists into two categories—selfish and unselfish rapists (Hazelwood, 1987). The FBI conferred the following features for selfish rapists:

- They show high levels of aggression and violence.
- There is indication of sexual dominance.
- There is display of self-confidence.
- The offender shows signs of insensitivity towards the victim.
- There is engagement to anal sex, followed by fellatio.
- There will be intense use of offensive, demeaning, irreverent, indecent, obscene language.

Contrarily, the unselfish rapists display the following features:

- There will be minimum display of violence or force.
- There will be no display of self-confidence.
- It is highly likely the rapist meant no physical harm towards the victim.
- There is established evidence of some kind of intimacy towards the victim.
- It is highly likely that the offender may ask the victim to perform some kind of sexual acts and use intimate, comforting, involved, and decent language.

A classification of such categories helps in the understanding of traits shared by rapist offenders. It further sustains in choosing the appropriate interrogation strategy. In addition to the above two categories, the FBI classified more categories of rapists. Hazelwood (1987) provided four other types of rapists.

Power Reassurance or Compensatory Rapist: It has been observed that this particular type of rapist is inclined to exhibit his virility and carnal competence and, thus, shows signs of an unselfish rapist. For the offender, the rape is a way of reassuring himself that there is no sexual inadequacy in him. This placation maybe short-lived, leading the rapist to find another victim in a few days or weeks. Such instances usually occur within the same vicinity or district, and the perpetrator is likely to remove an item of clothing or other possession from his victim as a 'trophy', and/or maintain a record of their conquests. Since the primary motivation is an attempt to remove insecurity, it is unlikely that the offender will stop until caught (Ainsworth, 2001).

It has been found that such type of rapists commonly prey during early mornings or late evenings when the victim is most likely to be alone or with young children. Such rapists commonly target a victim of his own age or race (Ainsworth, 2001). This kind of rapist also believes that the victim is 'liking' the rape. It appears though the rapist displays a bit of remorse and concern for the victim. Holmes and Holmes

(1996) claimed that this kind of rapist is likely to be single, social loner and live with their parents, is non-athletic, silent, and indifferent, has limited education, is often engaged in a boring job, likes to visit adult bookstores or porn sites, has a propensity to explore with sexual gender roles such as cross-dressing, possibly a fetishist, indulges in voyeurism, excessive masturbation and exhibitionism, tends to attack within their own neighbourhood, and was likely raised by a single, dominant, aggressive maternal figure. In addition, the rapist suffers from low self-esteem, and the control he exerts on another human being, usually by using force against them, acts to satisfy his ego, and validate his importance, even if temporarily (Holmes & Holmes, 1996).

Holmes and Holmes (1996) have recommended a particular style of interviewing such a rapist in order to elicit their sense of 'masculine chivalry', positing that the victim 'has not suffered "undue" trauma', and that the police are aware that the rapist did not mean to harm his victim. Such a statement could establish a 'sympathetic' relationship, making the rapist feel secure enough to reveal information about the rape currently under investigation and any other previous rapes committed by him.

Power Assertive or Exploitative Rapist: The power assertive rape interprets the rape as a symbol of superiority and masculinity. This rapist falls under the selfish category and exhibits no sign of sexual inadequacy in his act. He is prone to vicious violence, even treating his victim's clothing and carrying out multiple, repeated sexual assaults rather than one. Each act compounds his need for feeling virile and dominant (Ainsworth, 2001).

What has been observed in this category of rapist is the casual acceptance of rape in these offenders. They do not regard rape as a crime which makes it difficult while prosecution. Holmes and Holmes (1996) have observed that such kind of rapists are usually raised in single-parent households, having spent some time in foster homes. They may also have suffered physical abuse as a child, are most likely a high school dropout, have unhappy marriages and domestic problems, are heavy drinkers and are drawn to 'macho' occupations—construction or police work, and likely to choose a victim of his own race.

Holmes and Holmes (1996) recommended that the interviewer, when dealing with such rapists, needs to come across as a thorough professional, who is armed with full information about the crime. This includes details on how to place the suspect at the scene, physical evidence that directly implicates them of the crime and any other relevant information. It is imperative that the police be able to convince the offender, directly or indirectly, that they have enough evidence to prove that he committed the crime. A casual error—an incorrect fact or any hesitation or surprise that may cause the rapist to question his interviewer's competence—will make it unlikely that the rapist will cooperate further. No amount of intimidation, pleas for aid or appeals on behalf of the victim's will move the offender, once he detects the ambiguity in the investigator.

Anger Retaliatory Rapist: As suggested by the name itself, anger retaliatory rapist gravitates towards showing extreme anger and violence towards women. They commonly despise women and hence rape them in order to take revenge. Around 80% of such rapists are likely to have a childhood with a single female parent or caregiver (Holmes & Holmes, 1996). They view women as the source of their trouble, and hence direct their own rage and hostility towards them. In this way, the act of rape is a way of releasing the anger and deriving pleasure from their sadistic humiliation (Ainsworth, 2001). Such rapists are particularly selfish and use extreme violence. Holmes and Holmes (1996) have suggested that the interview should preferably be conducted by a male as such kind of rapists despise women.

Anger Excitement or Sadistic Rapist: It has been agreed upon by almost all researchers that the anger excitement or sadistic rapist is the most dangerous rapist of all. Such rapists plan the attack along with displaying extreme violence and murder through the act. For them, the act of rape is a source of pleasure and sexual excitement. The rapist is also more likely to carry rape paraphenilia to the location of the attacks. It has also been established that such a rapist is likely to come from a single-parent household, or with divorced parents, have a history of foster care and possible physical abuse in childhood, likely to be married and part of a middle-class family, have some level of college education, fall in the age group of 30–39, is employed in some white-collar occupation, display compulsive ritualistic behaviours, is likely to stalk their victims and eventually kill them (Holmes & Holmes, 1996). Holmes and Holmes (1996) believe that there is no correct method of interviewing such a rapist.

4.4.7 Profiling Inputs

Profiling inputs include all the important information that is integral to the crime—physical evidence, autopsy reports, indigenous factors such as weather conditions, political and social environment, witness and victim statements, crime scene photographs, and also police reports. By this stage, it is crucial to determine whether the crime was committed outdoors or indoors to be able to do a complete synopsis of the crime (Douglas & Burgess, 1986). Douglas et al. (1986) have outlined the following stages in the criminal profiling process—profiling inputs, decision process models stage, crime scene assessment, criminal profile, investigation, and apprehension.

4.4.8 Decision Process Models

During this stage, it is essential to determine the duration of time taken to commit the attack. At this stage, the profiler will also take note of the locations, patterns, and intentions and likely acts before and after the crime. The profiler then formulates "the input into meaningful questions and patterns"—what kind of murder—serial, mass, or spree murder (Douglas & Burgess, 1986).

Crime Scene Assessment: This is regarded as the most high-priority stage where the profiler needs to determine the likely intentions of the crime by now. Attempt must also be made to reconstruct the behaviour of the offender and the victim. It must also be kept in mind to resolve whether the crime scene was organized or disorganized in nature, the kind of injuries intended and the kind of weapons used.

Criminal Profile: The profiler at this stage creates an initial description of the most likely suspects. It is crucial to suggest the best method to apprehend the unknown offender. A criminal profile must ideally include all the following information—age, race, height, gender, marital status, kind of job, education, location, criminal record, military background, social life, sexual life as well as use of drugs or alcohol.

Investigation: A written report will be submitted to the investigators while focusing on finding the closest profile match to the suspect/s. Any new information made available at this stage will also be put together before the investigators.

Apprehension: An appropriate interview technique will be chosen if any suspect is apprehended. At this stage, the aim is to critically evaluate how the offender matches the profile.

It is to be noted that the FBI approach has been resourceful in various ways. As pointed out by Ainsworth (2001), the FBI approach comprises of 'the first systematic attempt to classify serial and serious criminals on the basis of behavioural characteristics'. In addition, the classification made it easier to link crimes that had similar characteristics and were probably committed by the same person. This would be helpful in allowing the police to combine all the evidence accumulated in the respective cases and build a whole picture of the offender. This classification would also assist the police in diagnosing when two crimes in the same area were unrelated, so that they can direct their resources accordingly (Ainsworth, 2001).

The FBI approach has also been criticized on various grounds. It has been regarded as being lacking scientific evidence and being intuitive and subjective in nature. Primary criticism is that the classification was devised based on interviews with only 36 convicted, American serial murderers. They form only one type of offender, statistically a rare kind in the USA, and it is not clear if these findings can be extrapolated to other types of offenders, or even those from other countries. Given that all the offenders interviewed had been convicted, it also raises the question if more successful offenders, i.e. those who have yet evaded the police, might have been characterized differently (Ainsworth, 2001).

4.4.9 The Investigative Psychology (IP) or Environmental Psychology Approach

In 1985, David Canter developed the investigative psychology approach. It was formulated with the aim to include psychology in assisting the police investigations. After constant shadowing of police investigations and observing criminal behaviour, Canter (1994) concluded that he could see how 'even elementary psychological principles could be used to help a major police investigation'.

Canter believed that the offender not only leaves physical traces, but also psychological traces at a crime scene. By investigating these psychological traces, the investigator can get an overall idea as to what kind of person is most likely to commit such a crime (Canter, 1994). Canter developed a five-factor model of offender behaviour based on his work on the five aspects of interaction.

Interpersonal Coherence: Canter believed that offenders operates in their own personal psychology. It relates to the understanding of how an offender's criminal actions mirror his or her reactions in normal non-criminal activities. Hence, the interaction between the victim and the offender reveals something about the offender, particularly regarding the people who are meaningful to the offender (Muller, 2011).

Significance of Place and Time: Canter was of the belief that offender commits crime in chosen locations which hold some significance in order to feel in control and be comfortable, most likely a place they live or work in (Muller, 2011). In addition, an analysis of the place and time of an attack may also inform about the scope of the offender's mobility. Analyse in the nature of the crime, the way it is committed, and the characteristics of the criminal; we can determine a profile that can guide the direction of the investigation (Egger, 1999a; b).

Criminal Characteristics: The main aim of this interaction is to determine the crime, the crime scene, and to classify the offenders. As mentioned earlier, there are numerous ways to classify offenders and crime scenes such as the FBI's classification into organized and disorganized offenders, and types of rapists.

Criminal Career: Attempts will be made in this interaction to determine if the criminal is a career offender or not. Presumably, most offenders stick to the same crime patterns.

Forensic Awareness: Canter believed that if the offender took conscious efforts to hide physical evidence, then such offender has experience with crime scene techniques. Thus, such an offender is likely to have criminal record prior to committing the present crime. This will enable the investigators to narrow their search of suspects.

4.4.10 Contemporarily Prevalent Techniques in Criminal Profiling

Criminal profiling is one of the many investigative techniques used by police to identify behavioural, cognitive, emotional as well as demographic characteristics of a known or unknown offender from a wide range of information. It is mostly used in three phases of the criminal justice process: investigation, apprehension, and prosecution. The techniques have evolved since its inception in the law enforcement dating back to 1956. Eventually, there were establishments of the Behavioural Science Unit (later renamed as the Investigative Support Unit) at the FBI which was popularized by John E. Douglas and Robert K. Ressler in the 1970s. Traditionally, only two disciplines used this technique: mental health practitioners, to look into the personality and actions of an offender through psychiatric concepts, and law enforcement, to determine the behavioural aspects through the investigative process. Because of the negative connotation, 'profiling' now goes by the name of various other overlapping nomenclatures such as behaviour analysis or criminal investigative analysis. In England, the term 'behavioural investigative analyst' (BIA) is used.

Till date, the most detailed criminal profiling procedures came from both Douglas and Ressler (Douglas & Burgess, 1986) who described a six-stage procedure to collect information and evidence. They categorized the following stages: profiling inputs, decision process models, crime assessment, criminal profile, investigation, and apprehension. Later, Holmes and Holmes (1996) also presented a model of profiling which emphasized the geographic and victim characteristics in the profiling process. Since then, various models have been developed which served as an adjunct to the traditional investigative techniques. Criminal profiling has been useful in various areas of criminal investigation such as hostage negotiation, identifying anonymous letter writers (Casey-Owens, 1984) and persons who make written or spoken threats of violence as well as in investigations of sexual homicides. Even with all the inputs, unfortunately, it does not provide the identity of the offender, but it does indicate the profile or the type of person most likely to commit the crime with the defining characteristics. Law enforcement personnel employ the use of psychological as well as geographical profiling to aid their serial crime investigations.

Many of the modern approaches are also heavily grounded in psychological theory and practice. The traditional approach was largely based on tangible evidence and observation. Although there is no one universally accepted method of criminal profiling, however, scientifically based profiling seems to be the current enterprise in contemporary times. Internationally, there are various approaches to criminal profiling. They are broadly divided into the following five types of profiling: crime scene, geographic, offender-based and psychological. All of these approaches have their own specific ideologies and methods. They often overlap during the course of investigation and encompass a wide range of assessments and investigations which are not mutually exclusive.

Crime scene profiling was the starting point, and one of the first systematic approaches to identify the various variables of an unknown offender was promoted by the FBI. They usually relied on the 'gut feelings' based on their extensive experience with crime investigation unlike in many other countries such as the UK, Australia, and Canada, where they still depend on the large database for statistical analyses of crimes. They routinely employ research-based typologies to provide a subjective description and offer investigate leads. Geographic profiling looks into the location and spatial relationships among various crime scene sites. Investigators identify 'hot spots' of criminal activity to follow the course of crimes in order to find the offender. Psychological profiling uses two assessments: threat assessment and risk assessment to identify and predict the dangerous individuals in the society. Threat assessment looks at the seriousness and credibility of a threat being carried out. Risk assessment is the process of evaluating an individual through various psychological measures, observations, and interviews about the chances of committing any damaging or violent act.

From the early origins of the technique, the field has grown rapidly across the world during the past 50 years. In recent times, there is an inclination towards the actuarial scientific approaches unlike the traditional (clinical) approach which was based on experience, expert knowledge with intuition. The actuarial method, as mentioned before, integrated more empirical knowledge about criminal behaviour. They use formal algorithms to make predictions. Many of the recent developments in the profiling field have been to include methods of experimental psychology as well as statistics to this applied field. This largely constitutes a scientific-based model to profiling. (Grove, 1996) More recent work includes interesting developments such as the emergence of Behaviour Evidence Analysis (BEA) as a new body of thought to profiling. BEA consists of a fusion of various criminological knowledge, philosophical concepts as well as the forensic sciences. It highlights the need to look at various combinations of factors for a particular crime and the generation of criminal profiles based on those unique factors. Another new technique of profiling is the 'case linkage analysis' which is typically conducted by police officers or crime analysts. It is also known as 'comparative case analysis', as a sub-type of behavioural analysis. It is defined as a process that aims to look at the behavioural similarities of the same suspect across various crimes. In other words, the crimes are then linked together to analyse the offender's characteristics in one crime which also showed similar patterns in other crimes, implying the possibility that many crimes have been committed by the same offender.

Some of the other alternative methods of criminal profiling provide varying degrees of theory and possibility (Wilson et al., 1997). There are three general types: diagnostic evaluations (DE), criminal investigative analysis (CIA), and investigative psychology (IP). The literature shows that CIA is the same as 'criminal profiling, except that it builds profiles based on studying groups of offenders rather than individuals. The goal is to determine any common features across offenses that might be helpful in identifying future offenders. It is ideally comprised of several steps such as: evaluating the criminal act, comprehensive analysis of the crime scene and the victim, and assessment of the preliminary police case files. This is then compiled together to develop a profile with critical offender characteristics and investigative suggestions. Another method is diagnostic evaluations which represent a description of all the services offered by mental health practitioners and professionals who gives profiling opinions on the offender, victims, and crime scene based on their clinical evidence. They are usually done on need basis. Last but not least is investigative psychology which is a research-based approach for the analysis of offender behaviour. The main advocate of this method is British psychologist, Dr. David Canter, who emphasized on five important factors: interpersonal coherence, significance of time and space, criminal characteristics, criminal career, and forensic awareness. It involves extensive examination of all these factors to test out patterns and trends for the police investigation. The application of criminal profiling has come a long way and has evolved with various perspectives and backgrounds. The various methods and applications of criminal profiling eventually help in assisting and improving our understanding of crimes.

4.5 Criminal Profiling in the East

As stated earlier, the field of criminal profiling has evolved steadily over the last 50 years. However, with the rise in terrorist attacks in the recent years, it has started to focus more on a suspect-based profiling. Suspect-based profiling has been controversial since it has targeted specific demographic features of individuals such as their race, ethnicity, and national origin. Public awareness about racial profiling heightened in the twentieth century.

In the light of such crimes, The European Union funded Border Management in Central Asia Programme (BOMCA 9) also conducted a National Workshop on Identification and Profiling of Travelers in the year 2016. It aimed to present good practices of modern techniques in profiling of border crossing persons such as criminal profiling, documents check, informative comparative analysis, and other profile development methods. Several tools were also developed for practical purposes, such as migrants' appearance, analysing first impressions and behaviours and characteristics as well as classification of travellers.

In the changing terrain of the post-Soviet region, there are several diverse trajectories for criminal investigations that have been developed as well. The Russian intelligence agencies are increasingly developing their own in-house profiling techniques such as crime reconstruction and analysis of the victim's wounds to determine the personality of the offender, his motives, and other models for prediction (Enikolopov, 2007). Ethnic profiling exists throughout Europe alongside arbitrary identity checks of persons from the North Caucasus in the Russian Federation.

Different methods of criminal profiling have been widely used as standard operating procedures in criminal investigations all over the world. Many sensor-based screening tools have also been developed. One such is the Future Attributing Screening Technology (FAST) which seeks to improve the behavioural-based procedures to enable investigators to make more informed decisions. Various machine learning algorithms are also used by police even though some are in an experimental phase, such as PredPol: used to predict where crimes may occur and how to allocate police resources, Correctional Offender Management Profiling for Alternative Sanctions (COMPAS) to forecast reoffending in order to make decisions to grant remand in custody and Harm Assessment Risk Tool (HART) to assess the risk of reoffending (Rights, 2019). They are increasingly becoming common although there are risks of data protection and privacy with the algorithm profiling. Keeping in mind the various discriminatory practices of profiling in the recent times, it is necessary to identify other existing profiling practices to increase accountability and transparency.

4.5.1 Criminal Profiling in India

Criminal profiling has so far been largely influenced by the work of United States' Federal Bureau of Investigations (FBI). In India, the field of criminal and behavioural profiling is, as yet, fairly new. It is still not used as a customary tool for the investigative process unlike the UK, Australia, and some European countries. Although the police are adopting new measures under the domain of psychological as well as behavioural techniques, there is still considerable scope for improvement. Currently, criminal profiles are largely prepared by the police with the help of few experts. Yet, scant efforts are made to make a much needed holistic assessment of the offender. Although it is still not widespread, conventional policing system which is known as the 'Kotwali' system has a system of analysing and recording behavioural traits of the criminal, similar to the methods used for offender profiling (Singh, 2016).

Policing in India still heavily relies on the traditional methods of reactive policing rather than being more proactive in using more modern scientific methods to predict criminal offending. There is still not well-defined roles and experts in the area. There is a need for more experts and roles for them in the investigative process to aid in scientific profiling of crimes. There is a need to assimilate data on the types of crimes and criminals in our country to create profiles in the Indian context. Governmental and non-governmental agencies can both simultaneously undertake such compilations. In recent times, the actuarial methods are more favoured, and investigators in our country could also undertake such statistically supported techniques to improve the current approaches. The Indian system is also stuck with information gathering and confessions rather than following scientific evidence.

Considering the dearth of literature on criminal profiling in India, it might be worthwhile that this specialized field be more utilized. The most obvious way is to improve the efficacy of the current techniques and provide police personnel and other stakeholders with relevant rigorous training in the area. It should be included in the higher education system, especially in the studies of law, criminology, and applied psychology. On the basis of curriculum, adequate training could be implemented to the existing police personnel for necessary training. Lastly, criminal profiling is still an unexplored area in India and investigations would benefit immensely if they opened up more research opportunities and collaborations in this area. It can also become a relevant tool for criminal investigation with an increased awareness about it.

4.5.2 Recent Deliberations in the Field of Criminal Profiling

In present times, the simplicity of the techniques and methods of criminal profiling has been questioned by various scholars and practitioners. The validity of criminal profiling has detected its flaws in theoretical and empirical effectiveness (Bourque et al., 2009; Snook et al., 2010). All the body of work that has proposed criminal profiling since the establishment of Behavioural Science Unit (BSU) at FBI in the 1970s have failed to present its accuracy and contribution to solving crimes. A multitude of complications were highlighted by researchers in the very act of criminal profiling carried out by FBI agents—there was no indication of any formal training or expertise of research design received by the agents, lack of representation of serial killers during that time and interviews based on convenience and relatively ad hoc (Canter et al., 2004; Risinger & Loop, 2002). Subsequent research on the typology of offenders by Hazelwood and Douglas in a short article called 'The Lust Murderer' in 1980 was critiqued for its lack of clear distinction between organized/disorganized offenders and little empirical value (Canter et al., 2004; Hazelwood & Douglas, 1980).

Similar techniques such as the criminal investigative analysis have originated after public infatuations with profiling and series of crime novels, wherein the FBI had redeveloped and polished its approach to criminal profiling. But such techniques have met with similar criticisms from the scientific research community. Hence, through recent literature on profiling a word of caution is issued to the use of criminal profiling in criminal investigations. As it currently stands, criminal profiling has expanded its popularity either as an investigative technique or in popular media. However, it still showcases poverty in terms of scientific assessment and rigorous evaluations.

References

Ainsworth, P. B. (2001). *Offender profiling and crime analysis*. Willan.

Badcock, R. (1997). Developmental and clinical issues in relation to offending in the individual. In J. L. Jackson & D. A. Bekerian (Eds.), *Offender profiling: Theory, research and practice* (pp. 9–42). Wiley.

Bourque, J., LeBlanc, S., Utzschneider, A., & Wright, C. (2009). The effectiveness of profiling from a national security perspective. Canadian Human Rights Commission.

Canter, D. (1994). *Criminal shadows*. HarperCollins.

Casey-Owens, M. (1984). The anonymous letter writer—A psychological profile? *Journal of Forensic Science, 29*, 816–819.

Canter, D., Alison, L., Alison, E., & Wentink, E. (2004). The organized/disorganized typology of serial murder: Myth or model? Psychology. *Public Policy and the Law, 10*, 293–320.

Davis, J. A. (1999). Criminal personality profiling and crime scene assessment. *Journal of Contemporary Criminal Justice, 15*, 291–301.

Douglas, J. E., & Burgess, A. E. (1986). Criminal profiling: A viable investigative tool against violent crime. *FBI Law Enforcement Bulletin, 55*, 9–13.

Douglas, J. E., & Olshaker, M. (2000). *The cases that haunt us*. Simon & Schuster.

Douglas, J. E., Ressler, R. K., Burgess, A. W., & Hartman, C. R. (1986). Criminal profiling from crime scene analysis. *Behavioral Sciences & the Law, 4*, 401–421.

Ebisike, N. (2008). *Offender profiling in the courtroom: The use and abuse of expert witness testimony*. Praeger.

Egger, S. A. (1999a). Psychological profiling. *Journal of Contemporary Criminal Justice, 15*, 242–261.

Egger, S. A. (1999b). Psychological profiling: Past, present and future. *Journal of Contemporary Criminal Justice, 15*(3), 242–261.

Hazelwood, J., & Douglas, J. (1980). The lust murderer. *FBI Law Enforcement Bulletin, 49*(2), 18–24.

Hazelwood, R. R. (1987). Analyzing the rape and profiling the offender. In R. R. Hazelwood & A. W. Burgess (Eds.), *Practical aspects of rape investigation: A multidisciplinary approach*. Elsevier.

Holmes, R. M., & Holmes, S. T. (1996). *Profiling violent crimes: An investigative tool*. SAGE.

Homant, R. J., & Kennedy, D. B. (1998). Psychological aspects of crime scene profiling. *Criminal Justice and Behavior, 25*, 319–343. Retrieved from https://issuu.com/torchmktg/docs/bsr

septoct16, https://www.coe.int/en/web/commissioner/-/ethnic-profiling-a-persisting-practice-in-europe.
Kocsis, R. N. (2006). *Criminal profiling: Principles and practice*. Humana Press.
Muller, D. A. (2011). Qualitative approaches to criminal profiling as ways of reducing uncertainty in criminal investigations. *Policing: A Journal of Policy and Practice, 5*, 33–40.
Ressler, R. K., Douglas, J. E., Burgess, A. W., & Burgess, A. G. (1992). *The crime classification manual*. Simon & Schuster.
Risinger, D. M., & Loop, J. L. (2002). Three card monte, monty hall, modus operandi and "offender profiling": Some lessons of modern cognitive science for the law of evidence. *Cardazo Law Review, 24*, 193–285.
Snook, B., Eastwood, J., Gendreau, P., & Bennell, C. (2010). The importance of knowledge cumulation and the search for hidden agendas: A reply to Kocsis, Middledorp, and Karpin (2008).
Wilson, P., Lincoln, R., & Kocsis, R. (1997). Validity, utility and ethics of profiling for serial violent and sexual offenders. *Psychiatry, Psychology and Law, 4*, 1–12.

Chapter 5
Mental Disorders, Violence, and Crime

Sanjeev P. Sahni and Karishma

Abstract Mental disorders are identified by a set of signs and symptoms causing significant clinical distress or impairment in an individual's functioning. The relationship between mental disorders and crime has been a topic of research and heated controversy since many decades. There is a consensus advocating a link between the two. However, the exact nature of the relationship is quite complex. Though individuals with mental disorders are frequently perceived as the perpetrators of crime, emerging research shows that they are more likely to be victimized than committing a crime. Moreover, mental disorders cannot be perceived as a singular variable and need to be understood as distinct categories with different levels of sense of judgement, touch with reality, decision-making, and so forth. To understand the culpability of such individuals, these aspects need to be established clearly. This chapter elaborates upon the categories of mental disorders that are frequently associated with crime namely psychotic spectrum disorders, addiction disorders, personality disorders, dissociative disorders, and sexual disorders, and their respective association with criminal offending.

Keywords Mental disorder · Antisocial · Violence · Crime · Personality disorder

5.1 Introduction

In 1999, Andre Goldstein abruptly hurled Kendra Webdale off the platform of a Manhattan subway station, in front of a train (Rohde, 1999). Mr. Goldstein's defence pleaded not guilty by reason of insanity towards the murder charge. He was a schizophrenic and had discontinued taking his medicine at the time of the attack. What followed was a controversial case of whether this man was responsible for his actions or not. Though the answer seems to be very simple, such questions remain very complicated for the criminal justice system to address. To determine the level

S. P. Sahni (✉) · Karishma
Jindal Institute of Behavioural Sciences, O.P. Jindal Global University, Sonipat, Haryana, India
e-mail: drspsahni@jgu.edu.in

S. Sahni et al. (eds.), *Criminal Psychology and the Criminal Justice System in India and Beyond*, https://doi.org/10.1007/978-981-16-4570-9_5

of loss of control and understanding that any mental disorder could have on an individual during the commission of a crime is a tricky assessment. To understand this, we delve into understanding the nature of mental disorders and how they affect a person's actions and cognition.

A mental disorder is a 'significant disturbance' in an individual's thinking, emotions, or behaviour that reflects a 'dysfunction in the psychological, biological or developmental processes underlying mental functioning' (American Psychiatric Association, 2013). It can be identified by significant distress or socio-occupational dysfunction. However, the responses to a common stressor such as grief cannot be identified as a mental disorder. Additionally, socially deviant behaviour, unless it is an outcome of dysfunction, is also excluded from being considered as a mental disorder (American Psychiatric Association, 2013).

Crime, violence, and mental disorders have been linked to each other for centuries. Philosophers such as Socrates and Benjamin Franklin have been proponents of the theory that individuals with mental disorders are dangerous to the society (Marzuk, 1996) but it has been only in recent decades that the scientific community began to examine the correlation (Hodgins, 1998).

From the legal perspective, it is extremely crucial to understand this link to prove *mens rea*, also interpreted as intent to commit a crime (Johnson & Elbogen, 2013). However, the exact nature of the relationship is extremely complicated and evades clear understanding due to various reasons. There are certain mental disorders such as schizophrenia that do make a person more prone to commit an act of aggression or violence, because the individual is paranoid and disconnected with reality. So can an act committed by such a person be considered a crime? Then, there are certain personality disorders that are classified as psychiatric illnesses; however, there is an emerging consensus reconceptualizing personality disorders as lack of societal value judgements rather than illnesses (Ghiasi & Singh, 2019; Kendell, 2002).

Despite the common belief that people with mental disorders are more likely to commit crime, emerging literature shows that the people with mental disorders are more likely to be victims of crime (Ghiasi & Singh, 2019). This chapter aims to understand the nature and phenomenology of psychotic disorders (especially schizophrenia), addiction disorders, personality disorders, dissociative disorders, and sexual disorders to be able to comprehend their intricate pathway and concurrence with the crime, especially violent crime.

5.2 Various Mental Disorders and Crime

Paul W. Tappan (1960) conceptualized crime as 'an intentional act or omission in violation of criminal law (statutory and case law) committed without defence or justification, and sanctioned by the state as a felony or misdemeanour'. This definition clearly mentions 'intention' and 'justification'. Here, we aim to understand the presenting nature of a mental disorder to be able to deliberate an individual's incapacity of reality orientation and lack of judgement between right and wrong.

5.2.1 Schizophrenia Spectrum and Other Psychotic Disorders

> "I am a 31 year old engineer working in a multinational company. I got married 4 years ago. Since a few months ago, I came to know that my wife is having an affair with one of my friends. I saw them smiling in 'that manner'. I tried to shrug it off, but I couldn't, I just knew. I told my parents too, they refused to believe me; I realized she had hypnotized them. I just knew. Last month, I came to know that my wife and her lover had hired a hit man to kill me. I informed about this to my family, but they didn't believe me. In fact, my mother took me to a faith healer. I went to the police but I realized that the police had already been bribed and bought off. I started planning my escape as I was very scared. I even saw some facebook posts about it, there were hidden meanings in her wall updates. Some people asked for concrete proofs but I just knew by intuition.
>
> This morning while taking a metro, I realized that there was a man following me. I tried to escape him but he kept on following me, and kept on pretending to read the newspaper. I saw him going for a gun in his pocket so I attacked him…I had to attack him otherwise he would have killed me. The police arrested me and said he didn't have a gun, they have now brought me to a hospital where a lot of people are pretending to be nurses and doctors. I am sure the police and these people are my wife's and her lover's accomplices and they all want me dead. I am afraid they will kill me now…."

In this case study, the man is convinced that his wife is having an affair with another man, and that they have conspired to murder him along with his family and law enforcement agencies. He was brought to the psychiatric services after he tried to attack a man at a subway station and became violent with the hospital staff claiming that they were 'imposters and want him dead'. On gathering detailed history from his family, it was found that he had been acting 'strangely' for the past year; being paranoid and suspicious of his wife without any proof. He also stated that his co-workers are bugging his office and want to get him fired. He stopped sleeping and eating properly and started having arguments with family, friends, and co-workers without provocations.

This class of disorders—different types of schizophrenia disorder, persistent delusional disorder, transient psychotic disorder, etc.—is generally identified by delusions, hallucinations, negative symptoms, and gross distortion in thought and perception (APA, 2013). Individuals with schizophrenia have bizarre experiences reflecting disordered consciousness, identified by disruptive thought process, perception, emotional responsiveness, and social adjustment. There are still no clear etiological factors or biomarkers predicting the course and treatment of schizophrenia, and it is still best understood through its clinical phenomenology. The most valid assessment symptoms are the five-factor model based on Positive and Negative Syndrome Scale (PANNS)—psychotic symptoms, negative symptoms, disorganized behaviour, agitation, irritability, and lack of insight (Kay et al., 1987; Sadock et al., 2017).

Psychotic Symptoms Though any one particular psychotic symptom cannot singularly justify the diagnosis of any psychotic disorder or schizophrenia, yet with the easier identification and uniqueness of such symptoms, psychotic features remain the fulcrum in understanding schizophrenia. The main psychotic symptoms can be classified as hallucinations (visual, auditory, gustatory, tactile, and olfactory) and delusions (Sadock et al., 2017). Though hallucinations are often linked with psychosis, hallucinations can occur in various disorders and conditions (Noll, 2009). There have been cases where individuals have heard voices of the God or the Devil commanding them to kill.

The classic definition of delusion is 'a false, unshakeable belief that is out of keeping with the patient's social and cultural background and is due to internal morbid process' (Fish et al., 2007). Delusions are identified by the fact that they are 'held with extraordinary convictions, are impervious to other experiences and counterargument and their content is impossible' (Sadock et al., 2017). Delusions are not just limited to forms of psychotic disorders but can occur in various other conditions such as delirium, dementia, and affective disorders. Thematically delusions can be classified into many types such as persecution, grandiosity, pregnancy, infidelity, and infestations (Kiran & Chaudhary, 2009). In the case given above, the man had unshakeable belief that his wife was cheating on him and that people were out to kill him. No amount of conviction from society, including that of family and loved ones, could convince him otherwise. A similar example of delusion in context of crime is an individual convinced that another particular person (maybe a celebrity, friend, stranger, etc.) is in love with them. There have been multiple reports of delusional cases where an individual would be convinced that a particular celebrity is married or in love with them.

Negative Symptoms Though positive symptoms such as hallucinations and delusions remain the core diagnostic variable of various psychotic disorders, negative symptoms are also extremely important because of their stability over the course of illness and their subsequent role of predicting the level of short and long-term disability especially an individual's social functioning (Sadock et al., 2017). Negative symptoms have been defined as 'diminution of normal behaviour and functions that results in emotional dullness, failure of mental activities, loss of mastery over volition, of endeavour, and of ability for independent action' (Buchanan, 2007). Negative symptoms include alogia (diminished verbal expression) blunted affect (diminished emotional expressiveness), asociality (diminished involvement in social interactions and relationships), avolition (diminished subjective interest in desires, goal-oriented activities, purposefulness, etc.), and anhedonia (inability to experience pleasure) (Kirkpatrick et al., 2006; Mitra et al., 2016).

Disorganization The disorganization syndrome is a set of symptoms that include formal thought disorder, inappropriate affect, catatonic, and bizarre behaviours. Formal thought disorder is dysfunction in the language production and alterations. FTD is a disorder of the 'form of thought' rather than the 'content of thought' (Kircher et al., 2018). Nancy Anderson (1986) in her landmark paper conceptualized formal thought disorder as 'disorders of thought, language and communication'. FTD includes poverty of speech, poverty of content of the speech, distractible speech, increased spontaneous speech, oblique and tangential speech, derailed and disjoined speech, etc. Catatonia can be defined as a psychomotor syndrome identified by a set of symptoms: retarded and excited. Retarded symptoms would include immobility, staring, mutism, automatic obedience, etc. Excited catatonia is identified by psychomotor agitation (Rasmussen et al., 2016).

Some of these symptoms can be present in almost all schizophrenic patients, but with some patients, disorganized symptoms are more prevalent and intense and as such patients are usually diagnosed with hebephrenic schizophrenia (Sadock et al., 2017). Understanding these symptoms is essential for clinicians and law enforcement as they could help in identifying malingering by an individual.

Agitation and Hostility Agitation is one of the least understood symptoms in schizophrenia and unfortunately linked with violence. Agitation, impulsivity, uncooperativeness, and irritability are common features of the psychotic spectrum and are more commonly found in males (Sadock et al., 2017).

Insight People with many severe psychotic disorders often lack the insight, i.e. the acceptance and awareness of their signs and symptoms, subsequently denying the need for treatment and medical adherence (Buckley et al., 2007). Lack of insight might be the most crucial care giver burden (Noll, 2009) and the underlying reason of agitation and aggressive behaviour by the individuals with schizophrenia (Linoln & Hodgins, 2008).

Case Analysis

The man in the case can be diagnosed with paranoid schizophrenia. Paranoid schizophrenia is the subtype of schizophrenia identified by prominent delusions and hallucinations. The delusions are generally of persecutory or grandiose nature accompanied by suspiciousness. These psychotic symptoms are generally in presence of optimal cognitive functioning (WHO, 1992). Persecutory delusions are the unshakable beliefs in which a person perceives that he/she is being subjected to maliciousness, hostility, harassment, and victimization despite contradictory evidence (Mental Health Daily, 2015). Delusion of infidelity could be referred as having false firm belief regarding one's spouse's infidelity (Graff-Radford et al., 2012). The individual in the case was displaying psychiatric symptoms over a period of at least one year before the incident occurred. Though his family did not understand that it was a psychiatric issue, they clearly understood that there was some sort of problem that warranted help (which is reflected by their referring to a faith healer). The man is of firm belief that his wife is having an extramarital affair and wants him dead. He sought legal help but that was denied to him. In such a situation, with his delusions and acute stress, he acted violently but his intention was to save his life.

The Schizophrenia Spectrum and Criminal Offending

There is ample literature investigating the link between schizophrenia and crime, especially produced over the last two decades. Yet the relationship between the two is highly controversial (Elbogen & Johnson, 2009; Bo et al., 2011). Traditionally, beliefs have held schizophrenia and violence as coexisting. These beliefs have been constantly fuelled by ignorance and stigma in the general public (Wehring & Carpenter, 2011) and distorted media reports (Angermeyer et al., 2005; Owen, 2012). Scientifically, these beliefs can also be attributed to flawed methodologies such as merging all types of violent acts into one amalgamated factor (Elbogen & Johnson, 2009) along with convenient and biased samples such as prison cohorts or already institutionalized cohorts (Douglas et al., 2009; Sadock et al., 2017). The contemporary research in the area is finding contradictory evidences. Firstly, a number of studies have suggested that comorbid substance abuse is the main etiological factor of the violence and crime among the psychotic disorder cohort (Soyka, 2000; Dolan et al., 2012). Fazel et al. (2009) in their meta-analysis of 20 studies, that included 18,423 individuals identified with schizophrenia and other psychotic disorders, found that though the risk of violence was increased, this risk of violence increased with the comorbidity of substance use disorders; but interestingly, the risk of violent outcomes in schizophrenia and other psychotic disorders with comorbid substance use disorders has no significant difference with the individuals diagnosed with substance use disorders. The study clearly established that there was no increased risk of violent crime in individuals with psychotic disorders.

Secondly, even with the convicts that could be identified with schizophrenia, it has been seen that majority of them have had no contact with mental health services. Morgan et al. (2013) used a whole-of-population design of an Australian cohort from 1955–69 and found that a substantial number of offenders with psychotic illnesses had their first point of contact with mental health services after their first arrest. Furthermore, research shows that individuals with schizophrenia are at a significant higher risk of being victimized and face violence rather than perpetrating violence (Fitzgerald et al., 2005; Sestoft, 2006; Wehring & Carpenter, 2011).

5.2.2 Addiction Disorders

> "I am M, a 20 years old man, hailing from a lower middle class family, having left school. The first time I ever used any substance was at the age of 14, when my school seniors pressurized me to just have a 'puff from a cigarette'. I started coughing and felt like vomitting, but my seniors started to laugh on me. So eventually I started trying to learn how to smoke a cigarette to appear 'cool' in front of them. Though I started smoking just to learn how to smoke, eventually I started enjoying it. In the beginning I used to smoke 2-3 cigarettes in a week, but I started craving for more. Gradually, within 1-2 years, I was smoking a whole pack. At this point, me and my friends also started consuming alcohol, though I used to drink alcohol only occasionally because of lack of money. If I ran out of money, I started using my stationery and books allowance for it or I started stealing petty change from my parents. If I couldn't get cigarettes, I used to substitute them with '*bidi*' (hand rolled cigarettes). At the age of 17, my friends bought some weed and we all tried it.

Within 5-6 months, I got bored of it and wanted to try something new but my friends were not interested. I got in touch with some street guy and befriended them. One of them got me '*chitta*'(synthetic drug produced from heroin and other substances) for free. I asked him what does he want in return, he said 'its okay between friends'. He kept getting me *chitta* for free for some days, gradually I started getting addicted. Once he was sure, I was 'hooked' he started charging me Rs. 2000–3000. First I took loans from my friends, but they stopped giving me money; so I tried to stop using it but I just couldn't; I used to get extremely restless, low…I felt like crying all the time. I was irritated all the time and I couldn't even sleep; Sometimes, I used to feel so hungry, I couldn't focus on anything. I kept on sweating and used to have uncontrollable vomitting and used to get excruciating pains; I even started having mild seizures. I just couldn't live without it. I stole my mother's gold bangles but she came to know of it and I was beaten up by my family. As I was not able to afford anymore *chitta*, my friend took me to his boss and he offered to supply me with *chitta* if I would help him sell it to various places. It was very easy, he started giving me *chitta* and some other drugs and all I had to do was go to parties and sell, I knew I was doing wrong but the thought of leaving *chitta* was very frightening. It was in one of these parties when the police arrested me…."

Addiction disorders can be accounted to a significant global disease burden having detrimental outcomes not only on health but also economy, social aspects and productivity. Addiction disorders also have one of the highest mortality rates among the psychiatric disorders (WHO, 2017; Degenhardt et al., 2018). The concept of addiction refers to a course in which a behaviour that can 'function both to produce pleasure and provide escape from internal discomfort and is employed in a pattern characterized by (a) recurrent failure to control the behaviour and (b) continuation of the behaviour, despite significant negative consequences' (Goodman, 1990). Traditionally, addiction or substance use disorders have deep moralized underpinnings, generally conceptualized as 'character flaws', but emerging scientific literature puts addictions at par with other chronic diseases. Addiction disorders, like many other chronic diseases, have the features of persistence, tendency of relapse, genetic etiology and are influenced by development, society and environment (M.H.S.A.U & Office of the Surgeon General, 2016). The National Institute on Drug Abuse (NIDA) (2007) states that addiction is 'a chronic, relapsing brain disease that is characterized by compulsive drug seeking and use, despite known harmful consequences. It is considered a brain disease because drugs change the brain—they change its structure and how it works. These brain changes can be long lasting, and can lead to harmful behaviours seen in people who abuse drugs'.

A breakthrough idea in the area of addiction research is that an individual can be addicted to a set of experiences or processes even in the absence of psychoactive drugs; these non-substance addictions can be called as behavioural addictions (Alavi et al., 2012; Peele & Brodsky, 1975). Therefore, addiction disorders can be classified into substance addictions and behavioural addictions.

Addiction Disorders: Substance Use Disorders

DSM-V defines substance use disorders as 'a cluster of cognitive, behavioural, and physiological symptoms indicating that the individual continues using substance despite significant substance-related problem' (APA, 2013). A substance or psychotropic drug is any drug 'capable of affecting the mind, emotions and behaviour' (Shiel, 2018). The medical classification system applies the diagnostic criteria of substance use disorders to various classes of substances that are: alcohol, tobacco, stimulants such as cocaine, caffeine, cannabis, hallucinogens, inhalants, and opioids (APA, 2013). The diagnosis often varies in relation to dose levels, presenting problems such as acute intoxication, harmful use, and dependence syndrome.

Dependence syndrome is 'a cluster of physiological, behavioural, and cognitive phenomena in which the use of a substance or a class of substances takes on a much higher priority for a given individual than other behaviours that once had greater value'. (WHO, 1992) The cynosure of dependence syndrome is a 'strong overpowering desire' to take the substance. The diagnosis of dependence is usually made if three or more of these criterion are present in an individual: (i) an overpowering compulsion to take the particular substance, (ii) lack of control in the substance taking behaviour, (iii) symptoms of physiological withdrawal when the substance is not being taken, (iv) developing tolerance, (v) abandoning alternative interests and pleasures, and (vi) persistence of taking the substance despite detrimental outcomes (WHO, 1992). The substance disorders that are seen linked to crime are described below.

Alcohol Use Disorders Mankind has been consuming fermented alcohol-like substance since at least 12,000 years, and almost all civilizations and cultures have mentioned the vices of alcohol consumption (Sadock et al., 2017). Yet, alcohol abuse remains one of the major social and health concerns of our times. National Mental Health Survey of India 2015–16 (2016) reports 4.65% prevalence rate of alcohol use disorders. Alcohol abuse can result in multiple short-term and long-term outcomes such as anterograde amnesia (in the form of blackout), impairment in sleep, increase in cholesterol levels and blood pressure, cardiovascular problems, and cancer (Sadock et al., 2017). Initiating drinking, developing dependence, and not quitting can be cause of multiple factors including genetic predisposition, religious and societal factors, personality dispositions, etc. (Karishma & Kumar, 2017). Among all psychoactive drugs, alcohol with its ability to impair judgement and lower inhibitions can be substantially linked to crime, especially binge drinking. Crimes often linked with AUDs are assault and violence including sexual assault, intimate partner violence, sexual violence, homicide, etc. (Galbicsek, 2019).

Cannabis-Related Disorders Cannabis is regarded as a 'schedule drug I', i.e. it has a high latency of abuse and no significant medical purpose (Patel & Marwaha, 2019). Nonetheless, cannabis use is highly prevalent all over the world especially with its legalization in multiple countries (Medrano, 2019) despite the scientific evidence demonstrating permanent neurological dysfunction with its persistent use (Meier et al., 2012). Cannabis abuse is significantly linked with criminal activity (Pedersen & Skardhamar, 2010). Moreover, cannabis has been stated to be the most prevalent illicit drug in the cases of impaired driving (Hartman & Huestis, 2013).

Opioid-Related Disorders It is believed that use of opium poppy predates the recorded history. Opioid in different forms can be prescribed medically for pain relief but is often abused. It is often used and abused as both: naturally occurring substance and as opiates (i.e. chemically synthesized) (Sadock et al., 2017). Scientific literature clearly demonstrates a strong correlation of opioid and opiate abuse with crime in terms of higher use showing higher criminal activities and opioid maintenance treatment showing reduction in crime (Darke et al., 2010; Bulten et al., 2011). However, factors such as poverty, discrimination, and use of multiple substances might be contributing factors (Hammersley et al., 1989; Sadock et al., 2017).

Case Analysis

The first point of contact for M with any kind of drug was a cigarette which he tried under peer pressure. Though his first experience was aversion, yet he kept on trying to learn to adjust in his social environment; but while learning to smoke, he developed tolerance and increased his intake. His tolerance increased to the level that he started getting withdrawal symptoms due to which he would even switch to *bidi* and would steal money. Gradually M switched to a synthetic version of heroin; this could be reason of a sensation seeking personality trait. It has been seen that people with personality traits such as impulsiveness, higher novelty seeking, lower conscientiousness, etc are more likely to indulge in addiction behaviors (Karishma & Kumar, 2017). Also, for M, cigarettes and alcohol have acted as a gateway drug to *chitta* (synthetic version of heroin). It has been seen that alcohol and nicotine often acts as pathways to more harmful substances such as cocaine (National Institution of Health, 2011; Kandel & Kandel, 2014). M eventually got addicted to heroin which is a class of opioids. Although he made repeated attempts to restrain from the drug, yet he would relapse because of acute physical and psychological withdrawal symptoms. As he was not able to manage his withdrawal symptoms, he was lured into easy criminal activities.

Behavioral and Process Addiction

Emerging scientific literature proves that the rewards systems in our brain work similarly in context to a behaviour, as they do with a chemical or a drug (Holden, 2001). This has led to emergence to a new area of research, i.e. behavioural addictions. Behavioural addictions (or process addictions) are the behaviours or activities (not involving substances) that produce short-term rewards and persistence in repeating the behaviour despite its detrimental outcomes. Behavioural addictions can include a wide range of behaviours such as pathological gambling, shopping, sexual addiction, and Internet addiction (Grant et al., 2010). The forms of behavioural addiction that are connected to crime are pathological gambling and Internet addiction that are explained below.

Pathological Gambling Pathological gambling is the first behavioural addiction to be included in the DSM-III. Though not researched as much, it can be as crippling as major psychotic and affective disorders. Moreover, with the augmentation of Internet being a medium, it is being seen that even recreational gamblers can slide towards pathological form of gambling (Sadock et al., 2017). The criteria of pathological gambling include (i) betting higher amounts of money to achieve excitement, (ii) withdrawal symptoms such as irritability when restraining from betting, (iii) failure at controlling gambling, (iv) persistence in gambling with an aim to get even when loosing, (v) remaining overwhelmingly preoccupied with gambling activities and thoughts, (vi) jeopardizing socio-occupational life, and (vii) lying about gambling (APA, 2013).

Internet Addiction Though not included formally and being stated as 'consideration for further study' in the DSM-V (APA, 2013), the scientific community especially mental health professionals and neuroscientists has extensively explored and reported the occurrence of Internet addiction and Internet gaming disorder (Brand et al., 2014; King & Delfabbro, 2014; Kuss et al., 2014). With the lack of recognition in either of the arbitrary classification systems, Kimberly Young (1998) developed a diagnostic criteria based on the DSM-V diagnostic criteria of pathological gambling. The set of criteria is as follows: (i) being preoccupied with Internet, (ii) presence of withdrawal symptoms' and developing tolerance, (iii) increasing amount of time indulging in Internet, (iv) failure in controlling in its usage, (v) jeopardizing relationships and work, (vi) using Internet as a medium of escape, and (vii) lying about Internet use.

Addiction and Criminal Offending

Crime, especially violent crime, is a quite commonly comorbid issue with substance use disorders (Dennis et al., 2006; Bennett & Holloway, 2009). The relationship between the two is well tabulated since ages as seen during the Opium War in the Nineteenth Century in China and Prohibition Era in 1920s in the USA (De la Rosa et al., 1990). It is highly important to comprehend the etiological pathways of the substance abuse and violence to be able to establish preventive measures. Goldstein (1985) in his landmark article conceptualized a tripartite framework to understand the 'drug-violence nexus'. He classified the drug-related violence into:

(i) Systemic violence, i.e. the violence involved in the drug market during the sale or distribution of the psychoactive substances. It is suggested that this type of violence occurs in the economically disadvantaged areas with lower social control mechanism.
(ii) Economic compulsive violence, i.e. the violent acts committed to procure means to support one's habit of substance abuse, and
(iii) Psychopharmacological violence, i.e. violent acts that occur due to physiological changes that occur after ingesting a psychoactive substance. These

changes can be due to (a) acute intoxication, (b) psychotic symptoms induced through psychoactive drugs, and (c) agitation linked with withdrawal symptoms (Copes et al., 2015; Oser et al., 2009).

Notably, another pathway found is that the individuals often use psychoactive drugs to transgress their values and morals while committing crimes. An intoxicated state of mind can help an individual in diminishing various emotions such as guilt and shame and inhibition, empathy, impulse control, thus enabling them violate their own moral codes and perform violent crimes (Havnes et al., 2014). Furthermore, tremendous amount of literature has established that substance abuse comorbid with psychopathology is also a significant causal pathway (Fazel et al., 2009).

In the domain of behavioural addictions, pathological gambling commonly results into non-violent crimes such as theft and embezzlement, usually to cover up the gambling losses (Pastwa-Wojciechowska, 2011; Rosenthal & Lorenz, 1992) Moreover, in some countries, gambling is illegal (Lawyermonthly.com, 2019). Another emerging issue in the area is the increasing prevalence of crime and violent acts associated with behavioural addictions especially Internet addiction and Internet gaming disorder. Although the field is in its infancy, there is some evidence that suggests further investigation. Internet addiction has been found to be positively correlated to crime especially because technology serves as an easy medium to engage in crime (Arasi, 2016; Nykodym et al., 2008). Internet addiction is also correlated to indulging in child pornography (Sitarz et al., 2014). Notably, a series of crime reports including that of homicides related to Internet gaming disorder (Kumar, 2017; India Today, 2018; The News Minute, 2019) also point out that there might be an interconnection between Internet addiction and crime that warrants attention.

5.2.3 *Personality Disorders*

R is a 24 year old doctor. Four years ago, when she was pursuing her under graduation, she started developing a crush on her professor. She never actually approached him but started stalking him, sending him anonymous letters and gifts. When she graduated from the course, she came to know that he is married, experiencing deep outrage and jealousy. She started slashing her arms at this point. After a couple of months, she started working in the same department in the hope of seducing him or making the professor fall in love with her. Eventually, he started being friendly with her; although she understood his friendly attitude as a reciprocation of her infatuation. One night, when they both were working late, she approached him sexually. Not only, did he not respond, he reprimanded her. Furious, she lodged a sexual harassment at workplace case against him. Though the professor's career and family life was at stake, she did not withdraw the complaint and felt no remorse.

R has had a history of multiple relationships and break ups; often she gets too friendly too quickly with people and this results in disastrous break ups, compounded by her overwhelming and suspicious nature. She often makes frenzied and obsessive efforts to cling to her friends and boyfriends, often threatening them with self-harm. Clinically, she has an extensive history with mental health services, after episodes of slashing her wrists, overdose of sleeping pills, binge drinking and threatening her family and friends.

Personality disorders are a group of disorders which can be identified by 'a person's pervasive, inflexible and dysfunctional pattern of thought, behaviour and functioning, causing subsequent problems in one's socio-occupational and personal life'. Individuals with personality disorders often do not have insight or have poor insight into their behaviours (Mayo Clinic, n.d). Individuals with personality disorders have an enduring pattern of abnormality in social functioning and self that deviates distinctly from cultural expectations (Gask et al., 2013).

The concept of personality disorders evades the objective scientific perspective, and there is strong scientific evidence that suggest personality disorders are not mental disorders. Most of the personality disorders that remain in DSM-V and ICD-10 pertains to 'value judgements' and seems to border on 'extremities' and 'eccentricities' when compared to 'social and cultural norms' (Sadock et al., 2017). Another distinction of personality disorders from other mental disorders is that they are enduring over the period of adult life. On the other hand, mental disorders are the outcome of some kind of morbid process, have more clearly demarcated and lucid onset, precipitation and course (Gask et al., 2013; Kendell, 2002). The etiology of personality disorders is as complicated as their nature: there is still dearth of empirical evidence providing concrete understanding; rather, the causes of personality disorder are presently understood through speculative theoretical models. Though scientific evidence suggests genetic similarity between certain personality disorders (schizoid, schizotypal and paranoid) and schizophrenia spectrum, there is still no clear understanding (Tyrer & Simonsen, 2003).

The DSM-V classifies personality disorders into three clusters based upon their descriptive resembling patterns: (i) Cluster A consists of paranoid, schizoid, and schizotypal personality disorder. Cluster A is marked by 'eccentricity and odd behaviour'. Individuals with these personality disorders also tend to be 'socially indifferent and suspicious'. (ii) Cluster B comprises of antisocial (ASPD), borderline (BPD), histrionic, and narcissistic personality disorders. This cluster is identified by impulsive, dramatic, erratic behaviour, attentions seeking, and unstable behaviour. (iii) Cluster C comprises of the avoidant, dependant, and obsessive–compulsive personality disorders. This cluster can be identified by perpetual anxiety, fearfulness, inhibitions, and submissiveness (APA, 2013; Sadock et al., 2017). Clusters A and B personality disorder have been explained below in regard to their association with criminal behaviour.

Cluster A Personality Disorders

Paranoid personality disorder can be identified by 'a pervasive distrust and suspicion', interpreting the motives of others as 'malevolent, deceitful, exploitative, or harmful'. Such individuals can be identified by traits like 'a disinclination to confide in others and preoccupation with baseless suspicion about the trustworthiness of their friends or fidelity of their spouse'. They tend to hold grudges from minor benign incidents and perceives personal attacks or covert threats into issues that are not so apparent (APA, 2013).

Schizoid personality disorder is relatively less encountered and difficult to diagnose, as the person in question remains quite comfortable with the symptoms and does not express any discomfort (Dobbert, 2007). It can be identified by a 'pervasive pattern of detachment and restricted range of expression of emotions in interpersonal settings'. Individuals with schizoid personality disorders do not have interest in close relationships or sexual relationships, lack confidantes, show indifference to appreciation or criticism, and manifest emotional coldness and flattened affect (APA, 2013).

Schizotypal personality disorder is identified by 'markedly illogical thinking, unusual ideas, or odd beliefs that are not consistent with prevailing ideas' (Harvard Health Publishing, 2019). Individuals with schizotypal personality have a longstanding pattern of 'interpersonal deficits marked by acute discomfort with, and reduced capacity for, close relationships as well as by cognitive or perceptual distortions and eccentricities of behaviour'. It can manifest in varied contexts such as ideas of reference, magical thinking, odd thinking, odd speech, eccentric behaviour or appearance, and lack of close friends or associates (APA, 2013).

Cluster B Personality Disorders

Antisocial personality disorder, also called as 'psychopathy', 'sociopathy', and dissocial personality disorder, can be defined as 'a pervasive pattern of disregarding and violating rights of others'. ASPD is further identified by the consistent failure to conform to societal norm and law, perpetual deceitfulness, recklessness and aggression in terms of disregard of the safety of others, history of physical violence, chronic irresponsibility and extreme lack of guilt and remorse. DSM-V further states that the patterns generally start appearing from the age of 15 years (APA, 2013). The justification of adding the age criteria is the scientific evidence in terms of longitudinal studies that show 40–70% of children identified with conduct disorders will convert into ASPD as adults (National Collaborating Centre for Mental Health, 2010).

Borderline personality disorder is identified by a longstanding pattern of 'interpersonal relationships, self-image, and affects, and marked impulsivity'. Individuals with BPD manifest this pattern by 'frantic efforts to avoid real or imagined abandonment, identity disturbance, and deliberate self-harm, marked reactivity in mood, dissociative symptoms, and inappropriate anger, impulsive in terms of sex, binge drinking, etc.' (APA, 2013). BPD is said to be result of adverse traumatic experiences during early age. The BPD symptoms have been attributed to a tripartite etiological model that includes biological vulnerability, early trauma, and triggering events (Sadock et al., 2017).

The core features of histrionic personality disorder are 'excessive emotionality and attention seeking'. The diagnosis is generally made with these features: being uncomfortable in any situation if one is not the centre of attention, interactions are often coloured with inappropriate sexual behaviour, shallow and quickly rapidly shifting emotional expression, easily suggestible by others or current trends, self-dramatization, etc. (APA, 2013).

The hallmark features of narcissistic personality disorder are 'pervasive pattern of grandiosity, need for admiration, and lack of empathy'. Individuals with NPD manifest sense of grandiosity and entitlement; exaggerations and over estimation of self-importance and achievements, believing themselves to be 'special' or of higher status than others. Further, these individuals are preoccupied with limitless power or success, and demands constant admiration. They have tendency to be exploitative, and arrogant in interpersonal relationships, lack empathy, and are often envious of other people (APA, 2013).

Case Analysis

R's multiple break-ups of her relationships and deliberate self-harm can be understood in terms of borderline personality disorder. Secondly, she has a habit of clinging to relationships and binge drinking. Also, her instant 'obsession' and consequent revenge from the professor can be symptomatic of BPD in terms of 'alternating between extremes of idealization and devaluation'. Though most of the features suggest BPD, her deceitfulness, lying and lack of remorse can be suggestive of co-morbid ASPD.

Personality Disorders and Criminal Offending

A substantial number of individuals who commit crime are likely to manifest personality disorders; these personality disorders may be clearly diagnosable as one particular category of personality disorder or may exhibit traits of multiple categories (Stone, 2007). Among all the three categories, individuals with cluster B personality disorder are significantly more likely to commit violence and criminal offending (Coid et al, 2006; Eher et al., 2010). However, minor deviance from the 'normal continuum' is not enough to be an excuse or a distinguishing factor from other offenders. Moreover, the dysfunctions characteristic to the personality disorders is often in one's volitional control, and only in extremely rare cases, can they be viewed as a cause of removal of an individual's capacity to make a decision (Johnson & Elbogen, 2013).

The legal system does not accept personality disorders as mental disorders or an excuse for criminal behaviour, because of many reasons such as: (i) it does not manifest psychotic symptoms such as delusions or hallucinations (Pickard, 2015); (ii) there exists extreme high prevalence of personality disorders, i.e. 50% of individuals assessed in clinical settings and 10% in the general public (Sperry, 2016), who are diagnosed but may never offend; (iii) overlapping subclassifications especially in concerned population combined with the high rates of comorbid personality dysfunction with other major mental illnesses often leads to confusion in legally defining mental incapacity within the criminal justice system; (iv) hard to determine how much variation would be accepted as illness; (v) personality disorders such as ASPD reflects the concept of criminality too closely (Johnson & Elbogen, 2013); (vi) unlike other mental disorders, the prognosis of treatment is poor and extremely complicated, especially with antisocial personality disorder (ASPD) (National Collaborating Centre for Mental Health, 2010).

Though there is a strong relationship between personality disorders (especially Cluster B) and crime, there are two factors which the legal and scientific field should be mindful of in establishing linkage on case-to-case basis. Firstly, the findings and subsequent classification are based on substantial data collected from prison and forensic settings which can be deemed as biased sample (Lowenstein et al., 2016). Secondly, the clinical classification systems and the legal system should mutually accept the ongoing categorical approach of personality disorders. However, latest scientific debate is whether to amalgamate dimensional understanding in the field. Dimensional approach is the perspective which can shed light on the extent to which individuals possess certain traits that can be identified as personality disorders. This approach might alleviate the significance of personality dysfunction or vice versa. With advancing technology in neurology and genetics, it is expected that there will be breakthrough in understanding dimensional extents, and that might change the whole scientific and legal framework (Dressing et al., 2008).

5.2.4 Dissociative Disorders

Dissociation can be conceptualized as 'a disruption, interruption, and/or discontinuity' of the 'normal, subjective integration of potentially any aspect of experience and cognition, including behaviour, memory, identity, consciousness, emotion, perception, body representation, and motor control' (Sadock et al., 2017). In other words, dissociation can be said to be occurring when an individual's psychobiological functions are not coordinated. Dissociation is fundamentally a response to chronic developmental stress as a majority of the patients report some kind of child abuse. The dissociative symptoms can be precipitated suddenly or gradually, they can be either transient or chronic. Though a distinct category in itself, it is to be noted that dissociative symptoms might be present in other psychiatric disorders as well (Sar, 2011, 2014). The DSM-V classifies dissociative disorders as dissociative identity disorder (DID), dissociative amnesia, depersonalization/derealization, other specified dissociative disorders, and unspecified dissociative disorder (APA, 2013). The first three subtypes are explained below in regards to their relationship with crime.

Dissociative Identity Disorder Dissociative identity disorder (DID) is one of the most disputed psychiatric issues, in terms of its prevalence, etiology, especially its validity and scientific status. On the one hand, it is claimed that it is a 'fad', over-diagnosed, caused by the medical treatment/psychotherapy itself, etc. It is also claimed that there is a lack of modern scientific research in the area. Yet, there exists a stance that there is enough historical evidence, along with some current scientific research, consolidating DID as a fully fledged psychiatric condition. Nonetheless, it has been included in various versions of psychiatric classification systems (Boysen & Van Bergen, 2013; Dorahy et al., 2014; Brand et al., 2016; Paris, 2019). DSM-V identifies it as 'disruption of identity characterized by two or more distinct personality states, which may be described in some cultures as an experience of possession' along with significant discontinuity in 'in sense of self and agency' accompanied by 'related alterations in affect, behaviour, consciousness, memory, perception, cognition, and/or sensorimotor functioning'. It is further recognized by recurrent gaps in remembering day-to-day events, personal information, traumatic events, etc. The symptoms are to cause significant distress and cannot be imputable to medical conditions or to outcomes of substance use (APA, 2013).

Globally, DID prevail in two main forms: possession form and non-possession form. In the former, the alternative personalities are experienced as 'external agents' typically being supernatural entities such as spirits. Generally, this form of DID is observed in individuals from a socio-cultural milieu where such supernatural agents are considered to be real. In the non-possession DID, the possessing personalities are generally 'internal aspects' of an individual such as stemming from different stages of life or a biographical role (childhood or a protector-figure) (Sadock et al., 2017).

Dissociative Amnesia

Dissociative amnesia, earlier known as psychogenic amnesia, can be identified by a marked disturbance in the ability to 'recall important personal information, usually of a traumatic or stressful nature, that is too extensive to be explained by ordinary forgetfulness'. This disturbance does not account to outcomes of substance abuse or any neurological/organic medical condition as well as psychiatric conditions such as DID, and PTSD. A subtype dissociative fugue is identified by 'sudden, unexpected travel away from home or one's customary place of work, with inability to recall one's past, along with confusion about personal identity or assumption of a new identity' (Spiegel et al., 2013).

Depersonalization/Derealization Disorder

Depersonalization can be conceptualized as a 'hard-wired inhibitory response'—a human psychobiological survival attempt during a trauma by 'preventing overwhelming flooding of consciousness'. Hence, it allows an individual to assuage anxiety and hyperarousal, thus conserving adaptive behaviour and resources in the situation of threat. It can be defined as a 'distorted experience of self, associated with a sense of unreality or strangeness and profound detachment'. Though its precipitates during a sudden trauma, it may persist beyond the immediate threat where it was triggered (Gentile et al., 2014). It is also to be noted that during depersonalization, reality orientation remains intact (Spiegel et al., 2013) which differentiates it from psychosis.

Dissociative Disorders and Criminal Offending

Among the various types of dissociative disorders, dissociative identity disorder (earlier known as multiple personality disorder) is most ingrained in the public mind via media and popular culture for ages. Starting from R.L. Stevenson's nineteenth-century classic *The Strange Case of Dr. Jekyll and Mr. Hyde* to myriad number of movies, this disorder has usually been misrepresented in media (Farrell, 2011; Rose, 2017). DID has a controversial place in the criminal justice system and ambiguity in psychology compounds the confusion.

There are three main reasons as to why DID is not usually a successful insanity plea:

(a) Not having 'personal control over one's behaviour' is the mainstay of establishing 'insanity' as a defence. In many such cases, the judiciary goes on to explore which personality was in control during said offence and whether that particular personality fulfils the criteria of losing personal control/insanity.
(b) Often, DID evidence (including expert testimony) fails to meet the scientific standards of the judicial system in terms of reliability and validity (Farrell, 2011).

Dissociative amnesia in context of a crime is said to be an outcome of extreme emotional stress during the incident. In this view, extreme levels of arousal may inhibit the formation of autobiographical memory of that event. However, this viewpoint is objected as not all emotionally weighed down events result in amnesia. Clinical accounts of dissociate amnesia related to crime have been presented in partial (patchy memory around the main event) or full-blown forms. Some accounts are usually related to substance use; hence, 'blackouts' due to alcohol intoxication are to be understood distinctly from dissociative amnesia (Bourget & Whitehurst, 2007).

Literature shows a varied status of dissociative disorders in the criminal justice system. There are no generalized outcomes, and such cases are usually evaluated on their own merit (Porter et al., 2001). One significant reason is that dissociation in any form is easy to feign. There are numerous legal examples citing that suspects malingering dissociation (trying to fabricate the symptoms) (Paris, 2019). Moreover, a defendant's ability to remember the incident is the cornerstone variable in determining his/her competency. In such cases, 'not being able to remember' renders the defendant incompetent (Porter et al., 2001). Clinical and forensic assessments should involve critical analysis with extensive history from different sources. There is a great need for scientific research in the domain to improve the forensic evidence in this context (Bourget et al., 2007).

5.2.5 *Sexual Disorders*

Societal bifurcation of 'normal sexuality' and 'deviant sexuality' has varied over the centuries from culture to culture depending upon the moral code of the era or region. On the one hand, sexual behaviours such as masturbation and extramarital sex are forms of recreational sex and beyond the scope of the 'clinical abnormality' (Sadock et al., 2017); on the other hand, paraphilias in spite of their astonishing prevalence (Ahlers et al., 2011; Holvoet et al., 2017; Joyal & Carpentier, 2017) and non-distressful nature (in most cases) are considered as psychiatric issues (APA, 2013; WHO, 1992). Broadly speaking, any sexual behaviour, to be conceptualized as 'normal' should (a) involve primary sexual organs, (b) be pleasure inducing to oneself and one's partner leading to climax, at least quite often and (c) should not accompany compulsiveness and negative feelings such as guilt, shame, and pain. What further complicates the relationship of sexual disorders and crime is the inclusion and exclusion of some issues in the diagnostic and legal systems. For instance, homosexuality was classified as paraphilic in DSM-II (Silverstein, 2009) and a crime in many countries, including India, till just recently (The Economic Times, 2018). Moreover, activities such as consensual oral or anal sex are also considered a crime in many countries (Sadock et al., 2017).

Sexual disorders can be broadly classified into sexual dysfunctions and paraphilias. Sexual dysfunctions are mainly concerned with disturbances in psychophysiological changes in sexual response, desire, etc. associated with significant distress (Taborda & Michalski-Jaeger, 2012). Paraphilias can be defined 'any intense and persistent sexual interest other than sexual interest in genital stimulation or preparatory fondling with phenotypically normal physically mature, consenting human partners' (APA, 2013). Various forms of paraphilias are explained below in their association with crime.

Paraphilias

To explicate the 'atypical sexual interest' from a mental disorder, the DSM-V suggests that a diagnosis can be made if an individual (a) 'feel personal distress about their interest, not merely distress resulting from society's disapproval' or (b) 'have a sexual desire or behaviour that involves causing another person's psychological distress, injury, or death, or a desire for sexual behaviours involving unwilling persons or persons unable to give legal consent' (APA, 2013). It is to be noted that any deviant behaviour or desire would be considered as paraphilia only if it fulfils the second criterion. Different forms of paraphilias are: Exhibitionistic disorder can be identified by one's sexual gratification by exposing one's private body parts to an unsuspecting person or exhibiting one's sexual activities to others. Voyeuristic disorder, on the other hand, can be recognized by the urge viewing an unsuspecting individual's private activities (including sexual activities, undressing, etc.). Similarly, sexual gratification achieved by touching an unsuspecting or non-consenting person is called frotteuristic disorder. Fetishistic disorder can be identified by gratification to a particular object or activity. Pedophilic disorder is the sexual preference of prepubescent children. Sexual masochism and sexual sadism can be identified by sexual gratification by being humiliated, beaten, etc. to and vice versa, respectively. Transvestic fetishism can be described as getting aroused from clothes of the opposite sex (McManus et al., 2013).

Paraphilias, Criminal Offending, and and Sexual Offending
There exists a strong corelation between paraphilias and crime, especially in male offenders. However, with multiple studies suggesting the common presence of 'paraphilia associated sexual arousal pattern', it is accepted that they are not unusual and are under discussion for their place in psychiatric manuals (Taborda & Michalski-Jaeger, 2012). It has been frequently suggested that psychiatry should exclude paraphilias, especially paedophilia, so that it cannot be used as a defence in the courts. However, doing so would also exclude people who have such tendencies from seeking psychiatric help (Dreger, 2010). Though generally paraphilia cannot be deemed as 'requisite mental incapacity' to be used as an insanity defence, there definitely have been cases where a diagnosis of paraphilia has been successfully used as a defence, citing 'specific, serious, and highly unusual inability to control his actions that the law traditionally has considered this kind of abnormality akin to insanity for purposes of confinement'. Hence, if it is proven that the defendant at the time of crime was unaware of the wrongfulness of his acts and/or the acts were beyond his control — this might be used as a basis of mounting an insanity defence (Janofsky et al., 2014). Sexual crime is an elusive area as research in the field is limited because of absence of case–control studies or clinical trials, resulting from obvious ethical concerns. Further understanding in the area is required to prevent further victimization and burden on society (Taborda & Michalski-Jaeger, 2012).

5.3 Conclusion and Way Forward

The perception that individuals with mental disorders are essentially dangerous is quite ingrained in the mind of public and fuelled by distorted media and biased scientific evidence. The relationship between mental disorders and crime is extremely complicated. Firstly, mental disorders cannot be understood as one single variable. Mental disorders need to be understood in terms of distinct categories and dimensions, focusing on their level of disability, such as, if the individual was in touch with reality, if the individual possessed the capacity to distinguish from right and wrong, and so forth.

Secondly, the definition and conceptualization of crime should also be taken into account. Crime, though a legal variable, can vary in different cultures and time periods. For instance, suicide is usually a result of a mental illness but may be considered a crime in many countries as constructed by the dominant social and religious values. Similarly, historically, homosexuality has been considered a mental illness and is still considered a crime in many parts of the world.

Thirdly, evidence shows that individuals with mental disorders are more likely to be victimized rather than being the perpetrators of crime. It has also been seen that bias against the mentally ill prevails in the criminal justice system as well (Ghiasi & Singh, 2019; Varshney et al., 2016). Furthermore, it should be remembered that the substantial number of individuals with mental disorder when convicted had never had any contact with mental health services; this also sheds light on the fact that a huge percentage of crime can be prevented with improvements and availability of mental health services.

To understand the intricate connection of mental disorders and crime, to break this link and to be able to preemptively prevent crime—the need of the hour is to have robust research in the area to understand their exact relationship. In addition to that, public perception and stigma towards mental illness needs to be combated. Furthermore, there is an urgent need of multidisciplinary teams of mental health professionals and patient advocates to be able to assess the at-risk individuals, to educate and rehabilitate the patients already enmeshed in the criminal justice system.

References

Ahlers, C. J., Schaefer, G. A., Mundt, I. A., Roll, S., Englert, H., Willich, S. N., & Beier, K. M. (2011). How unusual are the contents of paraphilias? Paraphilia-associated sexual arousal patterns in a community-based sample of men. *The Journal of Sexual Medicine, 8*(5), 1362–1370.

Alavi, S. S., Ferdosi, M., Jannatifard, F., Eslami, M., Alaghemandan, H., & Setare, M. (2012). Behavioral addiction versus substance addiction: Correspondence of psychiatric and psychological views. *International Journal of Preventive Medicine, 3*(4), 290.

American Psychiatric Association. (2013). Diagnostic and statistical manual of mental disorders. *BMC Medicine, 17*, 133–137.

Andreasen, N. C. (1986). Scale for the assessment of thought, language, and communication (TLC). *Schizophrenia Bulletin, 12*(3), 473.

Angermeyer, M. C., Dietrich, S., Pott, D., & Matschinger, H. (2005). Media consumption and desire for social distance towards people with schizophrenia. *European Psychiatry, 20*(3), 246–250.

Arasi, N. K. (2016). Internet addiction and cyber crime engagement () f undergraduate students. *Journal of Gducational Research S 6xtension, 55*(5).

Bo, S., Abu-, A., Kongerslev, M., Haahr, U. H., & Simonsen, E. (2011). Risk factors for violence among patients with schizophrenia. *Clinical Psychology Review, 31*(5), 711–726.

Bourget, D., Gagne, P., & Wood, S. F. (2007). Dissociation: Defining the concept in criminal forensic psychiatry. *Journal of the American Academy of Psychiatry and the Law, 45*(2), 147–160.

Brand, B. L., Sar, V., Stavropoulos, P., Krüger, C., Korzekwa, M., Martínez-Taboas, A., & Middleton, W. (2016). Separating fact from fiction: An empirical examination of six myths about dissociative identity disorder. *Harvard review of psychiatry.*

Brand, M., Young, K. S., & Laier, C. (2014). Prefrontal control and Internet addiction: A theoretical model and review of neuropsychological and neuroimaging findings. *Frontiers in Human Neuroscience, 8*, 375.

Coid, J., Yang, M., Roberts, A., Ullrich, S., Moran, P., Bebbington, P., … & Singleton, N. (2006). Violence and psychiatric morbidity in a national household population—a report from the British Household Survey. *American Journal of Epidemiology, 164*(12), 1199-1208.

Copes, H., Hochstetler, A., & Sandberg, S. (2015). Using a narrative framework to understand the drugs and violence nexus. *Criminal Justice Review, 40*(1), 32–46.

Darke, S., Torok, M., Kaye, S., Ross, J., & McKetin, R. (2010). Comparative rates of violent crime among regular methamphetamine and opioid users: Offending and victimization. *Addiction, 105*(5), 916–919.

De la Rosa, M., Lambert, E., & Cropper, B. (1990). Drugs and Violence: Causes, Correlates, and Consequences, National Institute of Drug Abuse Research Monograph 103. *Rockville, Maryland: National Institute on Drug Abuse.*

Degenhardt, L., Charlson, F., Ferrari, A., Santomauro, D., Erskine, H., Mantilla-Herrara, A., ... & Rehm, J. (2018). The global burden of disease attributable to alcohol and drug use in 195 countries

and territories, 1990–2016: A systematic analysis for the Global Burden of Disease Study 2016. *The Lancet Psychiatry, 5*(12), 987–1012.
Dennis, M. L., Chan, Y. F., & Funk, R. R. (2006). Development and validation of the GAIN Short Screener (GSS) for internalizing, externalizing and substance use disorders and crime/violence problems among adolescents and adults. *American Journal on Addictions, 15*(sup1), 80–91.
Dobbert, D. L. (2007). *Understanding Personality Disorders: An Introduction: An Introduction.* ABC-CLIO.
Dorahy, M. J., Brand, B. L., Şar, V., Krüger, C., Stavropoulos, P., Martínez-Taboas, A., ... & Middleton, W. (2014). Dissociative identity disorder: An empirical overview. *Australian & New Zealand Journal of Psychiatry, 48*(5), 402–417.
Dreger, A. (2010). Of kinks, crimes, and kinds: The paraphilias proposal for the DSM-5. *Science and Society*
Dressing, H., Sartorius, A., & Meyer-, A. (2008). Implications of fMRI and genetics for the law and the routine practice of forensic psychiatry. *Neurocase, 14*(1), 7–14.
Eher, R., Rettenberger, M., & Schilling, F. (2010). Psychiatric diagnoses of sexual offenders: An empirical investigation of 807 delinquents imprisoned for child abuse and rape. *Z Sexualforsch, 23*, 23–35.
Farrell, H. M. (2011). Dissociative identity disorder: Medicolegal challenges. *Journal of the American Academy of Psychiatry and the Law Online, 39*(3), 402–406.
Fazel, S., Gulati, G., Linsell, L., Geddes, J. R., & Grann, M. (2009). Schizophrenia and violence: systematic review and meta-analysis. *PLoS medicine, 6*(8), e1000120.
Fish, F. J., Casey, P. R., & Kelly, B. (2007). *Fish's clinical psychopathology: signs and symptoms in psychiatry*. RCPsych Publications.
Fitzgerald, P. B., De Castella, A. R., Filia, K. M., Filia, S. L., Benitez, J., & Kulkarni, J. (2005). Victimization of patients with schizophrenia and related disorders. *Australian and New Zealand Journal of Psychiatry, 39*(3), 169–174.
Galbicsek, C. (2019, July). *Alcohol Related Crimes*. Retrieved from https://www.alcoholrehabguide.org/alcohol/crimes/
Gask, L., Evans, M., & Kessler, D. (2013). Personality disorder. *Bmj, 347*, f5276.
Gentile, J. P., Snyder, M., & Gillig, P. M. (2014). Stress and trauma: Psychotherapy and pharmacotherapy for depersonalization/derealization disorder. *Innovations in Clinical Neuroscience, 11*(7–8), 37.
Ghiasi, N., & Singh, J. (2019). Psychiatric illness and criminality. In *StatPearls [Internet]*. StatPearls Publishing.
Goldstein, P. J. (1985). The drugs/violence nexus: A tripartite conceptual framework. *Journal of Drug Issues, 15*(4), 493–506.
Goodman, A. (1990). Addiction: Definition and implications. *British Journal of Addiction, 85*(11), 1403–1408.
Graff-Radford, J., Whitwell, J. L., Geda, Y. E., & Josephs, K. A. (2012). Clinical and imaging features of Othello's syndrome. *European Journal of Neurology, 19*(1), 38–46.
Grant, J. E., Potenza, M. N., Weinstein, A., & Gorelick, D. A. (2010). Introduction to behavioral addictions. *The American Journal of Drug and Alcohol Abuse, 36*(5), 233–241.
Hammersley, R., Forsyth, A., Morrison, V., & Davies, J. B. (1989). The relationship between crime and opioid use★. *British Journal of Addiction, 84*(9), 1029–1043.
Hartman, R. L., & Huestis, M. A. (2013). Cannabis effects on driving skills. *Clinical Chemistry, 59*(3), 478–492.
Harvard health Publishing (2019, March). *Schizotypal Personality Disorder*. Retrieved from https://www.health.harvard.edu/a_to_z/schizotypal-personality-disorder-a-to-z
Havnes, I. A., Clausen, T., Brux, C., & Middelthon, A. L. (2014). The role of substance use and morality in violent crime-a qualitative study among imprisoned individuals in opioid maintenance treatment. *Harm Reduction Journal, 11*(1), 24.

Hodgins, S. (1998). Epidemiological investigations of the associations between major mental disorders and crime: Methodological limitations and validity of the conclusions. *Social Psychiatry and Psychiatric Epidemiology, 33*(1), S29–S37.
Holden, C. (2001). 'Behavioral'addictions: do they exist?.
India Today. (2018, October). *Delhi teen who stabbed parents 26 times was addicted to online game: Police*. Retrieved from https://www.indiatoday.in/india/story/delhi-teen-who-stabbed-parents-26-times-was-addicted-to-online-game-police-1366758-2018-10-12
Janofsky, J. S., Hanson, A., Candilis, P. J., Myers, W. C., Zonana, H., Irving, B., ... & Merideth, P. (2014). AAPL practice guideline for forensic psychiatric evaluation of defendants raising the insanity defense. *Journal of the American Academy of Psychiatry and the Law, 42*, S3–S76.
Johnson, S. C., & Elbogen, E. B. (2013). Personality disorders at the interface of psychiatry and the law: Legal use and clinical classification. *Dialogues in Clinical Neuroscience, 15*(2), 203.
Joyal, C. C., & Carpentier, J. (2017). The prevalence of paraphilic interests and behaviors in the general population: A provincial survey. *The Journal of Sex Research, 54*(2), 161–171.
Kandel, E. R., & Kandel, D. B. (2014). A molecular basis for nicotine as a gateway drug. *New England Journal of Medicine, 371*(10), 932–943.
Karishma, P. N. & Kumar, K. (2017). Is it Personality or the Alcohol that makes one an addict? In Chikkara, B.S. & Shanwal, V.K. (Eds), *Alcoholism: Causes, symptoms effects and treatment*. Manakin Press.
Kay, S. R., Fiszbein, A., & Opler, L. A. (1987). The positive and negative syndrome scale (PANSS) for schizophrenia. *Schizophrenia Bulletin, 13*(2), 261–276.
Kendell, R. E. (2002). The distinction between personality disorder and mental illness. *The British Journal of Psychiatry, 180*(2), 110–115.
King, D. L., & Delfabbro, P. H. (2014). Internet gaming disorder treatment: A review of definitions of diagnosis and treatment outcome. *Journal of Clinical Psychology, 70*(10), 942–955.
Kiran, & & Chaudhary. (2009). Understanding delusions. *Indian Journal of Psychiatry., 18*(1), 3–18.
Kircher, T., Bröhl, H., Meier, F., & Engelen, J. (2018). Formal thought disorders: From phenomenology to neurobiology. *The Lancet Psychiatry, 5*(6), 515–526.
Kirkpatrick, B., Fenton, W. S., Carpenter, W. T., & Marder, S. R. (2006). The NIMH-MATRICS consensus statement on negative symptoms. *Schizophrenia Bulletin, 32*(2), 214–219.
Kumar, A. (2017, December). *Experts examine if internet addiction led to Noida Teenage boy killing family members*. Retrieved from https://www.news18.com/news/india/experts-examine-if-internet-addiction-led-to-noida-teenage-boy-killing-family-members-1602619.html
Kuss, J. D., Griffiths, D. M., Karila, L., & Billieux, J. (2014). Internet addiction: A systematic review of epidemiological research for the last decade. *Current Pharmaceutical Design, 20*(25), 4026–4052.
Lawyer Monthly. (2019, October). *10 countries where gambling is completely illegal*. Retrieved from https://www.lawyer-monthly.com/2018/02/10-countries-where-gambling-is-completely-illegal/
Lowenstein, J., Purvis, C., & Rose, K. (2016). A systematic review on the relationship between antisocial, borderline and narcissistic personality disorder diagnostic traits and risk of violence to others in a clinical and forensic sample. *Borderline Personality Disorder and Emotion Dysregulation, 3*(1), 14.
Lincoln, T. M., & Hodgins, S. (2008). Is lack of insight associated with physically aggressive behavior among people with schizophrenia living in the community? *The Journal of Nervous and Mental Disease, 196*(1), 62–66.
M. H. S. A. U., & Office of the Surgeon General (US. (2016). *Facing addiction in America: The Surgeon General's report on alcohol, drugs, and health*.
Marzuk, P. M. (1996). *Violence, crime, and mental illness: How strong a link?*.
Mayo Clinic. (n.d). *Personality Disorders*. Retrived from https://www.mayoclinic.org/diseases-conditions/personality-disorders/symptoms-causes/syc-20354463

McManus, M. A., Hargreaves, P., & Lee Rainbow, L. J. A. (2013). Paraphilias: Definition, diagnosis and treatment. *F1000prime reports, 5*.
Medrano, K. (2019). *30 places where weed is legal*. Retrieved from https://www.thrillist.com/vice/30-places-where-weed-is-legal-cities-and-countries-with-decriminalized-marijuana
Meier, M. H., Caspi, A., Ambler, A., Harrington, H., Houts, R., Keefe, R. S., ... & Moffitt, T. E. (2012). Persistent cannabis users show neuropsychological decline from childhood to midlife. *Proceedings of the National Academy of Sciences, 109*(40), E2657–E2664.
Mental Health Daily. (2015). *Delusions of Persecution: Causes, Symptoms, Treatment*. Retrieved from https://mentalhealthdaily.com/2015/05/13/delusions-of-persecution-causes-symptoms-treatment/
Mitra, S., Mahintamani, T., Kavoor, A. R., & Nizamie, S. H. (2016). Negative symptoms in schizophrenia. *Industrial Psychiatry Journal, 25*(2), 135.
Morgan, V. A., Morgan, F., Valuri, G., Ferrante, A., Castle, D., & Jablensky, A. (2013). A whole-of-population study of the prevalence and patterns of criminal offending in people with schizophrenia and other mental illness. *Psychological Medicine, 43*(9), 1869–1880.
National Collaborating Centre for Mental Health (UK). (2010). *Antisocial Personality Disorder: Treatment, Management and Prevention*. Retrieved from https://www.ncbi.nlm.nih.gov/books/NBK55350/
National Institute of Health. (2011, November). *Why Nicotine is a Gateway Drug*. Retrieved from https://www.nih.gov/news-events/nih-research-matters/why-nicotine-gateway-drug
National Institute of Mental Health. (n.d). *Schizophrenia*. Retrieved from https://www.nimh.nih.gov/health/statistics/schizophrenia.shtml
National Mental Health Survey of India, 2015–2016. (2016). *Prevalence, Patterns and Outcomes, Supported by Ministry of Health and Family Welfare, Government of India, and Implemented by National institute of Mental Health and Neurosciences (NIMHANS) Bengaluru: In Collaboration with Partner Institutions*. Retrieved from http://indianmhs.nimhans.ac.in/Docs/Report2.pdf
Noll, R. (2009). *The encyclopedia of schizophrenia and other psychotic disorders*. Infobase Publishing.
Nykodym, N., Ariss, S., & Kurtz, K. (2008). Computer addiction and cyber crime. *Journal of Leadership, Accountability and Ethics*, 78.
Oser, C. B., Mooney, J. L., Staton-Tindall, M., & Leukefeld, C. G. (2009). The drugs—violence nexus among rural felony probationers. *Journal of Interpersonal Violence, 24*(8), 1285–1303.
Owen, P. R. (2012). Portrayals of schizophrenia by entertainment media: A content analysis of contemporary movies. *Psychiatric Services, 63*(7), 655–659.
Paris, J. (2019). Dissociative identity disorder: Validity and use in the criminal justice system. *Bjpsych Advances, 25*(5), 287–293.
Pastwa-Wojciechowska, B. (2011). The relationship of pathological gambling to criminality behavior in a sample of Polish male offenders. *Medical Science Monitor: International Medical Journal of Experimental and Clinical Research, 17*(11), CR669.
Patel, J., & Marwaha, R. (2019). Cannabis Use Disorder. In *StatPearls [Internet]*. StatPearls Publishing.
Pedersen, W., & Skardhamar, T. (2010). Cannabis and crime: Findings from a longitudinal study. *Addiction, 105*(1), 109–118.
Peele, S., & Brodsky, A. (1975). Love and addiction.
Pickard, H. (2015). Choice, deliberation, violence: Mental capacity and criminal responsibility in personality disorder. *International Journal of Law and Psychiatry, 40*, 15–24.
Porter, S., Birt, A. R., Yuille, J. C., & Hervé, H. F. (2001). Memory for murder: A psychological perspective on dissociative amnesia in legal contexts. *International Journal of Law and Psychiatry, 24*(1), 23–42.
Rasmussen, S. A., Mazurek, M. F., & Rosebush, P. I. (2016). Catatonia: Our current understanding of its diagnosis, treatment and pathophysiology. *World Journal of Psychiatry, 6*(4), 391.

Rohde, D. (October, 1999). Witness Tearfully Describe Fatal Subway shoving, *The New York Times.* Retrieved from https://www.nytimes.com/1999/10/09/nyregion/witness-tearfully-describes-fatal-subway-shoving.html

Rose, S. (January, 2017). From Split to Psycho: why cinema fails dissociative identity disorder. *The Guardian.* Retrieved from https://www.theguardian.com/film/2017/jan/12/cinema-dissociative-personality-disorder-split-james-mcavoy

Rosenthal, R. J., & Lorenz, V. C. (1992). The pathological gambler as criminal offender: Comments on evaluation and treatment. *Psychiatric Clinics, 15*(3), 647–660.

Sadock, B. J., Sadock, V. A., & Ruiz, P. (2017). *Comprehensive textbook of psychiatry* (10th ed.).

Sar, V. (2011). Epidemiology of dissociative disorders: An overview. *Epidemiology Research International, 2011.*

Şar, V. (2014). The many faces of dissociation: Opportunities for innovative research in psychiatry. *Clinical Psychopharmacology and Neuroscience, 12*(3), 171.

Sestoft, D. (2006). Crime and mental illness: It is time to take action. *World Psychiatry, 5*(2), 95.

Sheil, W. (2018). *Medical definition of psychotropic drug.* Retrived from https://www.medicinenet.com/script/main/art.asp?articlekey=30807

Sitarz, R., Rogers, M., Bentley, L., & Jackson, E. (2014). *Internet addiction to child pornography.*

Soyka, M. (2000). Substance misuse, psychiatric disorder and violent and disturbed behaviour. *The British Journal of Psychiatry, 176*(4), 345–350.

Sperry, L. (2016). *Handbook of diagnosis and treatment of DSM-5 personality disorders: Assessment, case conceptualization, and treatment.* Routledge.

Spiegel, D., Lewis-, R., Lanius, R., Vermetten, E., Simeon, D., & Friedman, M. (2013). Dissociative disorders in DSM-5. *Annual Review of Clinical Psychology, 9*, 299–326.

Stone, M. H. (2007). Violent crimes and their relationship to personality disorders. *Personality and Mental Health, 1*(2), 138–153.

Taborda, J. G., & Michalski-Jaeger, C. A. (2012). Sexual disorders and crime. *Current Opinion in Psychiatry, 25*(5), 370–374.

Tappan, P. W. (1960). *Crime, justice, and correction.* McGraw-Hill Companies.

The Economic Times. (2018, Septempber). *Section 377: Here is everything you need to know.* Retrieved from https://economictimes.indiatimes.com/news/politics-and-nation/sc-delivers-historic-verdict-heres-everything-you-need-to-know-about-section-377/articleshow/65698429.cms?from=mdr

TNM Staff. (2019, September). *Karnataka Shocker: 21-year-old allegedly beheads father for not letting play him PUBG.* Retrieved from https://www.thenewsminute.com/article/karnataka-shocker-21-yr-old-allegedly-beheads-father-not-letting-him-play-pubg-108613

Tyrer, P., & Simonsen, E. (2003). Personality disorder in psychiatric practice. *World Psychiatry, 2*(1), 41.

Varshney, M., Mahapatra, A., Krishnan, V., Gupta, R., & Deb, K. S. (2016). Violence and mental illness: What is the true story? *Journal of Epidemiology and Community Health, 70*(3), 223–225.

Wehring, H. J., & Carpenter, W. T. (2011). *Violence and schizophrenia.*

World Health Organization. (1992). *The ICD-10 classification of mental and behavioural disorders: Clinical descriptions and diagnostic guidelines.* World Health Organization.

World Health Organization. (2017). Alcohol and drug disorders: Global Health Estimates. Retrieved from https://www.who.int/substance_abuse/activities/fadab/msb_adab_2017_GHE_23June2017.pdf

Young, K. S. (1998). Internet addiction: The emergence of a new clinical disorder. *Cyberpsychology & Behavior, 1*(3), 237–244.

Chapter 6
Causes of Juvenile Delinquency and Treatment

Manjushree Palit and Bhavya Chhabra

Abstract This chapter will examine the psychological theories and constructs closely associated with juvenile delinquency, its causes, prevention, and treatment. First, the chapter explores two developmental theories, Urie Bronfenbrenner's ecological theory and John Bowlby and Mary Ainsworth's attachment theory. The former presents a contextual understanding while the latter takes an organismic approach to development. Besides this, we will review psychosocial constructs influencing juvenile delinquency and youth development, supported by empirical research such as aggression, emotional intelligence, and prosocial behaviour. The above developmental and psychosocial constructs will explore the causes of juvenile delinquency, prevention, and treatment.

Keywords Juvenile delinquency · Causes · Prevention · Ecological theory · Attachment theory

6.1 Juvenile Delinquency

The period of transition from childhood to adolescence is an important milestone. It provides the adolescent with opportunities and challenges and may place immense pressure on them and increase their susceptibility to risks. (Johns et al., 2016; Lloyd, 2005). Juvenile delinquency is a universal phenomenon and an equally pressing issue in both developed and developing nations of the world (Lloyd, 2005, p. 188). Most delinquency studies have focused on adolescence as a period of development when delinquency reaches its peak (Allen & Anderson, 2017; Fung, 2019; Nichols et al., 2006). Moreover, programmes and research in this area have perceived the youths as offenders. On the contrary, they are more often victims of continuous

M. Palit (✉)
Jindal School of Psychology and Counselling, O.P. Jindal Global University, Sonipat, Haryana, India
e-mail: mpalit@jgu.edu.in

B. Chhabra
Jindal Institute of Behavioural Sciences, O.P. Jindal Global University, Sonipat, Haryana, India

S. Sahni et al. (eds.), *Criminal Psychology and the Criminal Justice System in India and Beyond*, https://doi.org/10.1007/978-981-16-4570-9_6

criminal or delinquent acts. Therefore, such victimization since infancy has shaped their socialization, internationalization of their societal values, adherence to the law and social norms, career choices, and life trajectory (Lloyd, 2005, p. 190).

Overall, delinquency is an unwelcome action or behaviour that demonstrates lapses in moral values, strongly disapproved or rejected by society (Allen & Anderson, 2017; Fung, 2019; Krahé, 2013; Lloyd, 2005). In sum, juvenile delinquency closely resembles juvenile misconduct expressed in the forms of aggression and antisocial behaviour, which are legally unacceptable instead of societal norms (Allen & Anderson, 2017; Krahé, 2013). Such violent behaviours result from the complex interplay of multiple factors, which cascades over many aspects of the individual's life (Fung, 2019). Therefore, research has identified many causes of juvenile delinquency, such as socio-economic factors, cultural factors, urbanization, family, migration, media, exclusion, peer influence, delinquent identities, and offenders and victims (Agrawal, 2018; Lloyd, 2005). Juvenile delinquency varies across regions; for example, in Asia, urbanization is the leading cause of juvenile delinquency crime rates; whereas, in Africa, they are attributed to the economic, political, and social changes (Lloyd, 2005). Finally, a developmental perspective in delinquency research and prevention programmes helped understand the problem and identify support and resilience in the environment. In short, child development provides a well-rounded understanding of the phenomenon (Agrawal, 2018) and the role of multiple societal structures and their influence on the child's development (Bronfenbrenner, 1979; Lloyd, 2005).

6.2 Developmental Theories Related to Juvenile Delinquency

6.2.1 *Bioecological Model of Urie Bronfenbrenner*

Urie Bronfenbrenner is a pioneer of the ecological theory of human development. He emphasized a scientific approach to study the systems of interconnections within and between the multiple contexts that influences human development (Bronfenbrenner, 1977; Darling, 2007). Bronfenbrenner's bioecological model was initially formulated in the 1970s and continued to evolve conceptually until 2005 (Bronfenbrenner & Morris, 2007). It is one of the most widely used theoretical frameworks in human development studies (Darling, 2007; Soyer, 2019). Bronfenbrenner outlined three critical factors that influence human development: the process, person, context, and time. The person refers to the individual's genetic and biological characteristics that affect development, whereas the context refers to the immediate and remote environmental conditions surrounding the individual. Finally, time denotes the development throughout the various forms of the interactional process between the individual and the environment (Bronfenbrenner & Morris, 2007, p. 795). This model presents a contextual but complex understanding of human development.

This model's uniqueness is its focus on the mutuality of the interactions between the individual's biological dispositions and characteristics, and the multiple contexts or environments in which they lives (Bronfenbrenner, 1974; Bronfenbrenner & Morris, 2007). Individual and multiple contexts have a mutual and reciprocal relationship. The individual shapes the environment by evoking responses from the environment and, in turn, is shaped by the environment through the individual's responses to the wide-ranging environmental influences (Darling, 2007). Therefore, proximal and distal processes interwoven in multiple settings influence child development (Bronfenbrenner & Morris, 2007; Darling, 2007). Bronfenbrenner urged researchers to go beyond dyadic family interactions to include transcontextual parameters that influence child rearing (Bronfenbrenner, 1979, p. 845). Figure 6.1 is a representation of the nested bioecological model.

Accordingly, this theory proposed a nested structure with five layers of concentric circles (ecological systems). The person or individual in the centre of the concentric circle actively shapes the environment by evoking and responding to the environment. The five layers mentioned below are as follows:

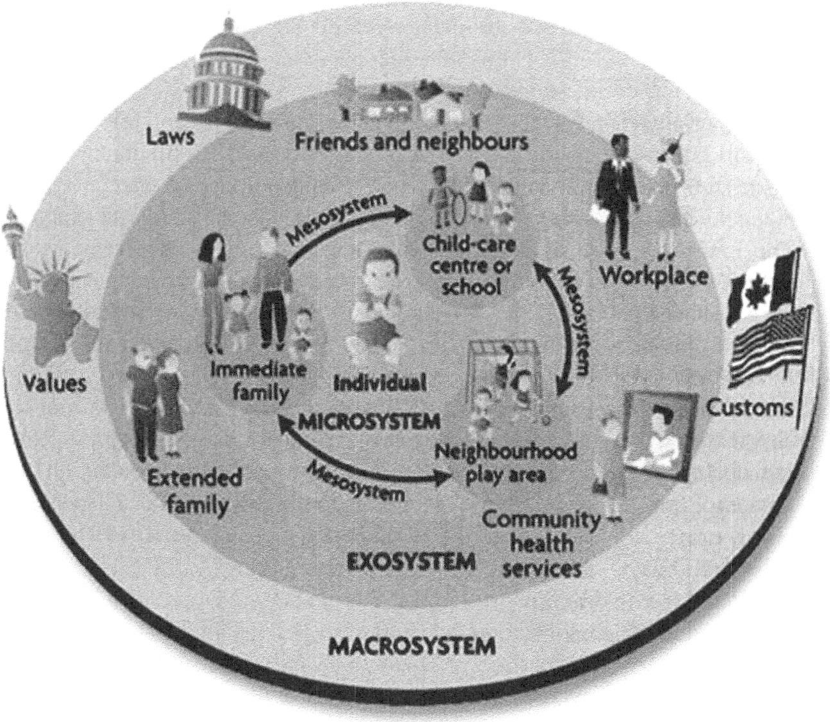

Fig. 6.1 Bronfenbrenner's ecological systems theory (in Berk & Roberts, 2009, p.28)

1. The first layer is the *microsystem*, and it is the innermost layer of the environment. It represents the child's interaction patterns with the immediate environment. A child's innate characteristics, temperament, physical, mental, emotional, and cognitive development interact daily with a range of immediate environments (Berk, 2013). These immediate environmental contexts are parents, siblings, school, teachers, close friends, and mentors (Bronfenbrenner, 1977). These are people that the child interacts with regularly, and they participate in the child's development for an extended time. Besides people, interaction with objects and symbols in the child's immediate settings influences their development (Bronfenbrenner & Morris, 2007). Bronfenbrenner (1977) stated, 'The factors of place, time, physical features, activity, participant, and role constitute the elements of a setting' (p. 514).
2. The second layer is the mesosystem, and it refers to the interactions between the child's two microsystems and their impact on the child's development. He suggested that alienation of children and youth and its destructive developmental sequelae reflect a breakdown of the interconnections among the various segments of the 'child's life- family, school, peer group, and neighbourhood' (Bronfenbrenner, 1979, p. 849).
3. The third layer is the exosystem; it refers to the interactions which do not directly involve the child but includes people in the child's immediate settings. These are formal or informal social structures, such as parents' workplace, neighbourhood, local, state, national agencies, mass media, and informal social networks. Exosystem is an extension of the mesosystem (Bronfenbrenner, 1977, p. 515). For example, changes in the school administration and rules enforced do not include the child directly but will indirectly impact the child's development.
4. The fourth layer is the macrosystem. This layer represents the general or larger societal structures such as the culture, technological growth, educational, economic, and political policies that influence the overall growth of the different settings. For example, the broad ideologies of the Indian culture might differ from an urban to a rural location, consequently impacting the child's development. The macrosystems' prevalent social structures explicitly and implicitly define the rules, acceptable and unacceptable behaviours, and activities, thereby influencing the child's diverse contexts and, in turn, affecting the child's development (Berk, 2013). Therefore, more extensive political, social, and economic changes have impacted the rise of juvenile delinquency in the African region (Lloyd, 2005).
5. The final layer is the chronosystem, which refers to time and adds a temporal dimension to the ecological model (Berk, 2013). This dimension explores the continuity and the changes in experiences of the individual, micro-, meso-, exo-, and macrosystems. Gradual or sudden changes in the interactional patterns in the interconnected systems influence the child's development, such as a death in the family and loss of employment (Darling, 2007).

This theory was revised thrice; initially, in the 1970s, it was known as the ecological model, later amended as the bioecological model, and finally, it evolved into the process-person-context-time (PPCT) model in 2005. In the beginning, Bronfenbrenner's bioecological model attempted to understand the systemic influence of the stressors and supports available to the family. These influencers impacted the child-rearing system and a child's development (Bronfenbrenner, 1977). Therefore, early intervention can play a more significant role in shaping a child. The latter model, the PPCT, stressed the process of continuous development of the individual (Bronfenbrenner, 2005; Bronfenbrenner & Morris, 2007; Rosa & Tudge, 2013) in an interrelated and nested system of layers that are bounded by context, culture, and history (Darling, 2007, Rosa & Tudge, 2013).

6.2.1.1 A Bioecological Perspective to Juvenile Delinquency

Bronfenbrenner's work has significantly contributed to the understanding of child development, family research, and child- and youth-care practitioners (Derksen, 2010). For example, fifty years ago, the head start programme was built based on this theoretical premise. Bronfenbrenner was a part of the team that established this programme in the USA (Soyer, 2019). The focus was on early childhood education and social justice for marginalized families from diverse backgrounds. They recognized that a child's development is shaped not only by their psychology, genes, and family, but also by the ecological systems, such as culture, society, politics, and economy (Hinitz, 2014). Similarly, this framework allowed researchers, such as Harris and colleagues, to focus on the impact of neighbourhood on juvenile re-offending. Here, families and neighbourhoods are two microsystems. Interactions between these microsystems comprise the mesosystem's structure (Berk, 2013; Bronfenbrenner, 1979). The proximal processes in these immediate settings (the mutual interaction between family and neighbourhood that form the mesosystem) influenced children's development in that neighbourhood. Harris and colleagues found that juvenile re-offending is dependent on the spatial characteristics of the neighbourhood. Therefore, low-income and segregated neighbourhoods with limited resources were highly susceptible to juvenile offending and re-offending.

Furthermore, juvenile re-offending in drug crimes was higher for juveniles from drug neighbourhoods than others (Harris et al., 2011). Therefore, using Bronfenbrenner's socio-ecological framework, the researchers could connect juvenile reoffending, in general, to the neighbourhood's spatial characteristics, and how neighbourhood characteristics influenced the reoffending rate in drug-related than other crimes. Similarly, they also found that paternal criminality in families increased the risk of juvenile delinquency among adolescents in microsystem interactions. Coupled with paternal criminality, vulnerable neighbourhoods with a history of discrimination, poverty, and crime further increased these children's risk (Harris et al., 2011). In an ecological study of prolific offending, Ellis, a participant and a juvenile offender in custody, mentioned 'all my boys are in there … so it makes it easier' (p. 12) represents the constellation of negativity surrounding these children at homes, peers, and neighbourhood (Johns et al., 2016). This cycle of negativity in the microsystem, mesosystem, and exosystem encouraged juvenile delinquent gangs' influence and power in the neighbourhood. These delinquent gangs were feared, rejected, and distrusted by their community as it initiated and recruited youth members. Therefore, multisystemic proximal interactional processes occurred between microsystems, mesosystem, exosystem, macrosystem, and chronosystem, and they continuously shaped the adolescent over a lifetime (Bronfenbrenner & Morris, 2007; Harris et al., 2011; Johns et al., 2016). Besides, unstable or dysfunctional surrounding environments (such as a neighbourhood) influenced the proximal processes and led to dysfunctional outcomes for youth in that community.

On the other hand, a stable or advantaged environment influences positive outcomes and competence among the youth (Bronfenbrenner & Morris, 2007, p. 803). Bronfenbrenner's model can be used to identify the problems in the multiple systems surrounding the child and identify the resources that can encourage resilience in the environment and reduce delinquency (Ungar et al., 2012; Johns et al., 2016). Hence, the bioecological model not only identifies problems but also provides a strength-based theoretical framework. It has been aptly used by practitioners and researchers to enhance their understanding of human development (Bronfenbrenner & Morris, 2007; Derksen, 2010; Johns et al., 2016) and support social work, social justice, and child welfare practices (The Social Justice, no date). This framework is flexible, and other suitable models and programmes can be integrated with the bioecological model to provide timely and impactful services and inspire social and legal policy changes (The Social Justice, no date). The advantage of this perspective is that it provides a broader lens to view child development. Using this framework, one can identify both deficits and strengths in the systems (Bronfenbrenner & Morris, 2007; Johns et al., 2016). Discover positive ways of working with adolescents and young adults in strengthening their bond with the families and the community, shifting the focus from the negative or problem-centred approach to the positive or strength-based approach. Develop programmes to strengthen the interaction in the immediate or proximal processes or find ways to build competence in the immediate settings. Consequently, these programmes increase a sense of belongingness among youths, encourage positive identity development, and prevent delinquency (Bronfenbrenner & Morris, 2007; Johns et al., 2016).

In conclusion, a relationship-oriented, systemic approach provides an effective guide to working with youth and juvenile delinquents (Johns et al., 2016). Bronfenbrenner's model emphasizes a reciprocal and nested interaction system between the individual and the environment which provides a multifaceted understanding of development (Berk, 2013). For practitioners worldwide, this theory has been noteworthy because of its emphasis on the reciprocal nature of minute interactions and how child- and youth-care practitioners can foster interactions and attachment with the children and shape their development (Derksen, 2010; Johns et al., 2016). Practitioners, policy-makers, and social workers can use this framework to implement changes both in the immediate and larger settings, such as society, economy, social and educational institutions, and culture. Juvenile delinquency prevention programmes focusing on immediate settings such as family, school, and neighbourhood are limited in scope when they ignore the broader contexts such as culture, socio-economic, and political stability that influence juvenile crime and delinquency

(Lloyd, 2005). In sum, the bioecological model encompasses a multisystemic view that can truly capture the full gamut of causes and treatment of juvenile delinquency (Bronfenbrenner & Morris, 2007; Derksen, 2010; Harris et al., 2011; Johns et al., 2016).

6.2.2 *Attachment Theory by John Bowlby and Mary Ainsworth*

Another developmental framework that has been explored by juvenile delinquency researchers is attachment theory. This theory, developed by John Bowlby, presents an ethological or organismic perspective to development. An infant and the caregiver are biologically predisposed to form an emotional tie to ensure the newborn's survival (Bowlby, 1969; Berk, 2013; Papalia et al., 2004). This emotional and reciprocal relationship between the infant and caregiver helps build trust in this relationship. It influences the infant's sense of emotional security and the capacity to build trust in future relationships (Berk, 2013). These influence the emotional and behavioural adaptability of the infant. 'Both the infant and the caregiver contribute to the quality of the relationship' (Papalia et al., 2004, p. 192). The onset of specific emotional patterns during infancy shapes the individual's personality (Berk, 2013; Papalia et al., 2004). They also serve various purposes. Firstly, they help the individual share what is going on inside them, i.e. share their inner world of emotions with others and help the individual fulfil their needs. This form of signalling also generates a reciprocal and sensitive response from the caregiver. Secondly, emotions provide guidance and help navigate the experiences such as fear, anger, joy, curiosity, and sadness with the outside world (Papalia et al., 2004, p. 180). Therefore, the nature of an individual's attachment to the caregiver will determine the sense of security and trust experienced by them in a trusting relationship (Berk, 2013). Attachment influences the emotional and instinctual processes as vehicles of transmission in close intimate relationships in the family (Benson, 2005, p. 382). In short, this theory emphasizes that attachment is a lifelong construct (McElhaney et al., 2006, p. 44).

The cornerstones of this theory are as follows: (a) the four phases of attachment, (b) the four essential components of attachment, (c) the four styles of attachment, and (d) the internal working model of attachment. A 'child's attachment to the caregiver develops in the initial years in four phases such as the (i) pre-attachment phase (birth to 6 weeks), (ii) attachment in the making phase (6 weeks to 6 to 8 months), (iii) 'clear-cut' attachment (6 to 8 months to 2 years), and (iv) formation of reciprocal relationship or the phase of the goal-corrected partnership (18 months to 2 years and on) (Ainsworth et al., 1978; Berk, 2013). These phases allow the child to use the parent as a secure base and influence the child's expectation of the attachment figures' availability to meet his/her needs, which then becomes the template for future interaction with others. The attachment also has four basic components: safe haven, secure base, proximity maintenance, and separation distress (Berk, 2013;

Bowlby, 1969; Papalia et al., 2004). These components are essential in attachment formation; infants use their caregiver as a safe haven when they are fearful, they use their caregiver as a secure base and explore the world around them, they want to be in proximity with their caregiver, and when separated from their caregiver, infants experience separation distress (Bowlby, 1969). Ainsworth and colleagues (1978) proposed three attachment styles: secure, ambivalent, and avoidant attachment. Later, researchers identified a fourth disorganized attachment found among children with trauma. These four styles were developed based on the 'Strange Situation Test' conducted in a laboratory setting with toys. The styles were developed based on the child's emotional reaction to the mother leaving the room and then reuniting with the child after a short lapse of time (Ainsworth et al., 1978). The first attachment style is the only secure and healthy attachment, whereas others are insecure attachments. Several factors influence attachment styles' formation, and they are early availability of consistent caregiver, quality of caregiving, the baby's characteristics, and the family context, including parent's internal working models (Berk, 2013, Papalia et al., 2004).

The consistent interaction pattern is organized instinctually and internalized by the infant, which shapes the infant's future interactional processes. Bowlby termed this process as the *internal working model* (Bowlby, 1969). The internal working model (IWM) serves as a template for close relationships and determines the individual's emotional, cognitive, behavioural, and relational expectations and engagement based on their past experiences (Bowlby, 1969; Bretherton & Munholland, 2018). According to Bowlby, attachment leads to 'affectional bonds' (1969, p. 224); it also helps the infant create a mental representation of the environment and the relational bonds with the attachment figures. In other words, the IWM is a dynamic representation of the child's experiences and expectations about the attachment figures' availability to meet their needs. IWM records information on the individual's response to his/her attachment figure, such as feeling confident or doubtful about their attachment figure. The IWM developed in the first year of life tends to persist for the long term. Based on the IWM in the child-caregiver dyad, each will try to evoke responses from the other based on their expectations. With exposure to new life experiences and skillsets, the IWM is dynamic and evolving in its constellation (Bretherton & Munholland, 2018). A securely attached child to the caregivers is more likely to develop a sense of security, confidence and fairly adapt to the developmental and environmental challenges during adolescence (Benson, 2005, p. 383). Overall, attachment is closely associated with emotional regulation and healthy adjustment.

6.2.2.1 An Attachment Perspective to Juvenile Delinquency

The prominent attachment figures in the life of a child are family and peer group. One of the well-known causes of juvenile delinquency is a poor relationship with attachment figures and lack of adequate parental supervision (Lloyd, 2005). Attachment to parents plays a crucial role in predicting juvenile delinquency among adolescents (Kim, 2017; McElhaney et al., 2006). The cause of dysfunctional family settings is manifold. They are child abuse, neglect, absent parents either physically or mentally or both, high conflict families, marital conflict, domestic violence in the parental relationship, and lack of monitoring and supervision by parents (Lloyd, 2005). Juan and colleagues studied disadvantaged families and found that exposure to violence in the parental relationship negatively influenced the parent–child attachment. A child's exposure to violence in the parental relationship in the first three years of life increases the risk for childhood aggression by the time the child reaches age five and nine years (Juan et al., 2020). Parent–child attachment had a mediating effect on the influence of violence in the parental relationship and aggression among nine year olds (Juan et al., 2020). Therefore, exposure to violence in the parental relationship increases the risk of violence in children at a young age, as early as the first three years, and negatively influences the child and the parents' secure bond. Prevention programmes can benefit from this knowledge. Early detection and prevention of partner violence in the parental relationship in the first three years of the child's life can minimize the child's exposure to violence and strengthen the parent–child relationship. The parent–child relationship has a buffering effect against juvenile delinquency (John et al., 2016). There is a strong link between attachment and delinquency in both boys and girls, and strengthening attachment bond with same-sex parents can increase resilience in the children and families (Hoeve et al. 2012).

The parent–child relationship also provides a template for social relationships (Bowlby, 1969; McElhaney et al., 2006). The strength of the parent–child relationship influences peer attachment, which influences children's social and emotional abilities among children between 7 and 18 years (Suatin & Wijayanti, 2020). Children form attachment representations, which influences their experiences of attachment in peer relationships. McElhaney and colleagues (2006) found that the quality of attachment, especially attachment styles, influenced friendships in moderately risky adolescents and predicted engagement in delinquent behaviour. Therefore, the styles of attachment influenced delinquency among adolescents with a specific approach to attachment. Adolescents with preoccupied or ambivalent attachment style engaged in attention-seeking behaviours and had distant peer relationships. In meeting their intense need for relationships, these adolescents were at high risk for negative friendships and delinquency because they would go to any extent to seek attention from their parents and peers. The attention-seeking behaviour increases their risk and negative friendships (McElhaney et al., 2006). Although the parental attachment is a supportive and positive factor in the prevention of juvenile delinquency, exposure to parental violence in the early years of life has a damaging impact on the child and encourages aggressive behaviour among children (Juan et al., 2020). Therefore, partner violence in the parental relationship affects both young children and adolescents (p. 17). On the other hand, increasing supportive relationships with parents and peers reduced adolescents' risk with preoccupied or ambivalent attachment and non-dismissive attachment (McElhaney et al., 2006). Overall, children's social and emotional competence is shaped by their secure attachment with parents and peers, serving as a protective factor from juvenile delinquency (Suatin & Wijayanti, 2020).

A significant risk factor is that disadvantaged families are segregated and have low resources for income and support. This condition increases their children's susceptibility to juvenile delinquency, such as immigrant families or socially excluded families, with limited economic and social support (Johns et al., 2016; Juan et al., 2020; Lloyd, 2005). Moreover, the environment also influences the parent–child relationships (Bronfenbrenner & Morris, 2007). For example, migration and urbanization weaken parental monitoring and social support of the families—similarly, countries in conflict influence the family dynamics in terms of time and resource availability. Therefore, parents cannot meet the children's emotional, cognitive, behavioural, and relational needs. Children may not resist the temptation of delinquent gangs and acts in the neighbourhood in such scenarios (Lloyd, 2005).

On the other hand, adolescents with strong and secure relationships with parents fight the attraction towards delinquent acts or groups due to the IWM of parental expectations and emotional and cognitive responses, which acts as a barrier (Kim, 2017). In a longitudinal study of juvenile offenders of serious crimes, Kim (2017) found that when emotional regulation improved, there was a decline in aggressive behaviour among adolescent offenders. Both consistent caregiving by parents and adequate emotional regulation moderated aggression and delinquent behaviour in adolescents. Therefore, Kim (2017) suggested that reforms and programmes should focus on families. Programmes that focused on parental relationships and parent–child relationships in the early years can prevent the risk of childhood aggression and juvenile delinquency (Juan et al., 2020). Programmes should help families repair their emotional and affectional relationship with their children and enable children to develop adequate emotional regulation that shapes their emotions, cognitions, behaviour, and relationships in the future (Kim, 2017). Early repair work is helpful, as researchers found that the link between attachment and delinquency weakens with age. Moreover, the connection between attachment and delinquency is stronger for same-sex parent–child relationships than cross-pairs; that is, programmes should focus on strengthening boys' attachment to their fathers and girls with their mothers (Hoeve et al., 2012).

6.3 Psychological Constructs Related to Juvenile Delinquency

6.3.1 Aggression

Youth gangs are becoming an increasing cause of concern globally because of the alarming rate of violent offences linked with them. Sometimes aggressive children become juvenile offenders and form adolescent gangs (White & Mason, 2006; Curry et al. 2002). Overt behaviour directed at someone with the deliberate intent to cause harm or injury is defined as aggression, and when a juvenile is the perpetrator of this misconduct, the behaviour is termed as delinquent (Allen & Anderson, 2017). When aggression is in the form of an emotional experience among juveniles, it includes feelings of revenge and rage, hostile attitudes, aggressive thoughts, and the desire to cause intentional harm. This aggressive affect is a precursor to the potential aggressive behaviour (Allen & Anderson, 2017; Geen, 2001; Krahé, 2013). Aggression takes various forms or classifications, and there are different types and subtypes of aggression (Krahé, 2013; Parrott & Giancola, 2007). The most common classification is verbal, physical, social, or postural (Allen & Anderson, 2017). The first category of aggression is verbal, which involves using words intended to harm another person disrespectfully. For example, shouting, swearing, screaming, or name calling. The second category of aggression, physical aggression, refers to physically causing harm to the recipient by hitting, slapping, punching, and stabbing. This aggression involves an experience of physiological hyperactivity (Nagin & Tremblay, 1999; Puhalla & McCloskey, 2020). Physical and verbal aggression is prevalent among juveniles (Siegel & Welsh, 2014; Tedeschi & Felson, 1994). The third category of aggression, relational or social aggression, involves hurting someone by harming their social connections or causing them to feel unaccepted or barred (e.g. spreading gossip or rumours, or advising others not to spend time with someone, and resulting in social exclusion) (Krahé, 2013; Martinelli et al., 2018). When a person is inclined to view the other person's behaviour as having hostile intent, it is termed as hostile attribution bias even when it is not the case. Criminal behaviour is positively associated with relational hostile attribution bias (Martinelli et al., 2018). The fourth category of aggression is postural aggression involves aggressively making uncomfortable gestures or invading another person's personal space without their consent (Allen & Anderson, 2017; Krahé, 2013).

There are also other forms of classifications of aggression, which includes the following: (a) direct versus indirect aggression, (b) active versus passive aggression, (c) hostile versus instrumental aggression, and (d) personological versus situational aggression. (a) When physical harm is caused directly in the victim's presence, it is direct aggression, whereas indirect aggression harm is caused in the victim's absence. For instance, punching somebody in the face is direct aggression, and recruiting a hired gunman to assassinate someone would be indirect physical aggression (DeWall et al., 2012). (b) Active aggression is deliberately employing harmful behaviours or overt acts (verbal or physical assault), for instance, kicking, threatening, or insulting someone. In contrast, passive aggression is like indirect aggression. When a person is furious or disturbed, he/she is unable to express their discontent and hold back their negative emotions to avoid conflict (Bushman & Huesmann, 2010). (c) Overt aggression refers to exceptionally noticeable conduct, like ridiculing somebody or pounding them before their companions. In contrast, covert aggression is moderately low in perceivability, such as leaving mean notes for an individual or spreading rumours about individuals despite their good faith (Allen & Anderson, 2017). (d) Hostile aggression refers to emotionally 'hot-blooded', 'impulsive', 'reactive', 'retaliatory' and 'affective' aggression (Allen & Anderson, 2017, p. 5; Muñoz et al., 2008, p. 15). The person displaying this form of aggression has heightened physiological reactivity with increased autonomic responses (Puhalla & McCloskey, 2020). Hostile aggression is accompanied by cognitive failure to comprehend social information like hitting somebody who has offended the person (Muñoz et al., 2008; Dodge et al., 1997; Berkowitz, 1978; Bushman & Anderson, 2001).

Conversely, instrumental aggression (otherwise called 'proactive' aggression) is aroused by a desire to accomplish an instrumental reward or a goal (e.g. cash or societal position) and commonly is portrayed as 'cold' conduct that is controlled, calculated, and determined. A good example of instrumental aggression is shooting the police to ensure secure escape from a bank burglary or carjacking (Bushman & Anderson, 2001; Poulin & Boivin, 2000). Juvenile delinquency, substance abuse, and criminality show stronger predictive associations with proactive aggression (Martinelli et al., 2018; Muñoz et al., 2008). (e) Lastly, personological versus situational aggressions, while experiencing personological aggression, the person is mainly influenced by person factors that increase aggressive behaviour. For instance, person factors include narcissism sex, where boys are more inclined to engage in violent or aggressive behaviours. Another factor is self-control, where adolescents who fail to control their impulses are more vulnerable to commit crimes. Lastly, person factors include perspectives and attitudes towards aggression, values, personal goals, and beliefs such as punching back is the logical reaction to being punched (Nagin & Tremblay, 1999). Situational factors act as antecedents that increase the likelihood of aggressive behaviours. Possession of arms or weapons, the experience of insult or offence that can result in aggressive retaliation, being provoked by others or bystanders, the experience of burn out (e.g. unable to achieve a goal), and being under the influence of drugs or alcohol, could be considered as situational factors that cause and reinforce aggressive responses (Caprara et al., 1992; DeWall et al., 2012).

6.3.1.1 Aggression and Juvenile Delinquency

Anger, which is misled by a flawed understanding of power and control, leads to a desire for retribution. Such anger obliterates healthy coping mechanisms and is highly likely to cause criminal behaviours (Agnew, 2001, p. 335). Aggressive children sometimes turn into juvenile offenders, who then form juvenile adolescent gangs. Youth delinquent gangs are becoming an increasing cause of concern globally because of the alarming rate of violent offences linked with them (White & Mason, 2006; Curry et al., 2002). Maladaptive developmental trajectories, such as disorderly conduct and aggressive patterns among juveniles, should be explored as they lead to delinquency (Nagin & Tremblay, 1999). Child abuse leads to a maladaptive developmental trajectory when a parent or caregiver's intimidating, violent, and aggressive behaviour intentionally hurts the child (Barrett et al., 2015). There are many forms of child abuse with their unique characteristics. Physical abuse refers to causing bodily injury to the child, for example, inflicting burn or pain. Emotional abuse occurs when parents inflict mental pain or wounds on the child that adversely affects his/her self-esteem and social communication, for example, when a parent or caregiver says derogatory and humiliating words to the child in a threatening or intimidating tone. In both cases, there is a deed or action conducted towards the child.

Neglect is also a form of child abuse, where the absence of care towards the child causes the damage (National Child Protect Agency, 2012).

Childhood abuse leads to deviant behaviours and emotional regulation problems, irrational thinking, alcohol, and drug abuse, violent approach with family, suicidal thoughts, and impaired social behaviourism leading to juvenile criminal offences (Osofsky, 1999; Dube et al., 2001). Existing literature suggests that a significant percentage of juvenile delinquents have experienced one or the other kind of child abuse (Wiebush et al., 2001). Abused children are more likely to engage in criminal acts and teenage delinquency than those who were not exposed to child abuse (Currie & Tekin, 2006; Hwang, 2009). The harmful effects of child abuse were reported by Hamilton and colleagues (2002). They found that criminal offenders who had inflicted violence and sexual harassment on people had been chronically abused in their childhood. Childhood abuse by caregivers causes trauma, resulting in deficits in internal states, emotional, behavioural, and psychological maldevelopment (Hamilton et al., 2002). The relationship between child abuse, juvenile delinquency, and aggression is not always a direct causal relationship. In fact, in many cases, there is a mediator in between which causes indirect effects. Child abuse has a secondary effect on the psychosocial development of a child. Emotional regulations and behaviour management are core aspects of psychosocial development. A consequence of maladjusted psychosocial development would be aggression. Consequently, childhood abuse leads to violent, aggressive behaviours, and short-temperament issues (You & Lim, 2015).

Furthermore, empirical evidence also suggests that aggression is a peripheral problem behaviour. Aggression is influenced by a history of child abuse, which may start from childhood and continues through adulthood (Chung & Lee, 2012; Hodgdon, 2009). Chung (2008) observed 904 adolescents from lower socio-economic classes in Korea and found that abused children were aggressive, engaged in delinquent behaviours, and isolated themselves from their peers. Another study from the Ministry of Health and Welfare (2012) advocated the high-risk children (for child abuse) had an increased tendency to be aggressive than the low-risk ones. Thus, minors exposed to psychologically aggressive parenting, domestic violence, and maltreatment have higher delinquency rates. They exhibit severe aggressive behaviour, were arrested for criminal behaviours, and reported serious delinquent acts. These acts serve as a precursor that resulted in antisocial, aggressive behaviour and paved the way for deviant acts. Abused children are nine times more likely to engage in severe violent activities and delinquent behaviours than non-abused adolescents. They are also less likely to engage in prosocial tendencies and other helping behaviours (Gold et al., 2011; Barrett et al., 2015).

Finally, there are several contributing factors to aggression, such as social, psychological, cognitive, and gender, which influence juvenile delinquents' aggression. Furthermore, male minors are more involved in criminal activities as compared to female minors. However, female minors experience amplified emotional problems compared to males (Fontaine et al., 2019). Additionally, research evidence suggests that male juveniles exhibit higher direct, hostile, and physical aggression, and their violent delinquent behaviours are usually at their peak (Salmivalli & Kaukiainen,

2004). On the contrary, female juveniles exhibit more significant indirect and social aggression levels with exacerbated delinquent behaviours. With this, female aggression and their disorderly conduct are also on the rise, and the differences between the two are almost diminishing now (Barrett et al., 2015; Salmivalli & Kaukiainen, 2004). Surprisingly, the rates of juvenile vandalism, gang membership, and recidivism have surged for female convicts compared to the male convicts. There has been a seven per cent increase in the felonies among female juveniles and a thirty-two per cent decrease in the male juvenile felonies (Nichols et al., 2006; Barrett et al., 2015).

6.3.2 Prosocial Behaviour

People are intrinsically and profoundly prosocial (Miller, 2018; Aknin et al., 2018). Prosocial behaviour is an act that benefits the other and not the doer, although it can be self-rewarding. Prosocial behaviour incorporates a myriad of helping acts, such as empathic listening, sharing personal resources, cooperating, volunteering, comforting, and helping (Dunfield, 2014; Millon et al., 2003; Snippe et al., 2018; Krettenauer et al., 2019; Kärtner, 2018). Children demonstrate helping and comforting behaviours when they see someone in distress in various sophisticated ways since infancy. Parental figures offer a positive role model when they are encouraging and provide interpersonal support to their children. They encourage replication and adaptation of such prosocial behaviour (Gallito & Steensen, 2019; Choudhary & Xavier, 2015). Additionally, positive parental responsiveness aids in cultivating rational decision-making processes and empathic concern among children. Such attributes positively influence the qualities that are related to prosocial competence and moral development (Gallito & Steensen, 2019; Kärtner, 2018). Emotions support toddlers' social development and socialization patterns. Therefore, emotions are considered the critical foundation of prosocial development among children (Hammon & Drummond, 2019; Gallito & Steensen, 2019).

A vital determinant of prosocial behaviour is empathy (Baron, 2008; Millon et al., 2003). Empathy is characterized by experiencing the emotional state of the victim, sentimental reactions, involving compassion, sympathy, and understanding their perspective (Baron, 2008; Van der Graaff et al. 2018; Lockwood et al. 2014). Positive emotions are empathic joy, elevation, happiness, gratitude expression, positive civic attitude, awe and love, and inspiring prosocial behaviour (Aknin et al., 2018; Baron, 2008; Krettenauer et al., 2019; Millon et al., 2003). This behaviour strengthens an individual's self-concept, confidence level, academic and social success, profoundly influencing a positive view of self and encouraging high-quality relationships (Van der Graaff et al., 2017; Aknin et al., 2018). On the contrary, people who have experienced social exclusion are less likely to be prosocial because they have a reduced propensity to feel empathy (Twenge et al., 2007). Juvenile delinquents also experience low empathic capacity and unemotional callous traits (Pechorro et al., 2015). Such people with callous-unemotional traits possess low cortisol levels, which is associated with empathy deficits (Miller, 2018; Pechorro et al., 2015), whereas high cortisol levels and cortisol reactivity are associated with greater social functioning. The latter prepares young adults and children to manage future challenges judiciously; however, hyperarousal may inhibit prosocial outcomes (Miller, 2018).

6.3.2.1 Prosocial Behaviour and Juvenile Delinquency

A child with prosocial beliefs is less likely to break the laws (Tarry & Emler, 2007). Engaging with non-prosocial peers increases the probability of drug abuse and property offending in juveniles and vice versa (Walters, 2019; Brook et al., 2011). It can also intensify the possibility of alcohol consumption and involvement in adolescent gangs (Jin et al., 2019). Lack of supportive and positive friendships puts the children at risk of developing psychological disorders, suggesting that one way to prevent juvenile delinquency and better coping skills is perhaps by having a friendship with prosocial peers (Wang et al., 2018; O'donnell & Barber, 2018). This stance is backed by *social control theory,* which states that positive social ties curb deviant behaviours (Bandura & Walters, 1959). Devotion to work, school, and family reduces the odds of juvenile crimes because these institutions encourage prosocial values and norms. Juvenile offenders are mainly low on emotional intelligence, self-efficacy, and possess poor moral judgement. For instance, young offenders have elevated levels of callous-unemotional traits, experience negative emotions with great intensity, and thus, find it extremely difficult to identify and acknowledge such emotions (Milojevic et al., 2016; Pechorro et al., 2015; Fontaine et al., 2019). These callous-unemotional traits mainly characterize early antisocial activity, aggression, negative feelings, superficial expressions of emotions associated with increased future delinquency rates (Pechorro et al., 2015; Dandreaux & Frick, 2009; Fontaine et al., 2019).

The antisocial youth experiences constant negative emotions, and there is a simultaneous escalation in violent delinquent behaviours. Delinquency consequently leads to socially devalued characteristics and negative social outcomes. Delinquency and negative emotions result in negative and unfavourable social outcomes, spiralling into lower social support (Fontaine et al., 2019). Convicted juveniles report self-induced delinquency, crime severity, aggression, psychopathic traits, lower empathic understanding levels, reduced prosocial tendencies, and social desirability. Thus, the greater the frequency of procriminal influence and criminal behaviour, the lower the prosocial altruistic impulses (Pechorro et al., 2015). On the other hand, a large body of evidence suggests that prosociality produces positive emotions, and interchangeably, positive affect spurs prosociality (Aknin, 2018; Dunfield, 2014; Van der Graaff et al., 2018). When people affiliate together in positive interpersonal synchrony, prosociality manifests behaviourally (Cirelli, 2018). Other researchers also found supportive evidence that adults who willingly volunteer to better society experience prosperity, compassion, happiness, and well-being (Aknin et al., 2018; Cirelli, 2018; Kärtner, 2018). Not only adults, but research evidence also supports that even children enjoy volunteering, which consequently fosters positive emotional consequences, social cognition, and affiliative behaviours (Aknin et al., 2018; Blake,

2018; Eisenberg & Mussen, 1989). For instance, twelve to fourteen-month-old infants are more willing to help a synchronous than an asynchronous social partner, which ultimately encourages prosocial tendencies (Cirelli, 2018; Kärtner, 2018).

How is prosocial behaviour helpful in everyday life? Prosocial behaviour instrumentally reinforces and sustains positive affect among people and increases social cohesion levels (Snippe et al., 2018; Cirelli, 2018). Positive states elicit advantageous behaviour early in life (Aknin et al., 2018; Hammond & Drummond, 2019). In short, positive childhood experiences, acts of gratitude, and modelling encourage prosocial tendencies, subsequently giving rise to another prosocial act. These acts reinforce the simultaneous result of emotional rewards experienced, succeeding the altruistic move (Aknin et al., 2018; Cirelli, 2018). A dynamic reciprocal consortium exists between positive affect and prosocial behaviour in everyday life. For example, a study that deciphered children's facial expressions found that children experienced happiness when sharing little treats with others. Though these findings are significant, they cannot be generalized (Baron, 2008; Lockwood et al., 2014). Numerous research findings have reported that prosociality is directly related to age in infancy, early childhood, and adolescence. This finding significantly aligns with the research on prosociality and that it is inherently rewarding (Aknin et al., 2018; Baron, 2008). Emotional states guide the prosocial tendencies, and the environmental conditions indeed guide these emotional states. For instance, a room that radiates positive vibes can build positive feelings, eventually elevates an individual's mood (Baron, 2008; Barasch et al., 2014). Such findings postulate that initiating a positive state of mind increases altruistic impulses, which is the very famous 'feel-good, do-good' effect. Reciprocally, the succinct formulation of a positive feedback loop elaborates that positive emotions evoke prosocial behaviour, and this generous act further restores the positive mood states (Snippe, 2018). Therefore, positively valenced situations, events, and objects evoke positively valenced emotions; this fosters altruism while learning and growing together (Baron, 2008; Hammon & Drummond, 2019).

6.3.3 Emotional Intelligence

Emotional intelligence (EI) has been defined in several ways. This concept was popularized by Daniel Goleman, who defined emotional intelligence as an individual's ability to recognize one's feelings and manage them effectively. It also includes motivating oneself to achieve goals by overcoming challenges and setbacks, recognizing emotions in other people, and managing them effectively (Goleman, 1995). Similarly, Mayer and Salvoy (1997) referred to emotional intelligence as a group of specific abilities that influenced an individual's ability to perceive and understand emotions and utilize emotions to arrange thoughts productively. In summary, an individual can recognize variations in self and others' emotions and proactively regulate and manage them. This seminal work of researchers, Salvoy and Mayer (1990) not only expanded the conceptualization of EI, but they highly recommended the scientific community to study the benefits of emotional intelligence (Mayer et al., 2008).

How is this relevant for children and their surrounding environment? In particular, high emotionally intelligent children are raised by socially and emotionally sensitive and non-judgemental parents. Such parents provide a safe environment for the child to freely discuss and explore their feelings and emotions and learn to cope with them effectively. In such a nurturing milieu, the child develops emotional expertise in their areas of competence: social competence, leadership, creativity, and moral and spiritual responsiveness (Mayer & Salovey, 1995). These EI researchers further delineated that individuals with high emotional intelligence were socially competent and enjoyed a better interpersonal relationship. As a result, such individuals established a healthy and supportive structural network of family, friends, and colleagues (Salvoy & Mayer, 1990).

6.3.3.1 Emotional Intelligence and Juvenile Delinquency

Comparatively, high EI is associated with positive outcomes, whereas low EI is associated with negative outcomes. Mostly, deficiency of EI is associated with a lack of adequate emotion and social functioning, which increases the susceptibility to at-risk behaviours (Goleman, 1995; Mayer & Salvoy, 1995). Mayer and colleagues (2008) reviewed the EI outcome trends in several studies and summarized EI's positive and negative outcomes for children and adults (Mayer et al., 2008, p. 525). EI was positively associated with good social relationships for children, whereas negatively associated with social deviance. In adults, high EI was associated with social competence and low EI with destructive interpersonal coping mechanisms. Empathy, social skills, and academic achievement were higher among children with high EI than children with low EI. Children and adults with high EI enjoyed better family and intimate relationships. Similarly, high EI leads to good workplace relationships during adulthood. Finally, higher EI resulted in better psychological well-being, self-esteem and life satisfaction, and low depression.

Conversely, children low on EI are at a greater risk for social deviance, poor interpersonal relationships, low academic achievement, destructive coping strategies, and poor psychological well-being (Mayer et al., 2008, p. 525). EI is related to the ability to differentiate and regulate emotions, thereby serving as a protective factor for delinquent adolescents (Chong et al., 2015). EI is strongly negatively associated with delinquent behaviour. This association was explored in Malaysia's research study, which explored the relationship between EI in delinquent behaviour among 300 adolescents in secondary schools between the ages of 15–18. Delinquent behaviours that were contextually relevant among adolescents in the Malaysian school system were misbehaviour at school, vandalism, pornography, dishonesty, and drugs. Such delinquent behaviour was negatively associated with emotional intelligence and its dimensions such as self-awareness, self-regulation, empathy, self-motivation, social, and spirituality (Chong et al., 2005). Delinquency prevention programmes would benefit from this knowledge; enhancing the deficient EI competencies would benefit delinquent adolescents (Chong et al., 2005; Kim, 2017).

Other theories, such as the attachment, confirm that emotion and emotional regulation starts from infancy. An infant's first bond with parents is influential in developing their emotions and self-regulation. Emotions serve a dual purpose, determining both the infant's survival and well-being and thereby performing both a communicative function and a guide for emotional regulation (Papalia, 2004). Emotions not only help children communicate with their caregivers and elicit a response from them for meeting their needs, but they also develop a characteristic pattern of emotional reactions with their caregivers since infancy. With ongoing development, children transition from external to internal emotional regulation, from being emotionally dependent on caregivers to self-regulating their emotions such as fear, curiosity, anger, and other emotions in response to their surroundings (Papalia, 2004). Therefore, children develop different attachment styles with their caregivers based on their emotional connectedness with them. Many researchers found a close relationship between attachment styles and emotional intelligence. They found that secure attachment is positively associated with emotional intelligence (Samadi et al., 2013). Therefore, attachment style influenced interpersonal emotional intelligence. Therefore, individuals with secure attachment had better interpersonal intelligence and individual outcomes such as better self-esteem, self-awareness, self-regulation, and self-actualization (which is the tendency to reach one's fullest potential) as compared to the three insecure styles of attachment: dismissive, preoccupied, and fearful (Samadi et al., 2013).

According to Bowlby, attachment styles influence self-regulation and children's internal working models (Bowlby, 1969). The child's internal working model represents the attachment figures, internal simulation relationship with caregivers, their expectations, response, availability, and acceptance of the child. These internal models evolve with developing the child's social, cognitive, communicative, and relational experiences. They influence the child's self-esteem, confidence, and relationship with self and others (Bowlby, 1988; Bretherton & Munholland, 2018). Early childhood experiences influence the internal models and influence the neural pathways for self-control (Tarullo et al., 2009). The early formative years between 3 and 6 years mark the development of the ability to control one's impulses, hold one's attention, and the ability to resist temptation, and wait for a reward. The brain regions that are involved in self-control are immature at birth and mature fully during adolescence. Although children continue to develop their self-control beyond six years, the formative years lay the early self-control foundation. While a conducive home environment encourages the development of this ability, conversely, an adverse home environment results in problems in children's self-control abilities. Self-control influences children's academic achievement, emotional, social, and behavioural problems. Chiefly, self-control influences antisocial and delinquent behaviour (Tarullo et al., 2009). Therefore, prevention and rehabilitation work with juvenile delinquents should focus on improving EI, emotional regulation, self-control, and parent–child relationships (Chong et al., 2005; Kim, 2017; Tarullo et al., 2009).

6.4 Conclusion

The developmental transition from childhood to adulthood is marked by multiple changes at an individual, relational, and social level. Several factors are responsible for the healthy and unhealthy development of an adolescent. These multifaceted factors vary due to changes in the socio-economic dynamics, family dynamics, societal, and community (Fontaine et al., 2019; Choudhary & Xavier, 2015). Any changes, such as restructuring traditional patterns of facing challenges and making choices impact the child's behaviour. Generally, juveniles are young minor adolescents under eighteen years of age who exhibit violent delinquent behaviours with unlawful misconduct. For instance, the most recent 'Bois Locker Room Case' reported by Cyber Crime Cell Police involved juveniles ('Boys Locker Room Case', 2020). A juvenile was convicted in the very famous 'Nirbhaya' rape case (Choudhary & Xavier, 2015). Essentially, delinquency refers to involvement in the activities condoned by society and the law. These activities include drug abuse and drug-related offences, underage consumption of alcohol, vandalism, having sex at a very young age, sexual abuse, teen pregnancy, truancy, smoking, marriage without consent, stealing, violation of the law, murder, 'gangs', and preoccupied with the illegal occupation are all commonly classified as delinquent behaviour (Choudhary & Xavier, 2015).

Our everyday activities and how we spend our day define and shape our behaviour (Cornish & Clarke, 2017). Involvement in unhealthy and unsupervised activities such as consuming toxic substances and juvenile victimization plays a significant role in facilitating juvenile delinquency (Tanner et al., 2015). Absence of supervision fuels a chain of juvenile delinquency acts and behaviour (Trinidad et al., 2019). Juvenile offenders are susceptible to difficulty in interpersonal adjustment (Tzoumakis et al., 2012). Family dynamics can determine the likely relation between juveniles and crimes (Jin et al., 2019). Strained interparental intimacy, interparental conflict, negative emotions, and indifferent attitude towards their parents have a positive correlation with juvenile crimes and problem behaviours (Chan & Chui, 2015). Juvenile criminals are often found to have edgy parent–child and interparental relationships (Jin et al., 2019; Henneberger et al., 2013). Marital clashes among parents can push a child into loneliness, violence, interpersonal aggressiveness, and communication impairment (Gottman & Notarius, 2000; Jin et al., 2019). The poor financial status also increases the likelihood of a juvenile becoming a delinquent (Jin et al., 2019). Furthermore, social, economic, and political factors, migration, exclusion, urbanization, dysfunctional family systems, peer influence, media, cultural factors, delinquent group identities, and offender and victims are some of the causes of juvenile delinquency. Hence, juvenile delinquency's causal factors exist at different social structure levels: individual, relational, and community level (Lloyd, 2005). Therefore, a micro and macrolevel developmental perspective is essential to understand the causes, prevention, and treatment of juvenile delinquency. Finally, a broad frame of reference based on Bronfenbrenner's socio-ecological perspective, Bowlby's attachment theory, and the psychosocial concepts such as aggression, prosocial behaviour, and emotional intelligence provides a well-rounded understanding of the risk and protective factors that influence the complex phenomenon of juvenile delinquency (Johns et al., 2016; Lloyd, 2005).

References

Agarwal, D. (2018). Juvenile delinquency in India- latest trends and entailing amendments in juvenile justice Act. People: *International Journal of Social Sciences, 3(3),* 1365–1383. Retrieved from https://doi.org/10.20319/pijss.2018.33.13651383

Agnew, R. (2001). Building on the foundation of general strain theory: Specifying the types of strain most likely to lead to crime and delinquency. *Journal of Research in Crime and Delinquency, 38*(4), 319–361.

Agnew, R., Matthews, S. K., Bucher, J., Welcher, A. N., & Keyes, C. (2008). Socioeconomic status, economic problems, and delinquency. *Youth & Society, 40*, 159–181. https://doi.org/10.1177/0044118X08318119.

Ainsworth, M. S., Blehar, M. C., Waters, E., & Wall, S. (1978). *Patterns of attachment: A psychological study of the strange situation*. Erlbaum.

Aknin, L. B., Van de Vondervoort, J. W., & Hamlin, J. K. (2018). Positive feelings reward and promote prosocial behaviour. *Current Opinion in Psychology, 20*, 55–59.

Allen, J. J., & Anderson, C. A. (2017). Aggression and violence: Definitions and distinctions. *The Wiley handbook of violence and aggression*, 1–14.

Bandura, A., & Walters, R. H. (1959). *Adolescent aggression*. Ronald.

Barasch, A., Levine, E. E., Berman, J. Z., & Small, D. A. (2014). Selfish or selfless? On the signal value of emotion in altruistic behaviour. *Journal of Personality and Social Psychology, 107*(3), 393.

Baron, J. (2008). *Thinking and deciding* (4th ed.). Cambridge University Press.

Barrett, D. E., Ju, S., Katsiyannis, A., & Zhang, D. (2015). Females in the juvenile justice system: Influences on delinquency and recidivism. *Journal of Child and Family Studies, 24*(2), 427–433.

Berkowitz, L. (1978). Is criminal violence normative behavior? Hostile and instrumental aggression in violent incidents. *Journal of Research in Crime and Delinquency, 15*(2), 148–161.

Benson, M. (2005). Parent-Adolescent relationships: Integrating attachment and Bowenian family systems theories. In V. L. Bengston, A. C. Acock, K. R. Allen, P. Dilworth-Anderson, & D. M. Klein (Eds.) in *Sourcebook of Family Theories and Research*, Thousand-Oaks, California; Sage Publications.

Berk, L., & Roberts, W. (2009). *Child development (3rd* (Canadian). Pearson Allyn and Bacon.

Berk, L. E. (2013). *Child development*. Pearson Education.

Blake, P. R. (2018). Giving what one should: Explanations for the knowledge-behaviour gap for altruistic giving. *Current Opinion in Psychology, 20*, 1–5.

Bois locker room case: Police file FIR after girl complains of 'offensive threat messages' online. (2020, June 09). Bois locker room case: Police FILE FIR after girl complains of 'offensive threat messages' Online. Retrieved from https://indianexpress.com/article/cities/delhi/bois-locker-room-case-police-file-fir-after-girl-complains-of-offensive-threat-messages-online-6449432/

Bowlby, J. (1969). *Attachment and loss v. 3* (Vol. 1). Random House.

Bowlby, J. (1988). *A secure base: Parent-child attachment and healthy human development*. Basic Books.

Bretherton, I., & Munholland, K. A. (2018). The internal working model construct in light of contemporary neuroimaging research. In J. Cassidy & P. R. Shaver's (Eds.) *Handbook of attachment: Theory, research, and clinical applications* (3rd ed.). Guilford Press.

Brook, D. W., Brook, J. S., Rubenstone, E., Zhang, C., & Saar, N. S. (2011). Developmental associations between externalizing behaviors, peer delinquency, drug use, perceived neighborhood crime, and violent behavior in urban communities. *Aggressive Behavior, 37*(4), 349–361.

Bronfenbrenner, U. (1974). Is early intervention effective? *Day Care and Early Education, 2*(2), 14–18. https://doi.org/10.1007/bf02353057

Bronfenbrenner, U. (1977). Toward an experimental ecology of human development. *American Psychologist, 32*(7), 513–531. https://doi.org/10.1037/0003-066X.32.7.513

Bronfenbrenner, U. (1979). Contexts of child rearing: Problems and prospects. *American Psychologist, 34*(10), 844–850. https://doi.org/10.1037/0003-066x.34.10.844

Bronfenbrenner, U. (2005). *Making human beings human.* Sage.

Bronfenbrenner, U., & Morris, P. A. (2007). The bioecological model of human development. *Handbook of Child Psychology.* https://doi.org/10.1002/9780470147658.chpsy0114

Bushman, B. J., & Anderson, C. A. (2001). Is it time to pull the plug on hostile versus instrumental aggression dichotomy? *Psychological Review, 108*(1), 273.

Bushman, B. J., & Huesmann, L. R. (2010). Aggression. In S. T. Fiske, D. T. Gilbert, & G.

Caprara, G. V., Barbaranelli, C., & Comrey, A. L. (1992). A personological approach to the study of aggression. *Personality and Individual Differences, 13*(1), 77–84.

Chan, H., & Chui, W. H. (2015). Social bond and self-reported nonviolent and violent delinquency: A study of traditional low risk, at-risk, and adjudicated male Chinese adolescents. *Child & Youth Care Forum, 44,* 711–730.

Choudhary, A., & Xavier, D. M. S. (2015). Juvenile delinquency in India: A Socio-Psychological Analysis.

Chong, A. M., Lee, P. G., Roslan, S., & Baba, M. (2015). Emotional intelligence and at-risk students. *SAGE Open.* https://doi.org/10.1177/2158244014564768

Chung, I. J., & Lee, J. Y. (2012). The pathways from child abuse and school bullying to depression and aggression in adolescence: With a special focus on differences in gender. *Studies on Korean Youth, 23*(2), 217–242.

Cirelli, L. K. (2018). How interpersonal synchrony facilitates early prosocial behaviour. *Current Opinion in Psychology, 20,* 35–39.

Cornish, D. B., & Clarke, R. V. (2017). The rational choice perspective. In R. K. Wortley & M. Townsley (Eds.), *Environmental criminology and crime analysis* (pp. 29–61). Routledge.

Currie, J., & Tekin, E. (2006). *Does child abuse cause crime? Andrew young school of policy studies. Research paper series.* Working Paper 06–31. Atlanta, GA: Georgia State University.

Curry, G. D., Decker, S. H., & Egley, A., Jr. (2002). Gang involvement and delinquency in a middle school population. *Justice Quarterly, 19*(2), 275–292.

Dandreaux, D. M., & Frick, P. J. (2009). Developmental pathways to conduct problems: A further test of the childhood and adolescent-onset distinction. *Journal of Abnormal Child Psychology, 37*(3), 375–385.

Darling, N. (2007). Ecological systems theory: The person in the center of the circles. *Research in Human Development, 4*(3–4), 203–217. https://doi.org/10.1080/15427600701663023

Derksen, T. (2010). The influence of ecological theory in child and youth care: A review of literature. *International Journal of Child Youth & Family Justice, 1*(3/4), https://doi.org/10.18357/ijcyfs13/420102091. Retrieved from: https://journals.uvic.ca/index.php/ijcyfs/article/view/2091

DeWall, C. N., Anderson, C. A., & Bushman, B. J. (2012). Aggression. In H. Tennen, J. Suls, & I. B.

Dodge, K. A., Lochman, J. E., Harnish, J. D., Bates, J. E., & Pettit, G. S. (1997). Reactive and proactive aggression in school children and psychiatrically impaired chronically assaultive youth. *Journal of Abnormal Psychology, 106*(1), 37.

Dube, S. R., Anda, R. F., Felitti, V. J., Chapman, D. P., Williamson, D. F., & Giles, W. H. (2001). Childhood abuse, household dysfunction, and the risk of attempted suicide throughout the life span: Findings from the adverse childhood experiences study. *JAMA, 286*(24), 3089–3096.

Dunfield, K. A. (2014). A construct divided: Prosocial behaviour as helping, sharing, and comforting subtypes. *Frontiers in Psychology, 5,* 958.

Eisenberg, N., & Mussen, P. H. (1989). *The roots of prosocial behaviour in children*. Cambridge University Press.
Fontaine, N. M., Brendgen, M., Vitaro, F., Boivin, M., Tremblay, R. E., & Côté, S. M. (2019). Longitudinal associations between delinquency, depression and anxiety symptoms in adolescence: Testing the moderating effect of sex and family socioeconomic status. *Journal of Criminal Justice, 62*, 58–65.
Fung, A. L. C. (2019). Adolescent reactive and proactive aggression, and bullying in Hong Kong: Prevalence, psychosocial correlates, and prevention. *Journal of Adolescent Health, 64*(6), S65–S72.
Gallitto, E., & Leth-Steensen, C. (2019). Moderating effect of trait emotional intelligence on the relationship between parental nurturance and prosocial behaviour. *Journal of Adolescence, 74*, 113–119.
Geen, R. G. (2001). *Human aggression* (2nd ed.). Open University Press.
Gold, J., Sullivan, M. W., & Lewis, M. (2011). The relation between abuse and violent delinquency: The conversion of shame to blame in juvenile offenders. *Child Abuse & Neglect, 35*(7), 459–467.
Goleman, D. (1995). *Emotional intelligence*. Bantam Books, Inc.
Gottman, J. M., & Notarius, C. I. (2000). Decade review: Observing marital interaction. *Journal of Marriage and the Family, 62*, 927–947.
Hamilton, C. E., Falshaw, L., & Browne, K. D. (2002). The link between recurrent maltreatment and offending behaviour. *International Journal of Offender Therapy and Comparative Criminology, 46*(1), 75–94.
Hammond, S. I., & Drummond, J. K. (2019). Rethinking emotions in the context of infants' prosocial behaviour: The role of interest and positive emotions. *Developmental Psychology, 55*(9), 1882.
Harris, P. W., Mennis, J., Obradovic, Z., Izenman, A. J., & Grunwald, H. E. (2011). The coaction of neighbourhood and individual effects on recidivism. *Cityscape, 13*, 33–55. Retrieved from https://www.jstor.org/stable/41426674
Henneberger, A. K., Durkee, M. I., Truong, N., Atkins, A., & Tolan, P. H. (2013). The longitudinal relationship between peer violence and popularity and delinquency in adolescent boys: Examining effects by family functioning. *Journal of Youth and Adolescence, 42*(11), 1651–1660.
Hinitz, B. (2014). Head Start: A Bridge From Past to Future. *YC Young Children, 69*(2), 94–97. Retrieved August 18, 2020, from www.jstor.org/stable/ycyoungchildren.69.2.94
Hodgdon, H. B. (2009). *Child maltreatment and aggression: The mediating role of moral disengagement, emotion regulation, and emotional callousness among juvenile offenders*. Temple University.
Hoeve, M., Stams, G. J. J. M., van der Put, C. E., Dubas, J. E., van der Laan, P. H., & Gerris, J. R. M. (2012). A Meta-analysis of attachment to parents and delinquency. *Journal of Abnormal Child Psychology, 40*, 771–785. https://doi.org/10.1007/s10802-011-9608-1. Retrieved from https://link.springer.com/content/pdf/https://doi.org/10.1007/s10802-011-9608-1.pdf
Hwang, H. (2009). A longitudinal study for the understanding of adolescents' delinquency: Focusing on general strain theory. *Journal of Korean Council for Children & Rights, 13*(1), 1–31.
Jin, C. C., Zhao, B. B., & Zou, H. (2019). Chinese delinquent and non-delinquent juveniles: An exploration of the relations among interparental intimacy, interparental conflict, filial piety and interpersonal adjustment. *Children and Youth Services Review, 103*, 148–155.
Johns, D. F., Williams, K., & Haines, K. (2016). Ecological youth justice: Understanding the social ecology of young people's prolific offending. *Youth Justice, 17*(1), 3–21. https://doi.org/10.1177/1473225416665611
Juan, S.-C., Washington, H. M., & Kurlychek, M. C. (2020). breaking the intergenerational cycle: Partner violence, child-parent attachment, and children's aggressive behaviours. *Journal of Interpersonal Violence, 35*(5–6), 1158–1181. https://doi.org/10.1177/0886260517692996
Kärtner, J. (2018). Beyond dichotomies—(m) others' structuring and the development of toddlers' prosocial behaviour across cultures. *Current Opinion in Psychology, 20*, 6–10.

Kim, Y. J. (2017). *Longitudinal relationship between emotion regulation and aggressive behaviour: The moderating effect of caregiving.* Doctoral Dissertation, University of Pittsburgh. (Unpublished). Retrieved from http://d-scholarship.pitt.edu/31658/

Krahé, B. (2013). *The social psychology of aggression* (2nd ed.). Psychology Press.

Krettenauer, T., Bauer, K., & Sengsavang, S. (2019). Fairness, prosociality, hypocrisy, and happiness: Children's and adolescents' motives for showing unselfish behaviour and positive emotions. *British Journal of Developmental Psychology, 37*(4), 505–518.

Lloyd, C. B. (2005). Juvenile delinquency. In United NATIONS: World youth report 2003: The global situation of young people. *Studies in Family Planning, 36*(4), 188–206.

Lockwood, P. L., Seara-Cardoso, A., & Viding, E. (2014). Emotion regulation moderates the association between empathy and prosocial behaviour. *PloS one, 9*(5), e96555.

Martinelli, A., Ackermann, K., Bernhard, A., Freitag, C. M., & Schwenck, C. (2018). Hostile attribution bias and aggression in children and adolescents: A systematic literature review on the influence of aggression subtype and gender. *Aggression and Violent Behaviour, 39*, 25–32.

Mayer, J. D., & Salovey, P. (1995). Emotional intelligence and the construction and regulation of feelings. *Applied and Preventive Psychology*, 197–208.

Mayer, J. D., & Salovey, P. (1997). What is emotional intelligence? In P. Salovey & D. Sluyter (Eds.), *Emotional development and emotional intelligence: Implications for educators* (pp. 3–31). Basic Books.

Mayer, J. D., Roberts, R. D., & Barsade, S. G. (2008). Human abilities: Emotional intelligence. *Annual Review of Psychology, 59*, 507–536. https://doi.org/10.1146/annurev.psych.59.103006.093646

McElhaney, K. B., Immele, A., Smith, F. D., & Allen, J. P. (2006). Attachment organization as a moderator of the link between friendship quality and adolescent delinquency. *Attachment & Human Development, 8*(1), 33–46. Retrieved from: https://www.tandfonline.com/doi/abs/https://doi.org/10.1080/14616730600585250

Miller, J. G. (2018). Physiological mechanisms of prosociality. *Current Opinion in Psychology, 20*, 50–54.

Millon, T., Lerner, M. J., & Weiner, I. B. (2003). *Handbook of psychology. Volume 5, personality and social psychology.* Wiley

Milojević, S., Dimitrijević, A. A., Marjanović, Z. J., & Dimitrijević, A. (2016). Bad past, gloomy future: The trait emotional intelligence profile of juvenile offenders. *Personality and Individual Differences, 94*, 295–298.

Muñoz, L. C., Frick, P. J., Kimonis, E. R., & Aucoin, K. J. (2008). Types of aggression, responsiveness to provocation, and callous-unemotional traits in detained adolescents. *Journal of Abnormal Child Psychology, 36*(1), 15–28.

Nagin, D., & Tremblay, R. E. (1999). Trajectories of boys' physical aggression, opposition, and hyperactivity on the path to physically violent and nonviolent juvenile delinquency. *Child Development, 70*(5), 1181–1196.

National Child Protect Agency. (2012). Child Maltreatment Report. Seoul: National Child Protect Agency.

Nichols, T. R., Graber, J. A., Brooks-Gunn, J., & Botvin, G. J. (2006). Sex differences in overt aggression and delinquency among urban minority middle school students. *Journal of Applied Developmental Psychology, 27*(1), 78–91.

O'donnell, A. W., & Barber, B. L. (2018). Exploring the association between adolescent sports participation and externalising behaviours: The moderating role of prosocial and risky peers. *Australian Journal of Psychology, 70*(4), 361–368.

Osofsky, J. D. (1999). The impact of violence on children. *The Future of Children*, 33–49.

Papalia, D. E., Wendkos, S. O., & Feldman, R. D. (2004). *Human development* (9th eds). McGraw-Hill.

Parrott, D. J., & Giancola, P. R. (2007). Addressing "the criterion problem" in the assessment of aggressive behaviour: Development of a new taxonomic system. *Aggression and Violent Behaviour, 12*(3), 280–299. https://doi.org/10.1016/j.avb.2006.08.002

Pechorro, P., Jiménez, L., Hidalgo, V., & Nunes, C. (2015). The DSM-5 limited prosocial emotions subtype of conduct disorder in incarcerated male and female juvenile delinquents. *International Journal of Law and Psychiatry, 39*, 77–82.
Poulin, F., & Boivin, M. (2000). The role of proactive and reactive aggression in the formation and development of boys' friend- ships. *Developmental Psychology, 36*, 233–240.
Puhalla, A. A., & McCloskey, M. S. (2020). The relationship between physiological reactivity to provocation and emotion dysregulation with proactive and reactive aggression. *Biological psychology*, 107931.
Rosa, E, M., & Tudge, J. (2013). Urie Bronfenbrenner's theory of human development: Its evolution from ecology to bioecology. *Journal of Family Theory & Review, 5*, 243–258. https://doi.org/10.1111/jftr.12022
Salmivalli, C., & Kaukiainen, A. (2004). "Female aggression" revisited: Variable-and person-centered approaches to studying gender differences in different types of aggression. *Aggressive Behaviour: Official Journal of the International Society for Research on Aggression, 30*(2), 158–163.
Salovey, P., & Mayer, J. D. (1990). Emotional intelligence. *Imagination, Cognition and Personality, 9*(3), 185–211. https://doi.org/10.2190/DUGG-P24E-52WK-6CDG
Samadi, R. G., Kasaei, F., & Pour, E. M. (2013). Attachment styles as a predictor of emotional intelligence. *Procedia - Social and Behavioural Sciences, 84*, 1712–1715. https://doi.org/10.1016/j.sbspro.2013.07.018
Siegel, L., & Welsh, B. (2014). *Juvenile delinquency: Theory, practice, and law* (12th ed.). Wadsworth.
Snippe, E., Jeronimus, B. F., Aan Het Rot, M., Bos, E. H., de Jonge, P., & Wichers, M. (2018). The reciprocity of prosocial behaviour and positive affect in daily life. *Journal of Personality, 86(2)*, 139–146
Soyer, G. F. (2019). Book review: the ecology of human development by urie Bronfenbrenner. *Journal of Culture and Values in Education, 2*(2), 77–80.
Suatin, W., & Wijayanti, N. T. (2020). Peer attachment and child's social competence. *Advances in Social Science, Education and Humanities Research*: Vol. 395, (pp. 314–317). Proceedings of the 5th ASEAN Conference on Psychology, Counselling, and Humanities (ACPCH, 2019). https://doi.org/10.2991/assehr.k.200120.068
Tanner, J., Asbridge, M., & Wortley, S. (2015). Leisure worlds: Situations, motivations and young people's encounters with offending and victimization. *Youth & Society, 47*(2), 199–221.
Tarullo, A., Obradović, J., & Gunnar, M. (2009). Self- Control and the developing brain. *Zero to Three, 29*, 31–37.
Tarry, H., & Emler, N. (2007). Attitudes, values and moral reasoning as predictors of delinquency. *British Journal of Developmental Psychology, 25*(2), 169–183.
Tedeschi, J. T., & Felson, R. B. (1994). Coercive actions and aggression.
The Social Justice (no date). Bronfenbrenner's Ecological model of human development and Signs of Safety. Retrieved from http://www.thesocialjustice.com/bronfenbrenners-ecological-model-of-human-development-and-signs-of-safety/
Trinidad, A., Vozmediano, L., & San-Juan, C. (2019). "Jumping at the opportunity": The role of situational and opportunity factors in juvenile delinquency in Southern Europe. *International journal of law, crime and justice, 59*, 100347.
Twenge, J. M., Baumeister, R. F., DeWall, C. N., Ciarocco, N. J., & Bartels, J. M. (2007). Social exclusion decreases prosocial behaviour. *Journal of Personality and Social Psychology, 92*(1), 56.
Tzoumakis, S., Lussier, P., & Corrado, R. (2012). Female juvenile delinquency, motherhood, and the intergenerational transmission of aggression and antisocial behaviour. *Behavioural Sciences & the Law, 30*(2), 211–237.
Ungar, M., Ghazinour, M., & Richter, J. (2012). Annual Research Review: What is resilience within the social ecology of human development? *Journal of Child Psychology and Psychiatry, 54*(4), 348–366. https://doi.org/10.1111/jcpp.12025

Van der Graaff, J., Carlo, G., Crocetti, E., Koot, H. M., & Branje, S. (2018). Prosocial behaviour in adolescence: Gender differences in development and links with empathy. *Journal of Youth and Adolescence, 47*(5), 1086–1099.

Walters, G. D. (2019). Peer influence or projection bias? Predicting respondent delinquency with perceptual measures of peer delinquency in 22 samples. *Journal of Adolescence, 70*, 1–12.

Wang, C., Williams, K. E., Shahaeian, A., & Harrison, L. J. (2018). Early predictors of escalating internalizing problems across middle childhood. *School Psychology Quarterly, 33*(2), 200.

Wiebush, R. G., Freitag, R., & Baird, C. (2001). *Preventing delinquency through improved child protection services*. US Department of Justice, Office of Justice Programs, Office of Juvenile Justice and Delinquency Prevention.

White, R., & Mason, R. (2006). Youth gangs and youth violence: Charting the key dimensions. *Australian & New Zealand Journal of Criminology, 39*(1), 54–70.

You, S., & Lim, S. A. (2015). Development pathways from abusive parenting to delinquency: The mediating role of depression and aggression. *Child Abuse & Neglect, 46*, 152–162.

Chapter 7
Gender and Crime

Tanay Maiti and Lukus Langan

Abstract Crime is a heterogeneous social phenomenon and does not merely reflect deviant behaviour that is incompatible with society's laws. Criminality can be used as a lens through which greater insight into a society's economic and moral values might be gleaned, but within the field of criminology, there seems to be a dearth of dedicated research into the relationship between gender and criminality. Indeed, gender-specific crimes tend to occur at higher rates within developing, low-, and middle-income countries, where one gender is committing or being victimized more so than another gender for specific crimes. Societal influences and cultural norms, as well as the role of the criminal justice system, undoubtably shape the ways in which women and men are able to be both the victims and the perpetrators of various criminal acts. By improving our understanding of this topic and by collecting further evidence of reliable predictors of criminality, research into the relationship between gender and crime will ideally contribute towards a society that may one day be described as 'equal'.

Keywords Crime patterns · Female offenders · Victimization · Gender gap · Domestic violence

7.1 Introduction

With the obvious exception of feminist scholars and criminologists, the complex dynamic of crime and gender has been historically disregarded within the field of criminology. The earliest advances in the study of criminal behaviour were typically androcentric in their assessments of class structure, social control, and deviance, with these studies being largely restricted to the study of male offenders (Daly & Chesney-Lind, 1988; Smart, 1976). However, this predilection for focusing on male offenders

T. Maiti (✉)
Department of Psychiatry, Jagannath Gupta Institute of Medical Science and Hospital, Kolkata, West Bengal, India

L. Langan
Jindal Institute of Behavioural Sciences, O.P. Jindal Global University, Sonipat, Haryana, India

S. Sahni et al. (eds.), *Criminal Psychology and the Criminal Justice System in India and Beyond*, https://doi.org/10.1007/978-981-16-4570-9_7

and deviants when constructing these early theories of crime may have been somewhat justified as a larger pool of more socially visible subjects would have attracted more focused study (Heidensohn, 2010). Men are more likely to commit a criminal act than women (DeLisi & Vaughn, 2016), and the majority of homicide cases have historically involved men murdering other men (Daly & Wilson, 1988). Interestingly, increased homicide rates have actually been found to be cross-culturally correlated with increased rates of gender inequality (Heirigs & Moore, 2018), although other factors—such as increased economic inequality—can also act as significant predictors (Koeppel et al., 2015). Indeed, it has been proposed that a societal decrease in gender inequality would likely contribute towards a corresponding decrease in societal violence, potentially even reducing motivations for various types of violence (Whaley & Messner, 2002).

7.2 Theories of the Crime–Gender Gap

While it is agreed that a pervasive and universal gender gap exists in criminality and criminal behaviour, it may be argued that the majority of contemporary criminologists do not adequately acknowledge gender in their examinations of criminality (Parker & Reckdenwald, 2008). To better recognize the gender inequalities that may contribute to criminality, the social construct of 'patriarchy' must first be examined. Typically denoting the subordination of women within social institutions and their disadvantaged position within broader society when compared to men (Belknap, 2007), patriarchy may be applied to private (e.g. familial and domestic inequalities) and public social spheres (employment, education, government, etc.; Atwell, 2002; Walby, 1990). While the intrenched patriarchal structure of Indian society overtly disadvantages women, the influence of patriarchal familial spheres cannot be understated; being a 'good daughter' can be threatened by deviations from traditional gender roles, and many young women subsequentially consider themselves to be burdens to their family, with their views often being undervalued (Choudhury & Choudhury, 2020).

Power–control theory (Hagan et al., 1985) emphasizes the role of private patriarchy in explaining the gender–crime gap, as the power and control relations between mothers and fathers are elaborated upon. Within more patriarchal families, children are typically socialized to adopt gender-specific roles that are most similar to the parent of the same biological sex and—with the father's authority exceeding the mother's—this is achieved through stronger control over daughters and weaker control over sons. Consequentially, a gender gap in childhood delinquency may be expected. Less patriarchal families, characterized by a balance of authority, are suggested to expose both sons and daughters to fewer controls, while encouraging children to take risks. As a result of this egalitarian approach, the delinquency gender gap is narrowed. Interestingly, although this model has received support from the initial researchers (e.g. McCarthy et al., 1999), there appears to be limited support from other researchers (e.g. Blackwell et al., 2002) (Fig. 7.1).

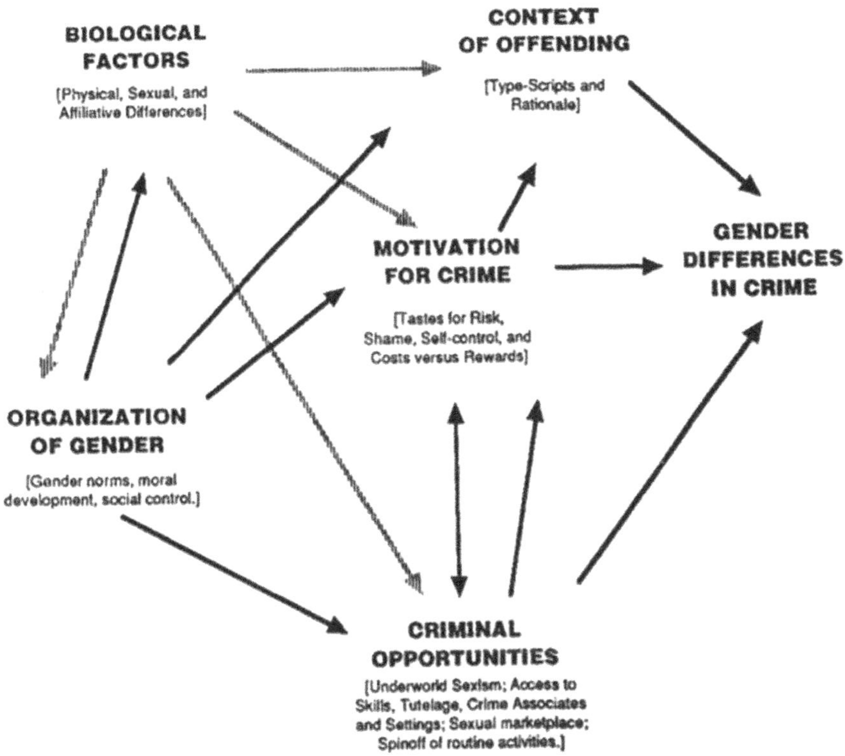

Fig. 7.1 Gendered model of female offending and gender differences in crime (Steffensmeier & Allan, 1996)

Broken line = weak effect.

The gender equality hypothesis proposes that as gender equality is steadily achieved, the gender–crime gap should also disappear, as pertinent social differences dissipate. Some have interpreted this as the 'darker side' of equality, with the gap being narrowed by 'women forcing their way into the world of major crimes' (Adler & Adler, 1975). This position has received heavy criticism (e.g. Steffensmeier, 1980), and it has been suggested that the narrowing gender–crime gap may be more related to decreases seen in male offending (Applin & Messner, 2015). Legal 'net-widening' may also be a cause, as once 'non-criminal' behaviours are deemed 'criminal' by societal institutions, and therefore become worthy of legal actions. The net-widening effect can be applied to familial structures as well, with more parents being willing to report their daughters to officials (Chesney-Lind & Shelden, 2014). Indeed, within Western countries, women account for a larger proportion of minor offences than of serious crimes, and this has disproportionately impacted the registered crime rates of female offenders, more so than their male counterparts (Steffensmeier et al., 2005).

7.3 Patterns of Victimization

When accounting for all criminal acts, women typically experience lower rates of overall victimization compared to men, but also tend to experience significantly higher levels of fear of crime. This discrepancy could be related to a statistical underrepresentation of female victimization, with a significant increase in documented crimes against women having been observed in recent years. Rather than a sudden spike in crimes being committed against women, this rise seems to be largely based on an increase in such crimes being reported to authorities (Iyer et al., 2012).

Women's increased fear of crime could also be explained by an underlying fear of rape that exacerbates their fear of other, more unrelated offences (Warr, 1985). Dubbed the 'sex-fear paradox', these higher rates of victimization for rape and other sexual assault-related criminal acts—a statistical exception to the 'rule' that men are victimized at higher overall rates—have been implicated as an underlying contributor to women's increased fear of all crimes, with the 'shadow of sexual assault' being subsequentially designated as a 'master offence'. Perceptually contemporaneous offences are associated with these master offences, as the more serious crimes (e.g. rape) can be cognitively connected with unrelated crimes (e.g. theft) and therefore will trigger a more intense fear to be attributed towards these perceptually related offences (Warr, 1984). In women, the most egregious master offence is arguably rape and other forms of sexual assault, but evidence has suggested that fear of assault is a stronger predictor of fear of crime for both men and women being regarded as the master offence for the general population. Furthermore, it is the fear of physical harm that seems to link both gender's fear, but due to the real-life prevalence rates of sexual assault impacting women, it is unsurprising that the threat of physical harm is specifically associated with rape (Ugwu & Britto, 2015).

Public transport is a common setting in which incidents of sexual harassment and assault can occur. Fears regarding safety can easily influence travel decisions, as particular bus stops and transit routes are avoided or only utilized during daytime hours; some even choose to avoid using public transport entirely (Loukaitou-Sideris & Fink, 2008). In India, buses are seen as the least safe form of public transport, although sexual harassment of women reportedly occurs in other public settings also (Phadke, 2010). Irrespective of the countermeasures that have already been taken (i.e. women-only Metro compartments), incidents of physical and verbal sexual harassment on public transport systems remain a prevalent issue. According to a study, 52.8% of 655 female student respondents in Chennai reported that they had been victims of sexual molestation on public transportation at least once, with 52.02% having reported repeated victimization within a 12-month period (Joseph et al., 2014); out of 200 female students in Lucknow, 100% of respondents reported having been both a victim and a witness to sexual harassment within a period of 6 months (Tripathi et al., 2017).

7.4 Patterns of Offending

In India, the majority of recorded murders are perpetrated by young men, while homicides committed by women are remarkably rare in contrast. It has been claimed that the 'three powerful stimuli' that motivate men to murder are '*zan, zar, and zamin*' translated as women, gold (money), and land (Edwardes, 1924), though these motivators have also been cited as provocation for a man to commit any crime. The comparatively rare incidences of women committing murder are potentially prompted by very specific provocations: infidelity and harassment (Drèze & Khera, 2000). Indeed, cases in which women murder their husbands, along with other male relatives, are purportedly in response to physical and/or sexual abuse (Lodha et al., 2018).

Female-on-female homicide is relatively rare compared to male-on-male homicide (Daly & Wilson, 1988), but dowry murders—in which a woman is murdered for not bringing sufficient dowry to the marriage—committed by mothers-in-law remain a fairly common example of female-on-female violence within India (Rudd, 2001). In addition to this, the abuse (physical, emotional, etc.) of daughters-in-law being prompted by insufficient dowry, inferior caste, etc., is also highly prevalent (Bajpai, 2005). Women prisoners comprise only 4.13% of the criminals convicted under the Indian Penal Code (National Crime Records Bureau (NCRB, 2018); however, there appears to be a trend of increased criminal behaviour among women and a rise in the types of crimes being committed (Lodha et al., 2018). The phenomenon of female criminality and its steady increase has been examined across the globe, with some suggesting that this is a result of numerous sociological, economic, cultural, and environmental factors, in addition to the contributory influence of rapid industrialization, urbanization, and westernization. This increase in women committing crimes has even been regarded as an attack on Indian social and cultural heritage, as well as impacting the very structure of society (Pattanaik & Mishra, 2001).

The end of childhood and the entry into adolescence is physiologically marked by the onset of pubertal maturation, but the onset of puberty is also a strong predictor of increased aggression—in both young men and young women. While men experience this onset by 10–12 years of age, in women, the surge of hormones marking the onset of adolescence typically begins by 9–10 years of age (Peper & Dahl, 2013). This early pubertal maturation has been visible in criminal statistics, with young women's offending peak occurring 2 years earlier than young men (Campbell, 1995, 2013). Older theories have also offered interesting explanations for what may motivate women to commit crimes: women are inherently manipulative and deceitful, and these characteristics are rooted in a number of physiological and social attributes (e.g. their ability to feign arousal; Pollak, 1950). Contemporary literature has since attempted to provide more nuanced explanations.

7.4.1 Biological Predictors

Compared to the average woman, the average man tends to be physically larger and stronger (Puts et al., 2016), an example of sexual dimorphism that has endured throughout our evolutionary history. However, although older biological theories have attempted to draw certain inferences between a person's physicality and their probability of criminality or deviancy (e.g. Sheldon et al., 1949), such factors do not directly contribute to a person's criminal likelihood and therefore cannot be used as a direct predictor of criminality. Regardless, many evolutionary theories have suggested that men's increased propensity to employ aggressive behaviours, especially towards other men (Archer, 2009), could be a hallmark of our species' approach to sexual selection and competition. Particularly when competing against other men, this increased willingness to employ aggressive and risky tactics—combined with increased physical size and strength—may contribute towards more favourable outcomes (social status, mating success, etc.). These biological components, as outcomes of historical and evolutionary selection processes, could be used to explain the greater prevalence of male offenders and the higher rates of violence between men (Puts et al., 2016; Durrant, 2019).

The 'female choice' as an intersexual selection process—in which the discrimination of prospective partners is exerted by a species' females (Darwin, 1871)—arguably encourages status-striving and/or aggressive behaviours in men, as these qualities supposedly demonstrate enhanced resource acquiring potential. According to the evolutionary neuroandrogenic theory, men developed a distinct inclination towards competitive and victimizing behaviours as a consequence of sexual selection pressures and the female-driven mating bias towards status-striving 'dominant' mates. Additionally, it is also argued that these evolutionary pressures predispose men to use deceptive or forceful copulation tactics (Ellis, 1989), with rape apparently being especially common among men with poor chances of becoming stable providers of resources (Ellis, 2005).

The Y chromosome present in the biologically male has been implicated as an underlying component of competitive, victimizing, and/or aggressive behaviours (Ellis, 2005). Men with an extra Y chromosome have been speculated to be 'hypermasculine' and more aggressive, with higher testosterone levels, and an increased likelihood to commit violent crimes than XY chromosome men (Jacobs et al., 1965). Although the overall risk of conviction seems to be increased in XYY chromosome men, this rate of conviction was found to be similar to XY chromosome men, once socio-economic parameters were taken into account. Additionally, these groups' testosterone levels do not appear to differ greatly. Interestingly, an increased frequency of sexual abuse convictions for men with XYY has been found, and it has been speculated that the contributory effects of XYY chromosomes are largely indirect, as the psychological conditions that might contribute to sexual offending (immaturity, interpersonal/sexual difficulties, etc.; Nielsen et al., 1973) are often present in XYY individuals (Stochholm et al., 2012), but there is insufficient evidence to support any concerns about exceptional risks of sex offending among these groups (O'Donovan and Völlm, 2018).

Despite beliefs to the contrary, estrogens (i.e. estradiol) and androgens (i.e. testosterone) are present in all genders and are produced by both testes and ovaries. Although average levels of estradiol do not differ between genders (van Anders, 2010), average testosterone levels are typically higher for men (Gillies & McArthur, 2010). Particular characteristics linked to increased criminality and exacerbated in men (dominance, intra-sexual aggression, etc.) may potentially arise due to the prenatal exposure of males to testosterone, in addition to other genetic and epigenetically mediated differences (McEwan & Milner, 2017). This has been disputed, as situational flexibility of hormone levels has been demonstrated (e.g. Oxford et al., 2010) and the gender variance in testosterone levels is much smaller than widely assumed, with a great deal of observable overlap within these average hormonal distributions (van Anders, 2010). Testosterone levels in both men and women can even be considerably influenced by other non-genetic factors: sexual thoughts (Goldey & van Anders, 2011), parenting behaviours (van Anders et al., 2012), relationship transitions (Dibble et al., 2017), etc. Ultimately, increased rates of criminality in men cannot be wholly explained by increased levels of testosterone.

7.4.2 Sociological Perspectives of Crime

A strong emphasis has historically been placed on the biological explanations that would better predict and elucidate differences between male and female criminality, but there are severe limitations inherent to relying upon such reductionist biological determinants. It is therefore suggested that a gendered sociology of crime be prioritized within criminological study. Only by understanding the impact of social control can the differences between men and women's deviant behaviour be more reliably accounted for (Heidensohn, 2010).

Despite greater societal progression and awareness, Indian women endure inequality at every stage of life (e.g. Choudhury & Choudhury, 2020), with equality not being experienced as it is stated within the Constitution (Mili & Cherian, 2015). Female criminality is potentially the product of strained interpersonal relations with familial entities (husbands, in-laws, etc.), their husbands' extra-marital relations, consistent deprivation, and a denial of basic needs (affection, security, etc.; Sharma, 1993). It is argued that thefts committed by Indian women are not the result of criminalistic tendencies, but are instead more strongly related to familial and economic compulsions (Mili & Cherian, 2015). Theories of 'family maladjustment' and the role of familial conflict have been used to better explain female criminality, but these private spheres are still subject to the broader socio-economic conditions enforced by more public spheres. The complex ramifications of economic poverty, as an example, contribute towards issues within the family, but may also motivate risk-taking, deviant behaviour, and delinquency (Chesney-Lind & Shelden, 2014). Indeed, poverty, illiteracy, gender inequality, and the legal system have been implicated as prominent contributors to female criminality in India (Kumari, 2009), but alternate theories have also been offered.

Masculinization theory refers to the attempt to understand women's behaviours by attributing male characteristics to their behaviours, rather than examining the sociological female experience, overarching structural pressures, or cultural environment. A popular application of this theory refers to the increase in female criminality that would arise from gender equality, as women's liberation would apparently make.

A woman thinks more like a man while committing a crime (Adler & Adler, 1975). Aside from the perplexing male-centred approach to female crime, this theory also lacks relevance to countries in which women are largely considered non-equal to men (Islam et al., 2014). Comparatively, the opportunity theory of female crime suggests that increased access to opportunities contributes towards increased criminal involvement; a complementary combination of opportunity and motivation—whether through desire or necessity—would explain increases in some offences (e.g. property crime) and decreases in others (e.g. violent crime; Simon, 1975). However, a distinct lack of economic (Saxena, 1994) and employment opportunities (Madhurima, 2009) often characterizes female offenders in India, with disparity in the economic sector being regarded as a prominent explanation (Lodha et al., 2018).

7.5 The Criminal Justice System and Intimate Partner Violence

'Male chivalry' within the justice system supposedly benefits female offenders. As gender biases and stereotyping are prevalent within the male-dominated judicial system, women are arguably treated more leniently by criminal justice personnel, being convicted less often and judged less harshly (Pollak, 1950). Though chivalry theory has some applicability within the justice system (e.g. Spohn & Beichner, 2000), it largely ignores more complex processes of gendering and tends to frame patriarchal influences as being beneficial to women. Instead, chivalry theory is better examined as an example of benevolent sexism—sexist gender evaluations that seem subjectively positive, but are negatively impactful to broader gender equality—that is derived from stereotypical notions of femininity (irresponsible, passive, etc.) and directly disadvantages both men and women.

The concept of 'double deviancy' (Lloyd, 1995) refers to the tendency for women to be sentenced in accordance to the court's assessment of them as wives, mothers, and daughters rather than by the actual seriousness of their offence; crimes deemed 'unfeminine' (crimes against children, murder, etc.) are often treated and represented more harshly in female offenders (Ballinger, 2000). Indeed, when a woman commits a crime, they are not only deviant from society but are also deviant from the socially constructed mandates of 'womanhood'. In women, behaving in a violent or sexually abusive manner is seen as antithetical to their femininity, but it is also the case that violence and sexual assault can be incorrectly regarded as components of masculinity (Ballinger, 2007).

One specific crime in which women are simultaneously less likely to be charged and also, less likely to be the offender, is domestic violence. Low-/middle-income women in South-East Asia (India, Sri Lanka, Bangladesh, etc.) have a higher prevalence of physical and/or sexual intimate partner violence through their lifetime than those living in low-/middle-income regions in the Western Pacific, Europe, and the Americas (World Health Organisation (WHO, 2013), and an estimated 4 in 10 Indian women experience at least one form of domestic violence (physical, sexual, psychological, control, etc.) in their lifetime (Kalokhe et al., 2016). A combination of intrenched patriarchal gender roles (Visaria, 2000) and propagated cultural views of female subordination (Gundappa & Rathod, 2012) undoubtably contribute towards this high frequency of domestic violence. While domestic violence perpetrated against women is the statistical norm, men are also victimized through intimate partner violence. Indeed, 326 out of 880 (37.05%) married women in Haryana had experienced domestic violence from their husbands: 26.9% reporting physical violence, 14.7% reporting sexual violence, and 27.2% reporting emotional violence (Nadda et al., 2018). Comparatively, 515 out of 1000 (51.5%) married men in Haryana had experienced domestic violence from their wives: 6% reporting physical violence, 0.4% reporting sexual violence, and 49.6% reporting emotional violence (Malik & Nadda, 2019). Gender differences in the kind of domestic violence experienced were also noted in these studies; the most common form of emotional violence against women was 'saying or doing something to humiliate her in front of others', while for men, it was being criticized. The most common form of physical violence perpetrated against both genders was being slapped by their spouses, although 46% of the cases of physical violence against men were bidirectional and initiated by the husband, whereas less than 5% of women initiated physical and/or emotional violence against their husbands. Intimate partner violence is a serious and traumatic ordeal for anyone to undergo, but the Protection of Women from Domestic Violence Act, 2005 applies only to female victims and—while women are more often the victims in such cases—male victims of abuse are largely ignored. The socio-symbolic relationships between genders ultimately impact the wider society's judgement of abuse survivors and determine whether victims of intimate partner violence are even recognized (Lelaurain et al., 2018); patriarchal preconceptions and ideologies propagate notions of male 'strength' and female 'weakness', to the detriment of both men and women.

7.6 Challenges for the Future

The influence of culture and society undoubtably shapes the ways in which women and men are able to be both the victims and the perpetrators of various criminal acts. However, this chapter has only examined the heterosexual, cisgender experience of criminal victimization and offending. This is an obvious failing in the discussion of crime and gender, as the LGBTQA + community has a long history of victimization and a complicated relationship with criminality, since being non-heterosexual/non-cisgender has been illegal at various intervals throughout world history. This complex topic deserves to be thoroughly explored, but doing justice to this critical area of study is decidedly beyond the scope of this particular exploration; a more nuanced approach by researchers with stronger ties to the LGBTQA + community and further dedicated research is certainly needed.

Poverty, illiteracy, gender inequality, and issues present within the legal system have been implicated as prominent contributors to female criminality (Kumari, 2009), but it is imperative that this knowledge be used for positive changes to wider society. The deep-rooted gender norms propagated by private and public spheres of influence must be questioned, and necessary amendments must be made to societies in which blatant inequality has been allowed to prosper. Indeed, by researching gender and crime, the findings can easily contribute towards a more 'equal' society.

References

Adler, F., & Adler, H. M. (1975). *Sisters in crime: The rise of the new female criminal*. McGraw-Hill.
Applin, S., & Messner, S. F. (2015). Her American dream. *Feminist Criminology, 10*(1), 36–59.
Archer, J. (2009). Does sexual selection explain human sex differences in aggression? *Behavioral and Brain Sciences, 32*, 249–311.
Atwell, M. W. (2002). *Equal protection of the law? Gender and justice in the United States*. Peter Lang.
Bajpai, A. B. (2005). *Female criminality in India*. Rawat Publications.
Ballinger, A. (2000). *Dead woman walking*. Ashgate.
Ballinger, A. (2007). Masculinity in the dock: Legal responses to male violence and female retaliation in England and Wales, 1900–1965. *Social & Legal Studies, 16*(4), 459–481.
Belknap, J. (2007). *The invisible woman: Gender, crime, and justice* (3rd ed.). Wadsworth.
Blackwell, B. S., Sellers, C. S., & Schlaupitz, S. M. (2002). A power-control theory of vulnerability to crime and adolescent role exits-revisited. *Canadian Review of Sociology and Anthropology, 39*, 199–218.
Campbell, A. (1995). A few good men: Evolutionary psychology and female adolescent aggression. *Ethology and Sociobiology, 16*(2), 99–123.
Campbell, A. (2013). The evolutionary psychology of women's aggression. *Philosophical Transactions of the Royal Society B, 368*(1631), 20130078.
Chesney-Lind, M., & Shelden, R. G. (2014). *Girls, delinquency, and juvenile justice* (4th ed.). Wiley Inc.
Choudhury, T., & Choudhury, R. (2020). The conversation: Understanding young women's childhood and its impact on mental health at the university counselling centre. *Journal of Humanities and Social Sciences Studies, 2*(4), 159–169.
Daly, K., & Chesney-Lind, M. (1988). Feminism and criminology. *Justice Quarterly, 5*(4), 497–538.
Daly, M., & Wilson, M. (1988). *Homicide* (5th ed.). Transaction Publishers.
Darwin, C. (1871). *The descent of man and selection in relation to sex*. John Murray.
DeLisi, M., & Vaughn, M. G. (2016). Correlates of crime. In A. R. Piqeuro (Ed.), *The handbook of criminological theory* (pp. 18–36). Wiley.
Dibble, E. R., Goldey, K. L., & van Anders, S. M. (2017). Pair bonding and testosterone in men: Longitudinal evidence for trait and dynamic associations. *Adaptive Human Behavior and Physiology, 3*, 71–90.

Drèze, J., & Khera, R. (2000). Crime, gender, and society in India: Insights from homicide data. *Population and Development Review, 26*(2), 335–352.
Durrant, R. (2019). Evolutionary approaches to understanding crime: Explaining the gender gap in offending. *Psychology, Crime & Law, 25*(6), 589–608.
Edwardes, S. M. (1924). *Crime in India (reprinted 1988)*. Printwell Publishers.
Ellis, L. (1989). *Theories of rape: Inquiries into the causes of sexual aggression*. Taylor and Francis.
Ellis, L. (2005). A theory explaining biological correlates of criminality. *European Journal of Criminology, 2*(3), 287–315.
Gillies, G. E., & McArthur, S. (2010). Estrogen actions in the brain and the basis for differential action in men and women: A case for sex-specific medicines. *Pharmacological Reviews, 62*, 155–198.
Goldey, K. L., & van Anders, S. M. (2011). Sexy thoughts: Effects of sexual cognitions on testosterone, cortisol, and arousal in women. *Hormones and Behavior, 59*, 754–764.
Gundappa, A., & Rathod, P. B. (2012). Violence against women in India: Preventive measures. *Indian Streams Research Journal, 2*(4), 1–4.
Hagan, J., Gillis, A. R., & Simpson, J. (1985). The class structure of gender and delinquency: Toward a power-control theory of common delinquent behavior. *American Journal of Sociology, 90*, 1151–1178.
Heidensohn, F. (2010). The deviance of women: A critique and an inquiry. *The British Journal of Sociology, 61*(s1), 111–126.
Heirigs, M. H., & Moore, M. D. (2018). Gender inequality and homicide: A cross-national examination. *International Journal of Comparative and Applied Criminal Justice, 42*(4), 273–285.
Islam, M. J., Banarjee, S., & Khatun, N. (2014). Theories of female criminality: A criminological analysis. *International Journal of Criminology and Sociological Theory, 7*(1), 1–8.
Iyer, L., et al. (2012). The power of political voice: Women's political representation and crime in India. *American Economic Journal: Applied Economics, 4*(4), 165–193.
Jacobs, P. A., et al. (1965). Aggressive behavior, mental sub-normality and the XYY male. *Nature, 208*(5017), 1351–1352.
Joseph, M. G. C., et al. (2014). Asian passengers' safety study: The problem of sexual molestation of women on trains and buses in Chennai, India. *Acta Criminologica: Southern African Journal of Criminology, 27*(1), 57–74.
Kalokhe, A., et al. (2016). Domestic violence against women in India: A systematic review of a decade of quantitative studies. *Global Public Health, 12*(4), 498–513.
Koeppel, M. D. H., Rhineberger-Dunn, G. M., & Mack, K. Y. (2015). Cross-national homicide: A review of the current literature. *International Journal of Comparative and Applied Criminal Justice, 39*(1), 47–85.
Kumari, N. (2009). Socio Economic profile of women prisoners. *Language in India: Strength for Today and Bright Home for Tomorrow, 9*(2), 134–259.
Lelaurain, S., et al. (2018). Legitimizing intimate partner violence: The role of romantic love and the mediating effect of patriarchal ideologies. *Journal of Interpersonal Violence*, Advanced online publication, 886260518818427
Lloyd, A. (1995). *Doubly deviant, doubly damned: Society's treatment of violent women*. Penguin Books.
Lodha, P., et al. (2018). Incentives of female offenders in criminal behavior: An Indian perspective. *Violence and Gender, 5*(4), 202–208.
Loukaitou-Sideris, A., & Fink, C. (2008). Addressing women's fear of victimization in transportation settings: A survey of US transit agencies. *Urban Affairs Review, 44*(4), 554–587.
Madhurima, N. (2009). *Women crime and prisoners Life*. Deep and Deep Publishers.
Malik, J. S., & Nadda, A. (2019). A cross-sectional study of gender-based violence against men in the rural area of Haryana, India. *Indian Journal of Community Medicine: Official Publication of Indian Association of Preventive & Social Medicine, 44*(1), 35–38.

McCarthy, B., Hagan, J., & Woodward, T. S. (1999). In the company of women: Structure and agency in a revised power-control theory of gender and delinquency. *Criminology, 37*, 761–788.
McEwan, B. S., & Milner, T. A. (2017). Understanding the broad influence of sex hormones and sex differences in the brain. *Journal of Neuroscience Research, 95*, 24–39.
Mili, P. M. K., & Cherian, N. S. (2015). Female criminality in India: Prevalence, causes and preventive measures. *International Journal of CrimiNal Justice Sciences, 10*(1), 65–76.
Nadda, A., et al. (2018). Study of domestic violence among currently married females of Haryana India. *Indian Journal of Psychological Medicine, 40*(60), 534–539.
NCRB (2018). *Prison statistics India 2018*. Accessed May 15, 2020 from https://ncrb.gov.in//prison-statistics-india-2018 (online)
Nielsen, J., et al. (1973). A psychiatric-psychological study of patients with the XYY syndrome found outside of institutions. *Acta Psychiatrica Scandinavica, 49*(2), 159–168.
O'Donovan, R., & Völlm, B. (2018). Klinefelter's syndrome and sexual offending—A literature review. *Criminal Behaviour and Mental Health, 28*(2), 132–140.
Oxford, J., Ponzi, D., & Geary, D. C. (2010). Hormonal responses differ when playing violent video games against and ingroup and an outgroup. *Evolution and Human Behavior, 31*, 201–209.
Parker, K. F., & Reckdenwald, A. (2008). Women and crime in context: Examining the linkages between patriarchy and female offending across space. *Feminist Criminology, 3*(1), 5–24.
Pattanaik, J. K., & Mishra, N. N. (2001). Social change and female criminality in India. *Social Change, 31*(3), 103–110.
Peper, J. S., & Dahl, R. E. (2013). Surging hormones: Brain-Behavior interactions during puberty. *Current Directions in Psychological Science, 22*(2), 134–139.
Phadke, S. (2010). Gendered usage of public spaces: A case study of Mumbai. In: S. Pilot & L. Prabhu (Eds.), *The fear that stalks: Gender-Based violence in public spaces* (pp. 51–80). New Delhi, India: Zubaan.
Pollak, O. (1950). *The Criminality of Women*. A.S. Barnes.
Puts, D., Bailey, D. H., & Reno, P. L. (2016). Contest competition in men. In D. M. Buss (Ed.), *Handbook of evolutionary psychology* (2nd ed., pp. 385–402). Wiley.
Rudd, J. (2001). Dowry-murder. Women's Studies International Forum,*24*(5), 513–522.
Saxena, R. (1994). *Women and crime in India: A study in sociocultural dynamics*. South Asia Books.
Sharma, B. R. (1993). *Crime and women: A pscyho-diagnostic study of female criminality*. Indian Institute of Public Administration.
Sheldon, W. H., Hartl, E. M., & McDermott, E. (1949). *Varieties of delinquent youth. An introduction to constitutional psychiatry*. Harper and Brothers.
Simon, R. (1975). *Women and crime*. Lexington Books.
Smart, C. (1976) *Women, crime and criminology: A feminist critique*. London, UK: Routledge and Kegan Paul.
Spohn, C., & Beichner, D. (2000). Is preferential treatment of female offenders a thing of the past? A multisite study of gender, race, and imprisonment. *Criminal Justice Policy Review, 11*, 149–184.
Steffensmeier, D. (1980). Sex differences in patterns of adult crime, 1965–77: A review and assessment. *Social Forces, 58*, 1080–1108.
Steffensmeier, D., et al. (2005). An assessment of recent trends in girls' violence using diverse longitudinal sources: Is the gender gap closing? *Criminology, 43*, 355–406.
Steffensmeier, D., & Allan, E. (1996). Gender and crime: Toward a gendered theory of female offending. *Annual Review of Sociology, 22*(1), 459–487.
Stochholm, K., et al. (2012). Criminality in men with Klinefelter's syndrome and XYY syndrome: A cohort study. *BMJ Open, 2*(1), e000650.
Tripathi, K., Borrion, H., & Belur, J. (2017). Sexual harassment of students on public transport: An exploratory study in Lucknow, India. *Crime Prevention and Community Safety, 19*, 240–250.
Ugwu, J., & Britto, S. (2015). Perceptually contemporaneous offenses: Explaining the sex-fear paradox and the crimes that drive male and female fear. *Sociological Spectrum, 35*(1), 65–83.
van Anders, S. M. (2010). Chewing gum has large effects on salivary testosterone, estradiol, and secretory immunoglobulin A assays in women and men. *Psychoneuroendocrinology, 35*, 305–309.

van Anders, S. M., Tolman, R. M., & Volling, B. L. (2012). Baby cries and nurturance affect testosterone in men. *Hormones and Behavior, 61*, 31–36.

Visaria, L. (2000). Violence against women: A field study. *Economic & Political Weekly, 35*(20), 1742–1751.

Walby, S. (1990). *Theorizing Patriarchy*. B. Blackwell.

Warr, M. (1984). Fear of victimization: Why are women and the elderly more afraid? *Sociological Science Quarterly, 6*, 681–702.

Warr, M. (1985). Fear of rape among urban women. *Social Problems, 32*(3), 238–250.

Whaley, R. B., & Messner, S. F. (2002). Gender equality and gendered homicides. *Homicide Studies, 6*(3), 188–210.

WHO. (2013). *Global and regional estimates of violence against women: Prevalence and health effects of intimate partner violence and non-partner sexual violence*. WHO.

Chapter 8
Serial Killings in India: Case Studies and Profiling Strategies

S. A. Deepak

Abstract The phenomenon of serial killing was the basis of criminal profiling in the West, and till date, there exists extensive literature on serial killers of the West. Yet, there is very little scientific research in this area from the East or South East. This chapter therefore specifically focuses on the study of serial killers in India. A content analysis of media articles published in both print and online databases brought to light around one hundred incidents of serial killings reported in the last forty years in India. These numbers should be considered as a 'tip of the iceberg', if one takes into account the vast population of India and its significant differences in reporting of serial crime by the media. The analysis shows that there are frequent incidences of serial killings in most states, but research into this abysmal phenomenon is in its infancy in India. The chapter discusses certain key strategies of criminal psychology which have significant bearings on investigation of serial killing and adds to our understanding of serial killing as a concept based on the nature of multiple murderers in the Indian prisons. Findings from previous global literature lend some understanding of the types of serial killers, modus operandi, characteristics, and motivation for killing. This information is contextualized with three case studies on serial killers conducted in a first-of-its-kind study in India. The chapter further introspects the ill-preparedness of the Indian criminal justice system in dealing with serial killers and emphasizes the need to adequately equip itself in dealing with such cases in future.

Keywords Indian serial killers · Criminal profiling · Criminal psychology · Case studies · Investigation

8.1 Introduction

Serial killing is a recurring phenomenon in India, but most of the literature available on serial killers in India is fictional and inspired by a minuscule percentage of the facts. From the case of Thug Behram in the eighteenth century, who is believed to have killed more than 900 people, to the case of Yerukali Sreenu who is accused of

S. A. Deepak (✉)
D.D.G.D. Vaishnav College, Chennai, India

S. Sahni et al. (eds.), *Criminal Psychology and the Criminal Justice System in India and Beyond*, https://doi.org/10.1007/978-981-16-4570-9_8

murdering 17 women in Telangana, India witnessed many incidences of serial killings in the past (Dash, 2005; Pallavi, 2015; Serial, 2019). Despite these reports, there is no statistics available on the occurrence or deaths caused specifically under this category. 'Crime in India', the yearly publication from the National Crime Records Bureau (NCRB), brings the statistics of murders in broad categories that do not specifically mention serial killings. This classification, if provided, would be useful in understanding the frequency and enormity of the problem and thereby help police and social scientists in devising measures in crime control and prevention.

A search for reported incidents of serial killings in India during the last four decades in the media fetched around one hundred separate incidents of serial murders in India from 1980 to 2020. These numbers should be viewed as a tip of the iceberg since there are vast and varying differences in the reporting culture of media in Indian states. For instance, the search did not reveal any serial killing cases reported from Mizoram, Manipur, and Meghalaya, which may be due to an absence of such cases in the North-East or more likely poor reporting or investigation of such crimes in these states. Another state which did not fetch any reported incidents of serial killings is that of Jammu and Kashmir. Again, this could be due to the limited media activism in the state and the prevailing focus on geopolitical issues in these regions. Serial killing is a borderless phenomenon, and there is no credible reason to believe that it is not taking place in certain states. Yet, in the absence of any official statistics on this particular class of homicide, an analysis of media reports is the only feasible way to understand the frequency and phenomena of such crimes.

Most of the literature available on serial killers in India comes from fiction, inspired by a minuscule percentage of real facts. India has produced a plethora of serial killer movies, while the real research on the subject abjectly stutters. While the West has invested considerably in researching serial killing since the 1970s, there is still a lack of scientific endeavours in this area in India. This ignorance is affecting the way the criminal justice system deals with the issue of serial homicides. The law enforcement agencies are often baffled at the onset of serial killing incidents. The lack of any reasonable motive for committing the offence makes the investigation that much harder. The unlawful killing of a human being is a grave offence and attracts severe forms of punishment in all legal systems around the world. It is even more imperative that multiple murders, such as in serial killing, should merit more close attention in empirical research than abstention.

8.2 Defining Serial Killing

The most common and broad definition of a serial killer is a person who has committed a series of murders. But, defining the broad concepts which characterize such killings can be tricky. Most researchers agree that a serial killer is a person who has intermittently committed a series of murders on different occasions with an interval between the murders. The points on which contentions may arise as to when to brand a person as a serial killer are as follows:

1. The number of murders a person has to commit to qualify as a serial killer,
2. The length of the interval between the murders,
3. The modus operandi of the murderer,
4. Motive of the person to commit the murder.

In defining a concept, we aim to understand the fundamentals of what it constitutes by obscuring all the complexities and clarifying comparisons. Undoubtedly, a definition is something that is dynamic and evolves with time, perception, and understanding. In the case of defining a serial killer, these suppositions are absolute.

8.2.1 Serial Killer: A Kind of Murderer

We embark on understanding the categorization of a serial killer by comparing them to other kinds of murderers—single murderers, double murderers, triple murderers, mass murderers, and spree murderers—and examining how they are different from each other.

A single murderer is a person who murders one person in an incident. A double and triple murderer is a person who murders two or three people, respectively, in the same incident at the same place. A mass murderer is a person who murders more than three in the same incident at the same place. A spree murderer is a person who murders several people in different places at the same stretch of time. Sometimes, a serial killer could commit mass murder, or, like most instances in the history of multicide suggests, a spree killer could commit mass murder also.

One of the important characteristics of a serial killer which allows for the serial nature of the crime is the presence of a 'cooling-off-period' between the murders. Once a serial killer commits a murder, he retreats to normalcy and stays without committing another murder for a while. The persistent and unyielding instinct to commit murder, again and again, after an interval, is the defining characteristic of a serial killer.

Prisons have a significant population of convicted murderers who are co-offenders in homicides. They may be career criminals or members of organized criminal units. There is also a significant number of convicts accused of multiple murders committed because of political motivation or as act of terrorism. Can they be considered as serial killers? This question maybe a matter of further, careful introspection, but in a broader context, political motivation or terrorism falls into a different category.

8.3 Investigation and Identification Strategies

Serial killings are different from other kinds of murders in particulars of the characteristics of modus operandi. Key characteristics of *modus operandi*, such as purpose of killing, identification of victims, and victim–offender relationship, may vary in serial killings. These differences may also arise from the motivation for the murders. However, the variance in motive and mode pose some major challenges for the investigation, making it more difficult and stressful.

8.3.1 Case Linkage

Case linkage is the connection made between different homicide cases based on similarities in the characteristics of crimes, such as unique evidence characteristic, proximity of events or victims, and localization of the murders. If the investigating officers fail to make a connection between multiple murders committed by the same offender in different incidents or jurisdictions, they risk allocation of resources in the wrong direction, giving the offender more time in persisting to commit such murders. Due to this, case linkage should be considered as the first step in an investigation strategy in cases where similar characteristics of active serial killing are involved.

Sometimes, it is a pretty straightforward case for investigators to recognize the connection between different murder cases with striking resemblance in characteristics of crime such as victims' characteristics, method of killing, time of offence, nature of crime scene, and distance. In many cases, it requires more than just the smartness of an investigating officer to track a serial killer with minimum evidence, fluctuating characteristics, and a broad geographical scattering of serial killing incidents. There are many incidents of serial killings in which case linkage hardly ever takes place, either due to jurisdictional or timeline distances. In such cases, the incidents continue as separate investigations until they are linked upon the arrest and interrogation of the offender. This proves an utter need for close coordination between officers from different jurisdictions.

Pattern recognition involves rigorous analysis of similar murders in a particular geographical area over a prolonged period of time to discern any case linkage and will require teams of trained professionals as well as other resources and funding that most investigative agencies struggle to allocate.

8.3.2 Modus Operandi

Modus operandi is the careful analysis of various aspects of the method a perpetrator applies to commit murder. This is important for recognizing the connection between perceived randomness of related incidents. Human beings tend to repeat their way of doing thing in a manner which they have already tested and succeeded, and serial killers are no different. Given that even the most carefully planned murder can offer various risks, serial killers tend to commit murders using tested methods which have succeeded in past.

An offender's *modus operandi* includes both pre- and post-murder behaviour. Pre-murder behaviour includes aspects such as scanning the scene, staking the victim(s), gathering weapons and other accessories, and deciding on victim-deception strategy. For example, 'Ripper Jayanandan', a serial murderer from Kerala, used to study his crime scenes for several days before he actually committed the murders. Once he identified his target families, he would carefully scope and study the routine and other relevant logistics of the inmates and house layouts before attack.

Most serial killers engage in elaborate inspection of victims or crime scenes before they engage the victims (Deepak & Ramdoss, 2020). 'Dupatta Serial Killer' from Goa who strangulated several women and 'Cyanide Mohan' who poisoned several women to death in Karnataka also had elaborate victim-deception strategies, including romantic relationships and gaining confidence of the victims with proposals for marriage, an elaborate ruse which sometimes lasted for several months (Mahanand spills, 2009; Siddiqui, 2020).

Post-murder behaviour involves aspects such as treatment of the corpse, evidence destruction, robbery, loot management, and staging. 'Killer Kuppusamy' from Tamil Nadu who is accused of murdering more than ten women used to engage in necrophilia. Both Kuppusamy and serial killer Ramesh from Tamil Nadu looted the gold ornaments of women they had murdered and sold it to fund their lifestyle of alcoholism and other expenses during their murder span (Deepak & Ramdoss, 2020).

There are a wide range of other aspects which need careful attention of the investigation team such as an offender's choice of victim, crime scene, time, location, weapon, and injury. Serial killing, regardless of motivation, is a hard act to keep up, and killers tend to rely on already tried and tested methods. That being said, a serial killer may gradually update their *modus operandi* by learning from the aspects of each murder or when faced with new challenges. There are many serial killers who alter their *modus operandi* depending upon the situation or to deceive investigators. Investigators also need to keep in mind variance in aspects of the *modus operandi* when trying to establish a connection between cases.

Signature is another concept which is closely associated with *modus operandi* of serial killers. Signature is explained as a ritual performed by a perpetrator at the crime scene as a part of the act or after, something which is not necessary for the execution of the murder but is done for the killer's whim and mental satisfaction (Douglas & Olshaker, 2019). Some researchers believe that although *modus operandi* can change over a period, signatures are more consistent and can be an essential clue in connecting murders. However, signature may not be present or identifiable for every serial killing, whereas *modus operandi* is more or less the same for all murders.

8.3.3 Criminal Profiling

Criminal profiling is the careful construction of the profile of an unknown offender through careful analysis of all information pertaining to the crime. The Federal Bureau of Investigation (FBI) attempted to classify violent offender's personality based on the scene behaviour, and this is believed to be the foundations of criminal profiling (Canter & Wentink, 2004). All investigators form a profile during investigation, even a vague one, to narrow down the personality of the offender. But such profiling is most effective if it is done by experienced criminal psychologists who are trained to understand criminal minds. An area of concern in criminal profiling is 'false positives and false negatives'. False positive occurs when investigators arrest an innocent person because of his resemblance with the profile, and false negative happens when the real offender escapes detection because of differences with the profile. There are many successful incidents of offenders being identified by profiles made by experts and many cases where profiling misled investigations. The best that one can do is to ensure that the criminal profile is constructed by someone with considerable knowledge in the subject area, and even then, profiles should not be viewed as conclusive, but only an investigation tool, to assist in combination with other strategies of investigation.

Investigating serial killing in India is not an easy task, with its large population, understaffed and inexperienced police forces, and lack of collated databases and proper coordination. In India, police are not provided with enough resources for a full-fledged investigation on a large scale, as serial killing cases would demand. There are also no permanent roles in most states and union territories for experts who work in this area. The role of forensic evidence in establishing connections between crime scenes is crucial in establishing linkage even when there are significant differences between various aspects of the cases. For this to happen, there should be effective coordination between multiple forensic science units, proper collection and management of evidence from all scenes, speedy examination and reporting, and a consolidated database that is accessible to forensic scientists and expert investigators across state borders. These require monumental upheavals and improvement to the current operations within the system. While the good work done by some brilliant investigators has resulted in apprehension of some serial killers, one may assume that for every offender captured, there are many other serial killers who skip detection and remain active.

Despite several studies on serial killing done internationally since the 1980s, the research into serial killing in India is in its infancy. There is a dearth of research-grade literature on serial killings, its causative factors, and characteristics from the Indian perspective.

8.4 Classification of Serial Killers

There have been initial attempts at classifying serial killers into different categories considering factors such as motivation, *modus operandi,* and other characteristics. Some classifications were developed as an aid for police investigations, while others were developed to understand the motive, victim–offender relationships, and other factors. Perhaps the most popular classification of serial killers is the one given by the FBI.

The FBI in 1986 classified serial killers into 'organized' and 'disorganized', mainly based on the crime scene behaviour of the offender (Ressler et al., 1986). As per this classification, the organized offender is described as leading an orderly life which is also reflected in the way he commits his crimes and that the disorganized offenders will reflect an overall sense of disorder and suggests little or no preplanning of the murder. This categorization has come into some critique recently for being overtly simplistic. Dietz (1986) constructed a typology which divided multiple murderers into five categories such as psychopathic sexual sadists, crime spree killers, organized crime functionaries, custodial killers, and psychotic killers. Holmes and De Burger (1988) classified serial killers into four categories such as 'the visionary motive serial murderer', 'the mission-oriented motive serial murderer', 'the hedonistic motive serial murderer', and 'the power/control-oriented motive serial murderer'. As an expansion of this work, Holmes and Holmes (2009) added another category to the hedonistic type naming it as the 'comfort killers'. Rappaport's (1988) typology describes serial killers into four types—sexual sadists, delusional killers, custodial killers, and utilitarian killers. In 1991, Barrett combined Holmes and De Burger's typology and the FBI's system for classifying serial rapists to form a new classification (Rossmo, 1987). Alan Fox and Jack Levin in 1995 proposed a modified Holmes and De Burger typology (Villalabos, 2005).

Most of these typologies work to understand the types of serial killers arrested and studied. In reality, many serial killers will not fit one type and may also exhibit the characteristics of multiple typologies. This is why there is a persistent need to update specific classifications of serial killers for a better understanding of the concept. Beers (2012) observed that 'our understanding of the phenomenon of serial murder is still limited and without extensive further research, typologies only cannot be said to provide any empirically valid or substantiated insight' (P. 21). Though these typologies are not effective in classifying every serial killer, the theories provide with interesting insights into the various concepts that explain a serial killer's action. While some of the popular studies classify these murderers according to the *modus operandi*, many others used motivation and other characteristics as the key element on which to distinguish.

8.4.1 Characteristics of Serial Killers

Holmes and De Burgers (1988) claimed that serial killers mostly choose strangers as victims and in most cases, there is a sexual element to the homicides. Keeney and Heide (1994) found some interesting differences in the characteristics of serial killers based on their genders; there were more differences than similarities between male and female serial killers. Similar findings were shared by Gavin (2015) after analysis of female serial killers. Canter (2004) underlined how similar a serial killer might appear to a normal individual in his social life. In her study of homicidal nurses, Field (2007) insisted that it is difficult to put serial killers into one-size-fits-all profile as it involves a diverse population of individuals. However, Mouzos and West (2007) found that the majority of the serial killers tend to be men, and the majority of their victims are almost always females.

8.4.2 *Modus Operandi*

Gransbury (2014), who studied black widows, found that most of them used poison to murder their victims. However, Myers et al. (2005) studied the case of Aileen Wuornos and found her *modus operandi* was similar to many male serial killers. Hickey (2013) proffered that most serial killers beat, stab, strangle, or torture their victims to death and only some victims are poisoned or shot. Mouzos and West (2007) also found that most serial killers used stabbing and strangulation, and in almost all the cases, the victims were abducted or killed at outdoor locations. Kim and Egger (2004) proposed the idea that a serial killer chooses a victim depending on the symbolic value they assign on their victims. Pinto and Wilson (1990) found that strangulation was the most common method used by serial killers to murder their victims, with stabbing and shooting following closely. Douglas and Munn (1992) emphasized on concepts such as signature and staging.

A brief analysis of the research on serial killing has revealed the existence of diversity among serial killers, the many different circumstances serial killing can take place, the various methods serial killers may adopt for committing murders, and most importantly, an array of factors causing serial killings.

8.5 Case Studies on Indian Serial Killers

Profiles and summaries of case studies of three Indian serial killers are drawn from a first-of-its-kind research on serial killers in Kerala and Tamil Nadu. The focus of the discussion is on the various aspects of their *modus operandi* (Deepak, 2016).

8.5.1 *Sebastian*

Sebastian (born 1981) aka Cheviathan Sebastian was an illiterate, single man who murdered more than four people between 1996 and 2005, in Thiruvananthapuram district of Kerala and Kanyakumari district of Tamil Nadu. The murders were characterized by kidnapping, paedophilia, strangulation, and robbery. His known victims were pre-pubescent girls within the age group of one to seven years.

Modus Operandi: The subject chose fishermen villages to commit the murders. Once he entered a village, he earned the trust of the villagers acting as a fisherman, while he searched for young pre-pubescent girls to sexually assault. He attacked his victims during the night. The subject kidnapped little girls from poorly built homes and sexually assaulted them in secluded locations, after which he strangled the victims, stole their ornaments, and threw away their bodies in the water after the assault. The subject would move on to a new village once he became aware that the villagers suspected him. On some occasions, the subject also had sex with his victims after murdering them. Except in the first case, where he dumped the body under a railway bridge, he dumped all his other victims in water bodies. The subject's victims were girls in the age group of one to seven years old, hailing from financially poor families. Only one of his murdered victims belonged to a migrant worker group from Tamil Nadu, while the rest were from fishing families. In one instance, subject used a towel to strangulate the victim. In the remaining cases, the victims died while he sexually assaulted them or were suffocated to suppress cries while he raped them. Because his victims were young children who were physically weaker than him, there was no specific weapon used in the murders. The subject had no proper place to stay in the village, giving him no private space to keep his victims. In the first crime scene, the subject was in search of a secluded location to rape the victim without any interference, and the railway underbridge was the nearest spot available. The other crime scenes included churches, where he committed one murder and nearly killed another. Big abandoned buildings with a lot of empty spaces served as a perfect spot for him to commit the offences. Two of the crime scenes were also at secluded locations on the beach.

8.5.2 Navas

Navas (born 1966), aka Motta Navas, was a single man, a primary school dropout, who had committed five murders in a span of 77 days from June to August 2012 in Kollam district of Kerala. Most of his victims were beggars and homeless petty workers who were bludgeoned and robbed as they slept at night in public places.

Modus Operandi: The subject roamed the streets as a rag picker during the daytime. He went to sleep early in Nehru Park of Kollam city and woke up late at night when most others in the city slept. He roamed the streets looking for potential victims sleeping on the streets. He would go through the pocket of his victims, and if they woke up and resisted, he would beat them to death with heavy stones or building blocks. The subject mostly robbed the victims of petty amounts, *beedi* (local cigarette), *ganja* (weed), etc.. If a police patrolling vehicle stopped him while he was roaming at night, he would fake mental disability by singing and dancing ridiculously and abusing them. Assuming him to be mentally ill, policemen would leave him alone. All his victims were beggars, homeless people, and poor labourers who slept on the streets. The victim's age ranged from 40 to 65, and most of them were old and defenceless, under the influence of alcohol or *ganja*. He never made any attempts to hide the bodies of his victims. The subject moved around on foot and targeted those areas in the neighbourhood where he could reach by walking. This explained the relatively small stretch of the area in the Kollam city of Kerala within which the murders were committed—a four-kilometre stretch in the city—and why the crime scenes were closer to the main road and the highway.

8.5.3 Killer Kuppusamy

Kuppusamy (born in 1973), aka Killer Kuppusamy, was a high school dropout who was married with no children at the time of the crime. From April to July 2009, he had committed more than 20 murders in a span of 85 days in Pudukkottai, Sivaganga, Dindigul, and Trichy districts of Tamil Nadu. His murders included rape, strangulation, necrophilia, and robbery, and his victims were women aged 18–70.

Modus Operandi: The subject would ride his two-wheeler, in a drunken state, through the deserted regions around his village, looking for lonely herdswomen. After zeroing in on potential victims, he followed them to secluded locations or waited until he figured out a spot where he could attack them. He used rope to strangulate his victims and raped them while they were struggling for life. The subject performed necrophilia on his victims in most of the cases. The subject threw away the ropes at the crime scene itself, along with the body, and bought a new one for the next murder. Only when the bodies of the victims were likely to be noticed easily by passers-by did he made some effort to hide it or drag it away to an obscure spot. All murders were committed between ten in the mornings to six in the evening. After killing, he would return to his village. He would sell the ornaments he had robbed from his victims at the same shop, either on the same day or within the next few days of the killings. Most of the money he obtained from this was spent towards drinking and gambling. The victims were from a wide range of age group, the youngest was 19-year-old, and the eldest was 70-year-old. The majority of them were herdswomen and women collecting wood or grass on government lands. The subject chose the victims primarily with the intent to assault them sexually, and in all cases, the victims were women to whom he was sexually attracted. His murder span lasted for two months and 24 days, during which time he is believed to have committed more than 20 murders. On an average, this means he committed a murder once every five days. Kuppusamy committed all his murders in the remote, deserted regions of Pudukkottai, Sivaganga, Namakkal, and Trichy districts of Tamil Nadu. These districts have many areas which are less populated and contain miles of unused lands with bushes and trees. There are many roads and paths where one can travel in the middle of the day for kilometres without seeing a single human being. The women folk he targeted happened to venture into these lands to graze cattle, get water or wood, and cut grass.

8.6 Comments on Serial Killing in India

The search for incidents of serial killings in India brought forth only a hundred cases of serial killings in the last forty years, assuming the real numbers to be even higher.

In the absence of official statistics, the frequency of serial killings cannot be established. The paucity of local research on serial killing in India is affecting the way the criminal justice system responds to such violent offenders. There are limitations in the application of western research on serial killers in the Indian scenario due to its vast social, political, cultural, economic, and geographical differences. The motivation, characteristics, and *modus operandi* of Indian serial killers can be significantly different from those in the West. Only by conducting rigorous local studies of such individuals will we be able to gain an in-depth understanding of Indian serial killers.

There are certain investigation strategies such as case linkage, modus operandi analysis, and criminal profiling, which can be utilized to improve investigation and identification of serial killers. For this to happen, there needs to be effective coordination between police all over India, which is presently lacking. There is an imminent need for improving the role of specialists like forensic scientists, criminal psychologists, and criminologists in the criminal justice system to deal with violent offenders. Their services can be utilized in legislation, investigation, and judicial sentencing and corrections. The insights thus gained can be utilized in future to devise effective strategies to improve the way we deal with such violent offenders.

References

Beers, E. D. (2012). Neat, plausible, and wrong: Examining the limitations of typologies in the study and investigation of serial murder. *Internet Journal of Criminology*. Retrieved from http://www.internetjournalofcriminology.com/dryerbeers_examining_the_limitations_of_typologies_in_the_study_and_investigation_of_serial_murder_ijc_july_2012.pdf

Canter, D. V. (2004). An empirical test of holmes and holmes serial murder typology. *Criminal Justice and Behavior, 31*(4), 489–515.

Canter, D., & Wentink, N. (2004). An empirical test of holmes and holmes's serial murder typology. *Criminal Justice and Behavior, 31*(4), 489–515. Retrieved from http://dx.doi.org/10.1177/0093854804265179

Dash, M. (2005). *Thug: The true story of India's murderous cult*. Granta Books.

Deepak, S. A. (2016). *Motivation for serial killing: Case studies on serial killers from Kerala and Tamil Nadu* (Ph.D).

Deepak, S. A., & Ramdoss, S. (2020). The unfathomable lives: Biographies of Indian serial killers.

Dietz, P. E. (1986). Mass, serial, and sensational homicides. *Bulletin of the New York Academy of Medicine, 64*, 477–491.

Douglas, J. E., & Munn, C. (1992). Violent crime scene analysis: Modus operandi, signature, and staging. Retrieved from https://www.ncjrs.gov/pdffiles1/Digitization/134597NCJRS.pdf

Douglas, J.E., & Olshaker, M. (2019). The killer across the table. Amazon

Field, J. (2007). *Caring to death: A discursive analysis of nurses who murder patients* (Ph.D.). The University of Adelaide.

Gavin, H. (2015). Female aggression. MA, USA: Wiley Blackwell.

Gransbury, A. (2014). Scamming black widow killers: Investigating a weirdly unexplored type of romance scam. *Internet Journal of Criminology*. Retrieved from http://www.internetjournalofcriminology.com/Gransbury_Scamming_Black_Widow_Killers_IJC_July_2014.pdf

Hickey, E. W. (2013). *Serial murderers and their victims. Wadsworth.* USA.

Holmes, R. M., & De Burger, J. (1988). *Serial murder*. Sage.

Holmes, R. M., & Holmes, S. T. (2009). *Serial murder* (3rd ed.). Sage.

Keeney, B. T., & Heide, K. M. (1994). Gender differences in serial murderers: A preliminary analysis. *Journal of Interpersonal Violence, 9*(3), 383–398. https://doi.org/10.1177/088626094009003007

Kim, & Egger, S. (2004). Victims of serial killers: The "Less-Dead". In M. S. Judith & M. Jack (Eds.), *Victimology: A study of crime victims and their roles* (pp. 09–32). Pearson Custom Publishing.

Mahanand spills more beans confesses killing Keri, Davorlim women (2009, May 28). Herald. Retrieved from https://www.heraldgoa.in/details.php?n_id=28295

Mouzos, J., & West, D. (2007). An examination of serial murder in Australia. *Trends & issues in crime and criminal justice*, 346.

Myres, W. C., Gooch, E., & Meloy, J. R. (2005). The role of psychopathy and sexuality in a female serial killer. *Journal of Forensic Science, 50*(3). Retrieved from https://www.ncbi.nlm.nih.gov/pubmed/15932102

Pallavi, S. (2015, July 21). Delhi serial killer held for murdering children, Necrophilia. *One India.* Retrieved from http://www.oneindia.com/india/delhi-serial-killer-held-for-murdering-children-necrophilia-1811462.html

Pinto, S., & Wilson, P. R. (1990). Serial murder. *Trends & issues in crime and criminal justice. Australian Institute of Criminology.* Retrieved from http://www.aic.gov.au/media_library/publications/tandi_pdf/tandi025.pdf

Rappaport, R. G. (1988). The serial and mass murder: Patterns, differentiation, pathology. *American Journal of Forensic Psychiatry, 9*, 39–48.

Ressler, R. K., Burgess, A. W., Douglas, J. E., Hartman, C. R., & D'Agostino, R. B. (1986). Sexual killers and their victims: Identifying patterns through crime scene analysis. *Journal of Interpersonal Violence., 1*(3), 288–308.

Rossmo, D. K. (1987). *Geographic Profiling: Target Patterns of Serial Murderers* (Ph.D.). Retrieved from http:C:Users/Dell/Downloads/b17675819%20(2).pdf.

Serial killer with 17 murders to his name in Telangana police net (2019, December 28). *Times of India.* Retrieved from https://timesofindia.indiatimes.com/city/Hyderabad/serial-killer-with-17-murders-to-his-name-in-t-police-net/articleshow/73001645.cms

Siddiqui, I. (2020, July 02). Prof Mohan Kumar, the man who killed 20 women with 'anti-pregnancy' Pill. Retrieved from https://bangaloremirror.indiatimes.com/bangalore/cover-story/prof-mohan-kumar-the-man-who-killed-20-women-with-anti-pregnancy-pills/articleshow/54758093.cms

Villalobos, T. (2005, November 10). Criminology: Typologies of serial killers (Web log post). Retrieved from http://moz333.blogspot.in/2005/11/criminology-typologies-of-serial.Html

Chapter 9
Perspectives on Internet-Based Crimes

Sweta Lakhani

Abstract With the advancement of technology and globalization, the natures of crime and criminals have also evolved. The recent surge in Internet-based crimes such as identity theft, financial fraud, money laundering, and piracy is the work of a different kind of criminal—more intelligent, less belligerent—than those studied up till now. This global criminality almost always exists in the virtual world and can cause huge losses to organizations as well as individuals. Even as we struggle to catch up with their modus operandi, the crimes and criminals continue to change and evolve. This chapter highlights the internet-based criminal profile and socio-psychological factors contributing to it. Furthermore, it has been noticed that technology laws struggle to meet the needs of the advancing digital world. The chapter observes that there is a significant need to introduce awareness programmes and policies that serve as a deterrent against such criminal tendencies. While there is undeniably more research to be done before we are able to consolidate a criminological profile for these crimes, this chapter will summarize the foundational indicators of this new criminal.

Keywords Cybercrime · Psychosocial · Behavioural · Cultural factors and law

9.1 Introduction

The Internet has brought great enhancement in the quality of life for everyone around the world. However, the fastest growing area of technological development has also become a salient issue in legal, economic, and political milieu (The World Information Society Report, 2007). Cyberspace has provided shelter to many criminal minds that hide and operate from behind their computers (Adler & Adler, 2006). With easy access to the internet, they can now commit crimes anonymously (Wall, 2005). Hence, e-security has become an issue of global importance and concern now.

In brief, 'Internet-based crimes' or 'online crimes' also popularly known as cybercrimes are crimes that cover all the criminal or illegal activities on computers or the

S. Lakhani (✉)
Jindal Global Law School, O. P. Jindal Global University, Sonipat, India
e-mail: slakhani@jgu.edu.in

S. Sahni et al. (eds.), *Criminal Psychology and the Criminal Justice System in India and Beyond*, https://doi.org/10.1007/978-981-16-4570-9_9

inter-web (Srivastava, 2012). According to Merriam Webster (2019), cybercrime is 'any criminal activity committed using a computer, especially to illegally access, transmit, or manipulate data'. Kshetri (2010) defined cybercrime as 'a criminal activity in which computers or computer networks are the principal means of committing an offence or violating laws, rules, or regulations'. Many of the reports have also categorized cybercrime into different categories to further define the kind of criminal activities that fall under its purview. The US Department of Justice has the following categories regarding cybercrimes, where:

a. The other computing device is targeted.
b. The device is used as weapon for committing the crime.
c. The device is used as an accessory to a crime.

With the phenomenal advancements in internet technology, today a cyber-criminal can achieve more with the click of mouse than with bombs; bytes are more lethal, dangerous, and disastrous than bullets in this information age. The purpose and motive of cybercrimes differ from case to case, crime to crime. While financial gain is the predominant one, theft of sensitive information is assuming huge proportions. In their quest for accessing privileged information, privacy is violated with impunity. Financial gain is achieved through stolen information violating privacy of individuals and their electronic assets (Bajpai, 2011).

The growing legions of violent cybercrimes such as cyber-terrorism, cyber-stalking, and cyber-bullying; and nonviolent cybercrimes like cyber-theft and cyber-frauds are a huge challenge to users, IT security professionals and cyber-cops. Rather than mere detection of cybercrimes, the real challenges lie in the prevention of such acts and taking appropriate reaction to them (Ainsworth, 2001). Therefore, digital technology that thrives on access to information also becomes the means to generate new tools for unauthorized use of the works. This rapid growth in the digital world and the subsequently increasing lag between technology and legal framework has been cited as a major factor in hindering the containment of the cybercrime problem. The swiftness of technology almost always exceeds the evolution of legal frameworks by many folds, thereby providing an upper hand to such faceless criminals. Overall, the concept of cyber-security is too technical in nature and understanding the nuances and consequences can be difficult for those with no background in this discipline.

Much research in this area focuses on the modalities of the crime and the aspect of security available in that context. In order to implement a holistic crime prevention approach towards cybercrime, there needs to be a balance in implementing policies including technology, law, and behavioural science. Criminologists and legislators studying online crime have noticed that it is a wholly different phenomenon than street crime or physical crime (Morris & Higgins, 2010). More often, crimes like online piracy do not face social stigma; so individuals are often unaware that they are indulging in criminal activity (Hsu & Shiue, 2008). It is also been seen that public awareness about laws against cybercrime, at large, does not deter such activities (Hsu & Shiue, 2008) unless the behaviour is socially unacceptable (Tunberg, 2004). Change their perception and attitude of people leads to consequent behavioural changes that meet the existing value system of society (Baron et al., 1984). When people's perception does not meet societal norms and values, there is a greater tendency for people to change their own value system accordingly. Hence, social acceptance is positively correlated with leniency when it comes to online crimes (Givon et al., 1985).

9.2 Behavioural Theories

The growth of information technology is increasing rapidly, becoming the most pervasive form of communication in the history of mankind and virtual anonymity has contributed highly to criminally active experiences in the online world. Data from the National Crime Records Bureau, Ministry of Home Affairs, India, suggests that in 2013, 'incidence of cybercrimes (as per the Information Technology Act and Indian Penal Code) had increased by 63.7% as compared to 2012 (from 3477 cases in 2012 to 5693 cases in 2013)'. The increase in the number of cybercrimes is concerning and shows that cyber-security is a real threat in the years to come.

The cyber-criminal is different—more intelligent, less belligerent—than those studied up till now. The chances of detection, apprehension, and prosecution over Internet are exponentially scarce. Studies have shown that online crime generates less outrage in people than physical theft (Zhang et al., 2009). While economic factors may count towards some reason for offenders to justify their actions, it is not the sole influencer of cybercrimes. The digital world offers an ethical filter between the criminal and society, creating psychological distance. Husted (2000) demonstrated that cultural variables such as power, distance, individualism, masculinity, and uncertain avoidance (the extent to which members of a culture feel threatened by uncertain and unknown situations) determine the rate of online crime in a region. The researchers in the field have formulated and explained various psychosocial, behavioural, and cultural theories that lead to criminal behaviour. Some of these theories can be linked with Internet crime behaviour.

Space Transition Theory Jaishankar (2008) has explained the concept of exploring the behaviour of a person in a physical and virtual space. He posits that the movement of a person from the physical world to cyberspace changes their actions, as well behaviour, towards others.

Neutralization and Justification It has been observed, in various studies, that the one committing illegal activities are quite aware of the repercussions of their act, yet they continue to indulge in the same by 'neutralizing' their guilt and justifying their actions. Neutralization techniques work in the following ways: deny responsibility ('it is not my fault'), deny injury ('no harm will result from my actions'), deny victimization ('nobody got hurt'), condemn those who judge ('how dare they judge me, as if they have never done so before'), and appeal to higher loyalties ('there is a greater and higher cause') (Sykes & Matza, 1957). According to some researchers, neutralization technique is more prevalent in organizational and white-collar crime where individuals excuse their criminal behaviour especially because they form a minority of those indulging in deviant behaviours (Maruna & Copes, 2005). Ingram and Hinduja (2008) proposed that neutralization offers a significant way to understand piracy. In a study, 90% of college participants believed that downloading music illegally is acceptable, citing a number of neutralization-based justifications for their behaviour (Ingram & Hinduja, 2008). The findings from a study involving 34 persistent pirates was that denial of responsibility was a common neutralizing technique (Halt & Copes, 2010).

Deviant Act and Behaviour An individual is more likely to offend if they are certain of not being penalized for it or of being identified as the doer. Also, less severe penalty for the act means that they will reoffend again, even if there is a chance that they will be identified. Therefore, severity and certainty of punishment do play an important role in offending and reoffending. The same was observed by various theorists in many studies (Higging et al., 2005; Peace et al., 2003; Hsu & Shiue, 2008; Hill, 2007; Limayem et al., 2004; Tan, 2002). According to Gottfredson (1987), the connection between deviant peer association and deviant behaviour is 'that people acquire the propensity to delinquency, find delinquent friends, and then commit delinquent acts, including serious criminal acts'.

Moral Beliefs and Justification An individual's actions is highly dependent on their moral beliefs; the sense of morality against wrong actions may prevent a person from contributing to an illegal act. Or, in other words, does holding high moral beliefs constrain themselves from indulging in deviant acts? In various studies conducted by Swinyard et al. (1990), Christensen and Eining (1991), and Tan (2002), it was concluded that ethical attitude negatively contributed to piracy rate. Most people would not steal something that did not belong to them (Loughlan, 2007). However, those committing software piracy was stealing someone else's property, but since this activity does not involve a physical product being lifted from a store, people tend not to consider it to be illegal. Also, in most cases, stealing someone's identity or work was not considered to be an act of theft at all, since there was no physical removal of items involved. This illustrates the 'morality gap' that people associated with crimes that are likely to take place online.

Moral Development The moral judgement of individuals towards internet-based crime can be understood by Kohlberg's three stages of moral development. The idea behind this theory is that when individuals grow intellectually, they also tend to grow morally (Fig. 9.1).

It has been established that individuals with lower ethical predispositions are more likely to get involved in such digital crimes that may include online bullying or financial frauds (Loughlan, 2007). For them, individual interest outweighs the moral issue in question (Konstantakis, 2010).

Social Learning Theory Akers (2011) postulates that association with like-minded people fosters learned behaviours, even criminal. In a social environment made of

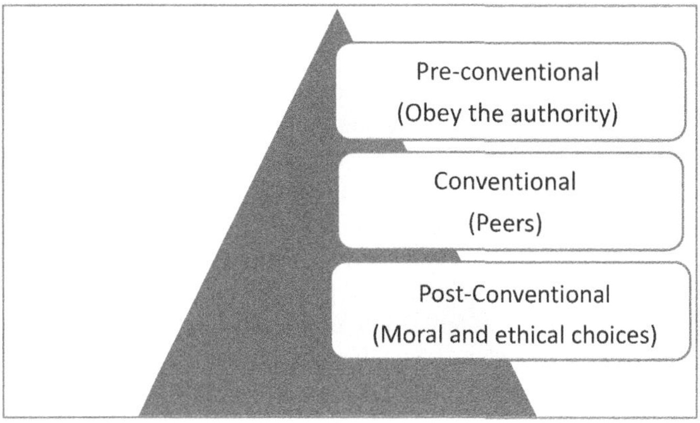

Fig. 9.1 Kohlberg's theory of moral development (1971)

people inclined to criminality, one may imitate and follow their peers. Any stimuli that reinforce deviant behaviour will only perpetuate it further. Akers also states that a person's models of behaviour, the presence of a conducive or aversive environment to crime commission, and 'differential reinforcement' influence the relationship between individual and social processes (Akers & Lee, 1996). Numerous scholarship present social learning theory as an appropriate framework to understand deviant online behaviour (Higgins & Wilson, 2006). In a survey involving 2000 university students, it has been suggested that deviancy can be predicted by the influence of both online media sources (chat rooms) and peers, explained by offline (friends, acquaintances, group discussion), and online communication (email, chat rooms, instant messaging programme) (Hinduja & Ingram, 2009).

Cultural and Religious Beliefs People within collectivist societies belong to 'in-groups' that take care of them in exchange for their loyalty to the group (Husted, 2000). Along the same lines, the behaviour amongst youth is also a result of the cultural factors and peer influences. Most cases of online bullying result from peer pressure. In a very recent experimental study conducted by Sulaiman and Rouibah (2009), it was observed that religious factors played a major role in de-incentivizing individuals from indulging in piracy. In the experiment, a group of religious people were informed that digital piracy is forbidden under their religious laws. Post the announcement, the number of cases of digital piracy within that group fell substantially.

9.3 Legal Challenges

In order to effectively deal with the cyber-issues, we have to not only understand the psychological motivations behind the culprits but also design implementable legal measures that incorporate this understanding. Legal response and policy should consider all stakeholders and participants operating in the network to prove effective.

One of the key issues in implementing cyber-reforms is that jurisdiction in cyberspace can realistically include several nations and hence carrying out and coordinating investigations of such crimes pose difficulties. Handling cyber-offence mainly relates to the scientific applications of crime but on the legal front, instruments to develop legal maturity and evolving effective ways to implement the existing laws still leaves a lot to be desired. Secondly, the variety of criminal activity which can be committed with or against information systems is surprisingly diverse. The systems are either instruments and/or targets of crime, and addressing the problems at all levels is intensive on resources, skills, and time (Kaushik & Chandra, 2009).

The need for preventive measures in the field of computer/data security is globally acknowledged, as we see a steady increase in the growth rate of computer crimes worldwide in the range of ~12–15%. Legal response to cybercrime in India has not been very effective as there is no agreed-upon policy addressing cyber-concerns. The Information Technology Act, 2000, is the only law on the issues of cybercrimes. However, this legislation is mostly meant to address matters relating to the regulation of electronic commerce and is not essentially equipped to work as a criminal law exclusively dealing with cyber-offences. In the Indian context, amendments in the Criminal Procedure Code, Indian Penal Code, Indian Evidence Act, Banker's Book Evidence Act, and Copyrights Acts have been made but more definitive and comprehensive legislations are needed to deal with cyber-crimes. One example could be the need for legislations on the lines of the European Data Protection Act for protection of personal data.

9.4 Third-Party Liabilities and Role in Law Enforcement

One of the major factors that have fuelled the growth of cybercrime is the availability of untraceable peer-to-peer networks and Internet connections at low costs, especially in countries like India, which have emerged to be the biggest hub of such activities.

The FBI, in collaboration with third-party entities such as online marketplaces, payment service providers, and advertisers, has expanded their efforts to prevent the activities of criminals. Third-party marketplaces offer competitive pricing and a sense of security to draw consumers to their sites, but criminal counterfeiters exploit these online marketplaces to gain an appearance of legitimacy, access to far-reaching advertising, and efficient sales transactions. Additionally, payment service providers (credit card payment processors, alternative payment methods) also give counterfeiters the false appearance of authenticity in terms of payment options, which may be mistakenly interpreted by consumers to enforce legitimacy. Further, criminals exploit online advertising as an additional revenue stream by attracting traffic to sites offering counterfeit products for sale or pirated digital content for download.

Working with third-party entities helps the investigation agencies' gain realistic awareness of the issue, gather information about and study latest crime trends, obtain investigative leads and collect evidence of criminal activity (Federal Bureau of Investigation, 2017). Internet Service Providers and search engines are now being tracked down in order to curb such crimes. Mike Weatherley, Intellectual Property Advisor to the Prime Minister of the UK, has stated that as the main provider of search facilities in the UK, it is widely felt that Google should take the lead in setting responsible industry standards (Guardian, 2014). The concern was that big players like Google have not taken adequate measures even after promising to do so (Guardian, 2010).

Researchers have concluded that efforts to encourage ethical behaviour should include training in ethical analysis and an enforcement of organizational code of ethics "since these measures exhibit the properties of public goods (efforts by one company can help all the other players), appropriate policy initiatives (consortium formation, public intervention, etc.) may be necessary for implementation" (Gopal et al., 2004).

9.5 Conclusion

One of the most logical ways to combat cybercrime is to spread awareness, via advertising campaigns and educational initiatives, about the illegality and consequences of the crime, expecting a deterring effect on the masses (Gopal et al., 2004). Several studies conducted in this area show that educational, legal, and media campaigns have achieved deterrent controls or back-end controls (Gopal et al., 2004). Deterrent controls include government-to-government negotiations, educational campaigns, and legal activity related to expanding or enforcing laws is focused on using legal sanctions to reduce crime. Supplement computer education in schools and colleges with Internet ethics might be an effective channel to ingrain good practices and make this a part of their discourse. This would consequently have a positive impact on peer association. Further, including ethics modules at introductory level in information technology courses, followed by frequent oral and written reminders can influence one's conscience and guide them in acceptable computer and network usage, in short, strategies that enhance moral misgivings and sensitize society should be employed (Ingram & Hinduja, 2008).

In case of music piracy, peer norms did influence future intentions to pirate, especially when there was little threat of punishment (Wingrove et al., 2011). Facilitating only authorized downloading within university settings can help stop rampant piracy. According to social learning theory, the same learned behaviour, operating within different social structure, interaction, and situation, produces both conforming and deviant behaviour. To a greater extent, the conforming behaviour is more apparent as being favoured. In simpler words, humans adapt their behaviour to their external stimuli and environment. When a university instils academic integrity and binds their students by a fair-use policy on the Internet, sooner or later the students will adapt and conform to an anti-piracy attitude. Thus, the social learning not only changes the nature of peer association to a positive influence but also assimilates an attitude that discourages such crime in future as well (Ingram & Hinduja, 2008).

References

Adler, P. A., & Adler, P. (2006). The deviance society. *Deviant Behavior, 2*, 129–148.

Ainsworth, P. B. (2001). *Offender crime profiling and crime analysis*. Willan Publishing.

Akers, R. L., & Lee, G. (1996). *A longitudinal test of social learning theory: Adolescent smoking*. The Selected Works of Gang Lee, 7.

Akers, R. L. (2011). *Social learning and social structure: A general theory of crime and deviance*. Transaction Publishers.

Bajpai, G. S. (2011). *Cybercrime and deviance: Concept and theory*. Serials Publication

Federal Bureau of Investigation. (2017). Intellectual Property Theft/Piracy. https://www.fbi.gov/investigate/white-collar-crime/piracy-ip-theft. Accessed December 7, 2017.

Gottfredson, M. R. (1987). The methodological adequacy of longitudinal research on crime. *Criminology, 25*(3), 581–614.

Higgins, G. E., & Wilson, A. L. (2006). Low self-control, moral beliefs, and social learning theory in university students. *Security Journal, 19*, 75.

Hinduja, S., & Ingram, J. R. (2009). 'Social learning theory and music piracy: The differential role of online and offline peer influences. *Criminal Justice Studies, 22*, 405–420.

Hsu, J. L., & Shiue, C. W. (2008a). Consumers willingness to pay for non-pirated software. *Journal of Business Ethics, 81*, 715–732.

Ingram, J. R., & Hinduja, S. (2008). Neutralizing music piracy: An empirical examination. *Deviant Behavior*, *29*, 358.

Jaishankar, K. (2008). Space transition theory of cybercrimes. In Schmallager, F., & Pittaro, M. (Eds.), *Crimes of the internet* (pp.283–301).

Kshetri, N. (2010). *The global cybercrime industry* (p. 3). Springer.

Kohlberg, L. (1971). Stages of moral development. *Moral Education*, 23–92.

Loughlan, P. (2007). You wouldn't steal a car: Intellectual property and the language of theft. In *Proceedings of the 7th International Conference on Electronic Commerce* (pp. 52–56). The World Information Society Report 2007. Available at: www.itu.int/osg/spu/publications/worldinformationsociety/2007/

Maruna, S., & Copes, H. (2005). What have we learned from five decades of neutralization research? In *Crime and justice* (pp. 221–320).

Merriam Webster. (2019). Dictionary Since 1828. *Definition of cybercrime*. https://www.merriam-webster.com/dictionary/cybercrime, Accessed on October 3, 2019.

Morris, R. G., & Higgins, G. E. (2010). Criminological theory in the digital age: The case of social learning theory and digital piracy. *Journal of Criminal Justice, 38*, 470–480.

Srivastava, S. (2012). Pessimistic side of information and technology: Cyber bullying and legislature Laws. *International Journal of Advances in Computer Science and Technology*. ISSN 2320–2602.

Sykes, G. M., & Matza, D. (1957). Techniques of neutralization: A theory of delinquency. *American Sociological Review*, 664–670.

Tunberg, L. (2004). Film piracy in the digital environment: Is it the wild, wild west? *Loyola Entertainment Law Review, 24*, 601.

Wingrove, T., Korpas, A. L., & Weisz, V. (2011). Why were millions of people not obeying the law? Motivational influences on non-compliance with the law in the case of music piracy. *Psychology, Crime & Law, 17*(3), 264.

Chapter 10
Mob Psychology and Crowd Control

Swikar Lama

Abstract This chapter will try to understand the intricacies of mob psychology. Mob control is one of the most difficult tasks which law enforcement agencies have to perform as it is a big challenge to control a mob or crowd without violating human rights. It is imperative that the law enforcement agencies study about the psychology of the crowd; else it will not be possible to control the crowd effectively by only wielding force. This chapter will discuss the various theories regarding crowd/mob behaviour, supplemented by case examples. The aim of this chapter is to help the readers understand the causes behind mob behaviour. Understanding mob psychology can help law enforcement agencies and mediators to observe and communicate with a mob in an appropriate manner. Mob psychology can help in the identification of leaders and rational people among the mob, facilitating effective communication, diversion, and cooperation with the mob. This chapter will attempt to unfold the intricacies of mob psychology which, in turn, will help the readers to understand why mob behaves in a particular manner and how they can be controlled in an effective manner.

Keywords Mob psychology · Mob control · Behaviour · Law enforcement

10.1 Introduction

There are various ways in which crime affects the public, and, in turn, the public are also important stakeholders in crime management and prevention. Educating the public is one of the most important strategies for preventing crime. Public perception and attitude also affect which crimes are considered more seriously by legislators. This was evident after the Nirbhaya rape case, when laws related to rape and juvenile delinquency were changed after the massive public outcry. Crime, in turn, also affects public perception as the large number of crimes against women in Delhi has led most people to label Delhi as the 'rape capital of India'. The various trends and patterns

S. Lama (✉)
Criminology and Police Studies, Sardar Patel University of Police, Security and Criminal Justice, Jodhpur, India
e-mail: swikar_lama@policeuniversity.ac.in

S. Sahni et al. (eds.), *Criminal Psychology and the Criminal Justice System in India and Beyond*, https://doi.org/10.1007/978-981-16-4570-9_10

of crime affect fear of crime among the public. Certain areas are seen to be risky or dangerous to visit due to the frequent occurrence of crimes in the past. Crimes create fear of crime and distrust among people. Most people are sceptical about being friendly with strangers while travelling.

These are some of the ways in which crime and the public affect each other, but there are other ways in which the public is directly involved in crimes. When a section of the public comes forward as a mob or a crowd, then their involvement can lead to horrific and brutal crimes like riots and mob lynching.

A crowd can be defined as a large group (mass) or multitude of individuals and small groups of people who have temporarily assembled in the same place with awareness that they are a crowd and have something in common. When you hear about the violence and damage done to property by mobs, one wonders whether those individuals, who are part of the mob, would behave the same way as separate individuals. In most cases, the de-individualization of members of the mob/crowd provides anonymity to the culprits and emboldens them to commit such crimes. Zimbardo (1969) has stated that the process of de-individuation takes place when people become part of a large anonymous group and lose their personal identity and subsequently lose their reservations in relation to violence.

The earlier view that all crowd members are intrinsically unreasonable and impressionable, and therefore potentially violent, is both incorrect and may be precarious. It is shown in the way policing strategies are implemented that respond to the crowd by suppressing all members, and in turn may cause all the members to feel that the police is intimidating and unlawful. In such a scenario, even those who were initially passive and against violence may support the violent crowd members, and this may lead to an escalation of violence that becomes uncontrollable. McDougall (1920), a renowned psychologist, said that a crowd is 'excessively emotional, impulsive, fickle, inconsistent, irresolute and extreme in action, displaying only the coarser emotions and the less refined sentiments; extremely suggestible, careless in deliberation, hasty in judgment, incapable of any but the simpler and imperfect forms of reasoning; easily swayed and led, lacking in self-consciousness, devoid of self-respect and of sense of responsibility .... Hence its behaviour is like that of an unruly child or it is like a wild beast.'

The mob has mostly been viewed as a disparaging unit by the law police, as it has caused many problems for them. The psychology of a mob is fascinating. Normal people who are law-abiding and passive can quickly become aggressive and unlawful and commit crimes when they feel that injustice has been done to them and the authorities are not listening to them. As a mob, people are capable of committing atrocious acts and causing a lot of damage to both people and property. In today's world of active human rights activism and widespread presence of media, the police are often criticized for use of excessive force when they are attempting to control a mob. It is a difficult task to control a crowd, which becomes even more complicated in a populous country like India, with its various religions, castes, classes, languages, etc., as the police is often criticized for being biased towards a particular group. This may lead to unnecessary violence or waste of resources. Hence, it would be really beneficial if the police were able to understand the psychology of a crowd and use this understanding to control the crowd psychologically.

10.2 Theories of Mob Psychology

During the nineteenth century, psychologists started focusing on crowd behaviour. Social psychologists such as Gustavo Le Bon and Gabriel Tarde opined that the impulse and mass imitation lead to the formation of crowds. Hence, 'mob psychology' as a theory of crowd behaviour was propagated by Le Bon. Later, Le Bon's theory made way for other new theories. These social psychologists have argued that behaviour in crowds is far more heedful, balanced, and socially organized than Le Bon thought to be. In addition to that, they have expanded the field to include the study of mob, riot, panics and rage, rumours, onlookers, and public and mass movements, under a new term 'collective behaviour'.

Psychologists, sociologists, and criminologists have come up with various theories to explain crowd behaviour. Emotions play a primary role in the behaviour of the crowd. Basic emotions like anger, fear, and rage exist within every individual. These common emotions actually cause the crowd to form, feel, and act in an uniform manner. This commonality creates a bond and facilitates communication (sometimes verbal and sometimes non-verbal) in certain environments. When people get engulfed in a crowd, these emotions are aggravated by the suggestion of leaders, by the usage of oral communication and other signs, the animated gesticulations of certain members, and the stressful situation and environment. These heightened emotions make the crowd easily susceptible to be influenced by leaders. In a crowd, mostly rationality becomes numb, and they agree to the most atrocious suggestions made by leaders.

Mob violence can also be ascribed to de-individualisation. Festinger et al. (1952) stated that in crowds, individuals are no longer guided by a sense of moral self-control. With the decline of individuality experienced by crowds also comes a major reduction or a complete elimination of rationality, accountability, and ethical restraints for individuals. Various experiments were done by Zimbardo to find out whether participants were ready to act with aggression towards other participants. Zimbardo sought to see if any of the participants in his experiments could be de-individualized in a way that would encourage a feeling of anonymity. The results of the experiments showed that the participants who had been de-individualized were much more prepared to give shock to the subjects for a longer duration than the participants whose identity was revealed through the use of tags with their names written on it and lack of camouflage. This proves that when individuals are de-individualized, they are capable of committing heinous acts.

Dehumanization has also been found to cause mob rage. Homer-Dixon (2010) says dehumanization causes members of the other group not to be seen as individuals. They are seen as outsiders, and people do not consider them members of their community. When mob lynching occurs, the victims are totally alienated by their transgressors and even by onlookers, leading to denunciation of their victimization, thus leading to brutal violence. In *Less Than Human: Why We Demean, Enslave, and Exterminate Others* (2012), it is said that those who commit mob violence are directed by group loyalties wherein one/some group(s) consider themselves as superior and others as inferior human beings.

10.2.1 Le Bon's Theory

Le Bon (2012) says that the individual identity melts away to form a group identity, with its own way of thinking and communication of emotions. This is the reason which causes mobs to commit heinous acts without any fear of the consequences. To be concise, the conscious, logical mind of the individual is replaced by the unconscious, illogical mind of the crowd. Due to this change from conscious to unconscious, logical to illogical, the collective mind of crowds becomes extremely inane. The mob is typically influenced by anonymity, suggestibility, and contagion to allow its members to commit extremely unbelievable acts of violence and cruelty. Le Bon suggests that a zealously stimulated mob can behave anonymously, which decreases the sense of individual accountability of the members of the mob for their wrong doings. Without the sense of responsibility, the crowd relies on primal instincts to guide their actions.

According to Le Bon (2012), the first and foremost proponent of crowd behaviour—the individual—starts to follow his basic instincts, which he would have otherwise kept under his control, if he was alone. Like an awestruck person, he is no more aware of his own acts. While certain sensibilities are damaged, other senses may be brought to an elevated degree of excitement. He is no longer himself, but has become a puppet that is no longer being directed by his rationale. When he is a part of the mob, he becomes a beast. He displays the impulsiveness, the viciousness, the fierceness, and also the zeal and valour of uncivilized human beings.

Le Bon formed the significant idea of 'group mind' to explain crowd behaviour. The group mind is not a simple assortment (or the summation) of the various minds of the members of a group. The group mind is an entity on its own working on each individual. Emotions, appeals, suggestions, and slogans are the factors behind its working. The mind of the crowd acts more emotionally and less rationally. It is a reckless mind, directing its thought on some promptly attainable objective(s). Its level of intelligence is very low, and it can be easily disconcerted. Le Bon stated that when society is weakened or fragmented, society is vulnerable to the group mind.

10.2.2 McDougall's Theory

The theory of the behaviour of disorganized crowd or groups given by William McDougall (1920) is almost similar to that of Le Bon's. He mentions two important factors influencing crowd behaviour, namely the heightening of emotions in a crowd which is simultaneously accompanied by the rationale level getting reduced. McDougall mentioned that the magnitude of the contagion is directly related to the number of people who exhibit the same emotions simultaneously. The individual comes under the influence of collective emotions and loses ability to resist it, thus succumbing to display the same emotion in himself. The common emotion becomes aggravated by shared communication among members. The heightening of emotion and the inability to remain unaffected by the effect of the crowd, in turn, hamper intellectual thinking and reduces logical thinking within the members of the crowd.

10.2.3 Freud's Theory

The explanation about escalation of emotion given by the theory of sympathetic induction proposed by McDougall does not find approval among many psychologists. In his essay, *Group Psychology and Analysis of Ego (1959)*, Sigmund Freud states that

> There is no doubt that something exists in us which, when we become aware of signs of emotion; … how often do we not successfully oppose it, resist the emotion and react in quite an opposite way? Why, therefore, do we invariably give way to this contagion when we are in group?' Freud maps it out to our indirect impulses. Freud states that every group is bounded by emotional ties especially relationship of love. He framed this as the principal phenomenon of group psychology.

Freud (1959) stated that, in a crowd, the individual members break away from their super ego, and come under the control of their basic Id and ego. Their self-control which is maintained by super ego is dominated by the influence of the crowd and their basic instinct or 'Id' impulses, which usually remains in the subconscious mind, takes charge of the individual. The Freudian theory is often criticized as its explanation for crowd behaviour cannot be verified through observation. Every now and then, the crowd behaviour may be a result of manifestation of suppressed drives, but it is not always the reason behind crowd behaviour. This theory is also unable to explain other characteristics of crowd behaviour.

10.2.4 Allport's Theory

McDougall's theory of sympathetic induction of emotion and behaviour was also criticized by F.H. Allport. He used two principles to explain crowd behaviour, out of which one is the principle of social facilitation (1924). This principle of social facilitation states that the behaviour of one person adds to the emotional response of another, but it did not induce it. Sometimes, we laugh in a group when others laugh without knowing the reason behind the laughter.

The second principle is that of interstimulation (Allport, 1924). A stimulus like verbal or non-verbal gesture can bring about suggestibility in crowds. A slogan or round of handclapping helps to break the barriers between individuals and brings about solidarity among them. Slowly and steadily, they exhibit the same mood and gestures. Every individual, therefore, stimulates the other. As a consequence, excitement grows and with it, the suggestibility of each individual. Skilled politicians and party manipulators use various techniques with a view to producing crowd rhythm and winning crowds to their purposes. This interstimulation among members of the crowd makes them feel invincible. Both the phenomena of interstimulation and social facilitation reduces the intellectual capacity of the individuals and makes them more suggestible. Subsequently, the members in a crowd exhibit behaviour which they would have never shown as individuals.

10.2.5 Turner's Theory

Sociologist Ralf Turner came out with a different perspective about crowd behaviour which was known as the emergent norm perspective. The core idea of this perspective is that even the most violent and dangerous crowds display some social interaction in which certain behaviours are acceptable, boundaries are defined, and lines of action are accepted and approved by the members of the crowd (Turner, 1964).

Emergent norm theory states that crowd behaviour is directed by certain social norms, which are agreed upon by the members of the crowd themselves. The emergent norm perspective states that the combination of similar individuals, anonymity, and shared emotion causes crowd behaviour. According to this theory, people come together with certain expectations and social norms, but during the interaction among the members of the crowd, new expectations and norms can emerge from this interaction. This causes the crowd to behave in a manner which would not have been exhibited in a normal situation. For example, some citizens may peacefully assemble to protest against something. During this peaceful protest, a few aggressive members of the crowd start abusing and start pelting rocks at the law enforcement agencies or at a property. Soon, shouting abuses and pelting stones is seen acceptable by the other members of the crowd, and within minutes, and the rest majority of the crowd members exhibit this aggressive behaviour.

10.2.6 Sighele's Theory

Sighele (2018) has mentioned that even though the mob has a heterogeneous nature, as it is often made up of people of different age groups, genders, classes, culture, and values and often formed on the spur of the moment, it exhibits collectiveness and unity to a large extent. Sighele also mentions that processes of imitation, moral contagion, and suggestion may lead the crowd to commit violence or crime. Sighele states that a mob has an objective and intention, but only the core people in the mob are able to comprehend this intention, whereas most of the members participate out of influence.

10.2.7 Tarde's Theory

Tarde in his work—'*Opinion and the Mob*'*(*1901*)*—mentioned about the low intolerance among violent members of a crowd, their ridiculous egotism, their susceptible vulnerability, the shocking sense of irresponsibility which emerged from their illusion of being invincible, and, lastly, the total loss of control as exhibited by the extreme kind of behaviour of some members of the crowd.

10.2.8 Jung's Theory

Jung has made various assumptions on the subject of mob criminality. He states that mobs are like wild beasts. The sudden explosion of the collective force of the mob brings about surprising changes in the state of mindset of the members (Jung, 1981). The members get converted from sensible human beings into wild animals. According to Jung, 'If one were to choose a hundred very intelligent men, together, they would soon form a stupid agglomeration!'. He states that every individual has a dark/primal side in them, and the conscious and the subconscious mind is always in conflict with each other. When an individual becomes a part of the mob, the subconscious mind gives him an illusion that he is all powerful. The mob engulfs the individual in its anonymity and makes him irresponsible.

10.2.9 Adler's Theory

Adler's theory was based on the concept of inferiority complex (Ansbacher & Ansbacher, 1956). He stated that people who have an inferiority complex about themselves give up this complex when they are a part of a mob. Their inferiority complex seems to get overcompensated as a part of the mob.

10.2.10 Espinas' Theory

According to Espinas (1878), an individual behaves differently when he is a part of the mob. He stated that a great public speaker can influence a crowd and bring them into a state of frenzy exhibiting acts like cheering, clapping, and hooting. This state of emotion brings about unity among the members of the crowd.

10.2.11 *Reiwald's Theory*

Reiwald (1947) stated that the aggression of individuals reaches their peak during wars, civil wars, or revolutions. A civilized society requires individuals to control their aggression. This is done through laws, so that individuals or mobs do not take justice in their hands. Although societies have been successful in putting control to such collective aggression, sometimes it does occur even during peace time in the form of mob lynching and riots.

From the various psychological theories regarding mob violence, one can deduce that mob violence is a manifestation of social learning that violence is a solution to problems, mob violence occurs because of sense of anonymity.

All the above-mentioned theories highlight one factor as the contributing reason behind crowd behaviour. Hence, these theories do not seem convincing or adequate. Crowd behaviour is caused by various factors such as stimulation, anonymity, suggestibility, emotionality, initiation, force of unconscious impulses, lack of volition, and contagion that may be the causes/factors behind the emergence of the distinctive behaviour of the crowd.

10.3 Mob Violence in South Asia: Case Studies

10.3.1 *Mob Violence in India*

Mob violence in India has occurred in various forms like mob lynching, riots, and agitations.

Mob Lynchings Most incidents of mob lynchings that have occurred in India are coloured by religious or caste intolerance. On 5 March, 2015, a mob gathered and took out Syed Farid Khan (a resident of Assam who was alleged to have raped a Naga girl) from the Dimapur Central Jail, Nagaland, and lynched him on the streets of Dimapur. The mob lynching in Dimapur was a case of de-individuation and collective aggression but also an aggression towards any group of outsiders or minorities as the perpetrator, in this case the accused was a non-Naga (a Bengali Muslim) and the victim was a Naga girl. The aggression of the mob was not because the accused had committed a heinous crime, but because the accused, being a non-Naga, had committed the crime against a Naga girl. This was evident since an accomplice of the suspect, a Naga man, was lodged in the same jail as well but was not targeted. Here, the out-group bias was evident, as the accused was dehumanized and brutally killed.

Pehlu Khan, a dairy farmer from Nuh district of Haryana, was attacked and murdered by a group of 200 cow vigilantes who pledged their affiliations with right-wing Hindutva groups in Alwar, Rajasthan, India. The mob lynching of Pehlu Khan was a case where rumour-mongering against one group aggravated the aggression towards them. The *gaurakshaks* (protectors of the cow) felt a sense of righteousness and moral obligation to punish the person who had desecrated the tenets of their religion by selling or eating beef. As mentioned in a report by Reuters, during the period between 2010 and mid-2017, 63 cow vigilante attacks have occurred (Kakvi, 2019).

In recent times, the other cause of mob lynching has been rumour-mongering of child abduction. This rumour-mongering has become rampant through social media. Notable incidents of such rumour-mongering is the case in Dokmoka in Karbi, Anglong, where two young tourists from Guwahati, who were actually engineers by profession, were brutally killed by a mob of local tribals on the suspicion that they were child abductors. Recently, two sadhus were lynched by a mob in Palghar on the suspicion that they were child abductors. Such rumour-mongering creates fear psychosis among the people which results in such tragic consequences.

Riots Across centuries, there have been numerous riots in our country starting from Parsee–Muslim riots in 1851 to the recent Delhi riots in early 2020. Most of them have been communal in nature, where one group was prejudiced against the other group. Brutal acts like murders, people being set on fire, rapes, and killings of children have been done during such riots. In such riots, members of the other group/religion are dehumanized, or even demonized, which leads to incomprehensible brutality.

Agitations There have been numerous agitations in India for various causes including political agitations, student agitations, farmer agitations, and agitations for reservation, Dalit agitations. Some of these agitations like the Jat agitation of 2017 in Haryana and some parts of Delhi turned violent, involving burning public property, beating of innocent people, looting stores, and even rape. Most of these agitations have occurred due to social stratification and societal inequality.

10.3.2 Mob Violence in Pakistan

Lorenz (1979) describes mob violence in these words: 'A shiver runs down the back and along the outside of both arms. All obstacles become unimportant ... instinctive inhibitions against hurting or killing disappear ... Men enjoy the feeling of absolute righteousness even as they commit atrocities'.

In the case of mob lynching of Mashal Khan, a mass communication student at Lahore in Pakistan, who was stripped naked and beaten with sticks and bricks, this feeling of righteousness was experienced by around 25 students of Abdul Wali Khan University. Mashal was accused of blasphemy as it was alleged that he had written something objectionable about Islam on his Facebook page and the mob took the onus to punish him. Ultimately, one of the students shot him dead. Mob violence, including mob lynching, in Pakistan is often related to blasphemy.

10.3.3 Mob Violence in Bangladesh

There has been a spate of mob lynching in Bangladesh where most of them were related to rumours regarding alleged and real child traffickers. People have certain preconceived notions that targets anyone who seems suspicious or who is vulnerable, which lead them to attack those targeted suspects. The mob becomes irrational in these cases. On 18 July, 2019 in Netrakona, an angry mob lynched a 28-year-old man when someone alleged that he was escaping with a bag holding the head of a child. After this incident, it was reported that five persons were beaten to death by mobs at different places across the country. The fear among people was flamed by rumours about child traffickers. According to Ain-O-Salish Kendra (ASK), a Dhaka-based rights watchdog, 53 people, all of them innocents, were killed in mob beatings in 2019.

10.3.4 Mob Violence in Nepal

On 23 May, 2020, an 'upper'-caste mob from Soti village, Chaurjahari municipality, Rukum lynched and killed a 21-year-old man. When Nabaraj B.K. went to the house of his girlfriend to elope with her, the upper-caste villagers lynched him and his friends. Out of the fifteen friends who had accompanied him, five of them were also killed and their bodies were thrown into the river. Apart from this incident, most of the mob violence is related to ethnic difference. Madhesis who live in the plains of Nepal and are considered to be of Indian descent have indulged in agitations and mob violence as they consider themselves to treated with inequality by the Nepal Government.

10.3.5 Mob Violence in Myanmar/Burma

June 2012 witnessed the start of widespread riots and clashes between Rakhine Buddhists and Muslims, largely supposed to be Rohingya Muslims. During these riots, 200 people were killed, and thousands were displaced. The riots started after the rape and murder of a young Buddhist woman who had been allegedly killed by Muslims. This incident caused a chain of riots to occur. After this incident, there have been several instances of mob violence against the Rohingya Muslims and now the violence has percolated even towards the local Muslims. A large population of Myanmar believes that the Rohingyas are outsiders who have migrated from Bangladesh and harbour deep resentment against them.

10.3.6 Mob Violence in Sri Lanka

In recent times, many instances of mob violence against Muslim people have occurred in Sri Lanka. Although instances of mob violence took place even before 2019, a recent series of bombings at various places like churches and luxury hotels on 21 April, 2019 by the Islamic State of Iraq and the Levant directed further anger towards the Muslims. The attacks on Muslims and mosques by mobs have since become more frequent. Many cases of mob violence against the Muslims have taken place in the recent years.

10.3.7 Mob Violence in Afghanistan

On 19 March, 2015, outside a holy shrine, in the main city of Kabul, a 27-year-old Afghan woman was beaten and burned alive, by a mob of angry men. A huge crowd silently witnessed the murder of Farkhunda Malikzada, a student of the Koran and Islamic Sharia law, while she was being ruthlessly lynched by a mob. A false rumour that Farkhunda had committed the sin of blasphemy against the Prophet Muhammad sparked the mob lynching. The reality was that she had a fight with a hawker who was selling charms to women. The hawker made a wrong accusation of blasphemy against her. When the crowd overheard this accusation, they attacked her. Some of the members of the mob dragged her by the hair; some others kicked her and punched her in the face. After dragging her to the banks of the Kabul River, the mob burnt her alive. As in Pakistan, most of the cases of mob violence in Afghanistan, including mob lynching, are related to blasphemy and religion.

10.3.8 Factors Behind Mob Violence in South Asia

As it can be observed, mob violence in all the countries in South Asia has occurred due to cultural conflicts, 'in-group–out-group' bias, and rumour-mongering. Social media has also played a huge role in spreading hatred and rumour-mongering. Mob violence in South Asia is entwined with factors like religion, caste, ethnicity, superstition, politics, etc. Most of the countries in South Asia are multicultural, and there are bound to be cultural conflicts between different groups. Tripathi (2016) states that 'collective violence occurs as a by-product of processes involved in the construction of a social identity, whereby members of different groups are in constant contestation with each other'. These contestations arise from the members' need to prove their loyalty to a community, a nation, or a culture. The process of 'othering', as Spivak (1984) says, essentially looks at how construction of one's identity in a social group is possible only with the construction of a group termed as the 'other'. The other is completely different from the self, exists outside the in-group and should be put down or condemned, in order to establish one's own identity as part of the in-group. The psychological construction of the 'other' is such that the 'other' is unnatural and needs to be eradicated from existence. Anything that is an aberration of this view is seen as violation of the group norm.

10.4 Methods of Crowd Control

Taking into consideration, the goal is to disperse the mob of armed protesters; the police have a few methods to choose from. Police officers need to consider cautiously the method they choose to employ, according to the threat level and the level of aggression of the crowd.

From mob psychology, we can understand that there are always some leaders in the mob who have a great influence on the crowd and also pacifiers or mediators who are more logical and understanding than the other members. The police officers need to identify these people among the crowd and attempt to negotiate with them or convince them to maintain a control over the crowd behaviour. If the leaders are hostile and threaten to take things in their own hand, law enforcement agencies must try to control these leaders and prevent the situation from going out of their hand. Even after repetitive warnings, if the crowd does not concede, the police should use minimum force to block the crowd or divert them from the path, by using shields and batons. If the crowd resorts to violence, use of tear gas, water hose, and rubber bullets are also advisable. Weapons should be used only in the rarest of rare cases when there is a high risk of injury or death to the police officers or other members of the public. While controlling the crowd, law enforcement agencies need to be tolerant and persuasive on one hand, while being active and swift on the other hand. Understanding the psychology of the crowd while dealing with them is a necessity. The police force needs to be led by a good decision-maker who should be impartial when dealing with the two parties in conflict.

There are various techniques designed to provide law enforcement agencies with choices for maintaining control over the crowd. The leader should select a combination of techniques that will produce the desired results within the framework of the selected crowd control option. Now let us discuss the most common techniques used for crowd control.

10.4.1 Observation

Observation includes the positioning of law enforcement personnel to the outermost periphery of a crowd in order to monitor the crowd's activity. The observation method includes collecting information on crowd size, location, and mood, and reporting about the developments to the authorities.

10.4.2 Communication of Interest and Intent (Pike, 2021)

In most cases, the law enforcement agencies can bring the situation under control by using appropriate communication with the leaders and participants in the crowd without using any force. Whenever the law enforcement agencies come to know that demonstrations, marches, or rallies are going to be organized, the leader of the police force or the officer in command in coordination with local authorities should meet with the organizers of those activities and communicate with them about the interest and intent of the police forces.

The officer in command and local authorities should make the activity organizers about their intention to deal with violence, illegal actions, and breaking of rules/restrictions imposed on the activity. It is expected that such kind of communication between the law enforcement agencies and activity organizers will ensure that the rally, parade, or demonstration will take place smoothly without any untoward incident happening, as a result of mutual cooperation between the stakeholders. On the other hand, if the law enforcement agencies communicate their intent as a threat or warning, things will not work out. Also, if the communication is incomplete and uncordial, law enforcement agencies will not be able to understand the plans of the organizers. If there is failure or lacunae in the communication, the demonstrators will conduct in such a manner that will display their defiance of the authority.

If the law enforcement agencies have properly communicated with the organizers, and the intent and nature of the activity of the crowd are known beforehand, the leaders of the crowd may be forced to move their demonstrations to another location. This will divert the crowd to another area which will help in reducing the disturbance caused to the community by the crowd, and it will also make things easy for the law enforcement agency.

10.4.3 Diversion

Control forces should make efforts to divert the crowd leaders from their planned and actual objective. When law enforcement agencies maintain communications with the leaders within the crowd, it can help them in their efforts. Law enforcement agencies can use direct techniques like blocking the area to be used in protests, or use indirect techniques like encouraging the crowd to opt for another location or another peaceful activity. Police forces should use diversion to provide assistance to them by lowering the intensity of the crowd or by encouraging the crowd to move towards an area which can be controlled by them in a better manner.

10.4.4 Cooperation

The cooperation of the leadership of the crowd can reduce the risk of an untoward happening. Whenever crowd leaders seek permission and require cooperation from the local government, officials should cease this opportunity. The cooperation can be formalized by communicating with the leaders and planning together in order to ensure that the protestors are able to demonstrate peacefully. Both the parties can also establish guidelines so that the other members of the society are affected to a minimum extent.

10.4.5 Proclamation of Dispersal Orders

Often, law enforcement agencies have to demand the members of the group to disperse from the site and go to their homes immediately. When law enforcement agencies make a proclamation stating that the actions of the crowd are unlawful, it can make the crowd aware about the intentions of the agency. A dispersal order is meant to disperse the crowd permanently and not to relocate it. When a proclamation of a dispersal order is made, it should be clearly stated that the crowd should leave the area immediately and failure to do so may compel the police to use force which can be painful or injurious to the members of the crowd.

The proclamation of the dispersal order should be done in such a manner that is heard and understood by the entire crowd. Depending on the situation, the law enforcement agencies may need to make proclamations from different locations in order to reach the entire crowd. Dispersal orders should be made in languages that are understandable to the crowd.

Dispersal orders may be announced in languages that are comprehensible to the audience. Not considering the method of deliverance, a record regarding the name of the person announcing the order and the date and time each order was announced should be kept by the law enforcement agency. Proclamation of dispersal orders should only be made after arrangements are made by the force to support crowd movement. Dispersal orders may be delivered or recorded through

- Amplified sound
- Loud speech
- Display of signage that indicates unlawful assembly and dispersal
- Drawing the attention of the crowd and documenting favourable responses of crowd members prior to the proclamation of dispersal order
- Placing law enforcement personnel to the rearmost side of the crowd to check and document the audible range of the dispersal order
- Attaining multiple-language capability
- Use of video/audio recording equipment for documentation of the dispersal order.

10.4.6 Show of Force

In cases of control operations towards civil disturbance, if the situation requires, it is advisable to use show of force. A force with proper and sufficient equipment and discipline may be marched in front of the crowd which can be used as a psychological ploy to influence the members of the crowd to disperse peacefully from the area. On the other hand, a show may result in more harm in certain situations. It may attract more people towards it and may provoke a non-violent crowd to become violent. When the law enforcement agencies are distributed all over the area to be controlled, the show of force may be conducted in the form of motor marches, saturation patrolling, and taking control of static posts.

10.4.7 Arrest of Crowd Members

Arrests should only be made when there is violation of law. During crowd control, sometimes the majority of the crowd violate the law and indulge in unlawful activities. When this type of crowd is dispersed, the crowd may become more aggressive and violent. In certain situations, the law enforcement agencies are not able to use water or riot control agents, leaving the control force with only option of arresting and removing the crowd members who are indulging in unlawful acts. In most cases, the arrests of the law violators should be made by the civil police officers rather than the military forces, but certain circumstances may necessitate the military forces to make the arrests. If mass arrests are to be made successfully and with minimum violence, it is utmost necessary for the leaders of the forces to properly plan, train, and comprehensively brief the police personnel. During mass arrests, the police have to face dynamic situations which require adequate planning and personnel. The processes used by the police must be adaptative enough to handle challenges according to the evolving situation. Police should be prepared to use different kinds of arrest tactics to tackle various kinds of unlawful crowd behaviour like passive confrontation, active confrontation, and assault and life-threatening altercations. Police should keep a proper record of the people who are arrested. The criminal act of each arrested person and the police officer who made the arrest should be mentioned in the arrest report. This should be done in order to help in criminal prosecution and reduction of civil liability of the arrested persons. All the agencies of the criminal justice system should put in a combined effort in order to ensure proper arrest, booking and prosecution of the persons who violate the law. Individual police officers should be made accountable to maintain evidence. Evidence should be collected in such a manner which can be useful in both criminal prosecution and civil litigation.

10.4.8 Use of Aggressive Measures

When all other measures have failed or the crowd is too violent, the police can use more aggressive tactics like barricades, water cannons, tear gas, batons, rubber bullets, etc. Use of bullets should be used as a last resort when there is eminent threat of life to other police officers.

10.5 Conclusion

The study of mob psychology is an important area, and now it becomes even more imperative that more research and study are done in this area because across the world because various nations are facing new problems related to crowd violence including mob lynching, riots, agitations, etc. THe existing and evolving theories of crowd/mob psychology can help us to understand the causes and factors behind crowd behaviour. This, in turn, can help the law enforcement agencies and negotiators/mediators deal with mobs and crowds without using excessive force.

References

Allport, F. (1924). The group fallacy in relation to social science. *American Journal of Sociology, 29*(6), 688–706. https://doi.org/10.1086/213647

Ansbacher, H. L., & Ansbacher, R. R. (Eds.). (1956). *The individual psychology of Alfred Adler: A systematic presentation in selections from his writings*. Basic Books.

Bon, G. (2009). *Psychology of crowds*. Sparkling Books Limited.

Espinas, A. (1878). *Des sociétés animales*. Baillière.

Festinger, L., Pepitone, A., Newcomb, T. (1952). Some consequences of de-individuation in a group. *The Journal of Abnormal and Social Psychology, 47*(2, Suppl), 382–389. https://doi.org/10.1037/h0057906

Freud, S. (1959). *Group psychology and the analysis of the ego* (J. Strachey, Trans.).

Homer-Dixon, T. (2010). *The upside of down*. Island Press.

Jung, C. G. (1981). *The archetypes and the collective unconscious* (R.F.C. Hull) (2nd Ed.). Princeton University Press.

Kakvi, K. (2019, April 27). *In a first, MP Govt to form law against cow vigilantes, imprisonment and fine on cards*. National Herald. https://www.nationalheraldindia.com/india/in-a-first-mp-govt-to-form-law-against-cow-vigilantes-imprisonment-and-fine-on-cards

Lama, S. (2021). *e-PGPathshala*. Epgp.inflibnet.ac.in. Retrieved 13 January 2021 from https://epgp.inflibnet.ac.in/Home/ViewSubject?catid=1608

Le Bon, G. (2012). *The crowd: A study of the popular mind*. Courier Corporation.

Lorenz, K. (1979). *On aggression*. Methuen.

McDougall, W. (1920). *The group mind, a sketch of the principles of collective psychology, with some attempt to apply them to the interpretaion of national life and character*. G.P. Putnam's Sons.

Pike, J. (2021). *MP1004 LESSON*. Retrieved 13 January 2021. https://www.globalsecurity.org/military/library/policy/army/accp/mp1005/lsn2.htm

Reiwald, P. (1947). Aggression und Aggressivität [Aggression and aggressiveness]. *Gesundheit (derendingen, Switzerland), 27*(9), 329–332.
Sighele, S. (2018). The criminal crowd and other writings on mass society. *University of Toronto Press*. https://doi.org/10.3138/9781487517359
Smith, D. (2013). *Less than human*. Martin's Press.
Spivak, G. (1985). The rani of Sirmur: An essay in reading the archives. *History and Theory, 24*(3), 247. https://doi.org/10.2307/2505169
Spivak, G. C. (1984). The rani of Sirmur. In F. Barker et al. (Eds.). (1985). *Europe and its others* (Vol. 1), *Proceedings of the Essex Conference on the Sociology of Literature*, July 1984, Essex
Swirski, P. (2012). *Less than human: Why we demean, enslave, and exterminate others* (review). *Philosophy and Literature, 36*(1), 263–265. https://doi.org/10.1353/phl.2012.0020
Tarde, G. (1901). *L'opinion et la foule*. Par G. (Jean Gabriel) Tarde. Alcan.
Tripathi R. C. (2016). Violence and the other: Contestations in multicultural societies. In R. Tripathi, P. Singh (Eds.), *Perspectives on violence and othering in India*. Springer. https://doi.org/10.1007/978-81-322-2613-0_1
Turner, R. (1964). New theoretical frameworks. *The Sociological Quarterly, 5*(2), 122–132. Retrieved 14 January 2021 from http://www.jstor.org/stable/4105100
Zimbardo, P. G. (1969). The human choice: Individuation, reason, and order versus deindividuation, impulse, and chaos. *Nebraska Symposium on Motivation, 17*, 237–307.

Chapter 11
Psychological Approaches to Detection of Deceit

Sanjeev P. Sahni and Lukus Langan

Abstract In this supposedly 'scientific age', deception detection tests have been offered as a solution to the inadequacies of the Indian criminal justice system. However, could it be possible that many of these approaches actually lack the scientific support necessary to validate their usage in any criminal justice system? The backgrounds, analysis procedure, and limitations of various psychophysiological methods will be discussed—namely the polygraph, brain-mapping, and narcoanalysis. The reliability of these methods will also be explored, and the appropriateness of their continued or prospective usage will be debated. This chapter will address the role of these approaches in the courtroom by discussing different legal cases from India where such measures were employed in trials and decision-making processes.

Keywords Deception · Detection · Techniques · Narcoanalysis · Polygraph · Brain-mapping

11.1 Introduction

The infrastructure of the Indian criminal justice establishment has been criticized, with aspects of criminal procedure, rules of evidence, and institutional organisation being seen as inadequate in this 'scientific age'. Indeed, some consider deception detection tests to be vital to the Indian Evidence Act (Pricilla & Arya, 2018). However, it must be acknowledged that many of these tests may lack the scientific support necessary to justify their implementation in criminal justice.

Although many people lie or omit the truth on a day-to-day basis, liars supposedly experience increased levels of negative emotion such as guilt, fear, shame,

The authors also acknowledge the contribution of Akshaya Krishnakumar for her assistance with the documentation and analysis of the case-studies used as examples in this chapter.

S. P. Sahni (✉) · L. Langan
Jindal Institute of Behavioural Sciences, O. P. Jindal Global University, Sonipat, Haryana, India
e-mail: drspsahni@jgu.edu.in

S. Sahni et al. (eds.), *Criminal Psychology and the Criminal Justice System in India and Beyond*, https://doi.org/10.1007/978-981-16-4570-9_11

etc. (DePaulo et al., 1996), with these strong emotional disturbances potentially producing specific expressions and behavioural changes. Common indicators allegedly include gaze aversion, increased bodily movement (e.g., fidgeting), speech disturbances (e.g., stuttering), sweating, inconsistency and incoherence with 'recalled' stories, etc. (Global Deception Research Team, 2006). While calmer behavioural cues are assumed to be expressed by those who are telling the truth, higher levels of nervousness supposedly correlate with the increased likelihood of a person being guilty and/or lying. Elements of these cues are typically measured and researched as: verbal cues (e.g., content of speech), paralinguistic cues that relate only to the qualities of speech (vocal pitch, hesitations, etc.), and nonverbal cues (i.e., body language and facial expressions) (Hartwig, 2011; Hartwig & Voss, 2017). False statements may be measured via verbal indicators, with liars talking for a shorter period of time and providing less details within their sentences. Additionally, liars are less likely to correct themselves spontaneously and are more likely to complain and express negative statements, with a decreased likelihood of admitting to not remembering something (DePaulo et al., 2003). Patterns of speech are an important indicator of possible deceit, but an individual's speech pattern can also be influenced by factors outside of broader cultural or linguistic differences, such as a sex, education level, intellect, mental/physical condition (Gottschalk, 1961). General disfluency in speech may actually be the more dependable indicator—deceptive responses are believed to be slower than truthful responses, with more hesitations, a higher frequency of pauses, and prolonged response times (Vrij et al., 2008). Observable body language can also provide an indication; whether they shift position in their seat or scratch themselves during the course of the interrogation. Brief facial expressions may also convey suppressed or concealed emotions, with the utility of these 'microexpressions' being emphasized within Ekman's (2009) emotional theory. This theory follows the leakage hypothesis, in which underlying felt emotions (fear, guilt, etc.) may be displayed or 'leaked' out for a brief moment before the onset of deliberate control—analogous to the 'tell-tale signs' that might give away a card player with a good or bad hand.

However, this theory appears largely unsubstantiated; liars do not manifest their underlying emotion through microexpressions or other 'tells', and there is little evidence to argue that leakage is an issue in deception. Evidence also suggests that 'common' behavioural and facial cues are poor indicators of potential deceit (Wiseman et al., 2012). Remarkably, the typical detection accuracy of the average person to differentiate between deceptive and true statements given by a stranger is only slightly above chance level—marginally better than flipping a coin, at 53–54% accuracy. Trained 'professionals' (police, judges, psychologists, etc.) do not demonstrate a statistically significant difference in accuracy of detection either (Aamodt & Custer, 2006; Bond & DePaulo, 2006, 2008), and there is also no evidence of outlier excellence in detection ability (i.e. 'human lie-detectors').

According to cognitive load theory (Zuckerman, DePaulo, & Rosenthal, 1981), concocting and maintaining a lie demands increased cognitive effort, with the increased executive control causing the deceiver to operate under a heavy cognitive load. Expending more cognitive resources leaves a liar with less resources to perform other cognitively complex tasks (Vrij et al., 2011). This manifests as longer pauses preceding answers to questions, increased speech errors, decreased bodily and peripheral limb movement (arms, fingers, legs, etc.), and a marked drop in eye blink frequency (Leal & Vrij, 2008). Indeed, liars tend to appear more tense and signs of cognitive strain have been noted to manifest as increased pupil dilation, higher voice pitch, and higher vocal tension (Porter & ten Brinke, 2008; Hartwig & Voss, 2017). Training based on this theory also appears to improve an interviewer's deception detection accuracy rate, jumping to 60–67% (compared to 42–47% with controls; Vrij et al., 2008, 2015) when cognitive demand level is enhanced and the suspect's cognitive strain is increased through reverse-order recall techniques (Hauch et al., 2016; Vrij et al., 2012).

11.2 The Polygraph

In 1921, John Augustus Larson developed the 'cardio-pneumo-psychograph', hoping to provide a more scientific approach to criminal investigation in the USA and end the wide-spread use of third degree methods to obtain a confession. As the 'lie-detector test' increased in popularity, Larson would go on to harshly criticise his own creation, calling it '*a Frankenstein's monster*', and his apprentice, Leonarde Keeler, would later rework, refine, and cross-culturally popularize the newly renamed 'polygraph' machine's usage in modern criminal investigation (Carlson, 2010). The modern polygraph continually charts an individual's cardiovascular changes (identified via an inflated blood-pressure cuff), heart rate (detected by a finger plethysmograph), respiration rate (measured through a pneumograph), and galvanic skin response (GSR; reflects variations in sweat gland activity though electrodes placed on the fingertips). This output of physiological indicators is produced on a graph paper/computer screen for the examiner to review in conjunction with the control, irrelevant, and relevant questions that would be interspersed throughout the interview (Sharma, 2014). Three of the more common questioning techniques used while conducting the polygraph test are: the relevant–irrelevant technique, control/comparison question testing, and guilty knowledge testing (National Research Council, 2003). The effort to conceal the 'mental excitation' caused by consciously lying arguably triggers a noticeable increase in particular physiological responses, derived from the stimulation of the adrenal gland and the secretion of adrenaline. Sometimes described as a 'defence mechanism' towards the fear of recognition and entrapment (or inaccurately as an indicator of guilt), the polygraph's output detecting these distinct psychophysiological changes potentially reflects the underlying internal perceptions and conscious processes related to lying (Rastogi et al., 2004; Sharma, 2014), which a polygraph examiner would later interpret as either a lie or the truth (Giannelli, 1985).

In India, the polygraph is a more frequently utilized technique. Indeed, when the police hit a dead-end in their investigations—being unable to find a murder weapon, locate a body, or find any other evidence that could provide a lead—use of the polygraph can be beneficial. In 2018, a woman was reported missing and was assumed to be dead, but the police had failed to locate the victim's body months after her initial disappearance. With a lack of other evidence, the investigation came to rely on the polygraph test results obtained from the victim's husband, who was accused of her murder, after receiving his consent (Kaushal, 2019).

The key issue with the polygraph is that it does not explicitly detect deception, rather it indirectly detects the arousal of emotions through the measurement of physiological changes that might immediately follow any sudden stressor (Goswami et al., 2016). If an examiner were to claim that a suspect was lying, this conclusion would merely be a subjective interpretation based on the data output. Indeed, being falsely accused or questioned about sensitive topics can trigger similar physiological phenomena, as would be evoked in a guilty suspect (Kleinmuntz & Szucko, 1982). The polygraph can also produce a 'false-positive' triggered by confusion, hypoglycaemia, psychosis, depression, substance usage (nicotine, caffeine, etc.), substance withdrawal, or unique emotional states (anger, sadness, etc.; Math, 2011). While most manuals explicitly state that a potential suspect should be in good mental and physical condition for the duration of the polygraph examination (Sharma, 2014), the margin for error is still unreasonably large. There is also the issue of suspects 'beating' the polygraph; persons sufficiently trained in various relaxation techniques (yoga, meditation, etc.) are suggested to have no difficulty in beating the test, as they would be able to control and/or suppress their physiological arousal symptoms (Math, 2011). Indeed, these countermeasures are easily learned and compromise the polygraph's effectiveness (National Research Council, 2003). Accomplished liars or individuals with a naturally 'flat' psychophysiological affect (i.e. some serial killers) are known to beat and even manipulate the results of the polygraph to their advantage—if you can control your body's stress response, you can pass the test. Interestingly, many government, law enforcement, and private sector representatives actually know that this tool is extremely fallible. However, the mere idea of its infallibility makes it useful, as the belief in and mystique surrounding the 'lie-detector' machine make an effective deterrent to potential liars. The fear of being caught in a lie can even prompt gullible criminals to offer a confession pre-emptively (Rastogi et al., 2004).

In late 2019, Delhi Police were able to finally crack a murder case which had been pending for almost eight years. A man had been murdered in March 2011, and the prime suspects were his new wife, her paramour, and her brother. After investigations failed to produce any conclusive evidence, police administered polygraph tests on them in 2012, but all three of the accused managed to passed the test. Along with their driver as accomplice, the wife and her paramour were later confirmed to be the actual perpetrators of the crime. However, precisely how the 'killer couple' initially beat the polygraph and kept the police at bay for many years, remains a mystery (Sunny, 2019).

11.3 Narcoanalysis Interrogation

'Truth-serum' compounds do not compel people to tell the truth. Real-life narcoanalysis procedures entail the controlled intravenous administration of specific psychoactive drugs to pharmaceutically supress suspects' reasoning abilities; ideally improving cooperation while under interrogation. In early twentieth-century Germany, the anaesthetic scopolamine was found to produce a state of 'twilight sleep' (Dämmerschlaf)—induced drowsiness, disorientation, and confusion—where patients would volunteer candid remarks and answer questions with remarkable accuracy and, in 1921, an obstetrician in Texas promoted scopolamine's usage in criminal interrogation across the USA (Gottschalk, 1961). Typically, barbiturate derivatives (amobarbital, secobarbital, etc.) have been used, but any chemical substance that alters higher cognitive functioning will do (ethanol, hallucinogens, etc.). The more popular 'truth serum' cited in contemporary Indian literature is the fast-acting barbiturate sodium pentothal. The dosage of sodium pentothal required to ensure a trance-like state (ranging around 0.25–0.50 g) is determined by an anaesthetist and throughout the narcoanalysis interrogation, visual and audio recordings are taken, so that any evidence obtained might be able to contribute to the greater investigation (Sharma, 2014).

Investigators in India have used narcoanalysis in numerous high-profile cases of murder, serial killings, and terrorism. Notable cases (the Nithari killings, Malegaon blast, 2006 Mumbai train blasts, etc.) have also implemented narcoanalysis. Indeed, during the investigations of the 1993 Bombay attack—in which thirteen bomb explosions sent the city to a standstill, resulting in the deaths of more than 250 people, and injured 1400 more (Karkaria, 2015)—use of narcoanalysis on an infamous gangster-turned-terrorist, in connection to the blasts and numerous other murders, led to the suspect confessing to various crimes that he and associates had committed (The Times of India, 2007). The confessions made during the test were not admitted as valid evidence by the Indian judiciary, but it did help the police to connect the missing dots and provided further leads for investigation.

While narcoanalysis is considered to be a useful technique, advocates of narcoanalysis have admitted that 'Unless supporting evidence is obtainable, the reliability of results of "truth serum" tests are open to serious question' (Muehlberger, 1951). Additionally, barbiturates like sodium pentothal have the tendency to produce verbal output that is contaminated with garbled speech, confusion, and fantasies. Information from the suspect's 'unconscious mind' surfaces during narcoanalysis, making suspects more likely to cooperate or communicate with an interrogator. But there is no way for an interrogator to control that flow of information being provided; mistaken beliefs, dubious stories or fantasies, irrelevant information, and false truths might be mixed with potentially useful information, with no method of distinguishing between them. Narcoanalysis lowers inhibitions, producing a 'twilight state' that makes it difficult to lie, but it does not make it impossible. Some suspects are able to maintain their cognitive functioning to the extent that deliberate deception is still possible despite being under the influence of powerful psychoactive compounds. Practiced liars or those who are firmly focused upon their false stories can even resist the drug's influence and will not reveal their deception. False memories and confessions can also be implanted in the drugged suspect. Given their extreme susceptibility to external influence, an interrogator can easily mislead a suspect without meaning to, causing them to clearly remember events that never happened or to even confess to crimes that they had no part in (Lakshman, 2007; Preethi & Nithin, 2011).

A young girl and a middle-aged domestic worker had been killed in the city of Noida in 2008, with suspicions being pointed at the girl's own parents and three other people, who were acquaintances of the second victim. Most of the forensic evidence at the scene had been destroyed and any existing evidence failed to yield promising results so the police later resorted to polygraph and narcoanalysis tests to aid in their investigations. The narcoanalysis test results would go on to play an important, yet controversial role in the case: all the accused persons admitted to being in the house where the crime had been committed, but each of the suspects gave a different sequences of events during the narcoanalysis test, one suspect even giving varying versions of their own account (Rattenpal, 2017). Allegedly, leading information about the case may had been presented to the accused before they underwent the narcoanalysis test, which could have easily influenced the results.

In contrast to other detection of deceit tests, only the implementation of narcoanalysis has been described as being tantamount to a third-degree interrogation procedure. Some argue that this analogue is inaccurate, as the drug itself causes no pain and has a calming effect on the subject, having been used as a 'therapy drug'—it is therefore 'blasphemy' to equate narcoanalysis to third degree methods (Khan, 2018; Sharma, 2014). However, in addition to no longer being used in modern therapeutic practices, this so-called 'therapy drug' was also formerly used in US lethal injections, and, outside of India, use of sodium pentothal is typically implemented as a general anaesthetic. India is one of the few democratic countries to allow narcoanalysis to be used on criminal suspects, despite strong internal and external condemnation (Preethi & Nithin, 2011). Additionally, the argument that narcoanalysis cannot be a form of torture as it does not inflict pain is blatantly ludicrous; the label of 'torture' may be applied to any method that is intended to damage/weaken the subject's personality or otherwise diminish their physical and/or mental capacity, regardless of physical pain or psychological damage (Jesani, 2002). Additionally, some accused persons have alleged to have also been more 'traditionally' tortured during their narcoanalysis interrogations (SAHDC, 2010; Ferreira, 2010). Overall, narcoanalysis has been considered to be an ineffectual and unethical technique for many years (Kala, 2007; Lokaneeta, 2018), but due to examples provided by institutes such as the Victoria Hospital, Bangalore, narcoanalysis has been undeservedly endowed with the dubious honour of being a scientific tool that might be used to solve any and all criminal investigations (Lakshman, 2007).

11.4 Brain-Mapping Tests

Within this 'scientific age', brain-mapping tests may offer an unequivocally objective and scientific method of deceit detection. In the case mentioned earlier, in which a 'killer couple' evaded capture by beating the polygraph test (Sunny, 2019), police managed to finally crack the case through evidence provided by a brain-mapping test. While the male suspect was purportedly confident that he would beat this test just like the polygraph years earlier, he showed positive responses to the test and revealed that the murder had been planned. The test's isolated experiential knowledge responses further established that the victim had been murdered through strangulation (Singh, 2019).

During the execution of a deceptive response, the frontal and parietal regions of the brain—areas related to enhanced cognitive control and executive functioning—are robustly shown to be engaged (Ganis, 2018; Ofen et al., 2017). Additionally, the superior temporal cortex and the temporal poles, which are implicated in the evaluation of social contexts, have also been associated with deception-related activation (Lisofsky et al., 2014). While these areas are likely essential to the ability to deliberately lie, this neurological 'signature' appears to differ depending on the content of the lie: whether they are lying about episodic knowledge or personal beliefs, as increased activation of the right temporal pole seems to correlate with lies about episodic personal experiences (Ofen et al., 2017). Frustratingly, there is a lack of consistency between various studies and a lack of certainty over the uniqueness of this neural 'signature'—though the activation of the frontoparietal neural network which seems to be an exception (Ganis, 2018).

Regardless, brain-mapping has been utilized as a form of 'lie-detection', with electroencephalography (EEG) being commonly used in these tests. The EEG is supposedly more reliable and more difficult to beat than other tests, given that it only reflects activity occurring in the brain (Meijer & Verschuere, 2017). EEG examinations are conducted by attaching electrode sensors to a person's scalp, through which their neurological electrical activity and impulses are detected. 'Brain fingerprinting', pioneered by Lawrence Farwell, uses EEG to measure the brainwaves that arrive approximately 300 ms after a subject is exposed to a familiar stimulus. This P300 wave is an event-related potential (ERP) with a positive peak arising in association with the parietal lobe; the P300's waveform size depends on stimulus frequency and reflects the reactivation of pre-established stimulus–response associations (Verleger et al., 2014, 2015). When a suspect recognises something significant (e.g., the murder weapon) within the presented context (e.g., amid sequentially presented irrelevant items), the EEG detects this unique ERP pattern—a larger average P300 response—and implicates a suspect's familiarity with that stimulus (Farwell, 2012; Lukács et al., 2016).

Brain-mapping was conducted by the Forensic Science Laboratory, Bangalore, in a multicrore fake stamp paper scam case, where the accused had been printing fake stamp papers and selling the fakes to various banks, insurance firms, and corporate firms. The investigators examined the accused's ERP responses toward neutral words (with no relation to the case), probe words (with direct relation to the case, intended to provoke a response), and target words (related to the findings and details of the case, but allow the investigators to put their theories to the test). Allegedly, the accused had received help from members of the police and politicians, and through ERP results, police were able to ascertain the involvement of numerous influential figures in the multicrore scam (Outlook India, 2004).

However, despite its increasing popularity in India and Australia, real-life application of the P300 test may be premature, as the current laboratory testing could not be applicable to real-life criminal cases (Brandom, 2015). Additionally, brain-mapping methods appear to be vulnerable to the same limitations as any other deception detection technique—namely learned countermeasures. P300 amplitudes are evoked by exposure to a deviant stimulus, but this makes it vulnerable to being 'beaten' by comparatively simple countermeasures. In concealed information tests, the 'irrelevant' items sequentially shown can be made significant through a deliberately increased P300 response. This manipulation severely reduces the diagnostic accuracy of the test and can even be taught within laboratory conditions, with participants 'imperceptibly wiggling the big toe' to ascribe a different neural significance toward otherwise insignificant stimuli options (Lukács et al., 2016; Rosenfeld et al., 2004). Some countermeasures also appear to be effective against other brain imaging techniques (e.g. fMRI), with the detection accuracy dropping massively, from 100% accuracy to a mere 33% (Ganis et al., 2011). If brain-mapping is to be practically used to better facilitate criminal investigations, then this promising technique must be beyond reproach.

11.5 Conclusion

Detection of deceit tests have been the subject of heavy debate regarding their actual effectiveness in real-world scenarios and their viability in the Indian criminal investigation process. There have also been many incidences of misuse with these techniques, which have led to serious human rights violations. The Supreme Court of India also observed that these techniques violate certain rights and, in the landmark case of Smt. Selvi and Ors v. State of Karnataka (2010), involuntary administration of these techniques was judged to be a violation of the right against self-incrimination, and right to life and personal liberty; which is granted by the constitution under Articles 20(3) and 21, respectively. The court saw this forcible administration as cruel and an invasion of mental privacy. The judgement also stated that these techniques could be used in investigations after getting due consent, but the results of these tests cannot be produced as evidence in the court of law. From scientific, human rights, ethical, legal, and constitutional perspectives, this decision has been described as admirable (Math, 2011). It is essential to keep a check on the misuse of these tests, as misuse can have severe ramifications for those being tested, as a false arrest or unwarranted suspicion from your community could be the least of the damages. Potentially, by developing a contemporary standard operating procedure for these deception detection tests, it could potentially allow these tools to be utilised in a more ethical and accurate manner.

Additionally, there seems to be a widespread assumption, particularly among communities that lack scientific backgrounds, that describing a particular technique or tool as 'scientific' somehow excuses it from outside scrutiny and criticism. Remarkably ignorant claims have even suggested that 'As long as the principles underlying the technologies are recognized as scientific, no parallel can be drawn with "torture"' (Khan, 2018). While scientific technologies, methodologies, and even theories have obviously been used to great effect in facilitating acts of torture and other contemptable atrocities, flawed science has also been allowed into courtrooms before, with bite-mark evidence and handwriting analysis being instrumental in the fates of both the guilty and the innocent. Interestingly, the notion that criminal elements within India might have taken advantage of particular advancements in technology has long been the impetus for proponents of detection of deceit tools being used within the Indian criminal justice system. Utilizing these tests in order to be on equal footing with the numerous faces of crime has been a popular rallying cry for public authorities to escalate their strategies in crime prevention and citizen protection (Barnwal & Sole, 2016). Therefore, it should be essential that rigorous research is undertaken to support reliability of deception detection tests, with premature application of these techniques being held back until the case findings are beyond all reproach. The current viability and reliability of these tests is not even close to the standards required to be considered as evidence inside or outside the courtroom. But by examining the objective truths surrounding these approaches to the detection of deceit, there is certainly hope for future investigations and development in this field.

References

Aamodt, M. G., & Custer, H. (2006). Who can best catch a liar? A meta-analysis of individual differences in detecting deception. *The Forensic Examiner, 15*(1), 7–11.

Barnwal, A. K., & Sole, A. N. (2016). Development of narco analysis test as investigation technique in the criminal justice system: An Indian perspective. *IOSR Journal of Humanities and Social Science, 21*(7), 97–102.

Bond, C. F., & DePaulo, B. M. (2006). Accuracy of deception judgments. *Personality and Social Psychology Review, 10*, 214–234.

Bond, C. F., & DePaulo, B. M. (2008). Individual differences in judging deception: Accuracy and bias. *Psychological Bulletin, 134*(4), 477–492.

Brandom, R. (2015, February 2nd). Is 'brain fingerprinting' a breakthrough or a sham? *The Verge*. Retrieved March 16th, 2020, from: https://www.theverge.com/2015/2/2/7951549/brain-fingerprinting-technology-unproven-courtroom-science-farwell-p300.

Carlsen, E., (2010). Truth in the machine. *California Magazine, Cal Alumni Association*. Retrieved March 16th, 2020, from: https://alumni.berkeley.edu/california-magazine/spring-2010-searchlight-gray-areas/truth-machine.

DePaulo, B. M., Kashy, D. A., Kirkendol, S. E., Wyer, M. M., & Epstein, J. A. (1996). Lying in everyday life. *Journal of Personality and Social Psychology, 70*(5), 979–995.

DePaulo, B. M., Lindsay, J. J., Malone, B. E., Muhlenbruck, L., Charlton, K., & Cooper, H. (2003). Cues to deception. *Psychological Bulletin, 129*(1), 74–118.

Ekman, P. (2009). *Telling lies: Clues to deceit in the marketplace, politics, and marriage* (Revised). W.W. Norton & Co.

Farwell, L. A. (2012). Brain fingerprinting: A comprehensive tutorial review of detection of concealed information with event-related brain potentials. *Cognitive Neurodynamics, 6*(2), 115–154.

Ferreira, A. (2010). Psychological third degree torture. *Frontier Weekly, 42*(52).

Ganis, G. (2018). Detecting deception and concealed information with neuroimaging. In J. P. Rosenfeld (Ed.), *Detecting concealed information and deception: Recent developments* (pp. 145–167). Academic Press.

Ganis, G., Rosenfeld, J. P., Meixner, J., Kievit, R. A., & Schendan, H. E. (2011). Lying in the scanner: Covert countermeasures disrupt deception detection by functional magnetic resonance imaging. *NeuroImage, 55*, 312–319.

Giannelli, P. C. (1985). Polygraph and deception tests. *Public Defender Reporter, 8*(1).

Global Deception Research Team. (2006). A world of lies. *Journal of Cross-Cultural Psychology, 37*(1), 60–74.

Goswami, H., Kakker, A., Ansari, N., Lodha, A., & Pandya, A. (2016). The deception clues in forensic contexts: The lie detection psychology. *Journal of Forensic Psychology, 1*(3), 113.

Gottschalk, L. A. (1961). The use of drugs in interrogation. In A. D. Biderman, & H. Zimmer (Eds.), *The manipulation of human behaviour* (1st edn, pp. 96–141). Wiley.

Hartwig, M. (2011). Methods in deception research. In B. Rosenfeld & S. Penrod (Eds.), *Research methods in forensic psychology*. Wiley.

Hartwig, M., & Voss, J. A. (2017). *Lie detection guide: Theory and practice for investment professionals*. CFA Institute.

Hauch, V., Sporer, S. L., Michael, S. W., & Meissner, C. A. (2016). Does training improve the detection of deception? A meta-analysis. *Communication Research, 43*(3), 283–343.

Jesani, A. (2002). Medicine betrayed: Again and yet again. *Indian Journal of Medical Ethics, 10*(4).

Kala, A. K. (2007). Of ethically compromising positions and blatant lies about 'truth serum.' *Indian Journal of Psychiatry, 49*(1), 6–9.

Karkaria, B. (2015, July 30th). How the 1993 blasts changed Mumbai forever. *BBC News*. Retrieved March 29th, 2020, from: https://www.bbc.com/news/world-asia-india-33713846.

Kaushal, Y. (2019, September 28th). Polygraph test raises suspicion on Panchkula Lawyer held for wife's murder. *Hindustan Times*. Retrieved March 20th, 2020, from: https://www.hindustantimes.com/cities/polygraph-test-raises-suspicion-on-panchkula-lawyer-held-for-wife-murder/story-mLRW6xFv9NWsk00vNpgasM.html.

Khan, G. F. (2018). Narco analysis test: A blessing to criminal justice system, its reliability and admissibility in light of various Judgements. *International Journal of Law, 4*(2), 311–317.

Kleinmuntz, B., & Szucko, J. (1982). On the fallibility of lie detection. *Law and Society Review, 17*(1), 85–104.

Lakshman, S. (2007). Narcoanalysis and some hard facts. *Frontlines, 24*(9).

Leal, S., & Vrij, A. (2008). Blinking during and after lying. *Journal of Nonverbal Behaviour, 32*(4), 187–194.

Lisofsky, N., Kazzer, P., Heekeren, H. R., & Prehn, K. (2014). Investigating socio-cognitive processes in deception: A quantitative meta-analysis of neuroimaging studies. *Neuropsychologia, 61*, 113–122.

Lokaneeta, J. (2018). Creating a flawed art of government: Legal discourses on lie detectors, brain scanning, and narcoanalysis in India. *Law, Culture, and the Humanities, 14*(3), 420–438.

Lukács, G., Weiss, B., Dalos, V. D., Kilencz, T., Tudja, S., & Csifcsák, G. (2016). The first independent study on the complex trial protocol version of the P300-based concealed information test: Corroboration of previous findings and highlights on vulnerabilities. *International Journal of Psychophysiology, 110*, 56–65.

Math, S. B. (2011). Supreme court judgment on polygraph, narco-analysis & brain-mapping: A boon or a bane. *The Indian Journal of Medical Research, 134*(1), 4–7.

Meijer, E. H., & Verschuere, B. (2017). Deception detection based on neuroimaging: Better than the polygraph? *Journal of Forensic Radiology and Imaging, 8*, 17–21.

Muehlberger, C. W. (1951). Interrogation under drug influence. *Journal of Criminal Law and Criminology, 42*(4), 513–528.

National Research Council. (2003). *The polygraph and lie detection* (pp. 11–28). The National Academies Press.

Ofen, N., Whitfield-Gabrieli, S., Chai, X. J., Schwarzlose, R. F., & Gabrieli, J. D. E. (2017). Neural correlates of deception: Lying about past events and personal beliefs. *Social Cognitive and Affective Neuroscience, 12*(1), 116–127.

Outlook India. (2004, February 10th). Telgi's brain mapping confirms payments to Chhagan Bhujbal. *Outlook* . Retrieved March 28th, 2020, from: https://www.outlookindia.com/newswire/story/telgis-brain-mapping-confirms-payments-to-chhagan-bhujbal/20065.

Porter, S., & ten Brinke, L. (2008). Reading between the lies: Identifying concealed and falsified emotions in universal facial expressions. *Psychological Science, 19*(5), 508–514.

Preethi, D. S., & Nithin, M. D. (2011). Truth serum: Boon or just a vain glory? *Journal of Karnataka Medico-Legal Society, 20*(2), 29–34.

Pricilla, H., & Arya, R. (2018). Polygraph and narco test in indian evidence law—Through case laws. *International Journal of Pure and Applied Mathematics, 120*(5), 125–145.

Rastogi, P., Kanchan, T., Das, S., & Daya, P. (2004). The truth behind lie detector. *Journal of Indian Academy of Forensic Medicine, 30*(3), 161–163.

Rattenpal, D. (2017, October 12th). The curious case of narco tests in Aarushi-Hemraj murder mystery. *The Quint*. Retrieved March 28th, 2020, from: https://www.thequint.com/news/india/the-curious-case-of-narco-tests-in-aarushi-hemraj-murder-mystery.

Rosenfeld, J. P., Soskins, M., Bosh, G., & Ryan, A. (2004). Simple, effective countermeasures to P300-based tests of detection of concealed information. *Psychophysiology, 41*, 205–219.

SAHRDC. (2010). The Ferreira case: All that is wrong with torture and narcoanalysis. *Economic and Political Weekly, 45*(21), 13–15.

Sharma, B. R. (2014). *Forensic science in criminal investigations and trials* (5th ed.). Universal Law Publishing Company Pvt. Ltd.

Singh, A. (2019, October 7th). Brain mapping test led to arrest of main accused. *Millennium Post*. Retrieved March 29th, 2020, from: http://www.millenniumpost.in/delhi/brain-mapping-test-led-to-arrest-of-main-accused-378350.

Smt. Selvi & Ors Vs State of Karnataka. Smt. Selvi & Ors Vs State of Karnataka Judgment on 5th May 2010. (Criminal Appeal No. 1267 of 2004).

Sunny, S. (2019, October 9th). Love story, murder, cover up: How cops cracked 8-yr-old murder case. *Hindustan Times*. Retrieved March 20th, 2020, from: https://www.hindustantimes.com/cities/bones-exhumed-to-crack-eight-year-old-murder-case/story-N36ptYDu7EeScZneXEJ6zH.html.

The Times of India (2007, August 17th). Abu Salem sings under narco test. *The Times of India*. Retrieved March 27th, 2020, from: https://timesofindia.indiatimes.com/india/Abu-Salem-sings-under-narco-test/articleshow/2286455.cms.

Verleger, R., Baur, N., Metzner, M. F., & Śmigasiewicz, K. (2014). The hard oddball: Effects of difficult response selection on stimulus-related P3 and on response-related negative potentials: Oddball-P3 and S-R mapping. *Psychophysiology, 51*, 1089–1100.

Verleger, R., Hamann, L. M., Asanowicz, D., & Śmigasiewicz, K. (2015). Testing the S-R link hypothesis of P3b: The oddball effect on S1-evoked P3 gets reduced by increased task relevance of S2. *Biological Psychology, 108*, 25–35.

Vrij, A., Fisher, R. P., & Blank, H. (2015). A cognitive approach to lie detection: A meta-analysis. *Legal and Criminological Psychology, 22*(1), 1–21.

Vrij, A., Granhag, P. A., Mann, S., & Leal, S. (2011). Outsmarting the liars: Toward a cognitive lie detection approach. *Current Directions in Psychological Science, 20*(1), 28–32.

Vrij, A., Leal, S., Mann, S., & Fisher, R. (2012). Imposing cognitive load to elicit cues to deceit: Inducing the reverse order technique naturally. *Psychology, Crime & Law, 18*(6), 579–594.

Vrij, A., Mann, S. A., Fisher, R. P., Leal, S., Milne, R., & Bull, R. (2008). Increasing cognitive load to facilitate lie detection: The benefit of recalling an event in reverse order. *Law and Human Behaviour, 32*(3), 253–265.
Wiseman, R., Watt, C., ten Brinke, L., Porter, S., Couper. S-L., & Rankin, C. (2012). The eyes don't have it: Lie detection and neuro-linguistic programming. *PLoS ONE, 7*(7), e40259.
Zuckerman, M., DePaulo, B. M., & Rosenthal, R. (1981). Verbal and nonverbal communication of deception. In L. Berkowitz (Ed.), *Advances in experimental social psychology* (Vol. 14). Academic Press.

Chapter 12
Investigative Psychology Through a Forensic Victimology Perspective

Poulomi Bhadra and Vipin Vijay Nair

Abstract This chapter would provide a critical and investigative outlook towards the victim–offender relationship as a penal couple. This chapter would address the investigative psychology issues faced in the study of victims of violent crimes. It would reflect forensic victimology as an applied discipline to examine, study, and interpret individual victim evidence in a scientific manner to address challenges in verification of facts presented in investigations and court proceedings. The chapter would talk about some of the theories and standard operating procedures that can be utilized by practitioners, experts and professionals towards victim profiling to facilitate crime investigation. The need for an informed perspective on forensic victimology would also be reflected in the chapter. Structured studies of victims within an investigative and forensic context will assist in an inclusive and accurate understanding of the role of each participant in the criminal justice system.

Keywords Forensic victimology · Victim profile · Investigative psychology · False allegations

12.1 Introduction

The Latin phrase *victima* has taken to mean, from the early times, a victim, whether animal or person, whose life was destined to be sacrificed to a powerful deity (Karmen, 2007). Historically, the term victim is loosely utilized to define an individual who has suffered any injury, loss, or damage over an incident usually committed by another person.

P. Bhadra (✉) · V. V. Nair
Jindal Institute of Behavioural Sciences, O.P. Jindal Global University, Sonipat, Haryana, India
e-mail: pbhadra@jgu.edu.in

V. V. Nair
e-mail: vvnair@jgu.edu.in

S. Sahni et al. (eds.), *Criminal Psychology and the Criminal Justice System in India and Beyond*, https://doi.org/10.1007/978-981-16-4570-9_12

12.1.1 Victimology Defined

Victimology has evolved as a sub-discipline of the existing field of criminology, and is described as 'the scientific study of physical, emotional, and financial harm, loss, or damage suffered by an individual based on any illegal activities' (Karmen, 2007).

The subgroups in victimology are categorized into general, penal, and critical victimology. General victimology caters to the study of those individuals or groups who have suffered harm, abuse, or loss irrespective of the incident being a crime, human rights violation, or natural disaster. Penal victimology or interactionist victimology is the study of the couple, i.e. the dynamic relationship of the victims and their offenders. Critical victimology is developed to understand the reactions explored by the other two subgroups and describes the established criminality and vulnerability to be a victim. These subgroups reflect the professional recourse to provide services towards the victims in terms of restoration, compensation, rehabilitation, etc.

12.1.2 Forensic Victimology

Forensic victimology is the idiographic and nomothetic study of victims of violent crimes. The discipline caters towards the investigative and forensic outlook within the criminal justice system. Forensic victimology is a subset of interactionist victimology, studying the loss, damage, and harm to violation of the law. It utilizes a comprehensive outline of the victim's lifestyle and situations that led to the event of injury and also evaluates the exact nature of any loss or harm.

The main objective of any professional in the field of victimology is to work towards victim assistance and victim advocacy. Their role is to restore and empower the victims back to the position before the harm instigated by the incident. Forensic victimology, in contrast, does not drive towards victim assistance, and is not sympathetic towards the victims. The forensic victimologist critically examines and evaluates victim evidence scientifically and assists the criminal justice machinery to corroborate the investigation and forensic proceedings.

The guiding philosophy in forensic victimology is that the victim's account can be plausibly flawed until corroborated with strong empirical evidence. The analysis and evaluation of victim testimony are tested scientifically to decipher the truth. The shepherding tenet in studying victims in the investigative domain is to provide a detailed and factual explanation of the magnitude of victimization over the crime scene. The utilization of scientific approach in evaluating victim testimony is the only way within forensic victimology to confirm the facts and provide dedicated proof in the court of law.

12.1.3 Role of Forensic Victimology in Investigative Psychology

As offender profiling developed as a means of assisting police investigation in identifying the type of criminal associated with particular crimes, there were also several psychological and practical issues that rose to the fore (Canter, 2004). The complexities of prediction and inference, as well as information management and decision-making, led to a new domain of applied psychology called investigative psychology. The focus of this field has primarily been to fulfil its main tenet—the classification of criminals and prevention of such criminal activities. However, the field struggled to find adequately robust and reliable schemes that could be used for this purpose. The latest advancement in overcoming this handicap included multidimensional scaling procedures that have been found to be the most useful approaches. In addition to the various approaches to criminal profiling, the model also urges to look at various aspects of the offender–crime–victim triad to decipher better ways of classifying offenders and their victims. This forms the premise of forensic victimology, which can be considered more as a branch of investigative psychology than forensic science.

Forensic victimology provides the criminal justice system with a scientific and empirical evaluation of victim evidence to reflect enlightened investigation practices. Forensic victimology dictates a neutral stance and provides information to identify criminality or susceptibility of a victim to crime. As described in Dienstein (2005; p.160), the criminal investigation is a process of collecting information and facts to be presented as evidentiary proof in the court. Without a proper and unbiased criminal investigation, it would be difficult to decipher the truth. In the investigative domain, forensic victimology focuses on the victim, delivering coherent identification, gathering, conservation, and documentation of victim evidence. Just as in criminal profiling, forensic evidence involves a dedicated empirical and scientific evaluation of facts and information that contribute as one of the most reliable pieces of evidence in building a victim profile (Turvey, 2011). A forensic victimologist essentially has a background in behavioural sciences, forensic science, and empirical methods, and provides a form of proof that complements various stakeholders of the criminal justice system in explaining the nature, scope, and depth of a case. They assist the crime scene and criminal justice system in the below-mentioned provisions (Turvey, 2011).

1. *Assistance in identifying the facets of crime*: By reviewing the victim, the relationship between victim and offender is better understood. It would analyse the various elements related to lifestyle, environment, and circumstances of a victim that constituted the crime.
2. *Understanding and creating the chain of events:* Acknowledging the timeline of the victim regarding the crime guides a better understanding of the relationship of various factors leading towards the occurrence of the crime.
3. *Reflecting the suspect pool:* In cases where the perpetrator is unidentified, a detailed victimological introspection scrutinizes various aspects of the victim's

routine that can ascertain the opportunity available to a potential offender to inflict harm towards the victim.

4. *Reflect investigative recommendations:* An in-depth victimological analysis would guide towards providing suggestions and guidance in identifying offenders, any lacuna in investigations, evaluation of witness, and evidence during the stage of the investigation.
5. *Aid in crime scene refurbishment:* Evaluating the victim's behaviour provides thorough guidance in reconstructing the crime scene and contributes to the establishment of the relationship between various elements of a crime.
6. *Gather factual information over victimization:* Collection of relevant information about the crime scene through victims help in establishing the truth or refuting the claim stated by the victim over victimization
7. *Deciphering modus operandi of the offender:* The familiarity of the victim's lifestyle contributes to understanding the modus operandi of the offender. For example, a stalker would inquire about the daily routine and lifestyle choice of a victim to increase the likelihood of vulnerability. This information from the victim would guide over the options decided by the offender.
8. *Deduce offender motive:* A comprehensive assessment of the victim and the description of the crime scene would contribute to understanding the motivation of the offender. For example, crime scene briefing by the victim would establish the harm, loss, or damage from the incident and determine the motive of the offender towards the commission of a crime
9. *Connect the missing dots of crime:* Investigator can corroborate various crimes depicting similar characteristics and link the behavioural pattern of a potential offender towards the crime. An analysis of different victims in multiple cases can illustrate a linkage towards a dedicated crime and their specific connection to the offender.
10. *Support towards public safety information:* Various crime prevention strategies establishes a prior outlook of different vulnerabilities and victim availability to the offender. This information, when circulated with the general public, will act as a public safety response and would prevent future susceptibility to being a victim.
11. *Advocacy towards the criminal justice system:* The active role of the forensic victimologist in the criminal justice system caters towards advocacy and information dissemination towards various stakeholders of the criminal justice system. It would act as precedent in future investigation and legal proceedings.

12.2 Theories of Victimology

12.2.1 Victim Precipitation

The term victim precipitation was first utilized by Marvin Wolfgang to depict a circumstance that was prompted by the victim, leading towards their untimely demise, harm, damage, suffering, or loss (Petherick & Sinnamon, 2014). The incident of victim precipitation views the victim as a protagonist of abuse or harm towards the offender at an earlier instance. The theory of victim precipitation does not attempt to blame the victim of their act, but provides a broader picture of the past circumstances that can describe an offender's behaviour.

Siegel (2008) talks about two variations of precipitation. The principal is passive precipitation, where the victim has qualities that bring out a reaction from their assaulter. The injured might be vulnerable or easily accessible, or may belong to a specific community with whom the wrongdoer has a prior issue. Then again, the attributes are misrepresented and fabricated to ones' advantage by the guilty party.

The second type is active precipitation, where the injured individual plays a functioning role and takes part in conduct that inspires a reaction. These are cases wherein the injured individual is the underlying assailant; however, they endures the most mischief or misfortune. Contingent upon the kind of conduct included if the unfortunate casualty prompted the occasion, it might be hard to figure out what each party did, why they did it, and the legality of their activities. Seemingly, this type acts as an active discussion over the role of precipitation.

John, working at ABC Limited, was a dedicated employee. He returns home late and is usually frusted from the overload of work. Miranda gets frustrated with the late arrival and expresses her displeasure with harsh comments. John, being an impatient person, get into argument and at times indulges in minor physical assault. On one fine day, the argument escalated to a scuffle between both and, in the heat of the moment, Miranda stabbed John to death. John would be identified as victim here and Miranda as the accused. Understanding the Victim Precipitation theory, one can recognize the role of John as an active precipitator towards the crime. He played a functional role and his conduct inspired reaction from Miranda.

12.2.2 Victim Facilitation

Between January 1948 and December 1952, Marvin E. Wolfgang led a principal methodical investigation on victim precipitation focusing on homicides recorded by the Philadelphia Homicide Department. He examined the victim and the guilty party as independent and as shared members in the homicide. Wolfgang, in his examination, found that 26 percent of criminal manslaughter were victim precipitated as per police records, and the injured individual was a determinantal factor in the wrongdoing. This research gave way to the theory of victim facilitation, which is less dubious vis-a-vis the victim-blaming approaches provided by Mendelsohn (victim culpability) and Hans Von Hentig (victim proneness). Schneider clarifies victim facilitation as a model that focuses only on the error of unfortunate interpretation of the victim's conduct by the guilty party. It is based on a symbolic interaction and does not relieve the guilty party of his/her responsibility (Wolfgang, 1959).

A 30-year-old, who is employed as a Royal Office worker, spent weeks walking around Exeter in the middle of the night looking for lone women. He approaches female Exeter University students coming out of clubs at late night. He targets girls who either take dark and empty roads or are stranded in the middle of nowhere. He then pretends to offer help and takes advantage of the situation. The cases of sexual harassment and rape increased over the year in Exeter. Few weeks later, a group of female students suspected a man's behaviour one night and reported to the police. The police took cognizance of the information and arrested the individual. The arrested individual turned out to be the serial rapist, charged for multiple rape charges. Understanding the victim facilitation theory, we can identify the interpretation of the victim's conduct as an opportunity by the guilty party.

12.2.3 Lifestyle Theory

Lifestyle theory expresses the risk involved in an individual's day-to-day routine that can reflect as an opportunity to depict victim availability and vulnerability. There are two kinds of risks-stable and dynamic risks-that are expected to contribute towards victimhood. Stable factors are generally unchangeable and moderately reliable aspects of the victim's everyday existence. These incorporate work and professional activities, social interactions (like the places where any social gathering of various groups), and different activities, for example, heading off to the recreational centre or hospital. These are explained as victim lifestyle exposure (Ferguson et al., 2010). The below mentioned explains stable risk factors: profession, residence, personality & behaviourism, and addiction or dependency.

Roger visited a self employed sex worker at a pre-decided location. They agreed on the payment time and concluded their professional commitment. They had a gala time with alcohol and mutually agreed leisure. At the time of payment, Roger handed over a sealed envelope and stated that the promised amount is inside the envelope. He asked her to open the envelope after he left and that she should trust her customer. He stated that he was getting late and had to catch the next train. She believed the customer and reached back to her apartment. As she opened the envelope, she noticed that the envelope was filled with fake bills. Understanding the lifestyle theory, we can identify that being in a profession of sex worker constitutes various risk factors towards victimization, ranging from fraud to rape and loss of life. The fraud by Roger highlights risk factors dictated by profession, personality, and dependency.

While there are certain aspects of a victim's way of life that are consistent, there are others that may change prompted by impulse and condition. A delay faced by traffic, malfunction in any technological arrangement (no network coverage on a cell phone), breakdown in machinery (phone battery dying) are few of them. These are conditions, activities, or occasions that the injured individual might not have made arrangements for or that may change regardless of fore-knowledge or because of typical predispositions. Therefore, these things are dynamic and contribute to a victim's incident exposure (Ferguson et al., 2010). Some other dynamic risk factors include mood and emotional reflection, injury or illness, and unforeseen circumstances.

Angelina was a jovial girl and an active participant in sports. She always maintained her calm and persistently indulged in sportsperson spirit. Nearing to a crucial match, she was keeping unwell and subsequently developed aggressive behaviour. On the day of a crucial match, she was bullied by competitor team mates consistently. Considering her circumstances, she stromed onto the opposite team members and initiated a fight, leading to severe injuries to the other team.

There can always be an overlap between the two risk factors. For example, the alcohol addiction of an individual (stable risk factor), when corroborated with an unforeseen circumstance (dynamic factor), can cause vulnerable to criminality or susceptible to be a victim.

12.2.4 Situational Exposure Theory

There are inherent similarities between lifestyle theory and situational exposure theory. The situational exposure theory suggests that an individual becomes more vulnerable when exposed to high-risk or dangerous situations. The degree of exposure correlates with various socio-demographic factors that influence the occurrence of crime. An individual exposure to low-risk places and association with high-risk persons are seldom on a common platform. These situations reflect the opportunity of individuals to be vulnerable to criminality or susceptible to be a victim.

Robert was a bike enthusiast and purchased a 750 cc racing motorbike. He planned for a road trip with his friends. On the road trip, Robert tried to race with fellow bikers and speed fast through narrow lanes. Robert crossed the speed limit of 150 km/hr when riding through a narrow street and lost his balance. He was seriously injured and suffered heavy trauma impact on his head. He was declared brought dead at the hospital. Understanding the situational exposure theory, we can identify that Robert made certain choices that exposed him to severe risk, leading to a fatal victimization.

12.3 Forensic Profiling of a 'Victim'

Weston and Wells (1974) provide a checklist for a victimological introspection of a crime scene analysis that can serve to be one of the most useful tools in gathering critical facts in an investigation. He suggested that the investigator should gather this information about the victim even before the first inspection of the crime scene. It includes questions such as-

1. Did the victim know the offender?
2. Does the victim have any suspicion against any individual, and why?
3. Has a history of crime been reported previously about the victim?
4. Was the victim equipped with any weapon?
5. Has any behavioural issues been reported with the victim?
6. Has the victim been available as a witness in any past police records?

Collecting information about various stakeholders in the crime provides a broader perspective to the investigation. Beginning investigation with the victim of crime provides ignition to the entire criminal proceeding and displays the tentative track of evidence collection. No single checklist can suffice the investigation entirely, thereby it is prudent to put the onus onto the forensic victimologist to shift through the various checklists and formulate evidence without any bias and prejudice. The below-mentioned profile depicts a more unified set of information that can be gathered by investigators or forensic victimologists in order to bridge any gap faced during the investigation.

Demographics: The basic profiling of a victim includes age, gender, height, weight, and any bodily feature that helps in establishing an accurate identification. The identification of the victim through profiling via clothing, jewellery, personal items, i.e. wallet, handbag, and other baggage on the day of crime provides assistance in crime scene investigation. For example, a demographic profile of a victim, namely the age, can guide the law enforcement agencies to limit the targeted offenders to a specific age bracket and their potential to offend towards the respective age group.

Legal history: The legal profile of the victim identifies any criminal history (orders, notification, warrants), testimonial history before officials or in court, and any interaction with the law enforcement in the past. This information contributes to diagnosing the victim's moral ethics and contributes to establishing the truth of the case by eradicating the possibility of false testimony.

Medical history: Profiling on medical grounds is relevant in cases involved with intoxication or any severe medical conditions. The profile provides an outlook over any role the medical state of the victim may have played towards the concurrence in crime. For example, the victim's tolerance for intoxication of the victim during the incident would be relevant information in understanding and recreating the entire chain of events, or proving validity of the victim's version of the story.

Intoxication and drug history: The understanding of the history of addiction and intoxication of the victim plays an integral part in discovering the contribution of the injured party who may have been inebriated state towards the commission of a crime. At times, the extent of intoxication can promote aggression and violent behaviour and leads toward violence. The history of addiction leading to crime can corroborate the theory of victim precipitation.

Psychological history: The psychological history of a victim provides an outlook towards the mental and behavioural state of the individual. This profile facilitates in understanding the psyche of the victim at the time of the incident and deciphers their part in the entire chain of events leading up to the crime. The psychological profile creates an understanding of any history of mental, personality, or mood disorder or any behavioural pattern that can incite any unacceptable behaviour.

Technological history: The digital profile of the victim would include all the details and history of any transaction performed with the possessed electronic items by the injured party that can be related to the crime. The pattern comprises call details, chats, photographs, videos from the cell phone, browser and social media history, documents, and records from the personal computer. This profiling reflects upon the activity of the victim, i.e. location, communication, history, etc., that may play a crucial role in the crime scene investigation.

Financial account: The financial profiling of a victim throws light upon the various monetary transactions performed by them, leading to the commission of a crime. These patterns include bank transactions, financial transactions associated with debit/credit/wallet cards, insurance policies, share market, and others. The identification of these transactions promotes a better understanding of any past malicious practices undertaken by the victim leading to the current scenario.

Locational reference: The residential or locational references of the victim provide a better understanding of the neighbourhood and the demographics of their living conditions. These elements help in identifying various underlying factors that would have contributed to the successful commission of the crime. The residential profile would include personal correspondence, details of the neighbourhood associated with the crime scene, and explicit blueprint of the crime scene.

Relational experiences: The past and current relationships provides an insight into the social and intimate state of affairs in an individual's life. Relationship profiling includes current and former intimate partners, provision of prior relationship counselling, and relation with various friends, relatives, and colleagues.

Employment data: The employment history of a victim provides an outline of both their educational and professional background. These profiles reflect the association, duties, roles, and responsibilities at the various workplace exhibiting an individual working style. The work environment and behaviourism at the workplace guides distinct possibilities and opportunities towards criminality or vulnerability to be a victim. These profiles can vary depending upon the affiliation of the individual ranging from students and faculty in school, scholars, and supervisors in university, employee and employer in an organization, and many others.

12.4 Identifying False Allegations

The data regarding false allegations is diverse under different jurisdictions, and in some, like in India, there is no reliable source to inform on the subject of false allegations of crime. It is generally agreed that false allegations are a persistent problem that lead to a significant drain on law enforcement resources (Turvey & McGrath, 2014). Additionally, there is a lot of critique for published research on false allegations and unofficial reporting of false report rates, especially about sexual assault. Because of the scarcity of data, in this chapter, we will talk predominantly about false sexual assault allegations, however empirical data collection regarding false reports in other crimes, and the motivations behind them, need to be studied further.

According to Epstein (2006), 'a false accusation must connote one of three phenomena: a report of forced sexual contact when there was no sexual conduct at all; a claim of forced contact where the actual encounter was consensual; or an accusation of a particular person when the complainant knows that her assailant was someone else'. Just as rape can cause significant damage to a victim's physical, psychological, and functional well-being, a false allegation of rape can also ruin the alleged rapist's professional and personal opportunities, temporarily or permanently, causing severe mental trauma.

The onslaught of feminism globally has also affected legal jurisprudence, owing to which the socio-economic and political aspects of rape as a crime has been redefined (Herman, 1990). Advancement in psychological treatment of rape victims and changes in legal policy have introduced new laws (such as the Rape Shield Laws) that protect victims from invasive defence tactics (Bryden & Legnick, 1997). While this safeguards the victim's personal and sexual history from taking the centre-stage for the defence plea, it also creates barriers that the forensic victimologist must safely navigate in order to construct a victim profile. Additionally, there are other socio-cultural barriers to reporting of sexual assaults, although these may vary between different countries. In India, for example, anecdotal interviews with police officers and lawyers in North India revealed that they estimate a higher percentage of false reports of rape among those that they investigate or prosecute. It is unclear the parameters which they use to define a 'false report' in this case, and this is clearly an area for further study and discussion. Many of these allegations may not formally translate into an investigation or a charge sheet if the complainant withdraws the complaint before an arrest is made, or if the initial interview discredits the complaint by revealing false claims or untruths in the victim's testimony or if initial investigation leaves the complaint unfounded. In a study conducted by Brown et al. (1997) on real and alleged rape victims who presented at a hospital emergency room, the rate of false rape reports, that turned out to be consensual sex, placed at 13.37%. In contrast, a study by Lisak et al (2010) focused on a university campus conducted for a period of ten years revealed that only 6% of the cases reported were false allegations. The prevalence of false rape allegation reporting is thus indeterminate and likely varies depending on geography and population demographics. At the same time, many rape survivors and their advocacy groups report that most sexual assaults are unreported because of fear of stigma, harm to reputation, professional and educational consequences, pressure from family or relatives, intimidation by rapist(s) or their associates, threat of bodily harm, etc. This is why, of those reported, false reports seem to form a higher percentage, negating the exceedingly high occurrence of actual incidents. There exists scarce scientific literature on the subject of false reports rates, especially in India, and one cannot infer, with any certainty, if institutional practices and social cultures create a risk of over-identification of false allegations by police and prosecutors.

12.4.1 Motivations for False Allegations

In matters of serious crimes such as sexual assault, the investigator must find that medical examination and arrest are very time-sensitive actions that must be undertake with urgent immediacy. However, interviewing the alleged victim should also form a crucial part of the investigation strategy. It is often seen that police as well as other intermediary bodies involved in such adjudications are often too willing to prosecute false reports of rape. Alleged rape victims are examined carefully, but the reports are often made less carefully or with rigour. This maybe because it is usually assumed, especially in patriarchal societies, that women will not make false allegations at the cost of their reputation (Turvey & McGrath, 2014). Additionally, rape advocacy in the last few decades has increased sensitivity among public, garnering a community support towards the victim from the start, regardless of investigation or proof. Some rape cases may draw extensive media attention, which brings its own hurdles of political sanction. There is also little to no legal consequence for having made a false report (Spilbor, 2003). These, and other factors, may influence an investigation into a reported rape.

It is common for even experienced investigators to assume that an accuser is a victim before *corpus delecti* has been proven, and they usually do not question their version of the story. This lack of scrutiny may be due to role effect bias, where one may be sympathetic to the victim to the extent of skipping investigative due diligence to avoid distress to the victim, or from ignorance of how to conduct investigations into potential false reports without coming across as doubtful of the complainant's account. Other kinds of bias such as confirmation or expectation bias may cause the investigator to not interrogate discrepancies in the victim's story. Even if one were suspicious, the lack of research and professional awareness about investigating false allegations means that there are no standardized tools available to assess the potential of false reports.

Before we begin to devise procedures to investigate false reports, it would be beneficial to understand the reasons why different people might make false complaints, and the socio-cultural and psycho-criminological theories within which they are contextualized. Some of these motivations may be common across many different types of crime reports, and some may differ depending on the premise of the crime being reported. Here, we shall highlight the motivations behind false sexual assault allegations. One of the most common reasons to claim to have been raped falsely is to conceal violation of morally, socially, or culturally expected norms of sexual activity, such as infidelity or losing one's virginity outside of marriage or contracting sexually transmitted diseases from 'unapproved' sexual activity (McGrath & Turvey, 2014). Although this kind of reporting is common with juveniles who may find themselves in a position of having to explain their sexual activity to their parents, it might also be common among adults who have to answer to their partner or family (Burgess et al. 2001). Another common reason, particularly among adolescents, is to claim abduction and/or rape as an explanation for missing curfew or being absent for an inexplicable length of time (such as partying late nights or running away from home). Such a desperate attempt at an alibi is produced to hopefully lessen severe consequences of their action (McGrath & Turvey, 2014). Not only as an alibi, a false allegation of rape can also be used as an excuse for relapsing into substance abuse. The motivation here can be fear of consequences or displacing the guilt over having failed those who were invested in their recovery; addicts may claim that they were forced to consume the substance during the rape act or that they took to it after the incident, as a way to cope with the pain and trauma (Burgess & Holmstrom, 1974). Those suffering from personality disorders may make false allegations to draw the attention and sympathy of their friends, family, acquaintances, or even the media (McGrath & Turvey, 2014). Additionally, alleging a false rape claim can also be an act of revenge to draw attention to oneself or suffer the other for a perceived wrong done by the accused to the accuser. In vicious custody battles, one parent can allege that the other parent indulged in sexual assault behaviour either towards any of their own or other children, thus compromising the accused's parental credibility (Green, 1986). Such allegations can also be suggested to susceptible children who may testify based on the tutored facts from their planted memory, almost as clearly as if it were true. Lastly, there are huge financial, material, and emotional costs to those accused of rape, regardless of whether it is proven true or not. The threat of a false allegation might cause irreparable damage to the accused, their family's or company's reputation. Many defence teams or corporate advisors may deem it prudent to provide monetary compensation to placate the complainant instead of risking a public and/or legal battle, regardless of whether their case had enough merit or not. Such reporters may make a habit of targeting reputed people with financial means and a public image to maintain to cop out and provide monetary or other forms of recompensation instead of letting law enforcement get involved and the investigation reveal the truth.

12.4.2 Tools to Identify Red Flags

In sexual crimes investigations, investigators walk a fine line between assisting the victim and scrutinizing their version to determine whether the report is false or not. This is done not only to weed out those cases that can be a waste of time and resources, but also to ensure that the investigator has all the true facts of the case so that they can do a complete investigation. Often, victims may leave out some information or misrepresent parts of their attack for many reasons that may not be intended to intentionally misdirect the investigators but will still impede the investigation. A lie about any one facet of the case does not mean that the complaint is unfounded but simply implies that the victim is reluctant to reveal the true facts about that aspect of the incident. It is the job of the investigator to sort out the inconsistencies, so that the prosecution's case, in case of a valid report, is not compromised.

One of the tools to assess false reports is the Baeza False Report Index (BAFRI) (Baeza & Turvey, 2002), although various experts have independently presented their own version of assessment tools to mark red flags in a suspect report (Dietz and Hazelwood, 1997). Most of these tools have been developed in the USA and may have the limitations of application depending on sociological and cultural factors influencing various jurisdictions. We have attempted to collate some of the dominant characteristics that appear in false allegation cases, urging researchers to conduct similar studies in this area to devise further socio-culturally valid tools.

Reporting: There might be delay in reporting the crime, ranging anywhere between a day to months. This may be due to any numerous reasons such as feelings of shame and guilt (self-blaming), fear of humiliation or other severe consequences, not registering that a sexual assault had happened, delays caused due to medical emergencies or other physical constraints, etc. It is very difficult to adjudge what may be considered as an unreasonable delay to raise red flags with the investigator, but it might be useful to look for delays that are unexplainable, since they are more likely to occur in false accounts. Delays are common in even legitimate reports, and by themselves, they are not enough of a red flag to alert the investigator. However, if the female or minor victim comes forwards after some amount of time and it is clear that they have been forced by an intimate partner or family to report the crime, it may indicate that closer scrutiny is needed.

Evidentiary Proof: The very nature of sexual assault crimes precluded the presence of witnesses, which means it may often come down to the victim's account versus the accused's version of events. Every aspect of both the stories should be verified by evidentiary proof, not only of the events of the crime, but also any details available about post- and pre-crime. One should also be wary of vague accounts of the assault, although temporary suppression of memory following traumatic events or drug-induced loss of memory is not uncommon in rape cases. Assistance from family, friends, and professionals must be sought, and all attempts must be made by the investigator to glean specifics about the incident. Reluctance to discuss specifics or misdirecting by vague answers can surely be inferred as suspicious behaviour. Avoiding giving details that can be verifiable can be strongly considered as a red flag. Exploring both accounts is important to avoid falling into the trap that the pseudo-victim would not go to great extents to make their story seem plausible to the investigators. Every evidence available should be testified to in consideration of the likelihood of both probabilities—that sexual assault has occurred, and second, that the complaint is unfounded. Additionally, greater scrutiny has to be given to interpretations drawn from all evidence, especially medical examination of the victim. Lack of defensive wounds when the victim claims to have resisted against one or more assailants should be explained by valid logic. The possibility of self-inflicted injuries or damages to clothes worn by the victim at the time of the crime must be considered when opining on the findings. Examiners must not work under the presumption that the victim's account is true or be eager to dismiss contradictory evidence as anomalies (confirmation bias).

Unknown Assailant: While it is not uncommon for offenders to target unfamiliar victims, accusing a stranger is an easy way to avoid getting caught in false report cases. Any report where a stranger is claimed to have assaulted the victim, especially where detailed descriptions have been provided, should be verified by supporting evidence, such as eyewitness testimony matching the suspect's description, video footage of predatory behaviour by a suspicious person, and trace evidence matching the description of the person or attack. The investigator must look out for indicators of paradoxical offender behaviour, such as assault in a public place or broad daylight, which is usually not characteristic of such crimes.

Psychological History: It is hard for an investigator to distinguish between traumatized victim response and the peculiarities in the personality of a pseudo-victim. This is where interviews of close family, friends, and workmates may help construct a viable victim profile that can help establish any red flags. Any previous history of the complainant making false allegations does not automatically annul their present case, some victims may find themselves to be more exposed to such offenders. However, a history of misrepresentation or false reporting must be treated as a significant red flag to consider when investigating further. A history of acting out or attention seeking behaviour, one of which may be to claiming falsely of having been sexually assaulted, may speak of underlying victimization from other sources. Even if the original complaint is unfounded, the investigator should dig deeper, or pass the case on to social workers who can, to diagnose the root problem and assist. Additionally, personal financial or professional issues should also be flagged, as false reports can be filed in hopes of getting a sizeable payout or coveted promotion in return for withdrawing the complaint later. In combination with the psychological history, the circumstances surrounding the event must also be reflected upon to determine if this maybe a case of the victim trying to escape severe consequences. For example, an underage victim who has missed curfew or an adult who has an unexplainable pregnancy or STD or a victim in rehab who has relapsed or missed curfew may lie about being assaulted in order to escape punitive actions.

Post-Behaviour: There is no ‘correct’ way that a rape victim should behave after the incident; the normal response observed in victims spans over a spectrum of behaviours. Some may shut down and ‘steel up’, and some may unravel in both mental and physical health. However, some behaviour that might be considered as suspicious is when the victim focuses too much on material gains—such as relocation to a new (and likely better) home or neighbourhood, especially for those victims who live in welfare states; or in initiating a lawsuit or obtaining monetary gains. Pseudo-victims may make false complaints to gain attention, sympathy, preferential treatment, or monetary gains from involved and uninvolved parties.

The above characteristics are by no means an exhaustive list, neither do these characteristics, in themselves or combined, provide a fool proof indicator that there has been a false report. While much interdisciplinary research needs to be conducted in this area, the information shared in this chapter is to only suggest that some cases sharing these characteristics may be false reports and that further investigation is needed. In criminal justice systems that operate within limitations of time and resources, and heavy workload, such guides may be helpful in training investigators to rule out false reports at an early stage.

It must be clarified here that the goal here is not to disprove or be sceptical of any reports made by victims. Power and socio-economic inequality notwithstanding, there are enough other reasons that deter real victims from report against their perpetrators. The aim of this investigative scrutiny to ensure that law enforcement resources are not wasted on fake complaints, and that the system can better focus on the needs of real victims. It also educates about the appropriate kind of support that false reporters may be given, in terms of mental health intervention, intermediary conflict management, or others, to prevent them from exploiting the criminal justice system for selfish gains.

12.5 Role of Professionals

The role of forensic victimologists is to analyse, contemplate, and construe evidence related to victim empirically. These examinations formulate definite proof over the crime scene investigation in the court of law. Over the above-stated role, there are two principal purposes of a forensic victimologist: the investigative and the forensic. In the investigative function, forensic victimologist gathers all information relevant to the case and relate the same with respective theories of crime. The admissibility of various evidence lies with the court, but the responsibility of an investigator in the collection of evidence without bias and prejudice requires due diligence. Forensic victimologists, in their forensic role, perform validation of various evidence through expert opinion and assessment.

Standard Practice

The main aim in defining the standard practice is not only to guide professionals to achieve their proficiency but also to provide various stakeholders with a benchmark to evaluate the diverse professional practice. These practices prevent any discrepancies, ignorance, and misinterpretation in the field of work. The standard procedure described by Ferguson and Turvey (2009) caters to the reduction of bias and encourages the utilization of empirical standards. Primarily, a forensic victimologist operates free from bias, despite working with the victim closely. They must evaluate the credibility of all material and non-material evidence connected to the crime, even visiting the crime scene if need be. A forensic victimologist's report should be fact based, and any inferences drawn must be achieved through scientific analysis, and rely upon logic and reasoning.

12.6 Conclusion

In the domain of the criminal justice system, a victim is an individual who has suffered any loss, damage, harm, or suffering because of a commission of a malicious incident by an individual or an organization. Victimology refers to the scientific study of victims, victimization, and reaction to both. It also looks into the relation of victim and offender in the entire criminal justice system. However, there are gaps in the literature that does not focus on the idiographic and nomothetic study of violent crime victims to contribute to the investigation and forensic proceedings (Turvey, 2008). These types of inquiries can be referred to the field of forensic victimology.

Forensic victimology is the study of victims, with a focus on unbiased and explicit details of the information of a victim's lifestyle and the sequence of events leading towards victimization. The purpose of forensic victimology is to describe the victim's information diligently for a better understanding of crime, offender, and various other legal constituents. Forensic victimology aims to assist the criminal investigation with scientific evidence regarding the victim that contribute towards an apprised legal outcome. Forensic victimology is a neutral and applied discipline to be utilized for independent scientific practice.

References

Baeza, J., & Turvey, B. (2002). False reports. In B. Turvey (Eds.), *Criminal profiling: An introduction to behavioural evidence analysis*, 2nd edn. Academic Press.

Brown, C., Crowley, S., Peck, R., & Slaughter, L. (1997). Patterns of genital injury in female sexual assault victims. *American Journal of Obstetrics and Gynecology, 176*, 609–616.

Bryden, D. P., & Legnick, S. (1997). Rape in the criminal justice system. *Journal of Criminal Law and Criminology, 87*, 1194–1384.

Burgess, A. W., Hazelwood, R. R., & Burgess, A.G. (2001). False rape allegations. In A.G. Burgess & R. R. Hazelwood (Eds.), *Practical aspects of rape investigation: A multidisciplinary approach*, 3rd ed. CRC Press.

Burgess, A. W., & Holmstrom, L. L. (1974). Rape trauma syndrome. *American Journal of Psychiatry, 131*, 981–986.

Canter, D. (2004). Offender profiling and investigative psychology. *Journal of Investigative Psychology and Offender Profiling, 1*(1), 1–15.

Dietz, P. E., & Hazelwood, R. (1997). Court TV. Report of the grand jury concerning the Tawana Brawley investigation. Online Legal Documents.

Dienstein, W. (2005). Criminal Investigation. In W. Bailey (Eds.), *The encyclopedia ofpolice science* 2nd ed. Garland Publishing.

Epstein, J. (2006). True lies: The constitutional and evidentiary bases for admitting prior false accusation evidence in sexual assault prosecutions. *Quinnipiac Law Review, 24*, 609–658.

Ferguson, C. E., Petherick, W. A., & Turvey, B. E. (2010). Forensic victimology. In W. A. Petherick, B. E. Turvey, & C. E. Ferguson (Eds.), *Forensic criminology*. Elsevier Science.

Ferguson, C., & Turvey, B. (2009). Victimology: A brief history with an introduction to forensic victimology. In B. Turvey & W. Petherick (Eds.), *Forensic victimology: Examining violent crime victims in investigative and legal contexts*, Elsevier Science.

Green, A. H. (1986). True and false allegations of sexual abuse in child custody disputes. *Journal of the American Academy of Child Psychiatry, 25*(4), 449–456.

Herman, J. L. (1990). Sex offenders: A feminist perspective. In W. L. Marshall, D. R. Laws, & H. E. Barbaree (Eds.), *Handbook of sexual assault issues* (pp. 177–193). Theories and Treatment of the Offender, Plenum Press.

Karmen, A. (2007). *Crime victims: An introduction to victimology* (6th ed.). Thompson Wadsworth.

Lisak, D., Gardinier, L., Nicksa, S. C., & Cote, A. M. (2010). False allegations of sexual assault: An analysis of ten years of reported cases. *Violence against Women, 16*(12), 1318–1334.

Petherick, W. & Ferguson, C. (2014). Forensic victimology. In *Applied crime analysis: A social science approach to understanding crime, criminals, and victims* (pp. 62–80). Elsevier.

Petherick, W. A., & Sinnamon, G. (2014). Motivations: Victim and offender perspectives. In W. A. Petherick (Ed.), *Profiling and serial crime: Theoretical and practical issues* (3rd ed.). Anderson Publishing.

Siegel, J. (2008). *Criminology: The core* (8th ed.). Wadsworth.

Spilbor, J. M. (2003). What if Kobe Bryant has been falsely accused? Why the law of acquaintance and date rape should seriously penalize false reports. *Findlaw's Writ*.

Turvey, B. (2011). *Criminal profiling: An introduction to behavioural evidence analysis* (4th ed.). Elsevier Science.

Turvey, B. E. (2014). Forensic victimology: Examining violent crime victims in investigative and legal contexts. Academic Press.

Turvey, B. E., & McGrath M. (2014). False allegations of crime in Turvey. In B. E. Turvey (Eds.), *Forensic victimology: Examining violent crime victims in investigative and legal contexts*. Academic Press.

Turvey, B., & Petherick, W. (2008). Victimology. In B. Turvey (Ed.), *Criminal profiling: An introduction to behavioural evidence analysis* (3rd ed.). Elsevier Science.

Weston, P. & Wells, K. (1974). In *Criminal investigation: Basic perspectives* (2nd ed.). Prentice Hall.

Wolfgang, M. E. (1959). Philadelphia and suicide by means of victim precipitated homicide. *Journal of Clinical and Experimental Psychopathology and Quarterly Review of Psychiatry and Neurology*, University of Pennsylvania Press.

Chapter 13
Investigating the Eyewitness: Accuracy and Fallacies of Memory

Mohita Junnarkar and Sweta Lakhani

Abstract Despite the advent of scientific evidence in criminal adjudication, eyewitness testimony continues to be widely prevalent in the criminal justice system for many reasons. From among the wrongful convictions that have been widely reported, it has been found that about 72% of these occurred due to eyewitness misidentification, among other reasons. This chapter unravels the various factors that affect the accuracy of eyewitness testimony and eyewitness identification. Different case studies from across the globe, including South Asia, are critically analysed to diagnose the fallibility in eyewitness testimony and determine the weightage that should be given to such evidence. Various cognitive psychological theories such as fuzzy-trace theory, source monitoring, verbal overshadowing, and models of misinformation (overwriting, misinformation, activation-based model) will be used to highlight the memory fallacies.

Keywords Eyewitness testimony · Memory · Reliability · Accuracy

13.1 Investigations and Eyewitnesses

Eyewitness is the legal term used to refer to individuals who were present at the scene of crime and likely observed the occurrence of the crime. The eyewitness is of immense significance to the criminal justice system. The recollection of the criminal incident that an individual narrates in front of the police and judge provides crucial information about the crime that would otherwise not be available to the investigation agency and is known as eyewitness testimony. The significance of eyewitness testimony was valued by the judicial system after the publication of '*On the Witness Stand*' by Munsterberg in 1908. The publication highlighted the role of psychology in the justice system, especially with respect to eyewitness testimony.

M. Junnarkar (✉)
Jyoti Dalal School of Liberal Arts, NMIMS Deemed University, Mumbai, India

S. Lakhani
Jindal Global Law School, O.P. Jindal Global University, Sonipat, Haryana, India

S. Sahni et al. (eds.), *Criminal Psychology and the Criminal Justice System in India and Beyond*, https://doi.org/10.1007/978-981-16-4570-9_13

Over the years, the study of eyewitness testimony became interdisciplinary in nature, including contributions from psychology, law, and criminology in the investigations of the significance of eyewitness testimony in the courtroom. The focus here has primarily been to identify the factors affecting eyewitness testimony and identification. To achieve this, the eyewitness, the interrogator, and the other stakeholders in the justice system were extensively studied to understand their role and interaction with each other.

Eyewitness testimony is predominantly relied upon by police officers and judicial system and is considered a tool powerful enough to heavily influence the verdict towards guilty (Kitaeff, 2011). The number of wrongful convictions contributed to mistaken identification is higher than the combined percentage attributed to the other factors causing wrongful convictions (Brandon & Davies, 1973; Loftus, 1979). In India, we know that the conviction rate is 81.3% (NCBR Report, 2010), but no data is available on false convictions.

There are several factors to consider when acknowledging the testimony of an eyewitness in the courtroom. For a significant period, memory recall has been considered as one of the reliable sources (Loftus & Palmer, 1974). Weightage on an eyewitness' rendition of the crime scene, the perpetrator, and all actions entailed within the act towards conviction, and sentencing in court was based on the assumption that they could recall this information accurately. However, there are significant challenges to this process, and numerous studies have presented such testimony to be unreliable, manipulated, biased, and subject to inaccuracies (Loftus & Palmer, 1974).

Depending on the jurisdictional protocols, the police generally employ investigative procedures—a three-step process—to isolate the potential perpetrator from the other suspects in a crime (Clifford & Davies, 1989). The investigation procedure starts with the police collecting verbal and written descriptive accounts from eyewitnesses. Such descriptions may also include a sketch created using the description of eyewitnesses (Clifford & Davies, 1989). Subsequently, the police is able to draw a pool of suspects based on the collective accounts by eyewitnesses and to establish a timeline of events leading up to, and after, the crime (Clifford & Davies, 1989). Finally, on apprehension, the eyewitnesses are required to confirm the identity of the perpetrator from a lineup of suspects. This is of extreme importance to both finding the perpetrator of the crime and dismissing the investigations against others who were suspected, but innocent, in the matter (Clifford & Davies, 1989).

The memory process, which is employed by investigative agencies, and the subsequent procedures reliant on it use evolving mechanisms by which authorities and the justice system determine the role of a suspect or an accused in a crime. Since recorded visual evidence may not always be present, eyewitness testimony becomes the greatest contributing factor in determining the identity of potential perpetrators. However, the criminal justice system treats memory traces very differently from physical evidence. Unlike physical evidence that follows prescribed guidelines and is collected by trained personnel, eyewitness evidence is often collected by an individual who lacks training in human memory (Bartol & Bartol, 2006). The police protocols for collecting, preserving, and interpreting eyewitness evidence have not integrated the findings of the body of ongoing research in eyewitness evidence by memory experts. Therefore, such mechanisms may be unreliable without regulations.

The primary focus of researchers working on eyewitness testimony is to reduce the false conviction rates by improving eyewitness identification accuracy. Here, we look at the legal use of eyewitness testimonies using a few landmark decisions to lay out the procedures of eyewitness accounts, the memory process, and the subsequent investigative proceedings. The chapter also examines the theories of eyewitness accounts that have surfaced to legitimize memory analysis of eyewitnesses. In addition, we will discuss the factors affecting such accounts in various circumstances. Lastly, we conclude that eyewitness accounts and memory theory are largely biased or distorted due to inherent functions and failures of memory itself.

13.1.1 Legal Perspective

The fundamental canon in criminal jurisprudence is that any accused is innocent until proved guilty. The accused is entitled to a just and fair trial under Article 21 of the Constitution of India. In the case Zahira Habibullah Sheikh v. State of Gujarat (AIR 2006 SC 1367), the court stated that the right of trial can be exercised not only by the accused or victims but also by their respective family, relatives, or society.

During trial, it is important that equality and fairness are balanced with accuracy and equality of arms in every case. The significant role played by evidence and testimonies majorly decides the fate of the case. Legally, the idea of best evidence is implicit in the Indian Evidence Act, 1872 (IEA). Under the act, evidence consists of statements made by a witness or contained in a document. Section 13.3 of the IEA specifically defines oral testimony as the person who has actually perceived something by that sense, and is rightfully capable of perception, should make the statement about it and no one else. Oral evidence majorly includes eyewitnesses and their testimony.

The landmark judgement in Padala Veera Reddy v. State of Andhra Pradesh and Ors. (Supp. (2) SCC 706, 1989) case outlined five golden principles to prove a case based on circumstantial evidence as follows:

1. The circumstances from which the conclusion of guilt is to be drawn should be unequivocally established.
2. The circumstances concerned 'must' or 'should' and not 'may' be established.
3. The facts established must solely support the hypothesis of the guilt of the accused only, that is to say, there should not be any alternative hypotheses possible except that the accused is guilty.
4. The circumstances should be of conclusive nature and exclude every possible hypothesis except the one to be proved; chain of evidence must be complete and unbroken, so as not to leave any reasonable ground for the conclusion consistent with the innocence of the accused.

5. And must show that in all probability, the act must have been done by the accused.

13.1.2 Credibility of Eyewitness Testimonies

The high-profile hit-and-run case, R. K. Anand v. Registrar, Delhi High Court (8 SCC 1, 2009), is infamous for many reasons, but mostly for the heavy reliance of the court on eyewitness testimonies in deciding the case. On 10 January, 1999, three young drunk men in a BMW car hit six sleeping pavement dwellers in Delhi. These three people were Siddhanth Gupta, Manik Kapoor, and the driver, Sanjeev Nanda, who was the grandson of former Navy Chief Admiral, S.M. Nanda, and son of arms dealer, Suresh Nanda. The police investigation found blood stains on the car tyres and oil leakage tracks on the road. Other than that, the only other evidence was a 30 min video recording prepared by the police, soon after the accident. But the video was produced in court after a few years, and the defence lawyer questioned the reliability of the evidence due to the lapse in time. Hence, the video evidence was not given much reliance in court. Most importantly, all but one eyewitness turned hostile during the trial. The role of media also played a very important factor in this case. The case had drawn a lot of attention, and the prime eyewitness was involved in conducting a sting operation, with the help leading news channel, to prove that he was being influenced by the parties to change the statement before the court. Ultimately, due to some pressure, he changed his testimony with vague details.

The judgement of this case revolved around the fact that it was hard to establish if the accused was driving the car or not, primarily because of the poor eyewitness testimonies. The only eyewitness who had not turned hostile later changed his testimony under pressure and refused to confirm the facts after a point. This leads to an essential conclusion that court should not rely too heavily on eyewitness testimonies, as there are many ways in which they can hugely weigh down the decision.

The criminal justice system's stand on eyewitness testimony is that such witnesses are believed to have no direct investment in the case or are confident about their testimony. Moreover, the evidence presented by the eyewitness is also verified, and if there are contradictions found in the evidence, it can be rejected by the court. Thus, the court concedes that one's personal biases or motives might unconsciously affect their accounts and does take active steps to minimize the inaccuracies.

In the last several decades, eyewitness testimony has majorly come under great scrutiny. Despite that, eyewitness testimonies continue to be the predominant form of evidence admitted in courts worldwide and has often been found responsible for unjust incarcerations of innocents. According to the Innocence Project, each wrongly convicted person has spent an average of 14 years in prison, and around 70% of such wrongful convictions in the USA were largely on the basis of eyewitness misidentification (Innocence Project, 2018). Other reasons were lack of legal representation to the parties, poor police investigation, and inadequate maintenance of records of evidence.

In Manson v. Brathwaite (432 U.S. 98, 97 S. Ct. 2243 (1977)) and in Sidharth Vashisht (aka Manu Sharma) v. State of Delhi) (6 SCC1, 2010) (popularly known as the Jessica Lal homicide case), prime eye witnesses to the crime turned hostile, thus allowing the reliability of eyewitness testimonies during the test identification parade, as is known in the Indian jurisdiction, to be challenged. Hostile witnesses compromise a lot of criminal cases in India. Some of the reasons for a witness turning hostile can be listed as follows:

Absence of protection: Despite several witness protection acts enforced within various jurisdictions, including India, the witnesses turn hostile before their testimonies in order to protect themselves and their loved ones from threats and intimidation, proving a lack of proper facilities and protection to witnesses.

Considerations offered by influenced party: The most common reason for a witness changing their testimony is monetary incitement or others offer tempting to testify in favour of one of the parties.

Regular adjournment in court proceedings: Another common dilemma ailing the judicial process is the prolonged and tortuous time taken to reach a verdict. Since the proceedings are dredged out for an extensive period of time, lawyers may be able to throw off or manipulate a witness's response through clever questioning.

In State of Punjab v. Jugraj Singh, (3 SCC 234, 2002), the court stated that relying solely on the information provided by the eyewitness is not recommended. Sir John Woodroff and Syed Amir Ali's '*Law of Evidence*' states that the admissibility of eyewitness testimony depends on the accuracy of the events observed and described in court, and the reliability with which the witness can remember the incident.

Additionally, in Bhajju Singh v. State of U.P. (RCR (2) Criminal 539 (SC), 2012), it was held by the Supreme Court of India that the 'decision will be taken cautiously at the time when witnesses turned hostile or go back from their earlier recorded statements'. However, the weightage of the testimony should be reassessed, and the credibility of the information provided by the eyewitness should also be scrutinized. In Jagdish Prasad v. State of M.P., AIR 1994 SC 1251, it has been stated that the verdict should not solely rely on eyewitness testimony.

While in India, jury trials are not a part of the legal framework, but in several other jurisdictions such as the USA, juries made of lay persons who are not well versed in law are much more susceptible to being influenced by the suggestible memories of witnesses. In a jury trial, jurors often tend to correlate the confidence level of the witness with the veracity of his/her testimony, and research with mock juries has illustrated that jurors often struggle to predict the accuracy of these testimonies.

13.2 Theories of Eyewitness Accounts

Several studies have demonstrated the ease with which people can be made to believe and testify about events and circumstances that they have not actually witnessed, and such studies have raised doubts about the reliability of the confident testimonies from eyewitnesses. Misinformation effect becomes more evident with passage of time after the event has taken place. This may be attributed to the fact that the memory of the event becoming considerably weaker with time. Additionally, it is seen that people will accept misinformation from the sources that they deem to be credible but will reject or resist from less credible sources, or those who are perceived to have an invested interest in the outcome of the event. The readiness of the people to accept misinformation is also heavily influenced by the presentation and attractiveness of the misinformation source.

There also exists an abundance of research in determining the factors that lend credibility to the witness. The age of the witness, for example, is an important variable. Younger children were found to be more suggestible when compared to young adults. Young adults displayed a remarkable ability to stay consistent and focused solely on the facts. Seniors (people at the age of 65 years or more) were more prone to memory distortion owing to post-event information.

In understanding the theories that function as the precursor to eyewitness accounts, psychologists and criminologists largely rely on the functions of memory. Eyewitness accounts are considered a function of long-term memory, a subject that has been independently studied in psychology and cognitive sciences. The process of retrieving information about an incident or event is a continuous, active process, where an eyewitness presents the stored information based on the development of that information in the subsequent period. In this section, we will delve into the various theories surrounding long-term memory that provide a classification system.

The first of such long-term memory processes is that of autobiographical memory, which basically stores the information within an individual regarding all physiological—physical and emotional—reaction and changes towards an instance or an event. The verbal narrative, illustrative narrative, and emotional interception within an individual that is formed during witnessing such an event forms the core function of autobiographical memory (Conway & Rubin, 1993). For example, if an eyewitness has witnessed a murder, the emotional and physical response to the scene becomes a part of their autobiographical memory (Conway & Rubin, 1993). It may be that physiological change hampers the memory recall; this naturally poses concerns regarding reliance on such memory. More analysis on autobiographical memory recall is discussed in the forthcoming section, which is an extension of memory theories known as the models of interference.

The two main theories that emerged out of autobiographical memory are interference theory and the constructivism approach. Interference theory suggests that the loss of long-term memory may occur when an attempt to recall is interfered with by other similar memories. Interference during recall can occur if the particular memory or its effects are recalled by other memories that have preceded and succeeded it. Past and present memories together lay the foundation of any resultant bias that may impact the recall procedure. The impact of past memories, those preceding the event being recalled, is known as 'proactive interference' and the impact of present 'memories' overshadowing the event is known as 'retroactive memories' (Ford et al., 1993). Retroactive memories become active in distorting accurate recall, when the succeeding memories are supplied with 'additional information' or 'misinformation' provided to the individual (Ford et al., 1993). For example, if an eyewitness is supplied with new information by the police or lawyers, he or she may include that within the retroactive process, thereby building a distorted picture of the actual events witnessed (Ford et al., 1993).

The 'constructivist approach' to memory recall was developed in the early twentieth century. The theory suggests the information from memory is 'constructed' in two steps. In the first step, when an event occurs, memory encodes the information in various forms (Bartlett, 1932). This is known as the construction of memory and is basically like the construction of a building, with the raw material being the information acquired by the individual. The second step—reconstruction—occurs when the same individual attempts to recall the information they have recorded (Bartlett, 1932). The recall process is greatly affected by the time between the recall and the event's occurrence, the organization of the information (in terms of priority and relevance to the subject), and the prior knowledge held by the individual.

Unlike the interference theory, the constructivism approach only uses the information preceding an event in the reconstruction process. The interference theory, however, considers information acquired both before and after the event and finds its application in understanding disproportionate recall process in eyewitness testimonies. Theories for recorded eyewitness testimonies have largely suggested reliance on short-term memory to be error-prone, making its inclusion in investigative procedures largely controversial. This is largely because short-term memory recall is associated with acoustic functions of the memory, which may be troubled and may not record accurate information due to the stress of the event (Conrad, 1964). However, long-term memory allows eyewitness time to organize information in a meaningful way and, therefore, provide a more accurate picture of an event.

13.3 Memory Processes and Investigation Procedures

The memory process is the central feature of information processing in human cognition and passes three distinct phases. The recognition of the same has allowed criminal investigations to employ memory as a tool for eyewitness accounts. The first process is the encoding of the information. The encoding process is the assimilation of different aspects, primarily visual and auditory, when an individual witnesses an event, say a crime. It is evident that there is a time difference between a memory encoding and its recall. Between the recall phase and the encoding phase, the memory is retained and is subject to severe reconstruction. Reconstruction of a memory is known to happen, but the mechanisms of it are not understood comprehensively, largely due to the subjective nature of the process. The loss of detail and inaccuracies adopted are largely during the retention phase and memories, therefore, may prove to be incorrect when recalled.

Within criminal investigations, largely a function of verbal dictum conducted by the investigating authorities. Research has proven that repeated collection of accounts from the same witness provides a change, in each instance, in the recollection of the crime (Odinot et al., 2008). Eyewitnesses do not do this deliberately, with some exceptions, but are compelled to change or modify due to reconstruction of memory. Considering the interference theory from the previous section, reconstruction may occur due to new information being supplied about the crime to the witness and, therefore, violate a more accurate memory retention. Further information may come from influences of society and media discussions on crimes and witnesses that may be subjectively biased towards, or against, certain details, aspects, and profiles (Odinot et al., 2008). This can lead to severe convolution of the investigative procedure and failure to discover the actual perpetrator of a crime.

The investigative proceedings, discussed earlier, include a three-step process that culminates in assembling a line of potential suspects who can then be excluded by eyewitnesses, thus isolating the perpetrator. The first step is the descriptive phase and involves eyewitness statements, either as a verbal record or statement, and if any visual recollection regarding appearances can be obtained, then a graphical sketch. The second step is the search phase. The search phase majorly relies on the information obtained from eyewitness accounts, which serve as the primary source of information about the crime (Clifford & Davies, 1989). If the eyewitness account is false, inaccurate, or misleading, the search phase may not yield results or lead to suspicion towards innocent individuals. The final phase is that of identification, a situation when potential suspects are scrutinized by eyewitness(es) to confirm identification (Clifford & Davies, 1989). This phase can be extremely compromised after severe reconstruction of memory has occurred, or if the eyewitness holds any form of bias against a particular suspect for any reason (Clifford & Davies, 1989). This can often lead to incorrect accusations and prosecutions. Having seen the results of failed memory recollections, modern forensics tends to reject the application of eyewitness accounts in identifying the perpetrator of crime.

13.4 Situational Effects on Eyewitness Accounts

Eyewitness memory can only be affected in two ways, internal processing of the information being encoded, and external factors which mainly force reconstruction of the encoded information. This section is going to discuss the situational effects on eyewitness memory in greater detail. The factors are spread across three primary classifications, namely memory processes, estimator variables, and impairment variables.

According to the memory processes discussed previously, any physiological effect that occurs in reaction to the event would be classified as a result of the event. For example, anxiety or stress arising from witnessing a traumatizing event. Any characteristic of the event itself would be classified as an event parameter. These parameters include the setting of the event, the time of the event (night or day), the available lighting in the scene, etc. In addition, the identity of the perpetrator can also be classified within this parameter, as a social parameter. The setting of the event that is the location also has an effect. Any audio interference that occur during the event, such as a gunshot, the sound of other surrounding objects can also cause information arrays in the eyewitness' memory. These characteristics are not in control of the estimator or impairment variables.

The estimator variables are the factors that are part of the justice system itself and the way they impact eyewitness' testimony. If the investigative procedure requires the eyewitness to recall information on multiple occasions, it may cause reconstruction of the information in the memory during the recall process. There are several aspects of estimator variables, some of which are recognized as the age of the witness, stress, and anxiety experienced by the witness during obtaining the statement, among others (Wells & Olsen, 2003). The period of retention—the time between the encoding of information and the recall period—further affects eyewitness accounts, as interference theory suggests that new information has a 'reconstruction effect' on the encoded information which may vary. Cross-race bias is another variable that must be considered as part of this analysis. Often social biases have an effect on eyewitness testimonies, and any prejudice may cause inaccuracies in the description and identification phases of the investigation. Intoxication, a purely physiological parameter, is another estimator variable and determines the dependency or accuracy of the information being provided by the eyewitness.

System variables, on the other hand, are not a part of either the eyewitness' own factors nor that of the estimator parameters previously discussed. The criminal justice system largely has control over these variables, which means that preventative measures can be taken to avoid the inclusion of any inaccuracies or erroneous statements being provided. These variables can be controlled to annul inaccurate descriptions or identifications provided by eyewitnesses resulting from the memory process or any other biases or conditions arising from estimator variables, such as intoxication or cross-race biases.

13.5 Comments and Theories Against the Memory Approach: Models of Interference

Previously, we established the parameters in memory, the theories of memory itself, and the relevance to investigative procedures. This section makes a brief statement regarding the failures of the eyewitness accounts theory and the memory theory. These arguments have been used to reject the reliance of criminal investigations solely or majorly on eyewitness accounts and alternatively, encourage use of 'impartial' scientific evidence. The constructivism approach and information interference form a basis of these theories.

Borrowing from the constructivist approach, the connectionist perspective states that new information recalled is often a product of past organized information preceding an event and similar to other cognitive functions. The connectionist perspective rejects memory recall among eyewitnesses suggesting that the process occurs in an inappropriate manner, largely through quick and automatic attributions made by the witness. Instead, proper recollection of the memory can only be made if the memory is recalled with deliberation and analysed under careful circumstances.

The fuzzy-trace theory (FTT) finds information is stored in memory across two modes, verbatim and in gist. Recall of information is based on either of the two modes (Loftus & Palmer, 1974). As per the theory, verbatim content is forgotten by the witness more quickly, in comparison with gist. Verbatim content refers to the surface copy of the characteristics of the event and cannot be recalled completely and accurately after sometime of the event. This includes the accurate information as the event occurred (Loftus & Palmer, 1974). The fuzzy-trace theory does not state that memory recall is incoherent, but instead suggests that the relationship between the acquisition of information and cognitive function when recall is initiated is a function of higher reasoning in humans (Loftus & Palmer, 1974).

Another critique of investigative procedures comes from the models of misinformation, which collectively state that misinformation provided to witness can often distort memory, and, therefore, causes irreversible reconstruction of the memory. Such processes may include misleading questions by authorities or lawyers to the witnesses. These models are further classified as follows. The first is the overwriting of information, which states that any new inaccurate information will cause irreversible damage to the memory recollection process of the witness, deeming any further account as incorrect (Loftus, 1975). The second one is the misattribution model, which states that inaccurate memories are a subsequent effect of distortion regarding the sequence of events (Linday & Johnson, 1989). Such disorder of the sequence hampers the abilities of the witness to accurately recall the main event itself. Finally, the models of information contain the activation-based model, which states that the activation of information, such as that arising from the supply of misinformation can be corrected if accurate information is again supplied to the individual in the matter. The eyewitness may then correct the sequence or the information stream for a more accurate description (Ayers & Reder, 1996).

13.6 Conclusion

The testimony of a witness plays an important part in a trial, and the account provided by a witness can, in many ways, decide the course of a case on trial. Although a witness' recollection of events is supposed to be accurate and detailed, that might not always be the case. The recollection of events is from the perspective of the witness describing it and that often introduces an element of subjectivity in the process. Historically considering a credible source, the eyewitness account has come under criticism of late. Researchers have now proven that memories and individual perceptions of the events can be unreliable, manipulated, and biased.

This chapter summarizes the scientific discourse that has been ongoing in the field of cognitive sciences and memory recollection, limited to the investigative procedures and criminal proceedings. Memory recollection and memory theories supplied investigative mechanisms to employ eyewitness theories as a major source of description and information regarding a crime. However, subsequent analysis has found that long-term memory recollection process faces significant reconstruction during the retention proceedings, largely due to new information or repeated information that may cause memory disturbances. Such disarray has led to the foundation of misinformation models that reject existing procedures that solely rely on the identification phase by eyewitness testimonies. New models must be generated within criminal procedures to ascertain the function of eyewitness accounts in the descriptive phase, until then, eyewitness testimony must be relied upon for corroboration and not the predominant determinant.

References

Ayers, M., & Reder, L. (1996). A theoretical review of the misinformation effect: Predictions from an activation-based memory model. *Psychonomic Bulletin & Review 5*(1), 1–21. Available at: https://doi.org/10.3758/BF03209454

Bartlett, F. (1932). "War of Ghosts"

Bartol, C. R., & Bartol, A. M. (2006). *Current perspectives in forensic psychology and criminal justice*. Sage Publications, Inc.

Brandon, R., & Davies, C. (1973). *Wrongful imprisonment: Mistaken convictions and their consequences*. Allen & Unwin

Clifford, B. R., & Davies, G. (1989). Procedures for obtaining identification evidence. In D. C. Raskin (Ed.) *Psychological methods in criminal investigations and procedure*. Springer.

Conrad, R. (1964). Acoustic confusions in immediate memory. *British Journal of Psychology, 55*(1), 75–84. Available at: https://doi.org/10.1111/j.2044-8295.1964.tb00899.x

Conway, M., & Rubin, D. (1993). The structure of autobiographical memory. In G. Collins, Conway & Morris (Eds.) Theories of Memory. Lawrence Erlbaum. Available at: https://philpapers.org/rec/CONTSO-13

Ford, D., & Zaid, M. (1993). *Eyewitness testimony, memory, and assassination research*. Marquette University. Available at: http://mcadams.posc.mu.edu/zaid.htm

Innocence Project. (2018). Retrieved from https://innocenceproject.org/justice-2018/ dated 19th May 2019

Kitaeff, J. (2011). *Handbook of police psychology*. Routledge.

Linday, S., & Johnson, M. (1989). The eyewitness suggestibility effect and memory for source. *Memory & Cognition 17*(3), 349–353. Available at: https://doi.org/10.3758/BF03198473

Loftus, E. (1975). Leading questions and the eyewitness report. *Cognitive Psychology, 7*(4), 560–572. Available at: https://www.researchgate.net/publication/240086683_Leading_Questions_and_the_Eyewitness_Report

Loftus, E. F. (1979). The malleability of human memory: Information introduced after we view an incident can transform memory. *American Scientist, 67*(3), 312–320

Loftus, E. F., & J. C. Palmer (1974). Eyewitness testimony. *Journal of Verbal Learning and Verbal Behaviour, 13*(5), 585–589. Available at: https://doi.org/10.1007/978-1-349-24483-6_46

Odinot, G., Wolterz, G., & van Koppen, P. (2008). Eyewitness memory of a supermarket robbery: A case study of accuracy and confidence after 3 months. *Law and Human Behaviour, 33*(6), 506–514. Available at: https://www.researchgate.net/publication/23186968_Eyewitness_memory_of_a_supermarket_robbery_A_case_study_of_accuracy_and_confidence_after_3_months

Wells, G., & Olsen, E. (2003). Eyewitness testimony. *Annual Review of Psychology, 54*, 277–295. Available at: http://public.psych.iastate.edu/glwells/annual_review_2003.pdf

Chapter 14
Is Forensic Evidence Impartial? Cognitive Biases in Forensic Analysis

Poulomi Bhadra

Abstract The presence of psychological biases that influence members engaged in the criminal justice process, specifically experts such as forensic investigators and analysts, is increasingly being discussed as an issue of concern regarding admissibility of scientific evidences and expert testimony. An overview of cognitive biases within forensic science highlights the vulnerabilities of the existing practices, and how they affect objective investigation and interpretation of results. These are presented in context of real case studies to highlight the key issues that compromise delivery of justice, and the need to recognize and mitigate the effect of these biases. Drawing from various existing empirical research and consequent policy recommendations, we discuss reformative solutions to minimize, control, or alleviate the impact of such cognitive biases on the individual expert as well as the collective forensic science disciplines to ensure credible and accurate decision-making.

Keywords Cognitive bias · Analyst bias · Forensic decision-making · Psychological contamination

14.1 Introduction

The process of cognition helps us make sense of the world around us through awareness, perception, and reasoning, and helps us arrive at decisions about how we go about in everyday life. Within the specific field of criminal investigation and trial, cognitive prowess helps speed up the decision-making process by drawing links between evidentiary proof and recognizable behaviour. However, if such linkages are based on illogical connections or prejudices, they lead to what we understand as cognitive bias (Haselton, 2005).

The presence of cognitive biases has been noted and empirically supported in both, everyday life, as well as other scientific fields such as medicine and data analysis.

P. Bhadra (✉)
Jindal Institute of Behavioural Sciences, O.P. Jindal Global University, Sonipat, Haryana, India
e-mail: pbhadra@jgu.edu.in

S. Sahni et al. (eds.), *Criminal Psychology and the Criminal Justice System in India and Beyond*, https://doi.org/10.1007/978-981-16-4570-9_14

Therefore, it is not surprising that despite the carefully crafted protocols and precautionary measures within forensic practices, scientific evidence has not remained immune to the pervasion of psychological biases. The operational costs of cognitive bias might result in a mistaken or exaggerated interpretation of an evidence or lead to derailing the course of investigation by pursuing a prejudiced lead.

While the literature on cognitive bias in psychological studies has been widely developed, its presence and impact on forensic sciences has been a subject of recent study, ongoing for a little more than a decade. These studies have used data from both controlled, laboratory-based experiments and real-life casework to understand the effect of such biases. Effective reforms to mitigate these biases are highly dependent on the training and analysis techniques of the respective forensic discipline in question. Discipline-specific studies have been done in fields such as forensic speech (Rhodes, 2014), forensic anthropology (Nakhaeizadeh et al., 2014), forensic document examination (Stoel et al., 2014), fingerprint analysis (Reese, 2012), digital forensics (Sunde & Dror, 2019), forensic mental health assessments (Zapf et al., 2018) among others. In this chapter, however, we will deal with the types of cognitive biases that commonly influence forensic sciences and the wider scope within which they operate.

14.1.1 *Role of Evidence & Expert Witnesses*

Given the prevalence of fallacies recorded in eyewitness memory, lawyers often rely on such testimony to be assisted or contradicted by forensic evidence. The scientific nature of most types of forensic evidence implies an objectivity that human witnesses may lack. However, the ability of scientific evidence to testify as close to the truth as possible is reliant on several factors, including the competency and training of the expert witness or forensic analyst.

Previously, not much attention was given to the role of human cognition in forensic work. Thus, it was easier to maintain that most forensic examiners and institutions involved in such examination and analysis operated from a place of objectivity, and therefore, their conclusions were trusted indubitably.

The nature of forensic analysis also requires knowledge and training in specific disciplines and techniques that the legal stakeholders–lawyers and judges-are not adept at comprehending. This lack of scientific literacy renders the courts handicapped in assessing the shortcomings of the expert testimony.

Even within forensic disciplines, some scientific techniques are more accurate and robust than others; for example, DNA profiling is a technique known for its accuracy and efficiency, in contrast to document examination and handwriting analysis, which can be a highly subjective assessment. Thus, an expert opining on DNA evidence is likely to garner more confidence from the judicial bench than a handwriting analyst. Even at the level of expert performance, one can observe inconsistencies in objectivity within experts, in that different examiners may differ in the confidence with which they opine on the same evidence (Dror, 2017). Not only between examiners, but differences may lie within the same examiner's assessment of an evidence done over multiple occasions, even if there is no change in other contextual information (Dror, 2017). Although this variance may result from factors other than cognition bias as well, bias is only one of the factors influencing decision-making.

Summarily, despite advances in scientific techniques, the human element plays an important role in interpreting evidences in context. Human fallibility may arise from subconscious biases, such as forensic scientists believing that they are operating on the righteous side of the justice system or from conscious biases, as in the case of Joyce Gilchrist and Fred Zain, who intentionally forged results to favour the prosecution, leading to conviction and execution of several accused who were possibly innocent. John Pitt Taylor wrote of partisan bias of experts in 1887, which may still hold true in current times—'Perhaps the testimony which least deserves credit with a jury is that of skilled witnesses. These gentlemen are usually required to speak, not of facts, but to opinions: and when this is the case, it is often quite surprising to see with what facility, and to what an extent, their views can be made to correspond with the wishes or the interests of the parties who call them'.

Over the last decade, the fallibility of forensic experts has dramatically changed the faith with which expert testimony is perceived. This new area of study in cognitive forensics has helped the forensic community recognize prevalent biases, and develop and deploy countermeasures to mitigate its effects on trial proceedings.

14.2 Role of Cognitive Biases in Analysis and Interpretation

The ubiquity of cognitive bias is now widely recognized by the forensic community, and various jurisdictions have published guidance policies to counter the effects of cognitive contamination on forensic decision-making. Some of the best regulations in this regard have been published by the United Kingdom Forensic Science Regulator (FSRG 217, 2015), the United States National Commission on Forensic Science ('Ensuring' 2015), and reports by the National Academy of Sciences ('Strengthening', 2009) and President's Council of Advisors on Science and Technology (PCAST Report 'Forensic Science in Criminal Courts', 2016).

Dr. Itiel E. Dror, one of the foremost scholars in cognitive forensics, has proposed a taxonomy of the possible sources of bias that may interfere with scientific observations and conclusions at various stages (see Fig. 14.1). The structure divides the sources of bias into three origins—those arising from the functioning of the human mind and its cognitive architecture, those arising from environmental and individual circumstances, and lastly, those arising from case-specific influences (Dror, 2017).

The bottom level of this hierarchy deals with the individual examiner's biases instilled during training and education, and those formed by the basic working of the human mind that predisposes us to biases. The latter has long been a widely studied premise within psychology.

At the next level, the environment, culture, and experience influence the examiner. Organizational factors relate to the kind of biases that originate from the organization

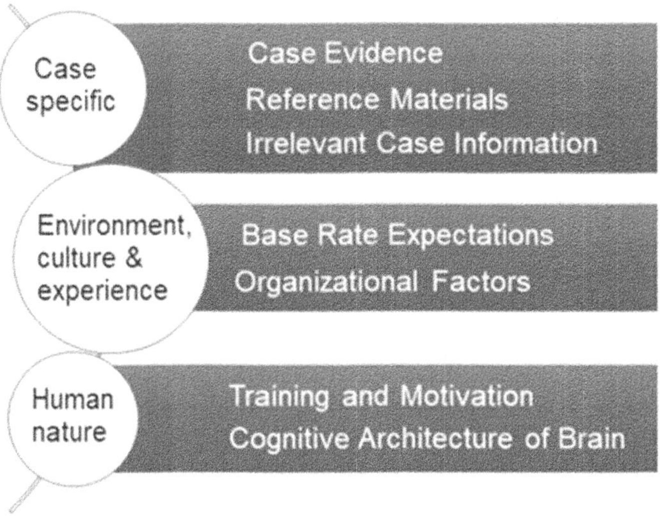

Fig. 14.1 A taxonomy of different sources of bias (Dror, 2017)

or the work culture that the forensic examiner is associated with. Most examiners may work closely with the investigation or legal team, and such interactions might build loyalties and allegiances that can create role effect or partisan bias, or lead to sharing of extraneous information between parties that might result in other biases. These influences are more general than case-specific and are likely built over time and peer-networking.

Base-rate expectations are prejudicial when past experiences in field analysis lead to a propensity to expect a particular result. This bias can also consolidate over time and is likely to carry over from past experiences to every new situation encountered by the examiner, compromising their objectivity to assess. For example, automated fingerprint identification system (AFIS) is an algorithm that generates a list of possible matches to a questioned fingerprint. It is usually seen that the closest matches are generally listed at the top of the list, and most examiners tend to invest more time in assessing the top matches instead of the ones at the bottom. This pattern often biases them to expect a match at the top of the list, leading to false positives, i.e. wrongfully finding a match because it appeared at the top of the list, under influence of base-rate expectations (Dror et al, 2012).

Lastly, the factors that contribute significantly to cognitive bias can arise from the case-specific evidence or case facts themselves. In some cases, the biasing aspect is strongly integrated with the evidence and cannot be separated. This is most prevalent in digital forensics, such as voice analysis or CCTV footage, where one cannot examine an aspect of the evidence without witnessing the related contextual information such as what is being said or done. On the other hand, in case of signature or handwriting analysis, it is possible to examine the questioned sample without exposing oneself to the contents of the entire document, which maybe irrelevant to the examination in question.

In some cases though, the context within which the evidence needs to be analysed is necessary for accurate interpretation. In such cases, the information revealed should be done judiciously so as to not allow irrelevant data to bias the examiner's interpretation or analysis. Irrelevant and extraneous information shared by the investigating police or legal counsel can influence the expert opinion negatively; examples of such information include details about the suspect's criminal past or personal history, information that eyewitnesses recognized the suspect at the scene or about any confession made by the witness, details about findings reported by other evidences or the personal opinions of the investigator, etc. Ideally, the evidence from the scene should not only be examined free from any contextual information regarding the targeted 'suspect', but also examined first, before examining the control sample taken from the suspect.

14.2.1 Types of Cognitive Biases

Even though cognitive bias is pervasive in regular lifestyles and work, the risks of such psychological contamination in forensic processes come at the cost of life and liberty of the people interacting with the criminal justice system. One of the first steps in forming effective countermeasures is to recognize the kind of bias and the stage of analysis at which it operates. Here, we will limit the discussion to the cognitive biases associated solely with the forensic processes and examination at crime scenes and laboratories, and not discuss those influence other participants of the criminal justice system, such as judiciary, jury, police and lawyers.

14.2.1.1 Motivational Bias

Motivational bias is often considered different from cognitive biases, since it involves a conscious judgement in favouring one of the litigating parties to win. Under this influence, the examiner will choose to favour one or the other party by faking results and reports, examining evidences that support the favoured party with lesser scrutiny, and intentional exaggeration of results and interpretation (Dawson, 2002). However, this motivational influence may also be based on a subconscious prejudice—namely the 'Avengers' complex—the misplaced motivation that they are the law, or on the right side of the law—or may be motivated by personal or political factors, such as pressure to give a favourable result for a politically important case or one receiving high media attention, closing case investigations with successful convictions in order to receive professional gains such as a promotion or other perks.

Fred Zain at West Virginia State Crime Laboratory and Joyce Gilchrist at Oklahoma City Crime Laboratory had both enjoyed being favourites with the regional prosecutors because they routinely delivered reports that favoured the prosecution, especially when other analysts were unable to find useable evidence or deliver favourable results. Later, both were independently tried for professional misconduct in which they were found guilty of manipulating results, withholding evidence and issuing false testimony for the prosecution, leading to wrongful convictions and sentencing (Giannelli, 2007).

14.2.1.2 Role Effect or Partisan Bias

When the motivation is subconsciously tied to the examiner's perception of their role in the criminal justice system, it can lead to role effect. Occupational socialization that leads to the building of support networks influences social conduct and attitude at shared workplaces (Saks & Van Duizend, 1983). Thus, it is not unknown for scientists to identify with the sides in the adversarial system that they might be presenting for. In India and many other jurisdictions, the forensic science services function under State governance, and many analysts work closely with State prosecutors and the police. In private laboratories, scientists might be working for either the State or a private party, representing either prosecution or defence. Although scientists are required to operate objectively, the close association with law enforcement or lawyers might create subconscious bias in favour of the team they identify with (Mills et al., 2004). This might particularly manifest in decision-making where some ambiguity in results exists. For example, in case of a footmark or tool mark, the probability of match may be presented more strongly in favour of the prosecution hypothesis, or in case of an ambiguous match of fibre analysis based on poor sample quality, the scientist might over-interpret the findings as supporting the view that contact had not occurred (defence hypothesis), rather than questioning the sample collection or demanding a better sample.

Cognitive Biases in the Indian Criminal Adjudication: Case Study

In May 2008, teenager Aarushi Talwar was found dead in her bedroom by her parents, and a day later, the dead body of their live-in house help, Hemraj Banjade, who was the police's initial suspect, was found on the terrace of the building. The post-mortem examination report on Aarushi, done on the day of discovery, did not mention any positive evidence of sexual intercourse or assault. After the discovery of Hemraj's body, the investigating police accused the parents of the double homicide, brewing up a scandalous story of wife swapping and sexual attraction between the 13-years-old Aarushi and 45-years old Hemraj, despite having no evidence to support this theory. The horrific death of the child in her own home and the sensational press release by the Noida Police garnered much media interest in the case. In the wake of this new information, Dr. Sunil Dhore, who conducted the initial autopsy revised his opinion to state that the child's vaginal cavity was abnormally open and that there was white discharge present on her underwear. This revision was made without a second examination of the body, which had already been cremated by then. Even though the High Court later rebuked the doctor for 'medical blasphemy', basing his revised opinion on no credible evidence, this incident presents the possibility of several cognitive biases in action. Firstly, the need to revise his opinion without a second examination demonstrates an inclination to produce favourable results for the prosecution—a classic consequence of motivational bias. This might also have been influenced by the doctor's close alliance with the police and their past working relationship, which may have subconsciously influenced Dhore to believe that the investigating police was correct in their conclusions. This can be termed as role effect, or partisan bias. Lastly, the need to confirm the new hypothesis of the Noida police would require evidence of sexual intercourse which the doctor provided in his revised opinion. He was either negligent in noting the appearance of the vaginal cavity during the first autopsy (because of expectation bias that young Indian girls are normally not sexually active) or the revised opinion was an exaggeration of what could be, at best termed as, an ambiguous result (confirmation bias). The other information presented to support the conclusion—the presence of whitish vaginal discharge—could imply the presence of semen but could also be a result of vaginal discharge, which is a normal occurrence in post-puberty females. The information should have been appropriately contextualized within both the alternative explanations, instead of being presented solely in a manner to support the prosecution's hypothesis.

14.2.1.3 Expectation Bias

This is the most common subconscious bias affecting scientists from all disciplines, where the evidence or results found seem to support a predetermined expectation of the analyst. Simply put, the scientist sees what they want to see; even if it comes at the cost of manipulating the data interpretation or exaggerating data that supports the hypothesis, and downgrading data that conflicts with it. For example, it has been observed that fingerprint analysts looking at the list of matches generated by the automated fingerprint identification system (AFIS) expect the best matches to be at the top of the list, and the degree of match to decrease as they go down the list. This expectation has led examiners to find (1) more false positives at the top of the list, i.e. tendency to find a (forced) match at the top of the list even if the correct match is present lower in the list, and (2) more false negatives at the bottom of the list, where the positioning of the correct match led the examiners to falsely exclude it as a match (Dror et al., 2012).

14.2.1.4 Confirmation Bias

Akin to expectation bias, examiners experiencing confirmation bias also look for evidence to confirm their hypothesis, but also ignore contradictory or conflicting information (Kassin et al., 2013). In the same case of the Aarushi-Hemraj double homicide, Dr. Naresh Raj who examined Hemraj's body noted that the deceased had a swollen penis and came to the conclusion that this was because 'he was in the middle of or about to have sexual intercourse just before he was murdered'. This conclusion was made by the experienced doctor despite exisiting evidence within medical literature confirming that between 18–34 h after death, the penis and scrotum are likely to appear enormously swollen (Yechury, 2017). This information was not presented to the court in the expert's testimony as an alternative explanation to his observation at autopsy. The tendency to ignore research-based evidence that would conflict with the prosecution hypothesis can be attributed to professional negligence resulting from confirmation bias.

14.2.1.5 Conformity Effect (Institutional Bias)

Within institutional power structures and expertise hierarchy, confirmation bias can also be exerted by the indirect influence of one examiner on the other. In cases of peer verification, the reviewing examiner can be influenced not only by knowledge of the initial expert's findings, but also by knowledge of the expert themselves—of their status or professional experience or their reputation. In the Madrid train bombing incident, the FBI wrongly identified Brandon Mayfield as the terrorist who planted the bomb, based off a poor quality fingerprint specimen retrieved from a damaged and soot-covered part of the explosive device used. This misidentification occurred despite the analysis having been reviewed by three experts. It is possible that prior knowledge of the previous expert having confirmed a match caused the other reviewers (one of them was even court-appointed) to scrutinize the report less thoroughly, leading to a conformity bias (Stacey & Unit, 2005).

14.2.1.6 Contextual Bias

One of the biggest problems is the influence of extraneous information that is irrelevant to the hypotheses under examination, but nevertheless affects the outcome of our consideration of the evidence, even if we are consciously aware that we should not take the information into account. One of the easiest ways to leak more than necessary information is by not screening the case facts that are sent to the examiner to assist in analysis. Other ways of such psychological contamination can be by oversharing information about the case with the forensic analyst that is not really needed to undertake the evaluation, such as revealing strong suspicions of the investigator regarding a suspect, divulging facts about the confession of the suspect or identification of the suspect by an eyewitness, or sharing the findings from other evidences found in the case.

14.2.1.7 Anchoring Effect or Focalism

This is when the examiner or investigator fixates on an initial piece of information and all the subsequent examination and interpretation is conducted relative to that information being true, excluding all possible alternatives that might also explain the results obtained. For example, the presumption that any violent crime is most likely to be committed by a male, or any such socio-economic stereotyping based on the crime circumstances, can lead to ignoring a lot of pertinent inferences that the evidence may offer, such as in the Yorkshire Ripper case (Byford, 1982).

14.2.1.8 Reconstructive Effect

Forensic professionals are required to take contemporaneous notes of what they do at the scene and in the laboratory, so that the case file reflects accurately the analysis performed on each evidence. This documentation is essential in diagnosing any procedural error or testing that might have implication on the outcomes reported to the court, particularly with regard to contamination or tampering. However, sometimes, simultaneous recording is not done by the examiners, who then later rely on memory for report writing or testimony in court. In such cases, there is an increased chance that they will fail to report what they actually did, and instead, influenced by protocol requirements, fill in the gaps in memory with what they believe they should have done, or happened. Such errors might raise red flags in terms of evidence integrity, compromising the counsel's case.

14.3 Conditions Impacting Risk of Cognitive Bias

While the risk of cognitive bias in forensic examination is ever present, it does not mean that it affects every case. Although, in real casework, the extent of the impact of cognitive bias, or a combination of these biases may be difficult to evaluate. Nevertheless, it has been noted that the risk of bias is greater in case of ambiguous results, such as when samples are of poor quality or when the assessment technique is unvalidated, ad-hoc and subjective to the examiner instead of a universally standardized procedure. Some biases (e.g. confirmation bias) may be present even in cases of methodical approaches; however, the occurrence is lower. The effect of biases is also found to be lower when the examination is conducted by trained and experienced examiners who adhere to standards of competence and scientific rigour, and the verification review is conducted independently and rigorously by equally competent peers.

14.4 Debiasing Countermeasures

The NAS and other subsequent reports have widely acknowledged the problem of cognitive biases in forensic examination and even recommended further investigation into this issue and systemic recommendations to safeguard the forensic processes and individuals working within the criminal justice system. However, the efficacy of these recommendations depends on the types of analysis methods prevalent within the disciplines, and the expectation and standards of the jurisdictional justice system within which they operate.

Even as we await comprehensive research to understand the extent to which cognitive biases affect criminal adjudication, there is a need to implement institutionalized, reformative measures. One of the most fundamental ways to control this prevalence is to educate the investigators and examiners about the existence of such biases and the risks associated with them. Although this does not effectively annul these biases, since they operate subconsciously, it does help to initiate awareness among practitioners and other stakeholders of the criminal justice system by giving them a working knowledge of these issues. In criminal justice systems like India, crime scene investigators come from modest educational backgrounds and may not be sufficiently trained in forensic sciences; additionally, there also exists a huge gap in academy training and ground-level practice of forensic protocols in the field. This gap especially needs to be addressed via innovative training programmes including practical or experimental components that will help to illustrate how even the most diligent investigator can be susceptible to bias and how the standardized protocols are developed to overcome such bias. Even without proof of bias within the system, it is advisable to implement the proposed reforms, as listed below, as they will indubitably improve the integrity of forensic science processes at a relatively low cost (Cole, 2013).

One of the effective ways to control contextual bias is by controlling the flow of information revealed to the examiner, what is popularly known as ‘linear sequential unmasking’ (Dror et al., 2015). Since task-relevant information is crucial for an accurate assessment and interpretation of evidence, the examiner cannot expect to get accurate results from conducting blind examination of the evidence samples alone, without any case-specific information revealed. However, in sequential unmasking, the examiner expects that the information they will receive will be managed and therefore also takes caution to avoid psychological contamination, such as by discussing the case facts with the investigation team or co-examiners before or during the assessment process. Any changes in opinion and analysis as new case information is disclosed should be recorded meticulously to help trace the decision-making process.

When it comes to the examination itself, the examination strategy should be efficient and robust. As far as possible, the examiner must rely on scientifically validated techniques rather than heuristic methods. It is also important that analysis follows a structured approach where the sample from the crime scene, or the 'questioned' sample, is examined first, and the features or test results are noted, before examining the reference or source sample. This prevents expectation or confirmation bias from creeping into the analysis. Making contemporaneous notes should be a mandatory stipulation, made habitual by practice during training.

Peer review of each analysis report should be done critically and independently, preferably without knowledge of the original examiner's identity or findings, and with as little background information given about the case as needed. Additionally, it is important to maintain strict organizational structures that streamline the flow of information and help sustain independent reporting, especially if the verification process is done by peers within the same institution.

Of course, there are other factors that can influence the reporting of an examination from analysis to trial, including new information about the case coming to light, new validation studies conducted to address the lacunas in that scientific discipline or technique, or improved expertise and knowledge capacity of the examiner resulting from experience and subsequent training since the initial reporting. Any or all of these factors may compel the examiner to revisit their opinion and such provisions must also be made available in legislation, when supported by adequate reasoning. However, law operates within limitations of time and a case can be made for limiting the number of revisions allowed, based on the confidence of the initial assessment (Dror et al., 2015).

In the broader scope, it must be acknowledged that different people will be differently susceptible to cognitive influences, and it might be helpful to consider assessing this potential during the recruitment process in forensic services (Charlton et al., 2010). It is also important that forensic laboratories and their professionals be constantly kept on their toes by proficiency testing, wherein accrediting bodies may conduct declared and undeclared blind testing using mock samples for which the outcomes are already known. There should also be strict measures within the organization to monitor and penalize misconduct as well as management structures and work culture that foster neutrality in evaluation, in the interest of the criminal justice system and not just for the prosecution or defence.

14.5 Conclusion

Cognitive biases are, by nature, caused by unconscious reasoning strategies and can often go unnoticed in practice, by self and peers. This makes their pervasion in the criminal justice process more problematic, especially when conviction and sentencing is reliant on evidence that has some component of subjective assessment. Alongside the advances in forensic techniques that make the technologies more efficient and accurate, it is imperative that laboratories impose interventions at all levels to minimize bias. Judges and lawyers must also be aware of the risks of psychological contamination in expert testimony and conduct a thorough examination of expert witnesses to ascertain the validity of their decisions, especially in case of ambiguous results.

References

Byford,. (1982). *Report by Sir Lawrence Byford into the police handling of the Yorkshire Ripper case*. Home Office.

Charlton, D., Fraser-Mackenzie, P. A., & Dror, I. E. (2010). Emotional experiences and motivating factors associated with fingerprint analysis. *Journal of Forensic Sciences, 55*(2), 385–393.

Cole, S. A. (2013). Implementing counter-measures against confirmation bias in forensic science. *Journal of Applied Research in Memory and Cognition, 2*(1), 61–62. https://doi.org/10.1016/j.jarmac.2013.01.011

Dawson, et al. (2002). Motivated Reasoning and Performance on the Wason Selection Task. *Personality & Social Psychology Bulletin, 28*, 1379–1387.

Dror, I. E. (2017). Human expert performance in forensic decision making: Seven different sources of bias. *Australian Journal of Forensic Sciences, 49*(5), 541–547. https://doi.org/10.1080/00450618.2017.1281348

Dror, I. E., Wertheim, K., Fraser-Mackenzie, P., & Walajtys, J. (2012). The impact of human–technology cooperation and distributed cognition in forensic science: Biasing effects of AFIS contextual information on human experts. *Journal of Forensic Sciences, 57*(2), 343–352.

Dror, I. E., Thompson, W. C., Meissner, C. A., Kornfield, I., Krane, D., Saks, M., & Risinger, M. (2015). Letter to the editor-context management toolbox: A linear sequential unmasking (LSU) approach for minimizing cognitive bias in forensic decision making. *Journal of Forensic Sciences, 60*, 4.

Forensic Science Regulator Guidance. (2015). Cognitive bias effects relevant to forensic science examinations. *FSR-G-217.*

Giannelli, P. C. (2007). Wrongful convictions and forensic science.The need to regulate crime labs. *North Carolina Law Review, 86*(163), 172–174

Haselton, M. G., Nettle, D., & Andrews, P. W. (2005). The evolution of cognitive bias. In D. M. Buss (Ed.), *The Handbook of Evolutionary Psychology* (pp. 724–746). Wiley.

Kassin, S. M., Dror, I. E., & Kukucka, J. (2013). The forensic confirmation bias: Problems, perspectives, and proposed solutions. *Journal of Applied Research in Memory and Cognition, 2*(1), 42–52.

Mills, S., McRoberts, F., & Possley, M. (2004). When labs falter, defendants pay: bias toward prosecution cited in Illinois cases. *Chicago Tribune.*

Nakhaeizadeh, S., Dror, I. E., & Morgan, R. M. (2014). Cognitive bias in forensic anthropology: Visual assessment of skeletal remains is susceptible to confirmation bias. *Science & Justice, 54*(3), 208–214.

National Academy of Sciences. (2009). *Strengthening forensic science in the United States: A path forward*. National Academies Press.

National Commission on Forensic Science. (2015). *Ensuring that forensic analysis is based upon task relevant information.* Washington (DC). Available from: https://www.justice.gov/ncfs/file/818196/download

Presidents' Council of Advisors on Science and Technology (2016) *Forensic science in criminal courts: ensuring scientific validity of feature-comparison methods.* Washington (DC). Available from: https://obamawhitehouse.archives.gov/sites/default/files/microsites/ostp/PCAST/pcast_forensic_science_report_final.pdf

Reese, E. J. (2012). Techniques for mitigating cognitive biases in fingerprint identification. *UCLA Law Review, 59*(5), 1252–1291.

Rhodes, R. (2014). Cognitive bias in forensic speech science. *Proceedings of IAFPA.*

Saks, M. J., & Van Duizend, R. (1983). *The use of scientific evidence in litigation*. National Center for State Courts.

Sanitioso, R., Kunda, Z., & Fong, G. T. (1990). Motivated recruitment of autobiographical memories. *Journal of Personality and Social Psychology, 59*(2), 229.

Stacey, R. B., & Unit, T. (2005). Report on the erroneous fingerprint individualization in the Madrid train bombing case. *Historian, 404*, 294–2647.

Stoel, R. D., Dror, I. E., & Miller, L. S. (2014). Bias among forensic document examiners: Still a need for procedural changes. *Australian Journal of Forensic Sciences, 46*(1), 91–97.

Sunde, N., & Dror, I. E. (2019). Cognitive and human factors in digital forensics: Problems, challenges, and the way forward. *Digital Investigation, 29*, 101–108.

Taylor, J. P. (1887). *A Treatise on the Law of Evidence as Administered in England and Ireland: With Illustrations from American and Other Foreign Laws: from the 8th English Edition* (Vol. 1). Blackstone Publishing Company.

Yechury, A. (2017, October 14). Aarushi Murder Case: Postmortem Doctor Suspected Aarushi, Hemraj Sexual Relations based on 'Own Experience'. News18 India. Retrieved from https://www.news18.com/news/india/aarushi-murder-case-postmortem-doctor-suspected-aarushi-hemraj-sexual-relations-based-on-own-experience-1545653.html

Zapf, P. A., Kukucka, J., Kassin, S. M., & Dror, I. E. (2018). Cognitive bias in forensic mental health assessment: Evaluator beliefs about its nature and scope. *Psychology, Public Policy, and Law, 24*(1), 1.

Chapter 15
Decision-Making in the Courtroom: Judiciary

Mohita Junnarkar and Kartik Adlakha

Abstract The verdict in all criminal cases is heavily reliant on judge's decision-making abilities. This, in turn, may be influenced by arguments from the litigating lawyers, eyewitness testimony, and comments from the arbitration panel; however, the lawyers are reported to generally hold maximal influence. This chapter will outline the various factors that influence the judges' decision-making process. We will discuss at length on psychological concepts such as short-term memory, schemas, language, emotions, persuasion, and their role in courtroom. In discussing various examples of the effective courtroom statements derived from international and Indian trials, we will also outline the various ways in which lawyers can successfully persuade a judge in the courtroom.

Keywords Judge · Decision-making · Persuasion · Language · Emotions

Box [Case study] starts

Opening Arguments in the People of the State of California V Orenthal James Simpson (O. J. Simpson Murder Trial, 1995):

Prosecution*:* 'We're here today, obviously, to resolve an issue, to settle a question, a question that has been on the minds of people throughout the country these last seven months. Did O. J. Simpson really kill Nicole Brown and Ronald Goldman? Well, finally, ladies and gentlemen, I am here in front of you this morning to answer that question. And we will answer that question from the witness stand, and from the exhibits you'll see in this case, and from the evidence. And when you see the evidence, and when you hear the witnesses,

M. Junnarkar (✉)
Jyoti Dalal School of Liberal Arts, NMIMS Deemed University, Mumbai, India

K. Adlakha
Student Researcher, Jindal Global Law School, O.P. Jindal Global University, Sonipat, Haryana, India

S. Sahni et al. (eds.), *Criminal Psychology and the Criminal Justice System in India and Beyond*, https://doi.org/10.1007/978-981-16-4570-9_15

and when you put it all together and consider the totality of circumstances in this case, the answer will be clear to you as well.

The answer to the question is yes. The evidence will show that the answer to the question is yes. O. J. Simpson murdered Nicole Brown and Ronald Goldman'.

Defence: 'None of us were out there on June 12, 1994. You can only deal with the witnesses as they were. It seems to me that this case, the prosecution's case, based on what we heard from the evidence, will show this case is about a rush to judgment, an obsession to win at any cost and by any means necessary'.

Closing Arguments:

Defence: 'The Defendant, Mr. Orenthal James Simpson, is now afforded an opportunity to argue the case, if you will, but I'm not going to argue with you, ladies and gentlemen. What I'm going to do is to try and discuss the reasonable inferences which I feel can be drawn from this evidence.

And so as we look then at the time line and the importance of this time line, I want you to remember these words. Like the defining moment in this trial, the day Mr. Darden asked Mr. Simpson to try on those gloves and the gloves didn't fit, remember these words; if it doesn't fit, you must acquit.

They don't have any mountain or ocean of evidence. It's not so because they say so. That's just rhetoric. We this afternoon are talking about the facts. And so it doesn't make any sense. It just doesn't fit. If it doesn't fit, you must acquit'.

Box [Case study] ends

15.1 Background

The above-mentioned opening and closing arguments have been taken from the trial of O. J. Simpson, a former NFL star, who was accused of murdering his ex-wife, Nicole Brown Simpson and another man, Ronald Goldman. It remains one of the most famous trials in history. The above-extracted paragraphs showcase how the prosecution and defence employed not only reason and logic, but also the art of persuasion, emotional argumentation, and courtroom theatrics to make their arguments. While the prosecution counsel in O. J. Simpson's case uses the art of rhetoric to make her arguments, the defence uses phrases like 'rush to judgment' and 'if it doesn't fit, you must acquit' to persuade the jury to acquit. The phrase 'if it doesn't fit, you must acquit', coined by Johnnie Cochran, O. J. Simpson's lead lawyer, was made a frequently used catchphrase during the case. The phrase was first used when O. J. was made to try the gloves found at the crime scene that the killer was allegedly wearing when committing the murders, and they were found to be too tight on O. J.'s hand. 'If it doesn't fit, you must acquit'—Mr. Cochran used this creatively rhymed catchphrase multiple times in his closing statement too. In the end, O. J. Simpson was acquitted of all charges, the theatrics of making O. J. try on the gloves in open court, an unusual move, and the phrase 'if it doesn't fit, you must acquit' seemed to have made a great effect on the jury deciding upon the O. J. Simpson case.

This chapter will delineate how lawyers, through effective persuasion, can affect the judge's (or jury's) decisions. In the first part, we will answer the question 'Why does psychology matter in the courtroom' by explaining the role of some psychological concepts in the courtroom and how certain activities of a lawyer can influence the judge. The second half will elaborate on the art of persuasion, which will outline the various methods by which a lawyer can cast a persuasive influence on the trier of facts.

15.2 Why Does Psychology Matter in the Courtroom?

Arguing a case in trial involves more than writing a legal brief outlining the arguments in favour of your case in front of a judicial authority. While cogent and sensible arguments made on points of law are definitely important, when it comes down to the judge's cognitive skills in choosing between two rational arguments, a lawyer's persuasive skills and psychological tactics play a considerable part. It is, therefore, necessary to understand the various psychological concepts and their interplay with the courtroom to understand how to use them in the courtroom.

15.2.1 Primacy and Recency Effect

Primacy and recency are two concepts that describe the effects of two sides of an issue, when presented one after the other. Which issue, do you think, has a more substantial impact on the audience, the one presented first or the one presented last? The primacy effect was discovered by Lund (1925) when he found that in an experimental set-up, if contrasting arguments around an issue were presented subsequently, the argument presented first had the most profound impact on the audience (Costopoulos, 1972). Opinions formulated initially by the audience were much less likely to change after hearing the second argument because of the primacy advantage afforded to the argument presented first. This is known as the principle of primacy which, simply stated, is the increased likelihood of people developing strong opinions in the first impression itself that are later unlikely to change.

Understanding the application of this principle brings to light how psychology plays an important and fundamental role in the courtroom. Following the principle of primacy, studies have been conducted to show that judges rely heavily on the arguments and evidence presented first when forming an initial opinion about the case. This opinion bias acts as a barrier that prevents proper consideration of the evidence presented in further stages of the trial, and therefore, it would be important for the trial lawyer to lead with his best evidence first.

Later, Cromwell (1950) found that, instead of primacy, recency was a much more important phenomenon that came into play here. He showed that there is an increased likelihood of people remembering and formulating strong opinions based on the arguments that they have heard last (Costopoulos, 1972; Kohler, 2007; Miller & Campbell, 1959). This came to be known as the principle of recency.

To this date, it not clear as to which principle should be afforded more weight but what is certain is that the order of presentation of your best evidence tips the scale in the courtroom. Whether you lead with the best evidence first or bring it in at the last moment, both would affect the judge's ruling.

Further research has proffered a list of variable factors, some of which produce a primacy effect, while some produce recency effect and some are free variable factors that could produce either of the two depending upon the manner in which they are used (Costopoulos, 1972). It has been found that the interesting or previously known topics to the receiver, when presented in form of arguments, tend to produce a primacy effect, while topics which are unfamiliar tend to produce a recency effect for the receiver. Weight and strength of the argument belong to the third category of free variable factors, a significantly stronger argument or evidence placed on record would be remembered, irrespective of the stage of the trial it appears at (Costopoulos, 1972). Generally speaking, cases that receive a lot of attention from media because of its high profile, controversial or sensational nature, such as the 2008 Aarushi-Hemraj double homicide, are likely to be interesting to both the public and judiciary alike, and present the prosecution with an advantage because they would be the first to present the opening statements and facts. But in case of an uninteresting, dry dispute like a taxation dispute that is too technical in nature, defendants would have the advantage, as it would be difficult for the judge to remember details of the arguments made at the beginning of the trial.

Generally, the prosecution is believed to have the advantage of primacy, and however, it can be easily offset by lengthening the duration of the trial, which is usually the case in India, where an overburdened judiciary can result in cases lasting over decades. The defence can also purposely offset primacy by presenting multiple witnesses and extending their examination, which would help lengthen the trial and build distance from the period when the prosecution evidence was introduced.

Considering all these factors at play, trial lawyers are advised to not present key evidence in the middle of a trial, as it would have the least substantial impact on the judge. Based on the advantages of primacy or recency effects, it would be advisable to start and end with a strong witness or evidence. As in the O. J. Simpson case, the defence counsel emphasized on the gloves not fitting the accused multiple times during the closing statement to get the advantage of the recency effect, and to ensure that the jury remembers most impressively that the defense had successfully thwarted the incriminating implications of a key prosecution evidence.

15.2.2 Placing Emphasis: Repetition, Duration, and the Von Restorff Effect

A trial lawyer should always be aware of which are the most relevant pieces of evidence to his argument, and should use techniques to emphasize their pertinence to the case, to present a stronger argument to the judge.

By spending more time on the examination of a particular evidence or witness and by reiterating the inference from that evidence frequently in court, the lawyer can successfully impress the importance of that particular evidence or argument upon the judge/jury. The more often you repeat an argument, the more easily it can be recalled by the audience hearing it (Lubet, 1997). Similarly, the more time and effort the lawyer spends on a particular evidence, the more important it will seem to a judge (Gold, 1987). This will also help the judge understand the lawyer's arguments better and more clearly. Johnnie Cochran, O. J. Simpson's defence lawyer, applied the same principles when he repeated the phrase 'if it doesn't fit, you must acquit' multiple times during the case, so that the message of this statement is embedded in the jurors' minds. This is a classic example of repetition and duration techniques.

Von Restorff principle states that events that are unique and different are almost unforgettable in nature (Voss, 2005). For example, one may not remember what they were doing on any particular day but they remember exactly what they were doing when they first heard about the 9/11 World Towers attack in the States or the 26/11 Mumbai terror attacks. Certain researchers have concluded that a person is substantially more likely to pay attention, remember what is said and be influenced by it when that particular person is told that they are about to hear something unique compared to a situation in which no such assertion is made (Voss, 2005). This is why, attorneys in controversial cases, use phrases like 'Today, I will reveal to certain facts that were left out of the investigative inquiry'. Use of such phrases tend to build curiosity and suspense relating to the fact that something unique or novel is about to be revealed, resulting in judges paying much more attention to the facts. Emphasizing techniques play an operative role in the courtroom, and however, they are only effective if used in moderation. Emphasizing frequently and almost every evidence would lead to all arguments being given the same amount of weight in the mind of the audience, which is antithetical to the aim of emphasis.

15.2.3 Value of Emotional Appeal

A courtroom does not function merely on plain logic and rationality, the value of emotional appeal and persuasion has their own clout in a courtroom. An experiment by George W. Hartmann proves that in some cases, emotional appeal can be more effective than a purely rational appeal (Coustopoulos, 1972).

Consider the closing statement below from the movie Shawshank Redemption (Darabont, 1994):

> "Ladies and gentlemen, you've heard all the evidence, you know all the facts. We have the accused at the scene of the crime. We have footprints. Tire tracks. Bullets scattered on the ground which bear his fingerprints. A broken bourbon bottle, likewise with fingerprints. Most of all, we have a beautiful young woman and her lover lying dead in each other's arms. They had sinned. But was their crime so great as to merit a death sentence?
>
> A revolver holds six bullets, not eight. I submit to you this was not a hot-blooded crime of passion! That could at least be understood, if not condoned. No, this was revenge of a much more brutal and cold-blooded nature. Consider! Four bullets per victim! Not six shots fired, but eight! That means he fired the gun empty…and then stopped to reload so he could shoot each of them again! An extra bullet per lover…right in the head. I'm done talking. You people are all decent, God-fearing Christian folk. You know what to do".

Usage of phrases like 'a beautiful young woman and her lover lying dead in each other's arm', 'revenge of a much more brutal and cold-blooded nature' indicate how the lawyer is using emotion with reason and logic to make his argument more persuasive and influential.

Therefore, lawyers should use facts, rationality and emotional appeal to come up with the most persuasive argument from a psychological perspective. Even if facts completely favour the State or prosecution's case, an argument based on an emotional appeal describing the circumstances and mindset of the defendant while committing the crime may help bargain a reduced sentence.

Psychologist Sannito (Sannito, 1981) carried out a combined study of emotional appeal, primacy and recency principles to work out techniques that would assist attorneys to strategize presentation of their arguments and evidences. He suggested that attorneys should begin with emotional evidence and arguments to get the primacy advantage, and factual evidence should be placed at last to get the recency advantage as the likelihood of forgetting factual evidence, which may sometimes be technical in nature, is more (Voss, 2005).

All the factors discussed above illustrate how the lawyer can, directly or indirectly, influence the court's decision-making process by structuring the presentation of evidences to favour primacy or recency, by laying emphasis on certain key pieces of evidence or by arguing to the emotional side of the audience. In the second section, we aim to understand how a lawyer can built the necessary skills for persuasive argumentation.

15.3 Art of Persuasion

Successful lawyers have mastered the art of persuasion, which can be defined as the art of influencing the will of others by arguments that appeal both to logic and emotions (Coustopoulos, 1972). However, persuasion is different from manipulation or coercion; the word 'persuade' refers to using verbal and non-verbal skills to move the audience, while 'manipulation' refers to controlling the other person for obtaining unfair advantage to oneself. Persuasion is a practiced skill itself which changes the decision of the one persuaded because the beliefs underlying the decision are changed by what one witnesses, and not through force or unethical tactics. In persuasion, there is no element of unwillingness or reluctance to change, the change in the decision comes from within the decision-maker, whereas in manipulation, a person reluctantly agrees with the manipulator.

Most countries, including India, follow an adversarial system where a typical case begins when the State charges a person with a crime. Upon levelling of the charge, the person becomes a defendant. Defendant engages a lawyer to appear for his trial or one is given to him by the state. The burden of proof lies on the State in most cases, where it must employ its own lawyer to prove beyond a reasonable doubt that the defendant has committed the crime. In an adversarial system, lawyers decide the kind of legal arguments to be made and the factual evidence that needs to be presented before the court. Apart from this, both lawyers also engage in a variety of persuasive skills to accomplish their point of view. There are a variety of persuasive skills that a lawyer can use to persuade the judge.

15.3.1 Know Your Judge

The first step in persuading your audience is knowing your audience. In a courtroom, the audience that matters most is the judge, so the trial lawyer needs to know as much as possible about the presiding judge(s) to prepare for a case. Professional background and personal information of judges are easily accessible in the public domain, but most lawyers do not pay attention to such information. Their social and cultural upbringing, the education they received, and the environments they frequently socialize or work within are all relevant factors when deciding a successful trial strategy. For example, a trial lawyer contesting a big corporation for environmental pollution and ecological degradation may find that the judge legislating the case has extensively worked on and written about environmental issues in university and could use that information to create a positive advantage in favour of themselves. This may be done by creating emotional arguments that resonate with the judge's stance on the subject or by citing the judge's scholarly publications in support of their written arguments. Therefore, carrying out basic due diligence about the judge is a thumb rule.

A lawyer should also try and gather information about the courtroom conduct preferred by the presiding judge, especially if it is their first time appearing before that judge. Knowing whether a particular judge favours certain behaviour in court or prefers adherence to some particular professional norms might be useful information that could assist the lawyer in creating a good impression on the judge. For example, some judges may frown upon chatter between lawyers in the court when one party is presenting, while some judges may not be affected by such behaviour. Creating a favourable impression helps the judge lend a kind ear to the lawyer's arguments.

Court personnel or staff that assist the court are invaluable sources of information, as they are most familiar with the workings of a court or a presiding judge. From personal preferences to ideological leanings, a smart lawyer who maintains relations with the court staff can gather a lot of good cards up his sleeve that might assist in preparing a successful trial strategy.

Studying the judges' past judgements and deciphering cognitive patterns can also help the lawyer chart out the judge's predominant ideology and opinions on issues. For example, Justice P. N. Bhagwati was a pioneer of judicial activism in India and was known to not only introduce but heavily promote public interest litigation in India. Similarly, Associate Justice Ruth Bader Ginsberg of the U.S. Supreme Court is known for her women rights and equality activism. This information would be relevant for lawyers who were presenting cases centred around the causes championed by these judges, as not only would they receive increased attention from the judges, but the judges would be better informed on the issues surrounding the dispute and are likely to make balanced and justified judgements in favour of the weaker party.

Expert testimony is an important feature of both civil and commercial trials. Lawyers should analyse previous court records to determine which experts are generally favoured by the judge, what kind of evidence does the judge give more weightage to, and what kind of qualifications are likely to impress the judge. This information will help the trial lawyer assemble and prepare the experts on their panel in a manner that would best assist the judge in comprehending their testimonies, hence adding weight to their evidence and helping secure a favourable decision at the end.

15.3.2 Physical Appearance and Believability

Social scientists have found that physical appearance has a strong correlation to believability (Lubet, 1997; Miller & Mauet, 1998; Reed & Bornstein, 2018; Voss, 2005). This is why most lawyers will ask their clients to dress for the cause, for example, if the ongoing trail is deciding on an issue of increment in rent, then lawyers advise their renter client to dress humbly for the court appearance so as to not give off an impression of affluence. The same reasoning flows into financial maintenance or child support lawsuits as well, where it is often found that the judge would subconsciously order higher maintenance to be provided by clients who were sharp dressers and resonated an impression of wealth and affluence.

Research also shows that people who are generally perceived as credible and attractive in appearance are more successful in persuasion than those who lack such characteristics (Voss, 2005). The words 'credible' and 'attractive' here, solely for the purpose of court presentation, imply that one is dressed neatly and professionally when appearing in court. It is also advised that one's appearance and mannerisms shows knowledge of and respect for the norms of the court. For example, if courtrooms prefer silence during proceedings, it is not advisable to be wearing shoes that click or screech when walking or moving about court. Taking care to move softly and silently settles well with the judge as it shows consideration and respect for the functions of the court.

Additionally, the size of the team present at each counsel's tables also influences which side he choose to be more sympathetic towards. In order to give an appearance of equality of arms, it is advisable that the lawyer should avoid bringing many team members to the counsel table in the court room. Any indication of an improper balance of power and resources could bias the judge towards the weaker-looking party.

15.3.3 Body Movement and Eye Contact

Research shows that judges rely on body language to determine the truth or honesty of the matter. Lawyers should avoid guarded postures, such as crossed arms, and favour less formal gestures that convey sincerity and openness, such as maintaining eye contact, showing open palms when speaking. Judges are known to more likely believe a lawyer who appears to be sincere, interested, and committed. Moreover, lawyers must be mindful of their body language at all times, even when the other party is presenting their case (Hart, 1992).

Lawyers should maintain comfortable eye contact with the judges when they are at the counsel table; when they are speaking, they should stand up straight and speak clearly, as it conveys credibility and confidence. The counsel table should be free from clutter and only hold relevant documents in an organized manner. The table should not be cluttered with files and notes, as not only does it distract the judge, it may also hinder eye contact, thereby conveying nervousness and unpreparedness.

Other gestures that indicate nervousness and untruthful behaviour are frequent blinking, continuous fiddling with hands, or a pen/pencil or rushed pacing across the courtroom. However, moving around slowly while presenting your case is encouraged as it demonstrates confidence and comfort in one's position; similarly, hand gestures that lend emphasis the point being made are encouraged. Psychologists suggest that moving around the courtroom while delivering their arguments helps the lawyer subconsciously assess and feel comfortable in the territory, thus enhancing confidence which helps the lawyer perform with more clarity in argumentation and increases agility and alertness to court proceedings (Blanck & Rosenthal, 1992).

15.3.4 Style of Speech

Research indicates that pattern and manner of speaking, choice of words, and style of speaking constitute effective persuasion tools (Voss, 2005). There are two channels through which information is imparted to the audience (the judge) in a courtroom scenario—the litigators and the witnesses. Both the lawyer and witnesses have to make conscious and deliberate choices about the words they use to convey their points in the courtroom. For example, when asked a question, a witness may respond with the phrase 'I think so' or 'Yes', which, in essence, would mean the same thing colloquially. However, in court, these two replies have completely different persuasive powers from the perspective of a judge. A definitive 'yes' conveys a lot more confidence and assertiveness than 'I think so'.

A powerful speech will help the judge have a credible and trustworthy impression of the speaker. One of the key characteristics of an impactful speech is that they do not use 'helper' words. 'Helper' words are usually filler words or phrases which convey no particular meaning but are used as connectors or fillers. Excessive use of 'helper' words are perceived as a lack of confidence and untruthfulness. In a courtroom, examples of certain words or phrases that a lawyer should be mindful when using too much would include frequent phrases like 'To tell you the truth', repeated use of 'Your Lordship', 'As you may know…', 'To the best of my knowledge…', and 'As far as I know…'.

When describing an incident to a judge or a jury, lawyers need to be mindful of the words they chose and how much details they include in describing the event. Consider the two types of descriptions mentioned below:

(1) The accident was an awful accident. It resulted in the death of Mr. and Mrs. Kumar.
(2) The accident was a terrible one, it resulted due to the collision of the car with the large truck, the front bumper was the car was totally smashed into the driver seat, and hood of the car got ripped off due to the numerous times the car flipped because of sheer velocity with which the truck had struck the car. The front bumper crushed Mr. and Mrs. Kumar who were sitting in the front seat splashing blood all over.

There is a substantial difference between the two descriptions of the same event. The first one only uses a single adjective to define the whole incident. The word 'awful', although descriptive enough, can have relative meaning and emphasis for different people; therefore, it fails to draw a vivid picture. However, the second description contains the use of combinations of nouns and adjectives that helps build a fairly accurate picture of what really happened, helping the judge visualize the event. The judge would be more likely to afford greater damages and even criminal penalties in the second scenario in comparison to the first one. Synonymous words like 'bumped', 'smashed', or 'crashed' tend to create different impressions of impact in the minds of the listener, and thus, trial lawyers should spend some time in deliberating about the words they are going to use during trial.

Lawyers should also be mindful of court etiquettes, especially if it helps to establish their reputation. Argumentative behaviour like speaking over the witness, cutting them off mid-testimony, engaging in verbal clashes with witnesses or any other behaviour that hinders or intimidates the witness should be avoided. Even if the witness turns hostile or aggressive, the lawyer should maintain composure and handle the situation professionally.

In the adversarial system, judges usually do not address the court during the ongoing trial. But should a judge have a question or a point, the presenting lawyer should immediately yield the floor to the judge. For the sake of an effective trial, it is also important that the layer listen carefully to the judge's input to the proceedings.

Psychologists and social scientists have always recommended listening genuinely and focused before answering but most people, even lawyers, fail at this. Pretentious listening would include frequent nods at the speaker, and pausing for effect when the speaker has finished, however, where it fails is when in response to the speaker's comment or question, the listener does not address the point that was just made, but continues to repeat what they were saying earlier, either using the same or different words. Genuinely listening would involve adopting the speaker's perspective, understanding where they are coming from and what they are trying to ask or convey, and then only responding to that. Verbatim repetition of the same point that the lawyer was making before the judge's comment is entirely infructuous and does not help move the case forward.

15.3.5 Persuading a Cold Judge

In an ideal criminal justice system, the sitting judge will be able to be prepare well ahead for all cases they are presiding over and devote as much time and attention needed to analyse all aspects of the case before delivering a verdict. In reality, the judicial machinery is significantly overburdened in both developed and developing countries. There are multiple cases to be heard each day, and the time afforded to each case is therefore very short, as a consequence of which, lawyers do not get much time to present their cases. To be able to plead successfully within the limits of time and attention on any given day in court, lawyers need to resort to a different set of persuasive skills (Bornstein, 2009).

Given the number of cases a judge hears per day, and the gap between one hearing and the next, especially in busy jurisdictions, it cannot be expected of the judge to recall the facts of the cases and the testimonies previously presented. So, in every hearing, a lawyer should use the first couple of minutes to introduce himself and revisit the important facts in issue at trial, the present stage of presentation at the case, the subject matter of hearing that day and the question(s) that the judge needs to pontificate upon. After this, the lawyer, should move on to the arguments outlining why he/she or his/her client should get the relief they are seeking. Even though it is the most essential question in business, jumping ahead to trying to answer that without revisiting the other information would result in improper communication. The judge may not have all the important facts that they need to consider at hand, and this could result in an unfavourable outcome at the end (Bornstein, 2009). It may be that some judges do come to court well prepared and do not require the recapitulation of events, a recap in such case may be a waste of time, that may not only annoy but also offend the judge. This is why it is important to do some background research on the presiding judge, as mentioned earlier. Courtroom history will inform you whether the judge prefers or dislikes a case recap, and acting accordingly would significantly help your case.

One might believe that persuasion starts and ends with verbal and visual factors, however, that is not the case. Another way to ensure clear communication of the important facts of the case that you intend to impress upon the judge is to prepare a trial memo or brief. A trial brief is an unofficial document, usually a page long and written in plain, simple English, that contains the key issues, the counsel's arguments and the relief claimed, put succinctly. However, one must be careful about presenting this document before the start of a trial, it could have two contradictory effects. One, it could be perceived as an attempt to gain an unfair advantage and compromise any leniency the judge might deem onto a counsel's case; or it could provide significant assistance to the judge to get up to speed on the case before a hearing and hence boost the counsel's credibility in front of the judge, while also allowing him/her to submit their closing statement before the judge in brief. Therefore, knowing the end goal of the arguments, the judge will likely be able to better follow the points a counsel makes and the stance they are advocating in court. Again, the adverse outcome of submitting a trial brief can be avoided by doing some groundwork research on the courtroom procedures preferred by the judge in question, as advised earlier.

15.4 Conclusion

The aim of this chapter is twofold: first to explain why and how psychology matters in the courtroom and second to illustrate practical techniques that a lawyer can use to subtly influence the judge and gain an edge over the opponents. An attempt has been made to contextualise the information in terms of real-life cases popular media and the reality surrounding the state of current judicial systems in many countries, and to explain to the readers how a lawyer can benefit from psychological techniques, over and above the evidence and facts that support his/her case, to influence the cognitive decision-making of the court.

References

Blanck, P. D., & Rosenthal, R. (1992). Nonverbal behavior in the courtroom. *Applications of nonverbal behavioral theories and research*, 89–115.

Bornstein, P. R. (2009). Persuading a cold judge. *Litigation, 35*(2), 27–31.

Costopoulos, W. C. (1972). Persuasion in the courtroom. *Duquesne Law Review, 10*(3), 392–393.

Cromwell, H. (1950). The relative effect on audience attitude of the first versus the second argumentative speech of a series. *Speech Monographs, 17*(2), 105–122.

Darabont, F. (1994) The Shawshank Redemption (n.d.). Retrieved November 29, 2019, from http://www.dailyscript.com/scripts/shawshank.html

Gold, V. (1987). Covert advocacy: Reflections on the use of psychological persuasion techniques in the courtroom. *North Carolina Law Review, 65*(3), 495.

Hart, A. J. (1992). On the sobriety of judges: Nonverbal influence in the courtroom.

Kohler, C. (2007) Order Effects Theory : Primacy versus Recency. Center for Interactive Advertising, The University of Texas at Austin. Retrieved 2007–11–04.

Lubet, S. (1997). Persuasion at trial. *American Journal of Trial Advocacy, 21*(2), 342–343.

Lund, F. H. (1925). The Psychology of Belief: IV. The Law of Primacy in Persuasion. *The Journal of Abnormal and Social Psychology, 20*, 183–191.

Miller, M. O., & Mauet, T. A. (1998). The psychology of jury persuasion. *The American Journal of Trial Advocacy, 22*, 549.

Miller, N., & Campbell, D. T. (1959). Recency and primacy in persuasion as a function of the timing of speeches and measurements. *The Journal of Abnormal and Social Psychology, 59*(1), 1–9. https://doi.org/10.1037/h0049330

Reed, K., & Bornstein, B. H. (2018). Objection: Psychological perspectives on jurors' perceptions of in-court attorney objections. *SDL Rev., 63*, 1.

Sannito, T (1981). Psychological courtroom strategies, TRIAL DIPL. J., Summer, 30.

O. J. Simpson Murder Trial (1995). The O.J. Simpson murder trial: Excerpts of opening statements by Simpson Prosecutors. (1995, January 25). Retrieved from https://www.latimes.com/archives/la-xpm-1995-01-25-mn-24229-story.html

Voss, J. (2005). The science of persuasion: An exploration of advocacy and the science behind the art of persuasion in the courtroom. *Law and Psychology Review, 29*, 306.

Chapter 16
Decision-Making in the Courtroom: Jury

Shankey Verma

Abstract Although the Indian criminal justice system is adversarial in nature, where the decision-making responsibilities are limited to the judges panel, there exist other federal systems where such responsibilities are shared between the body of jurors and the judge(s). This chapter encapsulates the existing literature from experts from different jurisdictions and legal systems that enlist the factors that can influence the cognitive decision-making functions of a body of jurors. We briefly discuss the psychological influences that are likely to be present at various stages of a criminal trial and how it may affect the jury, and what can be done to consciously avoid these prejudices.

Keywords Jury · Decision-making · Psychological factors · Courtroom psychology

16.1 Introduction

A jury is defined as a group of individuals chosen from a community, who collectively decide the outcome of a legal case (Hans, 2008). Trial by jury as a means of upholding the law was adopted by human civilization thousands of years ago, existing in ancient Egypt from 2000 BC. But it was in Athens where the proposition of right of a citizen to trial by jury of peers originated. The idea of jury then travelled across Europe from Athens. Normans introduced this concept to Britain in the middle of the eleventh century (Kapardis, 2003), when they invaded England, and it was Henry II who expanded it further to adjudicate private disputes as well (Nemeth, 1981). It has been in existence since then, evolving as a legal element.

According to one study, trial by jury in some civil and criminal adjudications is practiced in as many as 55 countries, including the USA, Britain, Russian, Australia, Argentina, Canada, and many others across the globe (Park, 2010). This system, which involves citizen participation in adjudicating legal cases, has been practiced in

---

S. Verma (✉)
Jindal Institute of Behavioural Sciences, O.P. Jindal Global University, Sonipat, Haryana, India
e-mail: sverma@jgu.edu.in

S. Sahni et al. (eds.), *Criminal Psychology and the Criminal Justice System in India and Beyond*, https://doi.org/10.1007/978-981-16-4570-9_16

countries such as the USA and Britain for centuries (Alschuler, Deiss, 1994), whereas countries such as South Korea and Japan have adopted this practice only about a decade ago (Park, 2010). It was only in 2008 that the South Korean government introduced trial by jury (Lee et al. 2013) and the process is still in the initial stage of development. Each nation practicing trial by jury has its own provisions and legal procedures based on its society and how its legal system evolved. The procedure for selecting the panel of jurors in any trial varies from case to case and country to country. For example, juries in countries such as England and Wales, the USA, New Zealand, Australia, and Canada have 12 members in their panel, whereas Scotland has 15 (Kapardis, 2003). Further, the types of legal cases that are subject to trial by jury also differ. For instance, in 2009, Russia eliminated jury trials for crimes against the State, which includes treason, revolt, sabotage, espionage, and terrorism (Stack, 2009). Britain is also in the process to disallow jury trial in complex and serious frauds (Rozenberg, 2002). The range of verdicts that a jury can deliver in the courtroom may also differ amongst countries. Verdicts other than guilty and not guilty are rare in American criminal law. Scotland judges and juries, on the other hand, can render three verdicts, i.e. guilty, not guilty, and not proven (Bray, 2005).

There exist divided opinions on whether jury trials should be practiced or not. Critics of the trial by jury system are of the opinion that jurors lack formal training and knowledge of the law and may become confused in complex trials due to absence of competence. They often get swayed by their individual understanding of legally irrelevant information which can lead to delivering unfair and partial verdicts (Vischer, 1987). Supporters of the jury system argue that it helps in maintaining checks and balances on the judiciary (Peterson, 1995), prevents tyranny, and acts as catalyst for legal reforms. Jurors are adequately responsible and competent enough in delivering just verdicts. It provides equal opportunity to the citizens to participate in the process of decision-making and leads to peaceful dispute resolution (Shwartzberg, 2018).

16.1.1 The Indian Scenario

As a British legacy, jury system was prevalent in India until late 1950s. It was only after the K. M. Nanavati versus State of Maharashtra, 1959 case that it was abolished by the Nehru government. The 14th report of the Law Commission of India, focusing on reforms in judicial administration, recommended the abolition of jury trials as they claimed that the decision of the jury can be easily influenced. The report argued that juries have religious biases and lack understanding of the law (Ramnath, 2013). Hence, juries may not always ensure justice to the victim, a principle enshrined in the preamble of the Constitution of India, 1950. However, this one and a half centuries old system is still being practiced by the Parsi community in India in divorce suits. Presently, the apex court of India is examining the validity of those divorces (Biswas, 2015).

Because jury system has long been out of prevalent practice in India, there is a dearth of research in understanding the psychosociological factors that may influence jury decision-making in colonial India, or within the few cases in the Parsi community. Much of the scholarship that we will discuss in this chapter is from the West and is presented as a succinct overview of psychological influences in the international criminal justice system. Interested readers may pursue this further by referring to the works of the authors mentioned hereafter.

16.2 Psychological Influences Affecting Jury

It is expected that jurors will be making their decision based on the evidence presented before them and the facts of the case. A fair trial is one where the decision of the jury is not influenced by anything other than the evidence presented in court. Although jurors are expected to be impartial and emotionally objective when giving their verdicts in any trial, they too can be swayed by various factors present inside and outside the courtroom. These can be individual, social, familial, religious, economic, or psychological factors that can come into play at any stage of the trial, i.e. pre-trial, during the trial or post-trial. This chapter shall discuss psychological factors that may influence the decision of any juror. These psychological factors broadly comprise the following:

16.2.1 Pre-trial Publicity of the Case

Exposure to extensive pre-trial publicity, whether positive or negative, has an effect on jurors' verdicts. This extra-legal information biases a juror's opinions of the case outside the courtroom (Ruva & McEvoy, 2008). Negative pre-trial publicity means publicity that paints the defendant in the negative light. It presents negative information about the defendant and the crime that can prejudice the outcome. On the other hand, positive pre-trial publicity is seen in cases where the defendant holds celebrity or other such highly visible status in the community (Ruva et al. 2011; Steblay et al. 1999).

Cases involving notoriety are likely to grasp both the media and public attention. Fuelled by this, media gives extensive coverage to such cases that may include the background of the defendant, particularly their past criminal record, if any. Often it may appear that media delivers a judgement on the morality of the defendant even before the case goes into trial; this can be fatal and goes against the principles of justice (Lieberman & Krauss, 2009). Due to the advent of media into the courtroom, there are many more people watching the progress of a trial than are present in the courtroom. The dexterity of the Internet and social media in reporting trial updates and recruiting 'experts' to opine on a public platform, regardless of whether such opinions are suitably qualified or substantial, also adds to the influential media coverage that is crucial to forming public perceptions for the defendant or victim (Datary-Kapur, 2014). The public image of the defendant or victim and how the media has portrayed them translates into public support, which is a significant factor affecting jurors' decisions.

Several researchers have demonstrated that, in cases where there is negative pre-trial publicity, jurors are likely to give guilty verdicts and rate defendants as less credible than victims. On the contrary, in case of positive pre-trial publicity, the percentage of guilty verdicts drops significantly, and jurors are likely to render not-guilty verdicts (Ruva & Guenther, 2015). Not only does the type of publicity affect decision-making, but also the amount of exposure given during publicity. An experiment conducted by Daftary-Kapur et al. (2014) correlated the extent of pre-trial publicity to the decision-making of jurors in favour of plaintiff or defendant. Jurors exposed to high amount of pre-trial publicity in favour of the plaintiff were more likely to render the defendants as guilty in comparison with jurors with low exposure. On the contrary, jurors exposed to high amount of pre-trial publicity favouring the defendant/s were more likely to render defendants as innocent as compared to plaintiffs who were less exposed.

16.2.2 Characteristics of Trial Participants

The participants involved in a trial include defendants, plaintiffs, jurors, judges, prosecution attorney, and defence attorney. Each participant differs from the other in various parameters such as race, religion, gender, age, sexual orientation, social and economic status, physical, and personality traits (Devine, 2012). These extra-legal factors can also prejudice the juror's decision unconsciously.

Race: There is a surfeit of research aimed at understanding the effect of these extra-legal factors on the decision of the juror. Pfeifer and Ogloff (1991) concluded that in rape trials where the victim was a white woman, jurors who participated in their study often rendered black defendants more guilty than white defendants. This was the scenario when jurors were not given any prior instructions. However, jurors did not discriminate racially when they were given prior instructions, specifically to be conscious of such a bias. This study also highlights the importance of instructions to jury and that they are effective in clearing ambiguity (Pfeifer & Ogloff, 1991). Similarly, Lynch and Haney (2009) found that there were differences in behaviour of jurors based on the race of defendant. Black defendants were more likely to receive capital punishment than White defendants. Race identity of defendant or plaintiff and even the juror can lead to impartiality in the verdict, and defence attorneys are using this tactic to entice case verdicts in their favour. This can be explained by a recent case in the USA where a police officer shot her neighbour, a Caribbean man, inside his apartment. The defence attorney in this case attempted to move the trial location from Dallas County, which has only 29% whites, to a neighbouring county which has a majority Caucasian population. It is evident that shifting the trial to this jurisdiction would affect the racial composition of the jury, which in turn, can affect the decision of the case in favour of the white defendant (Markis, 2019).

Religion: The role of religious beliefs of the juror in deciding guilt and severity of punishment is complex, at best. Miller and Bornstein (2006) noticed that although the prosecutor was ineffective in influencing juror decision by entreating jury members on Biblical notions, the defence attorney's biblical appeals did successfully move the juror's decision. Miller et al. (2011) could not find any relationship between the religious identity of the defendant and its effect on verdict. However, in their 2008 study, Miller and Hayward (2008) found that the decision of the jurors to award death penalty or not was acutely embedded in their religious beliefs.

Gender: Gender is another extralegal factor that can affect the decision-making process. In the meta-analysis of mock juror judgement studies, Mazzella and Feingold (1994) found that jurors recommended harsher punishment for male defendants when compared to female defendants. Further, in cases where the victim was female, defendants were treated more severely. However, no relationship could be established between gender and judgements of guilt. Ragatz and Russell (2010) made an interesting find while attempting to examine the effect of sexual orientation of defendants on the verdict in cases of crimes of passion. Their results revealed that female defendants who were heterosexual were given lower guilt ratings and shorter sentences. Michelini and Snodgrass (1980) tested the effect to attractiveness on juror's decision. They found that defendants with physically attractive traits were found less guilty as compared to the ones who were deemed to be less attractive. Quas et al. (2002) conducted a mock jury study on child sexual assault cases in 2002 that reported that there were more guilty verdicts from female jurors and also that women were more likely to believe the victim than men.

Accent: There has also been research conducted on how lingual accents affect the jurors' perception of the speakers. In a study, Dixon et al. (2002) found that after listening to a 2-min recorded conversation between a police officer and a person accused of robbery, jurors rated people with a Birmingham accent more likely to be guilty compared to a person with a standard British accent. Across the pond, Anwar et al. (2012) also examined how the racial composition of the jury determines the outcome of the trial in felony cases in Florida. After analysing the data of felony trials in Florida between the years 2000–2012, they inferred that when there are no black jurors in the jury pool, black defendants were more likely to be convicted as compared to the white defendants. With only one black juror in the jury pool, the conviction rates for both black and white defendants were similar.

16.2.3 Emotional Impact

The decisions of the jurors are sometimes based on emotions and feelings, rather than adequate comprehension of law and facts of the case. Occasionally, jurors may form a pre-conceived notion about the defendant or victim, based on the nature and intensity of the crime committed. This can be explained by an example where the defendant who is accused of rape charges is presented before a panel in which one of the jurors is a female who is a strong advocate leading the fight against sexual harassment of women for years. In this case, the juror might be prejudiced against the accused at an early stage of the trial, even before the presentation of evidences, based on emotional reactions and attachment to a social cause she is passionate about. She might find it easier to be sympathetic towards the victim of rape and likewise unforgiving towards the accused, even before knowing the circumstances and facts of the case. These emotions might also develop based on media reports and public reactions. This pre-constructed notion about the defendant or plaintiff at an early stage, based on emotions rather than facts of the case, is known as 'primacy effect' (Boyll, 1991). Schutte and Hosch (1997), in their meta-analysis, noted that in sexual assault cases, female jurors were more likely to convict the defendant as compared to male jurors.

The impact on the emotions of the jurors can also be a product of emotional testimony from the witnesses and their emotional reactions to the incident/s in question. The exposure of jurors to these reactions may bias them against the defendant. Paternoster and Deise (2011) found that exposure to victim impact statement aroused anguish and acrimonious, vengeful feelings towards the defendant. It also resulted in feelings of pity and empathy towards the victim. These jurors were more likely to impose death penalty on defendant in comparison with the jurors who were not exposed to victim impact statement. Matsuo and Itoh (2015) also documented a similar effect of emotional statement and horrific photographs on jurors' decision. According to their study, when the jurors were exposed to emotional statements and shown horrific photographs, they delivered more guilty verdicts as compared to jurors who were not exposed to emotional statements and were not shown horrific photographs of the crime. Similar effect of victim impact statement was also seen in the study by Wevodau et al. (2014), where jurors who were shown only victim impact statements advocated for lengthier sentences to defendant.

16.2.4 Social Loafing

Not all psychosocial influences affecting the jury's decision-making capabilities are as proactive as discussed above. People working in a group, such as in a jury, can also exhibit a phenomenon called social loafing, which is the reduction in motivation and efforts when individuals work collectively as compared to when they work individually or coactively (Karau & William, 1993). In this phenomenon, individuals put in less effort in achieving the collective goals and are heavily dependent on the efforts of other members of the group for success. While deliberating, jurors are working towards achieving a common goal, a unanimous decision. Lack of participatory contribution in group deliberations can result in a loss of collective information processed by the group collectively. It is also directly proportional to the number of members present in the group. As the size of the group with which they are making a decision increases, individuals may encode information with less effort (Henningsen, Cruz & Miller, 2000). It is important to understand the impact of social loafing on jurors' decision-making process as that is a collective outcome, represented as the shared opinion, to which each juror is in agreement. The reason most juries comprises more than one member is because it is presumed that a group is a better arbitrator of the facts than an individual.

16.2.5 Comprehension of Judicial Instructions

Because there are multifarious complexities involved in trials, there are a set of instructions delivered to jurors by the judge before the commencement of trial. These can be categorized as explanatory, cautionary, limiting, written, oral, verdict-directing, curative, pattern or preliminary (Tanford, 1990) and are procedural in nature, including intricate sentences, legal jargon, and atypical words (Severance & Loftus, 1982). The hurdles in comprehending judicial instructions include the complex nature of laws, jurors' knowledge of law, and the huge amount of information presented in a trial (Daftary-Kapur, Dumas & Penrod, 2010). Numerous studies have concluded that the arguments presented by prosecutor and defence counsel are beyond the capacity of juror to comprehend. This is because jurors are not legal experts while attorneys have had training in legal education and have usually been practicing this profession for years. In contrast, jurors receive no special legal training prior to the trial. In some cases, there may be multiple plaintiffs and defendants, which may have an increasingly confounding effect on jurors. Therefore, jurors are expected to possess high analytical capacity and problem-solving skills to untangle the convolutions. Intellectual ability, in this case, is defined as critical thinking skills required to reason between disciplines, and problem solving skills include abilities that adapt to new or changing situations. They must be intellectually capable of following complex threads of logic and possess adequate critical reasoning to rationally factor in the evidences and testimonies offered in court. In the absence of such skills, jurors may misunderstand or misinterpret the instructions and not be able to comprehend the information presented during the trial. Jurors may be unable to apply these instructions to the law. This may compromise the verdict of the trial and deprive plaintiff or defendant of their right to fair trial.

Severance and Loftus (1982) found that nearly a quarter of jury included in their sample had difficulty in comprehending instructions. The most common was definition of 'intent' and 'reasonable doubt'. Similarly, in a study conducted by Forston (1973), it was established that there was insufficient understanding of basic rules of evidence and 'burden of proof' in 80% of his subjects. Reed (1980) also concluded that jurors' decisions were affected by judge's instructions. In his study, jurors who were not given any instructions were more likely to vote 'guilty' or 'cannot decide' compared to the jurors who were given instructions.

16.2.6 Conformity

Discussion within the group during deliberation often has effect on the decisions of the group members in the jury. The reason for this change can be explained by two types of influences—normative social influence and informational influence.

Normative social influence is defined as an influence to conform to the positive expectations of another (Deutsch & Gerard, 1955). It generally occurs in order to foster likeability, fit in, and avoid rejection by the other members of the group. Informational influence is defined as an influence to accept information obtained from another as evidence of reality. This type of influence occurs when an individual does not possess adequate knowledge or is not confident of what they know and relies on their group members for guidance. An acknowledgment of what one does not know in depth is also accompanied by the presupposition that other members of the group are knowledgeable and therefore right. Normative influence may result in behavioural change in overt accordance with other jurors, whereas informational influence may result in real cognitive change as it arises from communication of ideas, facts, impressions, data, etc. (Devine, 2012). Similarly, shifts in the opinions, preferences, and decisions of jurors are also subject to changes after discussion and deliberations with the other members present in the jury.

16.2.7 Foreperson Influence

When the process of *voir dire* is completed, jurors have to elect a foreperson. *Voir dire,* meaning ‘to speak the truth’ or ‘to see them talk’ (Suggs & Sales, 1980), is an initial stage of jury selection during which the competence of jurors is examined to determine whether they are appropriate and competent to hear the case in court (Jones, 1987). The foreperson is *primus inter pares* in a jury, i.e. all jurors are equal, but the foreperson is first amongst equals (Deosaran, 1993). He is seen as the leader of the group, and his views can play an important role in shifting the decisions of other jurors, especially in ambiguous situations or hung juries. As the presiding member, the foreperson can influence the deliberations and decision-making of the jury. Bevan et al. (1958), through his study, showed that the opinion of an effective leader is reflected significantly in the opinion of the group. In his study, the high prestige, autocratic foreperson was the most influential in brining unanimous decisions of the jury followed by low prestige, autocratic foreperson, high prestige, democratic foreperson and low prestige, and democratic foreperson (Bevan et al., 1958). However, in a research on Korean jurors conducted by Lee et al. (2013), it was found that forepersons who gave jurors equal opportunity to participate in the group deliberations, succeeded most in managing the discussion well. In his study, forepersons gave each juror a chance to talk in 50% of the cases, requested the jurors to provide rationale behind their argument 72% of the time, and were effective in managing the jurors’ discussion in 77% of the cases.

Social status of an individual plays a prominent role in being selected as the foreperson. Strodtbeck et al. (1957) argued that males with a higher occupational status are expected to be the foreman because their views and comments are generally regarded to have greater value, which is, in turn, extrapolated from the substantive knowledge and high interactional skills required in higher status occupations. Study by Baldwin and McConville (1980) found that during the foreman selection process, less preference is given to females and young jurors as compared to jurors who have professional, managerial, and intermediate occupations. However, they could not find any relationship between verdicts and social attributes of foremen in juries in their study.

16.3 Conclusion

As seen from the above review, numerous psychological factors present inside and outside the courtroom have a biasing effect, directly or indirectly, on the decision of the case. The extent to which these factors influence varies according to the memory, perception, interpretation, persuasion capacity, emotions, and intellectual ability of the juror and what kind of environment surrounds him/her. Though many researches done on psychology of jury trials have explained the impact of these factors on jurors' decisions, several others yielded no significant relation between the both. Even after years of scientific research, it remains unclear whether jurors are actually influenced by the any of the above-mentioned factors. Despite the many areas that have already been looked into, there remain various other psychological domains which have not been explored by the psychologists and researchers. These may have implications for enhancing jury trial procedures and psychological research in their decision-making. Further, much of the research prevalent in this field originates from the USA. There is a limited contribution to similar research in this area from other countries.

Jurors are expected to be unbiased consumers of evidence and even-handed evaluators. Since jury is entrusted with a daunting task of deciding the fate of the defendant as well the plaintiff, a caveat must be mentioned here that utter importance should be given to the fact that the principle of justice and right to fair trial should not be compromised in any situation. Justice is sacrosanct and should not be interfered with. Updated efforts should be put by researchers in formulating interventions resulting in elimination of prejudices in decision-making of jurors and ensuring fair delivery of justice.

References

Alschuler, A. W., & Deiss, A. G. (1994). A brief history of the criminal jury in the United States. *The University of Chicago Law Review*, 867–928.

Anwar, S., Bayer, P., & Hjalmarsson, R. (2012). The Impact of jury race in criminal trials. *The Quarterly Journal of Economics*, 1017–1055.

Baldwin, J., & McConville, M. (1980). Juries, foremen and verdicts. *The British Journal of Criminology*, 35–44.

Bevan, W., Albert, R. S., Loiseaux, P. R., & Mayfield, P. N. (1958). Jury behaviour as function of the prestige of the foreman and the nature of his leadership. *Journal of Public Law*, 419–449.

Biswas, S. (2015, September 24). *Parsi matrimonial courts: India's only surviving jury trials*. Retrieved August 25, 2019, from BBC News: https://www.bbc.com/news/world-asia-india-34322117

Boyll, J. R. (1991). Psychological, cognitive, personality and interpersonal factors in jury verdicts. *Law and Psychology Review*, 163–184.

Bray, S. (2005). Not proven: introducing a third verdict. *University of Chicago Law Review*, 1299–1329.

Daftary-Kapur, T., Dumas, R., & Penrod, S. D. (2010). Jury decision-making biases and methods to counter them. *Legal and Criminological Psychology*, 133–154.

Daftary-Kapur, T., Penrod, S. D., O'Connor, M., & Wallace, B. (2014). Examining pretrial publicity in a shadow jury paradigm: Issues of slant, quantity, persistence and generalizability. *Law and Human Behaviour*, 462–477.

Deosaran, R. (1993). The Social psychology of selecting jury forepersons. *The British Journal of Criminology*, 70–80.

Deutsch, M., & Gerard, H. B. (1955). A study of normative and informational social influences upon individual judgment. *The journal of abnormal and social psychology*, 629–636.

Devine, D. J. (2012). *Jury decision making: The state of the science*. New York University Press.

Dixon, J. A., Mahoney, B., & Cocks, R. (2002). Accents of guilt?: Effects of regional accent, race, and crime type on attributions of guilt. *Journal of Language and Social Psychology*, 162–168.

Forston, R. F. (1973). Justice jurors and judges' instructions. *Judges Journal, 12*, 68.

Hans, V. P. (2008). Jury systems around the world. *Annual Review of Law and Social Science*, 275–297.

Henningsen, D. D., Cruz, M. G., & Miller, M. L. (2000). Role of social loafing in predeliberation decision making. *Group Dynamics: Theory, Research, and Practice*, 168–175.

Jones, S. E. (1987). Judge-versus attorney-conducted voir dire: An empirical investigation of juror candor. *Law and Human Behaviour* , 131–146.

Kapardis, A. (2003). *Psychology and law: A critical introduction*. Cambridge University Press.

Karau, S. J., & Williams, K. D. (1993). Social loafing: A meta-analytic review and theoretical integration. *Journal of Personality and Social Psychology*, 627–706.

Lee, J.-H., Woo, J., Rhee, J. W., Choi, J. M., & Shin, H. (2013). What's happening in the jury room: Analyzing shadow jury deliberations in Korea. *Journal of Korean Law*, 41–68.

Lieberman, J. D., & Krauss, D. A. (2009). *Jury psychology: Social aspects of trial processes*. Ashgate Publishing Limited.

Lynch, M., & Haney, C. (2009). Capital jury deliberation: Effects on death sentencing, comprehension, and discrimination. *Law and Human Behaviour*, 481–496.

Markis, J. (2019, August 30). *Duke professor researches how racial makeup of juries impacts criminal trials*. Retrieved September 4, 2019, from The Chronicle: https://www.dukechronicle.com/article/2019/08/duke-university-economics-professor-racial-makeup-juries-criminal-trials

Matsuo, K., & Itoh, Y. (2015). Effects of emotional testimony and gruesome photographs on mock jurors' decisions and negative emotions. *Psychiatry, Psychology and Law*, 85–101.

Mazzella, R., & Feingold, A. (1994). The effects of physical attractiveness, race, socioeconomic status, and gender of defendants and victims on judgments of mock jurors: A meta-analysis. *Journal of Applied Social Psychology*, 1315–1338.

Michelini, R. L., & Snodgrass, S. R. (1980). Defendant characteristics and juridic decisions. *Journal of Research in Personality*, 340–350.
Miller, M. K., & Bornstein, B. H. (2006). The use of religion in death penalty sentencing trials. *Law and Human Behaviour*, 675–684.
Miller, M. K., & Hayward, R. D. (2008). Religious characteristics and the death penalty. *Law and Human Behaviour*, 113–123.
Miller, M. K., Maskaly, J., Green, M., & Peoples, C. D. (2011). The effects of deliberations and religious identity on mock jurors' verdicts. *Group Processes & Intergroup Relations*, 517–532.
Nemeth, C. J. (1981). Jury trials: Psychology and law. *Advances in Experimental Social Psychology*, 309–367.
Park, R. Y. (2010). The globalizing jury trial: Lessons and insights from Korea. *The American Journal of Comparative Law*, 525–582.
Paternoster, R., & Deise, J. (2011). A heavy thumb on the scale: The effect of victim impact evidence on capital decision making. *Criminology*, 129–162.
Peterson, T. D. (1995). Restoring structural checks on judicial power in the era of managerial judging. *U.C. Davis Law Review*, 41–114.
Pfeifer, J. E., & Ogloff, J. R. (1991). Ambiguity and guilt determinations: A modern racism perspective. *Journal of Applied Social Psychology*, 1713–1725.
Quas, J. A., Bottoms, B. L., Haegerich, T. M., & Nysse-Carris, K. L. (2002). Effects of victim, defendant, and juror gender on decisions in child sexual cases. *Journal of Applied Psychology*, 1993–2021.
Ragatz, L. L., & Russell, B. (2010). Sex, sexual orientation, and sexism: What influence do these factors have on verdicts in a crime-of-passion case? *The Journal of Social Psychology*, 341–360.
Ramnath, K. (2013). The colonial difference between law and fact: notes on the criminal jury in India. *The Indian Economic & Social History Review*, 341–363.
Reed, R. (1980). Jury simulation: The impact of judge's instructions and attorney tactics on decisionmaking. *The Journal of Criminal Law and Criminology*, 68–72.
Rozenberg, J. (2002, July 18). *The Telegraph*. Retrieved August 19, 2019, from Juries to be scrapped in some trials: https://www.telegraph.co.uk/news/uknews/1401741/Juries-to-be-scrapped-in-some-trials.html
Ruva, C. L., & McEvoy, C. (2008). Negative and positive pretrial publicity affect juror memory and decision making. *Journal of Experimental Psychology: Applied*, 226–235.
Ruva, C. L., Guenther, C. C., & Yarbrough, A. (2011). Positive and negative pretrial publicity: The roles of impression formation, emotion, and predecisional distortion. *Criminal Justice and Behaviour*, 511–534.
Ruva, Christine L.., & Guenther, Christina C.. (2015). From the shadows into the light: How pretrial publicity and deliberation affect mock jurors' decisions, impressions, and memory. *Law and Human Behavior, 39*(3), 294–310. https://doi.org/10.1037/lhb0000117.
Schutte, J. W., & Hosch, H. M. (1997). A Gender differences in sexual assault verdicts: A meta-analysis. *Journal of Social Behaviour and Personality*, 761.
Schwartzberg, M. (2018). Justifying the jury: Reconciling justice, equality, and democracy. *American Political Science Review, 112*(3), 446–458.
Severance, L. J., & Loftus, E. F. (1982). Improving the ability of jurors to comprehend and apply criminal jury instructions. *Law & Society Review*, 153–198.
Stack, M. K. (2009, January 2). *New Russian law ends jury trials for 'crimes against state'*. Retrieved August 19, 2019, from Los Angeles Times: https://www.latimes.com/archives/la-xpm-2009-jan-02-fg-medvedev-juries2-story.html
Steblay, N. M., Besirevic, J., Fulero, S. M., & Lorente, B. J. (1999). The effects of pretrial publicity on juror verdicts: A meta-analytic review. *Law and Human Behaviour*, 219–235.
Strodtbeck, F. L., James, R. M., & Hawkins, C. (1957). Social status in jury deliberations. *American Sociological Review*, 713–719.
Suggs, D., & Sales, B. D. (1980). Juror self-disclosure in the voir dire: A social science analysis. *Indiana Law Journal*, 245–272.

Tanford, J. A. (1990). The law and psychology of jury instructions. *Nebraska Law Review*, 71–111.
Visher, C. A. (1987). Juror decision making—the importance of evidence. *Law and Human Behaviour*, 1–17.
Wevodau, A. L., Cramer, R. J., Clark III, J. W., & Kehn, A. (2014). The Role of emotion and cognition in juror perceptions of victim impact statement. *Social Justice Research*, 45–66.

Chapter 17
Criminal Psychology Through a Positive Psychology Lens: From a Deficit to Asset Perspective

Pulkit Khanna

Abstract This chapter explores important issues in the domain of criminal psychology through a positive psychology lens. In essence, the scope and importance of looking at crime prevention and criminal rehabilitation through a strengths-based perspective, beyond the conventional remedial approach, is discussed. This chapter is broadly presented in three segments. First, there is a brief introduction to the emergence and evolution of positive psychology, including the key aspects of happiness, wellbeing, and strengths, as well as their relevance in the area of criminal psychology. Next, the chapter focuses on the contribution of positive psychology to crime prevention and rehabilitation, by presenting existing theoretical and empirical work that has adopted a strengths-based approach. The final part of this chapter offers recommendations for future research and practice. Steps to bridge the gap between a deficit and asset perspective are elaborated. The chapter concludes by noting the prospects and benefits of applying principles of positive psychology to enhance wellbeing and reduce adverse outcomes for individuals, communities, and institutions.

Keywords Positive psychology · Crime prevention · Rehabilitation · Strengths · Wellbeing

17.1 Introduction

Criminal psychology is inherently characterized by a problem-focus, in examining the underlying motivations of deviance or utilizing psychological strategies to fix the problem. Maruna (2001) observed the scarcity of positive acknowledgement in the criminal justice system and termed it largely *negative* in its approach. In this context, it may be of benefit to change the lens from a deficit perspective and examine the subject matter through an asset or strength perspective (see Green & Haines, 2011; Linley et al., 2006). Such an approach would focus on potential, strengths, solution-orientation, and building hope and meaning (Rapp et al., 2008).

P. Khanna (✉)
Jindal Institute of Behavioural Sciences, O. P. Jindal Global University, Sonipat, Haryana, India
e-mail: pkhanna@jgu.edu.in

S. Sahni et al. (eds.), *Criminal Psychology and the Criminal Justice System in India and Beyond*, https://doi.org/10.1007/978-981-16-4570-9_17

This chapter examines an amalgamation of criminal psychology and positive psychology, delving into how the latter may be best applied in the realm of the former. Positive psychology and aspects related to it or drawing upon similar values and assumptions have received some attention in the area of criminal psychology (e.g. Gavrielides & Worth, 2014; Nikolic-Ristanovic, 2014; Ronel & Elisha, 2011; Ward & Stewart, 2003). Therefore, existing work that links these disciplines and proposes a stronger mutual connection has been reviewed, with a view to build upon the foundation and look at future applications. At the outset, a brief overview of positive psychology is presented to familiarize the reader with the background and scope of this discipline.

17.2 Emergence and Evolution of Positive Psychology

Seligman and Csikszentmihalyi (2000) described how psychology always had a holistic mission to deal with mental illness, on the one hand, and support human fulfilment and talent, on the other. However, the socio-cultural milieu following the World War II witnessed a shift in the emphasis of psychology, which became skewed towards repairing damage and illness (Seligman & Csikszentmihalyi, 2000). Facets of human thriving and other positive dimensions were neglected along the way. Seligman and Csikszentmihalyi (2014) noted that pathology had assumed centre stage in psychology, resulting in a bleak view of human beings, lacking dimensions of a positive life worth living. Park et al. (2016) acknowledge the utility of this problem-centred approach but at the same time challenge the myopic view of humans that it has resulted in.

This preoccupation with problem rectification has often bred the misconception that alleviating psychological distress is synonymous with ensuring optimal well-being. The distinction between absence of illness and wellness is one of the pivotal assumptions on which positive psychology has grown (Peterson, 2008). The science of positive psychology 'aims to discover and promote the factors that allow individuals and communities to thrive' (Seligman & Csikszentmihalyi, 2000). As positive psychology reiterated the vital pursuit of human flourishing, seminal texts in the area (e.g. Seligman & Cziksentmihalyi, 2000; Seligman et al., 2002) underlined the renewed focus on the aspects of a good life and the need for developing theory and explanation for what constitutes it (Peterson, 2008). These aspects of psychology carry immense potential in the domain of crime prevention, criminal rehabilitation, and corrective endeavours as well. This calls for targeted efforts to promote strengths and wellbeing (both at the preventive and reformative level), instead of limiting the role of psychological intervention to healing and repair. Psychology as a holistic discipline is meant to cater to both ends of the spectrum, rather than be disproportionately focused on specific human conditions. At this point, it merits clarification that positive psychology is neither opposed to, nor a substitute for the traditional understanding of psychology (Park et al., 2016). In fact, it is supplementary and symbiotic in its relationship with other branches of the discipline. This approach should be extended to its application with respect to criminal psychology.

Alongside its growing popularity and acceptance over the past few decades, the field of positive psychology itself has evolved (Lomas, Waters, Williams, Oades, & Kern, 2020). Contemporary literature suggests the emergence of a second wave positive psychology (see Lomas & Ivtzan, 2015; Wong, 2011; Wong & Roy, 2017), and more recently, a third wave in positive psychology (Lomas et al., 2020). This progressive understanding of positive psychology calls for a dialectical approach, encompassing individuals, and humanity at large as a whole—acknowledging both their positive and negative facets (Wong & Roy, 2017). Recent developments in the field embrace complexity, interdisciplinarity, and a renewed focus on systemic wellbeing (Lomas et al., 2020). A more balanced and inclusive approach like this inherently bridges the conceptual distance between some of the perspectives that are at the core of this chapter. Wong and Roy (2017) noted that this outlook could be utilized to 'meet clients in their dark valleys and use a variety of tools to help the clients overcome, transcend, and transform negatives into positives' (para. 63). Further, this evolution in positive psychology also looks at transcending cultural boundaries and being more universal in its appeal—thereby making it more amenable to application in diverse contexts. In view of Henrich et al.'s (2010) observation of the predominant representation of Western, Educated, Industrialized, Rich, and Democratic (WEIRD) populations in psychological research, this is a sign of advancement for the discipline.

After briefly tracing the emergence and evolution of positive psychology, the subsequent parts of the chapter describe how this discipline may be integrated with criminal psychology.

17.3 Beyond the Traditional Perspective of Criminal Psychology: What and Why

According to Ronel and Elisha (2011), the conventional focus of criminology anchored on the negative causes and consequences of deviance impedes the development of a more holistic and humane perspective of criminals and offenders. In a compelling call to shift focus to a strengths-based perspective, Prilleltensky & Prilleltensky (2007, p. 48) commented, 'reactive, individual, alienating, and deficit-based approaches that foster patienthood instead of health, citizenship, and democracy have dominated the field of health and human services for decades'. While negating the potential vulnerability of offenders, this perspective offers limited scope for positive change, and broader, more optimistic mechanisms for dealing with the issue at hand. In this context, Maruna (2010) emphasized relationships, employment, hope, motivation, and a sense of being able to contribute as important factors that could support desistance among criminals and offenders.

The widely used and empirically backed *Risk, Needs, Responsivity* framework (RNR; Andrews et al., 1990) is a popular approach for offender assessment and classification. However, approaches such as this usually focus on risks and related needs of offenders, neglecting their strengths and positive qualities that could be fostered to bring about positive change (Hunter et al., 2016). On the other hand, the *Good Lives Model* (GLM; Ward & Stewart, 2003) is an example of a strengths-based perspective towards offender rehabilitation. GLM suggests that offenders aspire to lead good lives and require support in this direction (Ward & Stewart, 2003). To this effect, GLM aligns with the humanistic school of thought (Maslow, 1968) that is often regarded as a predecessor of positive psychology as we understand it today.

This discourse builds the case for a revised approach: one that prioritizes wellbeing of not only victims but also transgressors; thereby offering the potential of greater good for a wider section of society. A better understanding of the psychological constructs of happiness and wellbeing is in order to gain insight into this area. While Diener (2000) conceptualized subjective wellbeing as a combination of affect (more positive affect, less negative affect), and life satisfaction, Keyes (2005) established the idea of a composite model of wellbeing encompassing emotional, social, and psychological wellbeing. Seligman (2011) proposed the five domains of positive emotions (P), engagement (E), relationships (R), meaning (M), and accomplishment (A) (PERMA) as building blocks of happiness or flourishing among people. Although space as well as the focus of this chapter precludes a detailed review of related literature, the reader may find abundant descriptions of wellbeing (e.g. Kahneman et al., 1999; Ryff, 1989; Younes, 2011) in positive psychology literature. Each of these facets of wellbeing seems to be a valuable pursuit for human beings at large. Nikolic-Ristanovic (2014) remarked that while most societies may regard the pursuit of happiness as a sacrosanct right of their citizens, yet it is not common to find systemic and organized efforts to attain this outcome. It is however important to note that all such pursuits while being intrinsically valuable for their own sake are also equally significant as means to an end—one of happier, more harmonious communities. It merits further research to understand how such societies fare in terms of crime and civic virtues.

Wong (2007) discussed how positive psychology that deals with aversive consequences could offer pathways of avoiding such outcomes as well as boosting well-being. Further, better psychosocial functioning, greater productivity at work, and lower costs of health care are correlated with happiness and wellbeing (Keyes, 2007). It is interesting to note that the link between wellbeing and many of these variables is often reciprocal. Study of such correlates of wellbeing must be extended to criminal psychology as well. The next section extends this discussion by detailing how positive psychology can contribute to the field of criminal psychology.

17.4 Positive Psychology: Contribution to Crime Prevention and Rehabilitation

Drawing from existing trends that suggest that happy people are less likely to commit crimes, or get victimized, Nicolic-Ristanovic (2014) advocates further exploration of the association between these correlates. An important manifestation of such thought is the emergence of the perspective of *positive criminology* (Ronel & Elisha, 2011). Ronel and Elisha affirmed that positive criminology is centred on fostering offenders' strengths—both individual and social, with a view to successfully rehabilitate and assimilate them within the community. This perspective is supported by work highlighting the need for criminal justice system to recognize personal as well as social strengths among offenders as a way to promote desistance (e.g. Bartels, 2017; Maruna, 2010; McNeill et al., 2012). A related approach with a holistic and inclusive focus is *positive victimology* (Ronel & Toren, 2012).

There is preliminary evidence to suggest that happiness and wellbeing can deter crime. A widely cited presentation of McCarthy and Casey's paper '*Get happy! Positive emotion, depression, and juvenile crime*' suggests that happier adolescents are less likely to be engaged in drug-related or criminal activities (e.g. Nauert, 2018; Nicolic-Ristanovic, 2014). Tweed et al. (2011) also recommended positive psychology-based practices to prevent youth involvement in crime and violence.

Beyond crime prevention, positive psychology interventions can facilitate reformative endeavours and inhibit recidivism (e.g. Hodgkinson, 2020; Huynh et al., 2015; Wittekind, 2018). White (2004) asserted that most correctional and rehabilitation techniques are rooted in the justice approach or welfare approach. He further discussed a bridge between the two approaches, namely restorative justice. Positive psychology informed correctional approaches could certainly fit well in the realm of welfare and restorative justice initiatives. Gavrielides and Worth (2014) recommend integrating positive psychology practices into the realm of restorative justice in order to accrue potential benefits for offenders, victims, and the community. White (2004) also discussed the aspect of community rehabilitation that utilizes supportive, skill-based and participatory interventions in order to positively alter criminal behaviour.

Ronel et al. (2013) explain that a comprehensive approach to criminal rehabilitation addresses diverse facets of an offender's life and encompasses physical, emotional, mental, and social health in a bid to prevent reoffending. Further, positive criminology encourages the development and use of programs aimed at rehabilitation via nurturing intrapersonal and interpersonal strengths. Many such programs are aligned with the basic goals of positive psychology and are presented in the next section. Some of these may be cautiously labelled as positive psychological interventions to the extent that they work to nurture positive emotions, behaviours, and/or thoughts, consequently enhancing wellbeing among individuals or groups (Parks & Biswas-Diener, 2013).

17.4.1 Applications of Positive Psychology in Criminal Population: Illustrations from Literature

This section presents some prominent documented work demonstrating the utility and impact of initiatives explicitly or tacitly based on the principles of positive psychology. The use of positive psychology interventions among offender population draws support from literature suggesting their benefits for disadvantaged people as being comparable to those outside of this group (e.g. Akhtar & Boniwell, 2010; Brayford et al, 2010). Extant literature also suggests that positive emotions that one experiences may give rise to an upward spiral or a positive spin—that in turn enables them to detach from a criminal spin (Bensimon et al., 2013; Ronel, 2013; Ronel & Segev, 2014) by widening their cognitive and behavioural capabilities. This brief review encompasses studies focused on enhancing wellbeing, preventing recidivism, as well as those promoting successful social reintegration of offenders. These studies are presented in chronological sequence to facilitate logical organization of information.

Cross et al. (2012) investigated the application of positive psychology approaches in case management and residential programming in a Canadian incarceration facility. Cross et al. presented both, the possibilities as well as limitations of this approach. They reiterated the importance of promoting readiness to change by nurturing responsibility and resilience among the offenders. Mapham and Hefferon's (2012) study in a South Africa-based offender rehabilitation program highlighted the potential of strengths focused programs in facilitating post-traumatic growth as a medium of desistance.

Norman (2015) discussed the potential of yoga as a tool to rehabilitate offenders, mitigate institutional violence, and foster better societal integration of prisoners after release. Interestingly, Norman (2015) also commented on the alternate viewpoint of denying yoga (viewed as a valuable positive activity) to prisoners. Clearly, there is a need to revisit this perspective and understand the benefits of such interventions towards the larger goal of correction and reformation and not just criminal or prisoner wellbeing.

Woldgabreal et al. (2016) established that positive psychological constructs like self-efficacy, optimism, hope, and psychological flexibility could promote offender supervision outcomes and reduce criminogenic risk factors. Based on their trial of the *Fresh Start Prisoner Reentry Program* in the USA, Hunter et al. (2016) recommended the paradigm shift from a risk assessment to strengths assessment framework. They also recommended building flexible programs encompassing family as well as community resources. Hunter et al. further supported the adoption of a strengths-based approach to prisoner reintegration by emphasizing how it nurtures a sense of self-worth and value among them, in turn motivating better intervention participation (Maruna & LeBel, 2003).

Kerekes et al. (2017) studied the impact of a ten-week long yoga program among a group of male and female prison inmates in Sweden. They reported beneficial results in terms of wellbeing and risk factors such as impulsivity and antisocial behaviour that are associated with recidivism among inmates. Further encouraging evidence for the use of yoga among prison inmates emerged from female participants in the *Yoga Prison Project* at two correctional facilities in South Carolina, exhibiting significant improvement in outcomes of depression, stress, and self-awareness after program participation (Danielly & Silverthorne, 2017). Sfendla et al. (2018) reported that yoga practice benefited participants in terms of specific physiological as well as psychological indicators.

Based on their literature review of yoga in prisons, Muirhead and Fortune (2016) affirm the potential of yoga programs in reducing offending behaviour, while also pointing to the need for better-planned and more rigorous studies in the field. Muirhead and Fortune further note that yoga could work by directly improving variables such as impulsivity and aggression (related to offending), as well as aspects like depression and emotional control, which in turn contribute to criminal behaviour. A systematic review by Wimberley and Xue (2016) supplements the research evidence for positive wellbeing effects associated with yoga interventions in incarcerated contexts. In fact, Auty et al.'s (2017) meta-analysis on the effects of yoga and meditation in correctional contexts revealed adequate evidence for the beneficial impact of these practices among inmates. Ronel and Ben Yair (2018) sum up the benefits of yoga in the area of positive criminology, pointing to the array of advantages such as interpersonal integration, development of a spiritual, humane, and pr-social perspective—cumulatively fostering the process of rehabilitation among offenders.

Bartels' (2017) balanced analysis of *Hawaii's Opportunity Probation with Enforcement* (HOPE) program offered a good example of application of hope in fostering desistance and better communities. It also emphasized the need for further research to better understand and build upon the scope for hope-based interventions in the realm of criminal justice.

Wittekind's (2018) case study of the Delancey Foundation (a residential rehabilitation centre for convicts and addicts in the United States of America) presents favourable evidence for the application of a PERMA-based approach (Seligman, 2011). Wittekind describes how positive emotions contribute to broadening the mental capacities and building resources as well as increasing resilience among convicts. Further, engagement emanating from flow experienced during some tasks facilitates skill development as well as focused attention. Building and nurturing relationships fosters a sense of belonging among inmates, while opportunities to recreate one's life story (in a positive manner) generate meaning. Furthermore, empowerment instilled through practice of these diverse activities generates a sense of achievement and accomplishment (Wittekind, 2018). Since literature suggests that people are inherently motivated to seek out the dimensions of PERMA as elements of well-being (Seligman, 2011), application of this framework seems appealing to bring about desired behavioural change among offenders.

Yang et al. (2018) examined the impact of six-week long gratitude and kindness interventions among Chinese male prisoners. They found that participants in both intervention conditions reported improved happiness and reduced negative affect as opposed to a matched comparison group. In another study of a six-week mindfulness training intervention among Chinese male prisoners, An et al. (2019) reported gains in mindfulness levels and reduction in perceived stress among participants when compared to a control group. Participants in a pilot prison yoga program in Australia exhibited statistically and clinically significant improvement in levels of depression, anxiety, goal-direction, negative affect, and various other indicators of wellbeing (Bartels et al., 2019). Kovalsky et al. (2020) reported the benefits of yoga in reducing recidivism, drawing on their study of a large-scale sample from Israeli prisons, followed up to five years after discharge from prison.

While this is by no means an exhaustive review of literature, it serves to provide an overview of the scope and potential of utilizing positive psychology in the domain of criminal psychology. A lot more could be done to allay criminal tendencies among people and to metamorphose criminals into flourishing members of the society. The final section of this chapter outlines some suggestions towards this end.

17.5 Recommendations for Future Research and Practice

Recommendations for future research and practice are proposed with a view to advance the asset and strengths-based perspective in criminal psychology. While some proposed suggestions are at a broader policy and big picture level, others pertain to specific actions and implementation.

17.5.1 Better Understanding the Links Between Happiness and Crime

There is growing evidence of studies that examine the association between happiness and crime, criminal recidivism, and victimization (e.g. Davis & Hinks, 2010; Moller, 2005). Nicolic-Ristanovic (2014) noted that extant research predominantly explores the relationships between happiness and victimization/fear of crime, happiness and offending, and the effect of incarceration on happiness, and reoffending. However, further research and application could better understand the links between happiness and crime prevention, as well as rehabilitation and mitigating recidivism. A deeper understanding of how nations and societies fare comparatively on indices of happiness on the one hand and crime on the other could reveal important patterns. Such findings could also facilitate channelization of resources to initiatives (such as wellbeing and happiness promotion among the community) that may otherwise lose prominence in the face of other urgent matters.

17.5.2 Exploring Relevance of Diverse Positive Psychological Constructs in Criminal Psychology

Further study of the association among different constructs from positive psychology and their role in preventing crime, promoting offender wellbeing and rehabilitation is recommended. As an example, the benefits of *forgiveness* are widely reported (e.g. Toussaint et al., 2015). Gehm (1992) dwelled upon the potential to work on incorporating forgiveness as part of individual and collective endeavours in the criminal justice system. The tendency to forgive is negatively correlated with aggression and vengeful rumination (Berry et al., 2005) and could also lower the extent of observed violence translating into aggression (Anderson et al., 2007). By extending the concept of forgiveness to encompass both interpersonal forgiveness as well as self-forgiveness, Suzuki and Jenkins (2020) explored the role of these dimensions in desistance and restorative justice.

Another relevant construct is *hope*. Maruna (2001, p.166) noted, 'societies that do not believe that offenders can change will get offenders who do not believe that they can change'. McNeill et al., (2012, p. 4) have also remarked that desistance 'implies valuing people for who they are and what they *could become*, rather than judging, rejecting or containing them for what they *have done*'. McNeill et al. go on to affirm that advancing hope and motivation should be a primary function of those involved in criminal justice. Further exploration of constructs including *meaning, resilience, empathy, grit, self-regulation,* and *prosocial behaviour* as mediating and moderating variables in crime prevention and promotion of other desirable outcomes among criminal offenders is recommended.

17.5.3 Proper Documentation and Scientific Evidence

Anecdotal evidence exists for various strategies to prevent crime and use an asset approach as corrective intervention among offenders. Practitioners on the ground may be utilizing such approaches as per their best judgement. However, robust documentation and scientific research is important to arrive at a reliable understanding of the efficacy and effectiveness of such strategies, and to make them more accessible to the larger community. This will advance existing knowledge and help stakeholders who may otherwise have limited access to reliable and empirically valid information. Propagation of biased, unscientific strategies could often be counterproductive and cause a drain on precious resources, without yielding desired results. To this end, Leadbeater et al. (2007) proposed increasing the involvement of practitioners and policy-makers in research to increase chances of implementation of research outcomes.

17.5.4 Utilizing Indigenous Best Practices

When introducing an asset perspective in advancing crime prevention, rehabilitation and desistance, it would be useful to optimally utilize indigenous and culturally rooted best practices. This implies recognizing and fostering practices that may be pre-existing in a given socio-cultural environment, instead of an exclusive focus on externally introduced strategies. Saleeby (1996) suggests that individuals and communities often possess pre-existing qualities that could contribute towards attaining desired goals. An example from Tihar jail (an Indian prison) was the practice of *Vipassana* meditation among prison inmates, leading to reduced hostility and improved hope and wellbeing among participants (Vipassana Research Institute, n.d.). In another study, Sureka et al. (2014) explored the impact of *Sudarshan kriya* and related practices among prisoners and reported significant gains in wellbeing, self-control, health, vitality, and general functioning. An example of a culturally rooted ritual from Indian society is that of *seva* (service) which also falls in the realm of prosocial behaviour—an important construct in positive psychology. Melton (2005) also proposed examples of indigenous justice systems in tribal societies, entailing forgiveness, and sincere community engagement as part of corrective interventions. Fostering such practices could offer the benefit of ready social assimilation and easier acceptance in a given culture. These homegrown practices may also be potentially useful for replication elsewhere.

17.5.5 Adopting Resource Efficient Mechanisms

For any interventions in the field of crime prevention and rehabilitation to be sustainable, it is imperative that they are resource efficient and not a drain on the existing systems and funds. This encompasses not only financial resources but also other aspects like human resources including time and effort. Towards this end, adopting collaborative efforts involving law enforcement agencies, prison departments, community stakeholders, and various other governmental and non-governmental agents is recommended. Moreover, mechanisms such as *peer mentoring* and *train the trainer* wherein participants are both recipients and further proponents of training could be utilized. This serves the twofold purpose of boosting social rehabilitation and employment of offenders and also improves the acceptance of initiatives. Additionally, it offers a promising example of reformation that may induce a sense of optimism and inspiration among current inmates. A good example is the Delancey Foundation case study (Wittekind, 2018) that has been described earlier in this chapter.

17.5.6 Promoting an Interdisciplinary Approach

A well-informed strengths-based approach may benefit from the influence of not only different disciplines within psychology but also other disciplines such as sociology, anthropology, and legal studies. In elaborating upon the scope of positive criminology, Ronel and Segev (2014) mention how this discipline is similar to yet different from positive psychology, detailing how the former encompasses sociological resources as well. To this effect, openness towards interdisciplinary approaches is recommended. While such distinctions may not be so rigid in practice, they do at times strongly delineate research endeavours. Interdisciplinarity could facilitate a holistic and well-rounded perspective towards dealing with (potential and proven) offenders in a more positive and constructive manner.

17.6 Conclusion

Through this chapter, support to transcend the deficit perspective and adopt a strengths-based focus in criminal psychology has been offered. Gavrielides and Worth's (2014, p.177) description of positive psychology practices in criminal justice as 'not a soft option …a balanced one' summarizes the importance of examining criminal psychology through a positive psychology lens.

Positive psychology is centred on the pillars of positive emotions, positive character traits, and enabling institutions (Seligman et al., 2005). Rich (2014) noted that the potential of positive psychology to impact global communities has gained acknowledgement by policy-makers. In conclusion, a synthesis of positive psychology and criminal psychology may benefit wellbeing at individual and group levels and advance the shared goals of both disciplines. At the *individual level*, participants of positive psychology informed programs and interventions would stand to benefit in terms of physiological and psychological outcomes. At the *institutional level*, budgetary allocation towards strengths-based initiatives in crime prevention and criminal rehabilitation could help reduce the budgetary burdens of prison maintenance and allied expenditures in the long- turn. At the *community level*, a happier, mentally healthy population, characterized by greater wellbeing and civic virtues presents itself as a desirable pursuit.

References

Akhtar, M., & Boniwell, I. (2010). Applying positive psychology to alcohol-misusing adolescents: A group intervention. *Groupwork, 20*(3), 6–31. https://doi.org/10.1921/095182410X576831

An, Y., Zhou, Y., Huang, Q., Jia, K., Li, W., & Xu, W. (2019). The effect of mindfulness training on mental health in long-term Chinese male prisoners. *Psychology, Health & Medicine, 24*(2), 167–176. https://doi.org/10.1080/13548506.2018.1510130

Anderson, C. A., Gentile, D. A., & Buckley, K. E. (2007). Violent video game effects on children and adolescents: Theory, research, and public policy. *Oxford University Press*. https://doi.org/10.1093/acprof:oso/9780195309836.001.0001

Andrews, D. A., Bonta, J., & Hoge, R. D. (1990). Classification for effective rehabilitation: Rediscovering psychology. *Criminal Justice and Behaviour, 17*(1), 9–52. https://doi.org/10.1177/0093854890017001004

Auty, K. M., Cope, A., & Liebling, A. (2017). A systematic review and meta-analysis of yoga and mindfulness meditation in prison. *International Journal of Offender Therapy and Comparative Criminology, 61*(6), 689–710. https://doi.org/10.1177/0306624X15602514

Bartels, L. (2017). HOPE probation: A new path to desistance? *European Journal of Probation, 9*(3), 248–266. https://doi.org/10.1177/2066220317741882

Bartels, L., Oxman, L. N., & Hopkins, A. (2019). "I Would just feel really relaxed and at peace": Findings from a pilot prison yoga program in Australia. *International Journal of Offender Therapy and Comparative Criminology, 63*(15–16), 2531–2549. https://doi.org/10.1177/0306624X19854869

Bensimon, M., Baruch, A., & Ronel, N. (2013). The experience of gambling in an illegal casino: The gambling spin process. *European Journal of Criminology, 10*(1), 3–21. https://doi.org/10.1177/1477370812455124

Berry, J. W., Worthington, E. L., O'Connor, L. E., Parrott, L., 3rd., & Wade, N. G. (2005). Forgivingness, vengeful rumination, and affective traits. *Journal of Personality., 73*(1), 183–225. https://doi.org/10.1111/j.1467-6494.2004.00308.x

Brayford, J., Cowe, F., & Deering, J. (2010). What else works—back to the future. In J. Brayford, F. Cowe, & J. Deering (Eds.), *What else works? Creative work with offenders* (pp. 254–268). Willan. https://doi.org/10.1111/j.1468-2311.2011.00661_5.x

Cross, L.E., Morrison, W., Peterson, P., & Domene, J. (2012). Investigating positive psychology approaches in case management and residential programming with incarcerated youth. *Canadian Journal of Counseling and Psychotherapy, 46* (2), 63–84. https://cjc-rcc.ucalgary.ca/article/view/59299

Danielly, Y., & Silverthorne, C. (2017). Psychological benefits of yoga for female inmates. *International Journal of Yoga Therapy, 27*(1), 9–14. https://doi.org/10.17761/1531-2054-27.1.9

Davis, S., & Hinks, T. (2010). Crime and happiness amongst heads of households in Malawi. *Journal of Happiness Studies, 4*, 457–476. https://doi.org/10.1007/s10902-009-9152-7

Diener, E. (2000). Subjective well-being: The science of happiness and a proposal for a national index. *American Psychologist, 55*, 34–43. https://doi.org/10.1037/0003-066X.55.1.34

Gavrielides, T., & Worth, P. (2014). Another push for restorative justice: Positive psychology and offender rehabilitation. In M. H. Pearson (Ed.), *Crime: International perspectives, socioeconomic factors and psychological implications* (pp. 161–182). Nova Science Publishers.

Gehm J. R. (1992) The function of forgiveness in the criminal justice system. In H. Messmer, H. U. Otto (Eds.), *Restorative Justice on Trial. Nato Science Series D: (closed) (Behavioural and Social Sciences)*, 64. Springer. https://doi.org/10.1007/978-94-015-8064-9_38

Henrich, J., Heine, S. J., & Norenzayan, A. (2010). The weirdest people in the world? *Behavioural and Brain Sciences, 33* (2–3), 61–135

Hodgkinson, R., Beattie, S., Roberts, R., & Hardy, L. (2020). Psychological resilience interventions to reduce recidivism in young people: A systematic review. *Adolescent Research Review*. https://doi.org/10.1007/s40894-020-00138-x

Hunter, B. A., Lanza, A. S., Lawlor, M., Dyson, W., & Gordon, D. M. (2016). A strengths-based approach to prisoner reentry: The fresh start prisoner reentry program. *International Journal of Offender Therapy and Comparative Criminology, 60*(11), 1298–1314. https://doi.org/10.1177/0306624X15576501

Huynh, K. H., Hall, B., Hurst, M. A., & Bikos, L. H. (2015). Evaluation of the positive re-entry in corrections program: A positive psychology intervention with prison inmates. *International Journal of Offender Therapy and Comparative Criminology, 59*(9), 1006–1023. https://doi.org/10.1177/0306624X14523385

Kahneman, D., Diener, E., & Schwarz, N. (eds.). (1999). *Well-Being: The Foundations of Hedonic Psychology*. Russell Sage Foundation.
Kerekes, N., Fielding, C., & Apelqvist, S. (2017). Yoga in correctional settings: A randomized controlled study. *Frontiers in Psychiatry., 8*, 204. https://doi.org/10.3389/fpsyt.2017.00204
Keyes, C. L. M. (2005). Mental illness and/or mental health? Investigating axioms of the complete state model of health. *Journal of Consulting and Clinical Psychology, 73*, 539–548. https://doi.org/10.1037/0022-006X.73.3.539
Keyes, C. L. M. (2007). Promoting and protecting mental health as flourishing: A complementary strategy for improving national mental health. *American Psychologist, 62*, 95–108. https://doi.org/10.1037/0003-066X.62.2.95
Kovalsky, S., Hasisi, B., Haviv, N., & Elisha, E. (2020). Can yoga overcome criminality? The impact of yoga on recidivism in Israeli prisons. *International Journal of Offender Therapy and Comparative Criminology. 0306624X2091189*. https://doi.org/10.1177/0306624x20911899
Leadbeater, B., Marshall, A., & Banister, E. (2007). Building strengths through practice-research-policy collaborations. *Child and Adolescent Psychiatric Clinics of North America, 16*(2), 515–532. https://doi.org/10.1016/j.chc.2006.11.004
Linley, P. A., Joseph, S., Harrington, S., & Wood, A. M. (2006). Positive psychology: Past, present, and (possible) future. *The Journal of Positive Psychology, 1*, 3–16.
Lomas, T., & Ivtzan, I. (2015). Second wave positive psychology: Exploring the positive-negative dialectics of wellbeing. *Journal of Happiness Studies*. https://doi.org/10.1007/s10902-015-9668-y
Lomas, T., Waters, L., Williams, P., Oades, L.G., & Kern, M.L. (2020). Third wave positive psychology: Broadening towards complexity. *The Journal of Positive Psychology*. https://doi.org/10.1080/17439760.2020.1805501
Mapham, A., & Hefferon, K. (2012). "I Used to Be an Offender—Now I'm a Defender": Positive psychology approaches in the facilitation of posttraumatic growth in offenders. *Journal of Offender Rehabilitation, 51*, 389–413. https://doi.org/10.1080/10509674.2012.683239
Maruna, S. (2001). Making Good: How ex-convicts reform and rebuild their lives. *American Psychological Association*. https://doi.org/10.1037/10430-000
Maruna, S. (2010). *Understanding Desistance from Crime*. UK Ministry of Justice. http://www.safeground.org.uk/wp-content/uploads/Desistance-Fact-Sheet.pdf
Maruna, S., & LeBel, T. P. (2003). Welcome home? Examining the "Reentry Court" concept from a strengths-based perspective. *Western Criminology Review., 4*(2), 91–107.
Maslow, A. H. (1968). *Toward a psychology of being*. Van Nostrand.
McNeill, F., Farrall. S., Lightowler, C., & Maruna, S. (2012). *How and Why People Stop Offending: Discovering Desistance*. Institute for Research and Innovation in Social Services. https://www.iriss.org.uk/resources/insights/how-why-people-stop-offending-discovering-desistance
Melton, A. P. (2005). Indigenous justice systems and tribal society. In D. W. McCaslin (Ed.), *Justice as Healing: Indigenous Ways. Writings on Community Peacemaking and Restorative Justice from the Native Law Centre*. 108–120. Living Justice Press. http://www.aidainc.net/Publications/ij_systems.htm
Moller, V. (2005). Resilient or resigned? Criminal victimization and quality of life in South Africa. *Social Indicators Research, 72*, 262–317.
Muirhead, J., & Fortune, C. (2016). Yoga in prisons: A review of the literature. *Aggression and Violent Behaviour, 28*, 57–63. https://doi.org/10.1016/j.avb.2016.03.013
Nauert, R. (2018). Happiness tends to deter crime. *Psych Central*. Retrieved on August 1, 2020 from https://psychcentral.com/news/2011/08/24/happiness-tends-to-deter-crime/28877.html
Nikolic-Ristanovic, V. (2014). Making people happy is the best crime prevention: Towards happy-making criminology. *European Journal of Criminology, 11*(4), 401–409. https://doi.org/10.1177/1477370814536323
Norman, M. (2015). Prison yoga as a correctional alternative?: Physical culture, rehabilitation, and social control in Canadian prisons. In I. Joseph, & W. Crichlow (Eds.), *Alternative*

Offender Rehabilitation and Social Justice. Palgrave Macmillan. https://doi.org/10.1057/9781137476821_5

Parks, A. C., & Biswas-Diener, R. (2013). Positive interventions: Past, present, and future. In T. B. Kashdan & J. Ciarrochi (Eds.), *The Context Press mindfulness and acceptance practica series. Mindfulness, acceptance, and positive psychology: The seven foundations of well-being* (p. 140–165). New Harbinger Publications, Inc.

Park, N., Peterson, C., Szvarca, D., Vander Molen, R. J., Kim, E. S., & Collon, K. (2016). Positive psychology and physical health: Research and applications. *American Journal of Lifestyle Medicine, 10*(3), 200–206. https://doi.org/10.1177/1559827614550277

Peterson, C. (2008). What Is Positive Psychology, and what is it not? *Psychology Today*. https://www.psychologytoday.com/us/blog/the-good-life/200805/what-is-positive-psychology-and-what-is-it-not

Prilleltensky, I., & Prilleltensky, O. (2007). Webs of well-being: The interdependence of personal, relational organizational, and communal well-being. In J. Haworth, & G. Hart (Eds.), *Well-being, individual, community and social perspectives* (pp. 61–78). Palgrave Macmillan. https://doi.org/10.1057/9780230287624

Rapp, C., Saleebey, D., & Sullivan, P.W. (2008).The future of strengths-based social work practice. In D. Saleebey (Ed.), (2006) *The strengths perspective in social work practice*, (4th Ed) Pearson Education.

Rich, G. J. (2014). *Positive institutions, communities, and nations: Methods and internationalizing positive psychology concepts*. In H. Águeda Marujo, & L. M. Neto (Eds.), *Cross-cultural advancements in positive psychology: Vol. 6. Positive nations and communities: Collective, qualitative and cultural-sensitive processes in positive psychology* (p. 17–32). Springer Science+Business Media. https://doi.org/10.1007/978-94-007-6869-7_2

Ronel, N. (2013). From a criminal spin to positive criminology. In K. Jaishankar & N. Ronel (Eds.), *Global criminology, crime and victimization in a globalized era* (pp. 335–351). CRC Press.

Ronel, N., & Ben Yair, Y. (2018). Spiritual criminology: The case of Jewish criminology. *International Journal of Offender Therapy and Comparative Criminology, 62*(7), 2081–2102. https://doi.org/10.1177/0306624X17693865

Ronel, N., & Elisha, E. (2011). A different perspective: Introducing positive criminology. *International Journal of Offender Therapy and Comparative Criminology, 55*(2), 305–325. https://doi.org/10.1177/0306624X09357772

Ronel, N., Frid, N., & Timor, U. (2013). The practice of positive criminology: A Vipassana course in prison. *International Journal of Offender Therapy and Comparative Criminology, 57*(2), 133–153. https://doi.org/10.1177/0306624X11427664

Ronel, N., & Segev, D. (2014). Positive criminology in practice. *International Journal of Offender Therapy and Comparative Criminology, 58*(11), 1389–1407. https://doi.org/10.1177/0306624X13491933

Ronel, N., & Toren, T. (2012). Positive victimology: An innovation or 'more of the same'? *Temida, 2*, 171–180. https://doi.org/10.2298/TEM1202171R

Ryff, C. D. (1989). Happiness is everything, or is it? Explorations on the meaning of psychological well-being. *Journal of Personality and Social Psychology, 57*(6), 1069–1081. https://doi.org/10.1037/0022-3514.57.6.1069

Saleeby, D. (1996). The strengths perspective in social work practice: Extensions and cautions. *Social Work, 41*, 296–305.

Seligman, M. E. P. (2011). *Flourish: A visionary new understanding of happiness and well-being*. Free Press.

Seligman, M. E. P., & Csikszentmihalyi, M. (2000). Positive psychology: An introduction. *American Psychologist, 55*(1), 5–14. https://doi.org/10.1037/0003-066X.55.1.5

Seligman, M. E. P., & Csikszentmihalyi, M. (2014). Positive psychology: An introduction. In *Flow and the Foundations of Positive Psychology*. Springer, Dordrecht. https://doi.org/10.1007/978-94-017-9088-8_18

Seligman, M. E. P., Steen, T. A., Park, N., & Peterson, C. (2005). Positive psychology progress: Empirical validation of interventions. *American Psychologist, 60*(5), 410–421.

Seligman, M. E. P., Snyder, C. R., & Lopez, S. J. (2002). Positive psychology, positive prevention, and positive therapy. In C. R. Snyder & S. J. Lopez (Eds.), *Handbook of positive psychology* (pp. 3–9). Oxford University Press.

Sfendla, A., Malmström, P., Torstensson, S., & Kerekes, N. (2018). Yoga practice reduces the psychological distress levels of prison inmates. *Frontiers in Psychiatry, 9*, 407. https://doi.org/10.3389/fpsyt.2018.00407

Sureka, P., Govil, S., Dash, D., Dash, C., Kumar, M., & Singhal, V. (2014). Effect of Sudarshan Kriya on male prisoners with non-psychotic psychiatric disorders: A randomized control trial. *Asian Journal of Psychiatry, 12*, 43–49. https://doi.org/10.1016/j.ajp.2014.06.010

Suzuki, M., & Jenkins, T. (2020). The role of (self-) forgiveness in restorative justice: Linking restorative justice to desistance. *European Journal of Criminology*. https://doi.org/10.1177/1477370819895959

Toussaint, L. L., Worthington, E. L., Jr., & Williams, D. R. (Eds.). (2015). *Forgiveness and health: Scientific evidence and theories relating forgiveness to better health*. Springer Science+Business Media. https://doi.org/10.1007/978-94-017-9993-5

Tweed, R. G., Bhatt, G., Dooley, S., Spindler, A., Douglas, K. S., & Viljoen, J. (2011). Youth violence and positive psychology: Research potential through integration. *Canadian Psychology, 52*, 111–121. https://doi.org/10.1037/a0020695

Vipassana Research Institute (n.d.) Available from: http://www.vridhamma.org/Psychological-effects-on-tihar-jail-inmates.

Ward, T., & Stewart, C. A. (2003). The treatment of sex offenders: Risk management and good lives. *Professional Psychology: Research and Practice, 34*, 353–360. https://doi.org/10.1037/0735-7028.34.4.353

White. R. (2004). Community corrections and restorative justice||, *Current Issues in Criminal Justice, 16*(1), 42–56. http://www.austlii.edu.au/au/journals/CICrimJust/2004/11.pdf.

Wimberley, A.S., & Xue, J. (2016). A systematic review of yoga interventions in the incarcerated setting. *Journal of Sociology and Social Welfare. 43*(4), 85–108. https://scholarworks.wmich.edu/jssw/vol43/iss4/1

Wittekind, K. (2018). *The Bottom Two Percent: Using Positive Psychology to Create Change Among Convicts*. Master of Applied Positive Psychology (MAPP) Capstone Projects. 143. https://repository.upenn.edu/mapp_capstone/143

Woldgabreal, Y., Day, A., & Ward, T. (2016). Linking positive psychology to offender supervision outcomes: The mediating role of psychological flexibility, general self-efficacy, optimism, and hope. *Criminal Justice and Behaviour, 43*(6), 697–721. https://doi.org/10.1177/0093854815620816

Wong, P. T. P. (2007). Viktor Frankl: Prophet of hope for the 21st century. In A. Batthyany, & J. Levinson (Eds.), *Anthology of Viktor Frankl's Logotherapy* (pp. 67–96). Zeig, Tucker & Theisen Inc.

Wong, P. T. P. (2011). Positive psychology 2.0: Towards a balanced interactive model of the good life. *Canadian Psychology, 52*, 69–81. https://doi.org/10.1037/a0022511

Wong, P. T. P., & Roy, S. (2017). Critique of positive psychology and positive interventions. In N. J. L. Brown, T. Lomas, & F. J. Eiroa-Orosa (Eds.), *The Routledge International Handbook of Critical Positive Psychology*. Routledge. https://doi.org/10.4324/9781315659794

Yang, Y., Zhao, H., Aidi, M., & Kou, Y. (2018). Three good deeds and three blessings: The kindness and gratitude interventions with Chinese prisoners. *Criminal Behaviour and Mental Health., 28*(5), 433–441. https://doi.org/10.1002/cbm.2085

Younes, S. M. (2011). Positive mental health, subjective vitality and satisfaction with life for French physical education students. *World Journal of Sport Sciences, 4*(2), 90–97.

The manufacturer's authorised representative in the EU is Springer Nature Customer Service Centre GmbH, Europaplatz 3, 69115 Heidelberg, Germany. If you have any concerns regarding our products, please contact ProductSafety@springernature.com

Printed and bound by CPI Group (UK) Ltd, Croydon, CR0 4YY
30/09/2026
02225290-0010